CHICAGO

CHICAGO
Metropolis of the Mid-Continent

FOURTH EDITION

Irving Cutler

With a Foreword by James F. Marran

SOUTHERN ILLINOIS UNIVERSITY PRESS

CARBONDALE

First edition published 1973. Fourth edition 2006

Printed in the United States of America

09   08   07   06   4   3   2   1

Frontispiece: Chicago's lakefront and Michigan
Avenue looking northward from Balbo Drive. Image
by Wernher Krutein; by permission of Photovault.

Figure 6.17 was taken by permission of the Board of
Trade of the City of Chicago, Inc. This publication
has not been reviewed by the Board of Trade, and the
Board of Trade makes no representation regarding the
accuracy of the content of the publication.

Library of Congress Cataloging-in-Publication Data

Cutler, Irving
Chicago, metropolis of the mid-continent / Irving
Cutler ; with a foreword by James F. Marran. — 4th ed.
     p.   cm.
Includes bibliographical references and index.
     1. Chicago Metropolitan Area (Ill.) — Economic
conditions. 2. Chicago Metropolitan Area
(Ill.) — History. 3. Chicago Metropolitan Area (Ill.) —
Population. 4. Regional planning — Illinois — Chicago
Metropolitan Area. I. Title.
HC 108.C4C83 2006
307.76'40977311 — dc22
ISBN-13: 978-0-8093-2701-0 (cloth : alk. paper)
ISBN-10: 0-8093-2701-5 (cloth : alk. paper)
ISBN-13: 978-0-8093-2702-7 (pbk. : alk. paper)
ISBN-10: 0-8093-2702-3 (pbk. : alk. paper)
                                        2005031343

Printed on recycled paper ♻

The paper used in this publication meets the minimum
requirements of American National Standard for
Information Sciences — Permanence of Paper for
Printed Library Materials, ANSI Z39.48-1992. ∞

In memory of my beloved wife, **Marian**,

whose unflagging assistance and support,

along with her smile and her courage, continue

to provide indispensable inspiration

Contents

Foreword

In 1973, when the first edition of *Chicago: Metropolis of the Mid-Continent* by Irving Cutler was published, the city still lived in the enduring shadow of Carl Sandburg's compelling assessment that Chicago was the nation's "City of the Big Shoulders," "Stacker of Wheat," and "Hog Butcher for the World." However, it hovered promisingly on the edge of a new era. In the more than three decades that have intervened between that edition and this one, Chicago has become a world-class city and a key player in the global community. Its economy has moved from a gritty industrial base that employed many thousands of workers in slaughterhouses, food processing plants, factories, and rail yards to one where the "new" Chicago in sleek skyscrapers provides every array of service to an eagerly awaiting world.

As Chicago has become a center of service and technology, it has also emerged as culturally sophisticated in ways that other cities envy and try to emulate. The arts are thriving in its museums, theaters, libraries, and music halls. Its lakefront parks and beaches attract thousands with their statuary, charming gardens and fountains, sprawling marinas, and multiple and varied seasonal attractions. But the city is more than its lakeside charm, downtown office towers, and glittering shops and department stores. The real Chicago is beyond the wall of high-rises along Lake Michigan. It is in the neighborhoods of the South, West, and North sides that cluster along the elevated lines, avenues, and boulevards; they define the city and connect it to its past. These places serve as a guide to the traditions and cultures of Chicago's diverse communities, proving that there is not one Chicago but many. Once thought of as a melting pot, the city is now seen as a multicultural milieu where differences are celebrated. As a city of changing demographics, Chicago is an anticipatory urban place because it already is what the United States is becoming: one of the most broadly multicultural places in the world.

This new edition of Irving Cutler's powerful story of the historical geography of Chicago provides a context for this twenty-first-century city by showing the physical and human processes and phenomena that make it work. This fourth edition continues to capture the intricate but revealing layers of a complex city. Dr. Cutler's updates of chapters fully encompass the characteristics of the metropolis and its hinterland. In addition, a new chapter about the city's cultural dimensions reveals its geographic variability, its dimensions as a desirably livable place, and its attractiveness to visitors from across the world.

To even the most casual reader, it is clear that the author's lifelong fascination with the city is enhanced by his significant professional, academic, and research experience. His descriptions and analyses of places and the cultural heritage they represent are presented in terms that are appealing for both their candor and their kindness. With this updated story of one of the planet's great cities, Irving Cutler continues to affirm that he is "Chicago's geographer." With his style, verve, and affection, he presents the city's physical and cultural geography with a perspective that joins space and time in ways both meaningful and memorable.

James F. Marran
past president, National Council for Geographic Education

Preface

The first edition of this book was published in 1973 on the occasion of the seventy-fifth anniversary of the Geographic Society of Chicago. It was distributed primarily to the Society's thousands of members and to school libraries in the Chicago area. When it became evident that there also was a large demand for such a book from educational institutions and from the general public, the Society brought out a second edition. A few years later a third edition was published by the Kendall/Hunt Publishing Company, followed now by this updated and greatly enlarged fourth edition. This broader treatment of the Chicago area based on more recent research and field work should be of value to students and others, both within the city and in its suburbs, who often know too little about the growth, characteristics, problems, and plans of their remarkable and dynamically changing "metropolis of the mid-continent."

This fourth edition has numerous new photographs and maps and increased chapter and appendix material, as well as recent U.S. census data. There is also an entirely new chapter—"Culture, Education, and Recreation."

Numerous individuals and organizations facilitated the writing of this book, and their help is gratefully acknowledged. Edward B. Espenshade Jr., as the chairman of the Seventy-fifth Anniversary Publication Committee, skillfully organized and guided the original project. A special acknowledgment must go to the representative of the Society for the project, Elizabeth Eiselen, for her wise counsel and scrupulous editing of the first three editions and to Irwin Suloway for his perceptive and careful editing, as well as his many valuable suggestions for this fourth edition. Joseph Kubal, a former student of mine, rendered needed cartographic assistance by producing or modifying many of the maps. Sections of the various editions of the book were critically read by my colleagues Joseph Chada, John Hobgood, Walter Kelly, Albert Logan, Herbert Rau, and Leonard Simutis, and by Dominic Candeloro, Edwin Cudecki, Andrew Kopan, Carolyn Levy, Mark Mandle, Leonard Mishkin, Burt Rhodes, Pearl Slaton, Henry Sokolow, Lori Stone, Leah Wexler, and Eugene Zucker.

Useful advice and recent data were supplied by Marc Thomas of the Northeastern Illinois

Planning Commission; Carol Sonnenschein, Michael Stiehl, Atakan Guven, and Leo Hernandez of Chicago Metropolis 2020; Thomas E. Palzer of the Chicago Area Transportation Study; and the people of various Chicago city departments and of the Chicago Jewish Historical Society. Valuable guidance and assistance were provided by Karl Kageff and Wayne Larsen, editors at Southern Illinois University Press, and Barb Martin, its design and production manager.

To my family I owe a debt of gratitude for their patience during the period of writing and for their help in so many ways. My son Dan helped with the photographs; he and my daughter Susie and her husband Joab Silverglade helped with the evaluation of the photos, maps, and text. Very special appreciation goes to my wife and coworker, Marian, for her tireless assistance, discerning criticism, manuscript preparation, and encouragement in bringing this book to completion in all of its editions.

The photographs and maps in the book came from many sources, which are indicated in the captions. The largest numbers of illustrations came from the Chicago Historical Society (name changed to Chicago History Museum in 2006), the Illinois Ethnic Coalition, and my own collection.

Through the years, I have had the opportunity to observe the changing city and its suburbs from diverse career vantage points, ranging from that of a taxicab driver to employment in the Chicago area with the U.S. Army Corps of Engineers, the U.S. Department of Labor, and the Office of Economic Opportunity. I also learned about the metropolitan area from the excellent writings and teachings of many scholars, particularly my former professor and mentor, Harold M. Mayer.

Finally, I am most grateful to the Geographic Society of Chicago for affording me the opportunity to write on a subject that has interested and fascinated me all of my life—Chicago!

CHICAGO

FIG. 1.1. Chicago Water Tower *(foreground)*, one of the few structures to survive the disastrous Chicago Fire of 1871. To the left, combining residential, retail, and office functions, is the one-hundred-story John Hancock Center, completed in 1970. To the right is the seventy-four-story Water Tower Place, opened in 1975, which contains an urban high-rise shopping center with many small shops and two major department stores, the 450-room Ritz-Carlton Hotel, and luxury condominiums. Photograph by Mati Maldre.

1

Introduction

Yesterday and Today

Stand on the busy Michigan Avenue Bridge
over the Chicago River, in the locale where
Chicago began, and look about you in any
direction. At once, you are aware of the vigorous growth and development of a great city.

From the north end of the bridge, where
once the old Green Bay Road originated and
the du Sable cabin stood alone in the wilderness, now stretches the renowned Magnificent
Mile affluent shopping district, crowned by
the John Hancock Center. This soaring one-
hundred-story skyscraper overshadows the
Water Tower, the last landmark of the great
fire that decimated the city well over a century
ago.

To the south, where once Fort Dearborn
stood, where the river arched sharply
southward, and where the lake washed
Michigan Avenue, now stand a beautiful
park built on the debris of the Chicago Fire,
skyscrapers symbolic of Chicago's commercial growth, and such cultural landmarks
as the Art Institute, the Symphony Center,
the Chicago Cultural Center, Adler and
Sullivan's Auditorium Building, and the new
Millennium Park, with its indoor and outdoor

theaters and its cluster of high-profile, engaging features.

Westward, along the Chicago River and
the newly reconstructed double-deck Wacker
Drive, where less than a century ago, produce
terminals and warehouses abounded, where
hundreds of ships and barges lined the
channel, and where the tragic capsizing of the
steamer *Eastland* occurred, there are now the
Merchandise Mart, Marina Towers, major
corporation headquarters, and three new
hotels.

And to the east, on the former sites of grain
elevators and the large McCormick Reaper
Works, is a growing array of skyscrapers, four
new hotels, and an inviting river walk. Farther
on is the double-deck Outer Drive bridge,
with its endless procession of vehicles; the
lock that helps reverse the flow of the Chicago
river; and finally, magnificent Lake Michigan,
Chicago's water gateway to the world.

Chicago's Geographic Attributes

Chicago's growth and change have been both
swift and dramatic. It is the youngest of the
world's largest cities and, with a population of
2,896,016 in the year 2000, it ranks third in

FIG. 1.2. Major asset of Chicago: its excellent location. Adapted from a map produced by the Chicago Association of Commerce and Industry.

the nation in size. The number of inhabitants in Chicago's burgeoning suburban area is now much greater than that of the city proper, resulting in a metropolitan area population of about nine million people—the twenty-seventh largest urban area in the world.

Chicago's remarkable population growth—greater than that attained by Paris in twenty centuries—was achieved in the last century and a half, although the area was first visited by Europeans more than three centuries ago. A bronze tablet on the Michigan Avenue bridge commemorates the event with this inscription: "In honor of Louis Jolliet and Pere Jacques Marquette, the first white men to pass through the Chicago River, September, 1673."

The Canadian explorer and the French missionary were returning to Canada after exploring the Mississippi Valley for France. The Chicago region they passed through was essentially a flat, poorly drained wilderness blanketed with prairie grass, wild onion, clusters of trees, and foul-smelling marshes. Native Americans would often pass through it in pursuit of game.

Despite the area's inauspicious setting, the essentials for its rapid growth were present when the first settlers arrived. These essentials included the following:

1. Location near the geographic center of the vast, flat, and fertile plains between the Appalachian Mountains to the east and the Rocky Mountains to the west. Chicago's situation enabled it to become the center of the most productive agricultural hinterland in the

world. The flat terrain permitted easy access to this rich tributary empire by all modes of transportation. For the city itself, it facilitated the layout of streets in all directions and the unimpeded expansion of urbanization.

2. Conveniently located and economically accessible important natural resources—the forests of the north, the iron ore of Minnesota and Wisconsin, the coal of Illinois and nearby states, and an unlimited supply of fresh lake water.

3. Location at the southwestern tip of the world's greatest lake system. This made possible exceptionally low transportation costs and a great range of domestic and overseas connections. In addition, Chicago's location is at a natural point of convergence for land traffic between the east and northwest that must find its way around the southern tip of Lake Michigan. Long before the coming of Europeans, numerous Native American trails joined at Chicago.

4. Short natural waterways of Chicago. These were eventually modified and extended to provide the only all-water connecting link between the Great Lakes–St. Lawrence Seaway and the rich Mississippi Valley. Louis Jolliet noted this important possibility when he portaged through the Chicago region in 1673. He wrote in his journal that "it would only be necessary to make a canal by cutting through but half a league of prairies to pass" from Lake Michigan to the Illinois River and on to the Mississippi River and the Gulf of Mexico.

FIG. 2.1. Limestone bedrock that underlies Chicago, evident at the more-than-a-century-old Stearns Quarry at Twenty-eighth and Halsted streets. Since 1971 the quarry has been used by the city as a dumping site for the residue of its incinerator operations. Plans call for the land, once it is completely filled, to be made into a city park. Photograph courtesy of the Material Service Corporation, Chicago.

2 The Physical Setting

In the Beginning

The natural landscape of the Chicago region, as viewed by Jolliet and Marquette and by the Native Americans before them, was the result of millions of years of geologic action—for although the chronicle of human beings in Chicago is brief, the story of the land on which metropolitan Chicago spreads began eons ago.

Many millions of years ago, the first living creatures appeared in the ancient tropical sea that covered the mid-continent. Through the millennia of geologic eras, the limy skeletons and the shells of countless sea creatures settled over the ocean bottom where, eventually, they formed the rock known as limestone. In time, the ocean receded, but the limestone remained to form the bedrock on which rest Chicago's skyscrapers.

The bedrock is visible in limestone quarries, some road cuts, and some waterway channels. The limestone from the numerous quarries in the area has provided a basic building material. In Chicago, the limestone bedrock is visible at the more-than-a-century-old former Stearns quarry at Twenty-eighth and Halsted (800 W.) streets and flanking the Kennedy Expressway around Addison Street (3600 N.). Large limestone quarries were opened in Thornton, McCook, and other places throughout the area. Southwest of the city, the bedrock is exposed along sizable segments of the Calumet Sag Channel and the Chicago Sanitary and Ship Canal.

In the mild and fertile swampy areas that bordered the receding shallow inland seas, giant fern trees took hold, forming thick jungles of vegetation. As the plants and trees died, layer upon layer of dead vegetation, often buried by sediment, decomposed into peat. Millions of years later, the peat was compressed into harder fuel, coal, which was eventually mined in the southwestern fringe of the Chicago region, just beyond Joliet, at Coal City and Braidwood.

Effect of the Glaciers

Many thousands of years ago, changes in climate brought on a glacial period. At least four successive ice sheets crept down from the far north and covered much of what is now the northern part of the United States, including most of Illinois. These glaciers, advancing and retreating, greatly altered the landscape.

FIG. 2.2. Gravel pit along U.S. route 45 in Lake County, Illinois, showing glacial till of the Valparaiso Moraine. Photograph by Irving Cutler.

FIG. 2.3. Toboggan slide in the steep side of the Valparaiso Moraine in the Palos Hills Forest Preserve. Photograph by Irving Cutler.

The moving ice masses ground down elevations, polished rough surfaces, and gouged and deepened such areas as the basin of Lake Michigan. The glaciers left behind a covering of glacial drift—a jumble of clay, sand, gravel, and boulders over the limestone bedrock. In some places this drift reached a depth of more than 150 feet, with an average depth of between fifty and sixty feet. Later, some of the drift was commercially quarried.

In the Chicago region, the last glacier receded about 13,500 years ago, having sculpted the basic landscape surface. Chicago now occupies a lake plain that is hemmed in by a series of concentric ridges of glacial drift, called moraines, which are aligned generally parallel to the lake. The largest and most significant, especially in regard to the drainage pattern, is the outer crescent-shaped ridge around the southern end of Lake Michigan, stretching from southeastern Wisconsin into southwestern Michigan. Its surface exhibits substantial diversity. Known as the Valparaiso Moraine, it borders the southern and western part of the Lake Plain. Its inner edge is now followed approximately by the Tri-State Tollway. It averages about fifteen miles wide and, in general, stands twelve or so miles from Lake Michigan. The elevation of the moraine ranges from less than a hundred feet to more than five hundred feet above the level of Lake Michigan. The steep front of the moraine is used for the toboggan slide in the Palos Hills Forest Preserve.

The northern part of the Valparaiso Moraine is rugged and irregular, with rounded hills and undrained depressions. In Lake County, Illinois, and into Wisconsin, many of these depressions are occupied by approximately one hundred small lakes and ponds. This inland lake region has become an important recreational and residential area,

with sizable settlements around some of the larger lakes, such as Fox Lake, Pistakee Lake, Diamond Lake, Round Lake, Long Lake, Grayslake, and Lake Zurich.

On the eastern side of the northern part of the Valparaiso Moraine is the much smaller Lake Border Upland, an elongated belt of nearly north-south ridges with a width of five to fifteen miles. The main segment extends northward from about Des Plaines and Winnetka, with a narrow extension south into the Lake Plain as far as Oak Park. Some ridges rise to about two hundred feet above the lake level and are interspersed with gentle sags occupied by several small streams and an occasional marsh, such as the Skokie Lagoons. Lakeward of the Valparaiso Moraine and the Lake Border Upland—except between Winnetka and Waukegan where the bluffs rise abruptly from Lake Michigan—spreads the flat Lake Plain on which Chicago is situated.

The Lake Plain

As the last glacier retreated, water drainage to the north was blocked by ice; consequently, the glacier meltwater filled the depression between the receding ice front and the Valparaiso Moraine. This created a lake, marginal to the ice, that at its highest elevation rose about sixty feet above the present surface of Lake Michigan. This enlarged version of Lake Michigan, geologically known as Lake Chicago, covered all of the present city of Chicago, as well as a portion beyond it. The lakeshore stretched from approximately what is now Winnetka through the present communities of Maywood, La Grange, and Homewood, crossing the state line at Dyer, and then continuing eastward beyond Chesterton, Indiana.

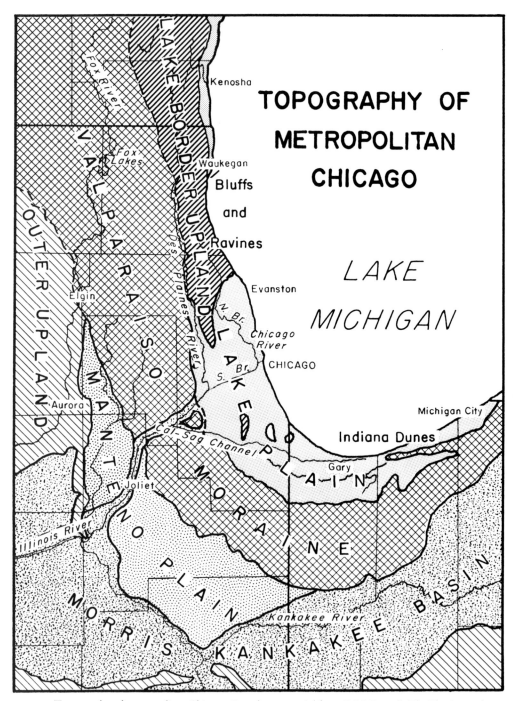

FIG. 2.4. Topography of metropolitan Chicago. Based on material from F. M. Fryxell, *The Physiography of the Region of Chicago;* from Rutherford H. Platt, *Open Land in Urban Illinois,* 1971; used with permission of Northern Illinois University Press.

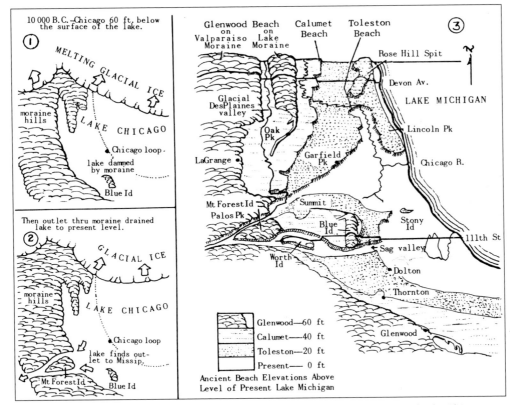

FIG. 2.5. Stages and development in the Chicago area of the three ancient beach levels of Lake Chicago. From W. J. Beecher, "Lake Michigan's Ancient Beaches," *Science Notes* (Chicago Academy of Sciences), n.d.

The accumulated water receded in stages, finding its way into the Illinois-Mississippi river drainage system by enlarging two outlets through the Valparaiso Moraine drainage divide. These outlets were later to become important transportation corridors. One of the outlets, which now holds the Calumet Sag Channel, was through the Sag Valley south and southwest of the city. The other outlet, to the southwest, sometimes known as the Chicago Portage, contained first the Illinois and Michigan Canal and later the Chicago Sanitary and Ship Canal, as well as other important transportation arteries, including railways and highways.

The drained bottom of Lake Chicago left the Chicago area remarkably flat—a lake plain—except for a few small islands that had existed in the lake, such as Mount Forest Island, Blue Island, and Stony Island, and some spits, sandbars, and crescent-shaped beach ridges that emerged as the water receded in three different stages (Fig. 2.5). These ridges stand about sixty feet, forty feet, and twenty feet higher than the present, approximately 580-feet-above-sea-level Lake Michigan. Driving away from the lake on an

FIG. 2.6. Looking east along 115th Street, where the street drops from the ancient beach ridge at the intersection of Michigan Avenue, 1895. Photograph by Henry R. Koopman; courtesy of Mrs. Walter Gindl.

east-west street, such as Devon Avenue (6400 N.) or 111th Street, will take one over each of the three beach ridges of Lake Chicago within a distance of ten to fifteen miles.

Because they were often the best-drained grounds in an otherwise marshy area, some of the sandy spits, bars, and beach ridges of the area became Native American trails, and some are now parts of modern roads such as Green Bay Road, Gross Point Road, Ridge Avenue, North Clark Street, Vincennes Avenue, U.S. routes 6, 20, and 30, and Interstate 94. The good drainage also made these areas attractive locations for cemeteries and golf courses. Both Graceland and Rosehill spits bear the names of large cemeteries on them.

Three small lakes near the Chicago-Hammond state-line boundary are isolated remnants of the glacial Lake Chicago. In recent decades, these lakes have declined in size because of marginal filling and drainage

alterations. Lake George, on the Indiana side, has virtually disappeared; Wolf Lake is a recreational area; and Lake Calumet has been developed as the major port of Chicago. Beach ridges separate the three lakes from Lake Michigan. A series of such ridges has hampered drainage in the Calumet district.

After the Glaciers

The basic topography of the Chicago area that developed through these ecological epochs resulted from the superimposition on the limestone bedrock of an uneven layer of glacial drift and, later, of the deposits of Lake Chicago. Since the Ice Age, a number of limited topographic changes have occurred. Through weathering, wind and water deposition, and vegetative growth, the present soils have been formed on the surface of the deposits of the glacial period. The soils are generally of good quality: very productive agriculturally, except where there are major drainage problems or where extensive sand deposits have accumulated, such as along the shore at the head of Lake Michigan, especially in parts of northwestern Indiana. A magnificent concentration of dunes has developed there owing to the continued action of the lake current and winds, which sweep sand southward.

A dune is formed when sand from the beach is blown inland until it strikes an obstruction, such as a bush or tree, and piles up on the windward side. In time, as the sand dune becomes higher, it may often kill or even bury the obstruction. The wind may blow sand from the windward slope of the dune over to the leeward side, creating a "moving" dune that migrates slowly inland. Small dunes are found several miles inland from Lake Michigan; large ones are close to the lake, some approaching heights of two hundred feet.

Another noteworthy postglacial change has been the result of shoreline erosion, which created scenic bluffs with deep ravines along the lake between Winnetka and Waukegan. Some of the bluffs are almost one hundred feet high, and many of the more than twenty major, deep, V-shaped ravines extend a mile or so inland. The ravines have been eroded by the downward cutting action of water runoff from the upland area into the lake below.

The effect of lakeshore erosion is dramatically illustrated by the following report:

FIG. 2.7. Lakeshore road in the dunes area of Beverly Shores, Indiana, damaged by high and powerful waves from Lake Michigan in winter 1973. Many homes on the side of the road adjacent to the lake were destroyed or badly damaged. Photograph by Irving Cutler.

In 1845 and for about ten years following there was a village located in the southeast corner of what is now the Fort Sheridan grounds. This village was known as St. Johns. The chief industry was brick making, the yards employing as many as eighty men. . . . North of the clay pit remnants of a foundation and of an orchard are at the very margin of the lake cliff. Reports differ as to the amount of land that has been cut away at this point, but all agree that it was more than 100 feet. Some old settlers insist that 300 to 400 feet have been removed, and that the cliff and even overhanging are reported by some to have been in the yard to the west of the westernmost house in the village. If this is true, the entire site of the village of St. Johns is east of the present shoreline.[1]

Today, except for adjacent St. Johns Avenue, even these meager traces of the village have vanished, prey to the attacking waves and currents.

The Chicago River

The Chicago River is the outstanding topographic feature of the rather featureless Lake Plain that contains the city of Chicago. Though short and sluggish (the important South Branch being only about six miles in length), the river has been a major factor in the establishment and growth of the city. It was the early connecting route between the East and the commercial wealth of the middle prairie. Early Chicago centered on the river and consisted mainly of the rectangular peninsula, about a mile square, that was enclosed on the north and west by the river and on the east by the lake. In the period of its greatest use, the river handled huge cargoes of grain, lumber, and manufactured goods. The river's main channel with its two branches forms a Y, with the junction near the Merchandise Mart. This configuration has, by tradition, divided Chicago into three broad sections—the North, South, and West sides.

The North Branch of the Chicago River originates in Lake County, Illinois, as three small streams that flow southward in the sags of the moraines of the Lake Border Upland. The three streams—the Skokie River, the Middle Fork, and the West Fork—join in northern Cook County and flow southeast toward the junction with the main channel. The North Branch is joined just south of Foster Avenue (5200 N.) by the North Shore Channel. This eight-mile channel was completed in 1910 by the Metropolitan Water Reclamation District of Greater Chicago to furnish an outlet for drainage and sewage for Wilmette, Evanston, and the adjacent area. Fresh water for the channel is drawn from Lake Michigan through the gates at Wilmette.

The South Branch was usually navigable only as far west as the present Leavitt Street (2200 W.). Often, however, during spring high water, it was possible to push canoes across the marshy divide all the way to the Des Plaines River (near Forty-ninth Street and Harlem Avenue [7200 W.]) by using seasonal Mud Lake, which bridged most of the six-mile portage between the two rivers.

The Chicago River has been greatly modified since it was navigated by the early explorers and was alive with fish, mink, muskrat, turtles, and wading birds. It has been straightened and widened in parts. The sandbar that blocked the river's mouth and caused it to bend southward and flow into

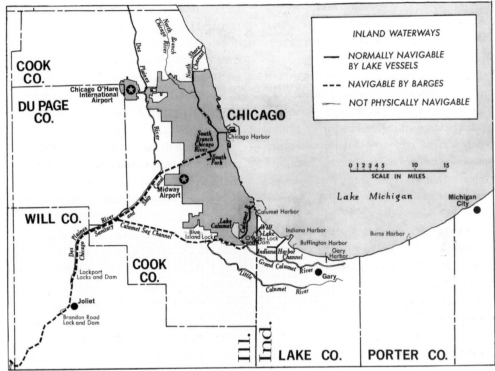

FIG. 2.8. Harbors and waterways of the Chicago area. Updated from University of Chicago Center for Urban Studies, *Mid-Chicago Economic Development Study* (Chicago: Mayor's Committee for Economic and Cultural Development, 1966).

the lake opposite the foot of Madison Street has been removed. An artificial island, Goose Island, was created and a sharp bend bypassed with the construction of the mile-long North Branch Canal. Most important, the portage was eliminated and the South Branch of the river was connected with the Illinois-Mississippi river waterway system, first by the Illinois and Michigan Canal in 1848, and later by the Chicago Sanitary and Ship Canal in 1900. In addition, the Chicago River was reversed to flow into these connecting waterways instead of into Lake Michigan, whose shoreline waters were being polluted by the unsanitary discharges of the river.

Unfortunately, during this period, the river was largely walled off by industrial development and its aquatic life was drastically curtailed. However, in recent years, various environment-conscious groups have promoted limited improvements and have dedicated themselves to the rebirth of the river as a multipurpose, clean, pleasant, life-supportive waterway that could serve as a vibrant artery through the heart of the city, as well as a controlled transportation and industrial corridor. As the river has become cleaner, new parks, residences, and short trails have developed along the waterway. The late mayor Richard J. Daley once predicted that the Chicago River would become so clean that people would be able to fish for their lunch along its banks. He undoubtedly would have been shocked to learn that in April 1992 one could catch fish swimming in the basement of City Hall as the result of a river bridge protection piling being pounded into part of the sixty-two-mile-long downtown freight tunnel, thereby unleashing 124 million gallons of water. The water flooded the basements of most Loop buildings, including the Marshall Field store on State Street and two Chicago Transit Authority subway tunnels. The floodwaters knocked out electrical and natural gas services, and some Loop facilities were closed for weeks. Damage and business losses amounted to at least a billion dollars.

The Calumet River

At the southeastern end of the city is Chicago's other important river, the Calumet. It is formed by the confluence of the nearly parallel Grand Calumet and Little Calumet rivers. Joined to the Calumet as a saclike attachment on Chicago's Far South Side is Lake Calumet—the site of Chicago's major port. Unlike the Chicago River, the Calumet River played an insignificant role in Chicago's early history. Later, however, it became one of the most industrialized rivers in the world—the "Ruhr of America"—and carried considerable tonnage, although that activity has been declining rapidly in recent decades.

The early settlers found the Calumet to be a strange, erratic, meandering stream that had formed an elongated loop parallel to the lake. The river flowed westward from its source in Indiana and then looped back into Indiana only two or three miles to the north, flowing in the opposite direction to empty into Lake Michigan near Miller, Indiana. Frequently, the

mouth of the river was nearly closed by sand drift.

Later, the Calumet River, like the Chicago River, was altered to suit human purposes. The mouth at Miller was blocked and a channel was dug from the river near Hegewisch to an outlet into Lake Michigan at about Ninetieth Street in South Chicago. The river was again altered in 1922 when the sixteen-mile Calumet Sag Channel was dug. The Calumet River was reversed to flow away from Lake Michigan into the Calumet Sag Channel and eventually into the Illinois-Mississippi river system.

The Drainage Pattern

The reversal of the Chicago and Calumet rivers altered the unusual drainage pattern of the Chicago region. In creating moraines parallel to Lake Michigan, glacial action also created a drainage divide parallel to the lake and relatively close to it. Water on one side of the divide flows into the Great Lakes–St. Lawrence River system, and that on the other side, into the Gulf of Mexico via the Illinois-Mississippi river system. The divide is less than four miles from the lake in the Waukegan, Illinois, area and, at its farthest point, south of Hammond, Indiana, about twenty miles from the lake.

A few short rivers on the eastern side of the divide, such as the Chicago and the Calumet, broke through sandbars to reach Lake Michigan, but major rivers such as the Fox, Des Plaines, and Kankakee never penetrated the moraines; instead, they flow into the Mississippi Basin. In places, the divide is less than one hundred feet above Lake Michigan. At its lowest point, the Chicago outlet at Summit, Illinois, the divide is a barely discernible fifteen feet above the lake.

The Kankakee, Fox, and Des Plaines rivers have the largest drainage basins in the area. The Kankakee drains the largest area—more than five thousand square miles—but only a small part, in Will County, is within the six-county metropolitan area. The river starts in Indiana, flows westward, and crosses the southwest corner of Will County, where it joins the Des Plaines River to form the Illinois River. In Indiana, the Kankakee is considered a drainage ditch, straightened and channelized to drain the old Grand Marsh, once one of the nation's most famous wildlife areas. The drainage project produced a million acres of rich Indiana farmland. In Illinois, the Kankakee is still a winding natural river, the home of a spectacular array of wildlife, where record-sized fish are caught. The river is an important source of drinking water and recreation along its Illinois portion and adds an estimated $50 million annually to the economy of the area. The differences in use of the river in Indiana and Illinois have, on occasion, led to friction between the two states over the "waterway with a split personality."

The Fox River arises in Wisconsin and flows seventy miles southward before entering the northwestern part of Lake County, Illinois. There it flows through the recreational Chain of Lakes, Fox Lake, and Pistakee Lake area. The river then continues southward through McHenry and Kane counties before angling to the southwest and joining the Illinois River at Ottawa, Illinois. The drainage area of the Fox covers almost two thousand square miles, about half of which is in the Chicago metropolitan area. In Kane County, the river is near the ever-expanding edge of the urban area, although some of the communities that straddle the Fox River, such as Elgin and Aurora, are industrial cities almost as old as Chicago itself.

The Des Plaines River starts in the sloughs and marshes near the boundary between Kenosha and Racine counties in Wisconsin and flows south some ninety miles through Illinois' Lake, Cook, Du Page, and Will counties before joining the Kankakee River to form the Illinois River. The Des Plaines River drains about a thousand square miles, mainly within the Chicago metropolitan area. It has two sizable tributaries, Salt Creek and the Du Page River, both of which flow parallel to the Des Plaines River for many miles. At Summit, the Des Plaines River turns to the southwest, descending toward Joliet. It is a small river in the relatively wide, deep, scenic valley formed by the mighty torrents that flowed through the Chicago outlet with the melting of the last glacier.

The twenty-five miles of the Des Plaines River valley between Summit and Joliet is a most interesting area, traversed also by the historic Illinois and Michigan Canal. Although dotted with scattered industry and settlements, the valley contains sizable natural areas and places of geologic and historic value. These include virgin prairie and wetlands, dense forest growth, Native American archaeological sites, interesting geologic formations, waters paddled by early explorers, rapids, river islands, abandoned spring-fed quarries replete with fish, historic trails, and towns, such as Lockport and Lemont, rich in history and beauty. This stretch of land is now part of the Illinois and Michigan Canal National Heritage Corridor. The Corridor was established in 1984 by the federal government as a ninety-six-mile-long linear route along the Illinois and Michigan Canal whose attractions draw increasing numbers of visitors. The Corridor is financed and administered by local government and private interests.

Because the land of so much of the Chicago area is flat, rivers tend to be sluggish and drainage of the land is poor, with some of the lowland river areas subject to occasional flooding. Layers of impermeable clay left by the glaciers also hampered the drainage of surface waters, created a high water table, and helped make early Chicago a virtual sea of mud for at least part of the year. To obtain adequate gradient for storm and sanitary sewers, the Metropolitan Water Reclamation District of Greater Chicago has had to provide more than a dozen pumping stations to enhance the flow to the extensive drainage canal system.

The Vegetation

The Chicago region is a transition zone between the vegetative patterns of the great eastern forests of North America and the prairies to the west. The transition zone once contained both forests and tall-grass prairies. An early settler, Gurdon S. Hubbard, wrote about the natural landscape with its grasslands and forests: "The waving green, intermingling with a rich profusion of wildflowers, was the most beautiful sight I had ever gazed upon. In the distance the grove of Blue Island loomed up—beyond it the timber on the Des Plaines River."

The solid stands of forest diminished westward in Illinois largely because of declining rainfall. The zone's average annual rainfall of 34.44 inches is substantially less than the forty to fifty inches farther east, which nurtured a beech-maple forest. However, there is enough rain to support drier oak-hickory stands and extensive tall-grass prairie. The percentage

of forestland generally increased to the east and to the north and was prevalent and more varied in wet bottomlands, especially adjacent to the rivers. Along the river floodplains stand elms, hackberries, and basswoods.

The preferred choice of the earliest farmers in the area usually was well-drained prairie land that was partly forested. The forest supplied construction timber and fuel and provided protection against winds and floods, but it also presented the problem of clearance. Later settlers had to choose mainly prairie, but such land generally was more productive than cleared forestland.

The natural vegetation of the Chicago area is indicative of its position as a meeting ground for plants of a number of regions.

The plants fall chiefly into three categories: "hangovers" of species of the North that have persisted locally since the glacial era; returned plant migrants from the southeastern states that had been driven out during glacial times; and a few species that migrated from the semiarid Southwest.

Within a generation or two of the start of intensive settlement of the area, most of the forestland and prairie grass had disappeared, except in a few isolated patches, on the moraines and along the rivers where drainage was often poor. Many of the remaining wooded areas, especially along the rivers, later became part of the extensive sixty-eight-thousand-acre system of the Forest Preserve District of Cook County.

The cosmopolitan character of the vegetation in the area was especially evident in the unusual and largely untouched Indiana sand dune region. Professor H. C. Cowles, a pioneer plant ecologist, developed largely from his studies of these dunes the concept of the dynamics of plant succession, especially the correlation between changes in vegetation and changes in landforms due to the action of wind, wave, and the presence of vegetation. The following is his description, early in this century, of the vegetation of the Indiana dunes:

There are a few places on our continent where so many species of plants are found in so small compass. This is in part because of the wide diversity of conditions prevailing there. Within a stone's throw of almost any spot one may find plants of the desert and plants of rich woodlands, plants of the pine woods, and plants of swamps, plants of oak woods and plants of prairies. Species of the most diverse natural regions are piled here together in such abundance as to make the region a natural botanical preserve, not only of the plants that are characteristic of northern Indiana, but also of the plants of remote outlying regions. Here one may find the prickly pear cactus of the southwestern desert hob-nobbing with the bearberry of the arctic and alpine regions. The commonest pine of the dunes, the jack pine, is far out of its main range, reaching here its farthest south. One is almost startled at the number of plants of the far north, many of which, like the jack pine, are not found to the southward of our dunes. Among such plants of the Canadian forest and tundra are the twinflower, the glandular willow, the poverty grass, and the northern rose. Northern plants are particularly characteristic of the dune swamps and embrace such interesting species as the larch, bunchberry, dwarf birch, sage willow, numerous orchids, cranberry, leather leaf, and many more. Many of these species are found nowhere for many miles outside of the dune region.[2]

The Climate

A major characteristic of the climate of Chicago is its variability from season to season and even from day to day. The seasonal change in temperature is due to the northern latitude and the interior continental location. Seasonally, the temperature ranges from an average daily reading of 24.3°F in January to 74.7°F in July, with a yearly mean of 49.2°F. Individual daily extremes have officially been recorded ranging from -27°F in 1985 to 105°F in 1934.

The day-to-day changes are mainly the result of a procession of high- and low-pressure areas that move across Chicago at intervals of a few days in a generally easterly direction. The succession of highs and lows gives to the weather its frequently changing aspects of warm and cold, rainy and snowy, cloudy and sunny.

The climate of the Chicago area is suitable for agriculture, and the region was once very productive, especially in dairying and truck farming. Agriculture declined with the spread of urbanization, although it still exists in the surrounding rural areas.

The region averages 183 consecutive frost-free days a year. Summers are warm, but the lake, in addition to its welcome breezes, exerts a moderating influence, keeping the city somewhat cooler than areas farther inland. The reverse occurs in the winter, when temperatures are higher near the lake than to the west. Despite Chicago's windy reputation, the breezes, which blow predominantly from the west, are moderate in velocity, with an annual average of 10.4 miles per hour. The "Windy City" designation is sometimes said to have been bestowed in 1893 by the editor of the *New York Sun*, Charles Dana, who was

FIG. 2.9. Dairy farm in Cook County, Illinois, 1969. The land is now the site of a large housing development. Photograph by Irving Cutler.

tired of hearing Chicagoans boast about the wonders of their World's Exposition (though some claim the nickname is even older and credit it to politicians).

Precipitation is adequate for productive agriculture in the area, with about one-third usually coming during May, June, and July. Droughts are rare, as are prolonged rainy periods. Annual seasonal snowfall is 39.7 inches, with extremes ranging from 9.8 inches in 1920–21 to 89.7 inches in the unusually severe winter of 1978–79. On the average, ten inches of snow is considered the equivalent of one inch of rain. The greatest single snowfall was twenty-three inches in 1967.

There is some evidence that Chicago has slightly more rain than the nearby suburbs and rural areas. A recent study showed that the city produces atmospheric changes that increase local rainfall slightly. Two factors seem to account for this increased rainfall. First, there is a greater prevalence of dust, water vapor, and other tiny particles over the city. These motes and droplets provide nuclei for cloud condensation. Second, more heat rises from city surfaces, buildings, and automobiles than from open land, and as this warm air rises, it is cooled and may form rain clouds over the city.

In summer, the Chicago area is subject to occasional severe thunderstorms with very strong winds. Once in a while, a tornado will develop and touch down, usually in a suburban area. In 1967, for example, a tornado touched down in the southwest suburban area around Oak Lawn, killing thirty-three, injuring five hundred, and causing $50 million in damage. A dozen tornadoes have been recorded inside the Chicago city limits, but so far, only one, in 1961, has resulted in serious damage. It moved across the South Side of the city from approximately Ninety-first Street and Hoyne Avenue (2100 W.) to Sixty-first Street and the lake, killing one person and injuring 115.

Two possible explanations have been given for central Chicago's relative absence of tornadoes. One is the "heat island" theory that suggests that the rising warmer air from the city creates updrafts that cause tornadoes to skip over central Chicago. The more widely accepted theory is that tornadoes thrive on flat land and their force is dissipated somewhat by building obstructions. The built-up suburban sprawl seems to have created a relatively safe zone in the central part of Chicago.

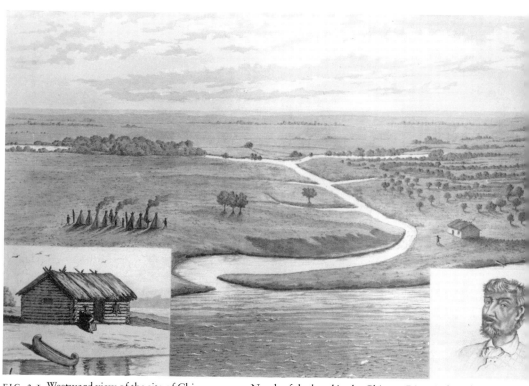

FIG. 3.1. Westward view of the site of Chicago, 1779. North of the bend in the Chicago River is the cabin of Jean Baptiste Point du Sable, the first permanent settler (du Sable and his home shown in insets). The sandbar at the river's mouth caused the river to bend southward and flow for almost a half mile along approximately what is now Michigan Avenue until it entered the lake at about the site of present-day Madison Street. In the distant center are the forks of the river where the South Branch and North Branch join, forming the main channel. To the left is a small Native American encampment. Chicago Historical Society, ICHi-05623.

3 The Evolution of Chicago

Early Settlement

A century after Marquette and Jolliet passed through the area in 1673, Chicago still had no permanent settlers. During the period of French rule, which lasted until the cession of the land to the British in 1763, there had been sporadic but limited activity in the area. Other explorers for France, notably René-Robert Cavelier, Sieur de La Salle, and his companion Henri de Tonti, had passed through the area around the 1680s. Later, because of its excellent geographic location and portage, a number of French voyageurs, trappers, and fur traders also traversed the area. Native Americans, mainly members of the Potawatomi, which was the most powerful tribe around the southern end of Lake Michigan, hunted, traded furs, and occasionally camped in the area they called "Checagou," evidently referring to the garlicky wild onion smell that permeated the air.[1]

The territory was under British rule for twenty years, until the Treaty of Paris in 1783 ended the American Revolutionary War and made the area part of the new United States. The British nonetheless lingered on illegally until the Jay Treaty of 1794 pledged British evacuation.

Native American resentment at being driven from their lands continued to make permanent settlement of the area hazardous. A turning point for the Chicago area came with the defeat of Native Americans at Fallen Timbers, Ohio, by the army of "Mad Anthony" Wayne. The ensuing Treaty of Greenville of 1795 forced the Native Americans to cede "one piece of land, six miles square at the mouth of the Chicago River." The treaty cleared the title to Chicago and opened to settlement a thirty-six-square-mile area encompassed today by the lake, Cicero Avenue (4800 W.), Fullerton Avenue (2400 N.), and Thirty-first Street. In 1803 the U.S. Army erected Fort Dearborn at an elevated point in the bend near the mouth of the Chicago River in order to secure the area and protect the important waterway linkage, which became even more important with the Louisiana Purchase that same year.

In the late 1770s, even before the building of the fort, Jean Baptiste Point du Sable built a cabin on the north bank of the river in the vicinity of the present Tribune Tower. Du Sable's father is believed to have been French and his mother a Negro slave. Du Sable

FIG. 3.2. Fort Dearborn, originally erected in 1803 by Captain John Whistler and a company of U.S. soldiers. It was burned by Native Americans in 1812. The site is now outlined by metal plaques embedded in the sidewalk at the intersection of Michigan Avenue and Wacker Drive. Chicago Historical Society, ICHi-21562.

described himself as a "free Negro."[1] His home was probably Chicago's first permanent dwelling; from here, for about two decades, du Sable carried on trade with the Native Americans. Later the house was occupied by another trader, John Kinzie, who was also a famous early settler of Chicago.

Despite the fort, settlement in this part of Illinois remained sparse, in contrast to southern Illinois, which was rapidly becoming occupied by settlers. A major reason was the persistent hostility of the Native Americans, who were angered by the continuing takeover of their lands. This anger was brutally manifested in the War of 1812, when a group of soldiers and settlers who had been ordered to evacuate Fort Dearborn in order to contract

the western military perimeter against the British were ambushed by Native Americans. This ambush took place in 1812 along the shores of the lake at about what is now Eighteenth Street and Calumet Avenue (344 E.). Fifty-three men, women, and children were killed. The Native Americans burned Fort Dearborn to the ground, and once again Chicago lapsed into a prairie wilderness.

In 1816 Fort Dearborn was reestablished after a treaty between Great Britain and the United States. News of the outpost's rebuilding attracted a few settlers, tradesmen, and agents to the vicinity of the fort. But large-scale settlement did not begin until the conclusion of the Black Hawk War in 1832. The treaty with the Native Americans provided for their relocation west of the Mississippi River in return for certain payments in cash and goods.

The Native Americans assembled in Chicago for their final payments in 1835. Also gathering there were a motley group of wayfarers—horse dealers and horse stealers, peddlers, grog sellers, and "rogues of every description, white, black, brown and red-half-breeds, quarter-breeds, and men of no breed at all." By ruse, whiskey, and thievery, they managed to separate the Native Americans from a good part of their money and goods. About eight hundred Native Americans joined in a last defiant dance of farewell before crossing the bridge over the South Branch of the Chicago River and heading westward until Chicago saw them no more.

Town and City

No longer impeded by fear of the Native Americans, the trickle of newcomers to the little military and trading outpost grew into a stream. The westward movement of people and trade was aided by the opening of the Erie Canal in 1825 and the subsequent establishment of regular, cheap, and convenient steamboat service from the East, via the Great Lakes. Migration was also helped by an improvement in land transportation to the Chicago area, as competing Atlantic ports fostered the building of canals and roads westward to tap the growing midwestern hinterland.

The rapid push westward to this area was also due to a variety of difficulties experienced in other areas—especially in the eastern United States and in western Europe. Men were drawn to Chicago by cheap land, jobs, and a speculative fervor stimulated by plans for a canal that would connect Lake Michigan with the Mississippi River.

Settlers came in increasing numbers, some fanning out into adjacent lands and some remaining in Chicago. In 1831 the first Methodist church in Chicago was established with a congregation of ten members. Services were held in a log cabin on Wolf Point, at the fork of the Chicago River. In 1833 the first Baptist, Catholic, and Presbyterian churches were established. Also in 1833, Chicago, with a population of around 350, was incorporated as a town. The town was only three-eighths of a square mile in size and centered on the main channel of the Chicago River. Its boundaries encompassed the present Kinzie Street (400 N.) on the north, Madison Street (N. and S. baseline) on the south, State Street (E. and W. baseline) on the east, and Des Plaines Street (700 W.) on the west. Also, in the same year, Congress appropriated twenty-five thousand dollars for major improvements to the harbor. In 1834 a channel was opened through the sandbar at the mouth of the river and, to protect the entrance to the harbor, five-hundred-foot piers were constructed on either side.

In the year of its incorporation, Chicago was described by the Scottish traveler Patrick Shirreff as follows:

Chicago consists of about 150 wood houses, placed irregularly on both sides of the river, over which there is a bridge. This is already a place of considerable trade, supplying salt, tea, coffee, sugar, and clothing to a large tract of country to the north and west; and when connected with the navigable point of the river Illinois, by a canal or railway, cannot fail of rising to importance. Almost every person I met regarded Chicago as the germ of an immense city, and speculators have already bought up, at high prices, all the building-ground in the neighborhood.[2]

Chicago's rapid growth was reflected in a number of ways. In 1833 black bears were still being killed on the fringes of what is today's Loop. Only four lake steamers entered the harbor that year; by 1836, the number had increased to 450. A parcel of land at South Water (300 N.) and Clark (100 W.) streets costing one hundred dollars in 1832 was sold for fifteen thousand dollars in 1835. And by 1837, when Chicago was incorporated as a city, the population exceeded four thousand people.

The city, at incorporation, encompassed some ten square miles. Its boundaries were North Avenue (1600 N.) on the north, Twenty-second Street on the south, the lake on the east, and Wood Street (1800 W.) on the west. Ten years later, as the population grew, the western boundary was extended to Western Avenue (2400 W.).

The author John Lewis Peyton portrayed the burgeoning Chicago of 1848 as follows:

The city is situated on both sides of the Chicago river, a sluggish slimy stream, too lazy to clean itself, and on both sides of its north and south branches, upon a level piece of ground, half dry and half wet, resembling a salt marsh, and contained a population of 20,000. There was no pavement, no macadamized streets, no drainage, and the three thousand houses in which the people lived were almost entirely small timber buildings painted white, and this white much defaced by mud. . . .

Chicago was already becoming a place of considerable importance for manufacturers. Steam mills were busy in every part of the city preparing lumber for buildings which were contracted to be erected by the thousand the next season. Large establishments were engaged in manufacturing agricultural implements of every description for the farmers who flocked to the country every spring. A single establishment, that of McCormick[,] employed several hundred hands, and during each season completed from fifteen hundred to two thousand grain-reapers and grass-mowers.

Blacksmith, wagon and coachmaker's shops were busy preparing for a spring demand, which with all their energy, they could not supply. Brickmakers had discovered on the lake shore near the city and a short distance in the interior, excellent beds of clay, and were manufacturing, even at this time, millions of brick by a patent process, which the frost did not hinder, or delay. Hundreds of workmen were also engaged in quarrying stone and marble on the banks of the projected canal; and the Illinois Central Railway employed large bodies of men in driving piles and constructing a track and depot on the beach. Real estate agents were mapping out the surrounding territory for ten and fifteen miles in the interior, giving fancy names to the future avenues, streets, squares, and parks. A brisk traffic existed in the sale of corner lots, and men with nothing but their wits, had been known to succeed in a single season in making a fortune—sometimes, certainly, it was only on paper. . . .[3]

By 1850, Chicago's population had grown to about thirty thousand, and its future role as a great transportation and industrial center was already clearly evident. The Illinois and Michigan Canal opened in 1848, connecting

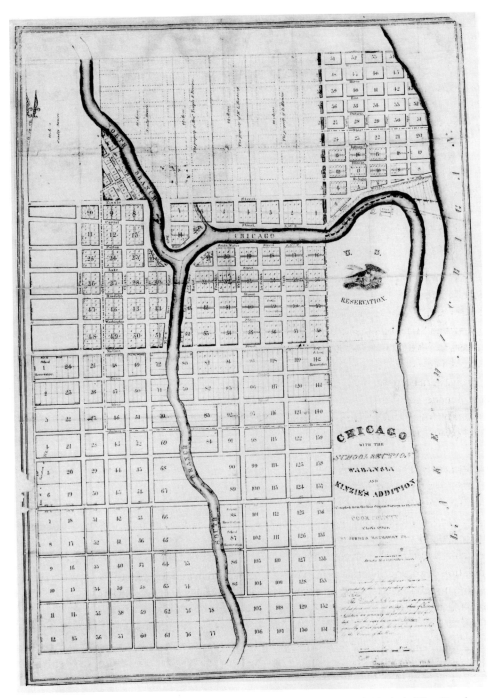

FIG. 3.3. Chicago streets and subdivisions, 1834. The U.S. reservation *(right)* included Fort Dearborn, along the bend in the river. The same year, an artificial canal was cut through the sandbar at the mouth of the river. Joshua Hathaway; Chicago Historical Society, ICHi-17663.

FIG. 3.4. View west, between Randolph and Washington streets, from La Salle Street, 1858. The photograph, taken by Alexander Hesler, a pioneer Chicago photographer, captures the clutter of retail establishments, livery stables, woodsheds, and cheap hotels. The four-story building on La Salle Street, in the foreground, housed an undertaker's business. The masts of several ships on the South Branch of the Chicago River are visible in the distance. Chicago Historical Society.

the Great Lakes with the Mississippi Valley. It was ninety-six miles long, from Chicago's Southwest Side near Ashland Avenue (1600 W.) and the South Branch of the Chicago River to the confluence with the Illinois River near La Salle, Illinois. Shortly thereafter, a period of vigorous railroad building brought railroad tracks to Chicago from almost every direction. By 1855, Chicago was already the focus of ten trunk lines. Ninety-six trains a day arrived or departed from the city, and on a single day, the Michigan Central brought two thousand immigrants into the city.

Chicago's location and its excellent transportation connections with the rich agricultural hinterland helped forge strong bonds of interdependence between the city and the farmers of the Midwest. The farmers funneled their produce to Chicago, and the city provided stockyards, food processing, and grain elevators, as well as ships and trains to deliver the commodities eastward. From Chicago, the farmers were shipped clothing, processed food, household items, lumber, and farm equipment. Much of the farm equipment was manufactured by the McCormick Reaper factory, which had been established in 1847 on the north bank of the river at the site of the former du Sable cabin. Cyrus McCormick from Virginia was among the first of a long line of commercial and industrial entrepreneurs who, together with their employees, were to help make Chicago "Hog Butcher for the World, Tool Maker, Stacker of Wheat, Player with Railroads and the Nation's Freight Handler."

On the whole, political and economic dominance was held initially by men from the eastern United States. With remarkable combinations of thrift, shrewdness, and drive, they acknowledged no barriers to the successful expansion of a wide range of enterprises.

Often with little regard for others in their climb to the top, they did what they thought had to be done to raise a city out of a swamp.

Among these early pioneer leaders was William B. Ogden of New York, who was elected the city's first mayor in 1837. One of the earliest of many Chicagoans to promote the building of railroads, he later was the first president of the Union Pacific. Potter Palmer arrived in 1852 from New York. He made a fortune in dry goods and cotton speculation, adding to his wealth by developing State Street. In 1867 Marshall Field, who came from Massachusetts, became part owner in the firm that was later to bear his name. Two farm youths from the East, Gustavus Swift and Philip D. Armour, helped make Chicago the meat packer of the nation. In 1892 the latter also founded the Armour Institute of Technology, now part of the Illinois Institute of Technology.

A new era in railroad travel began in 1864 when George Pullman invented the sleeping car. Later his shops for building passenger and freight cars spread over thirty-five hundred acres near Lake Calumet. Julius Rosenwald, a native of Springfield, Illinois, learned the clothing business, went to work for Sears, Roebuck and Company, and eventually became the president and board chairman, as well as one of the nation's great philanthropists. Sears' major competitor, Montgomery Ward, was founded shortly after the Chicago Fire of 1871 by A. Montgomery Ward, who had lost everything in the conflagration but sixty-five dollars and the clothes he wore. He later earned the nickname "watchdog of the lakefront" for his long but successful struggle to save the Grant Park area from being commercialized—thereby upholding an 1836 legal provision that designated the area as "public

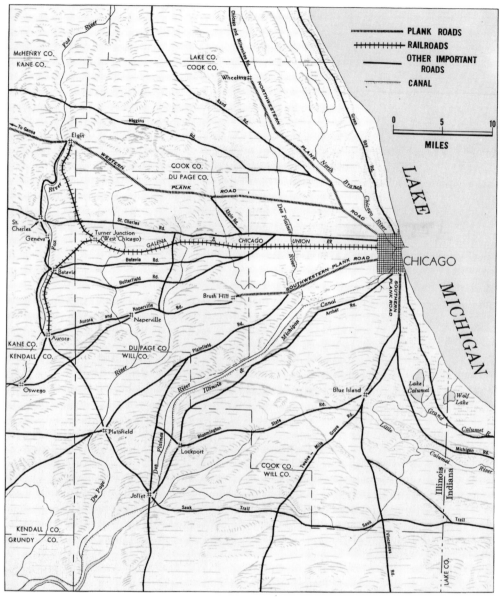

FIG. 3.5. Transportation routes of the Chicago area, 1850. Reproduced, with permission, from Harold M. Mayer and Richard C. Wade, *Chicago: Growth of a Metropolis*, © 1969 by the University of Chicago.

FIG. 3.6. Illinois Central Railroad, 1860. The tracks paralleled the lakeshore from the South Side to the Chicago River. The front row of buildings in the background is on Michigan Avenue. Lithograph by Jevne and Almini; Chicago Historical Society.

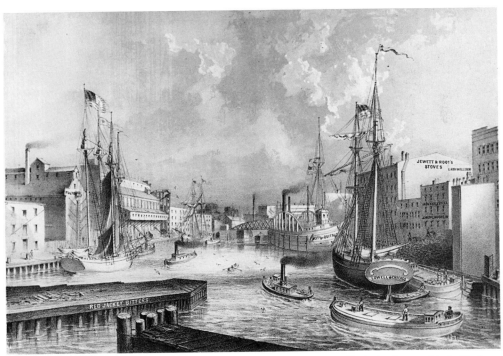

FIG. 3.7. Eastward view along the Chicago River from State Street, 1868. In the background is the Rush Street Bridge. On the left is the grain elevator of the Galena and Union Railroad, and in the lower righthand corner is a canal boat being towed from the Illinois and Michigan Canal. Lithograph by Jevne and Almini; Chicago Historical Society.

FIG. 3.8. Lock of the Illinois and Michigan Canal at Lockport. This photograph was probably taken between 1900 and 1910 when canal traffic already had declined sharply. Chicago Historical Society.

ground, forever to remain vacant of building." He is honored with a statue in the park.

The Street Pattern

Fundamental to Chicago's internal development was its street pattern. The Federal Ordinance of 1785, with its land survey provisions, imparted to early Chicago a basic functional pattern of land subdivision and roads. Even today, it is a strong determinant in the pattern of streets, traffic flow, commercial development, and arrangement of lots and parcels.

Surveyors divided the land into square-mile sections using a rectangular grid system. The section lines were a mile apart and ran either north-south or east-west. They became the city's main traffic thoroughfares and, later, the major routes of public transportation. The section-line streets also became endless ribbons of commercial development, which ultimately became too extensive and inefficient. Major shopping areas often developed at the intersections of section lines, such as Sixty-third and Halsted (800 W.), and Madison (N. and S. baseline) and Pulaski (4000 W.).

In Chicago there are typically sixteen short blocks to the mile in the east-west direction and eight long blocks in the north-south direction, although there are many variations from this pattern, especially in the older parts of the city. The street numbering system of Chicago was adopted in the early 1900s and, with a few exceptions, is based on a theoretical eight hundred numbers to the mile. Thus, there are section-line streets of Thirty-first, Thirty-ninth, Forty-seventh, Fifty-fifth, and so on, and in the other direction, such streets as Halsted (800 W.), Ashland (1600 W.), Western (2400 W.), and Kedzie (3200 W.). Frequently, half-mile streets, halfway between the section lines, became important thoroughfares and

FIG. 3.9. Chicago, 1860s. Prominent features of the city are its rectangular-grid pattern of streets and the great activity on its lake and river. Lithograph by Rufus Blanchard; Chicago Historical Society, ICHi-05665; creator Edward Mendel.

FIG. 3.10. State Street, south from Lake Street, in the late 1860s. Chicago Historical Society.

shopping streets, like California Avenue (2800 W.) and Fifty-first Street.

In time, as a result of tradition, zoning laws, and actual development, this rigid rectangular grid system became virtually fixed as the basic pattern of Chicago. This had an advantage in that the right-angle pattern eliminated travel dangers associated with streets meeting at acute angles. Chicago's few diagonal streets, such as Archer, Ogden, and Milwaukee, were major exceptions. Many of these had begun as Native American trails that followed higher and drier land. The subdividing of lots and the assigning of street addresses were also simplified by this rectangular street pattern.

On the other hand, this street pattern led to a monotonous uniformity, made virtually all streets "through streets," and fostered unneeded commercial ribbons. Furthermore, the grid system discouraged some pleasing patterns, such as distance-saving diagonals, curvilinear streets, cul-de-sacs, streets following terrain, drainage, or scenic conditions, and planned housing and shopping developments—features that have been adopted in many of the newer suburbs of the metropolitan area.

Mudhole of the Prairies

In their 1895 book, Joseph Kirkland and John Moses explain that mud was the main problem of the streets of early Chicago.

> [In 1848, Chicago] could boast of no sewers nor were there any sidewalks except a few planks here and there, nor paved streets. The streets were merely graded to the middle, like country roads, and in bad weather, were impassable. A mud hole deeper than usual would be marked by signboards with the significant notice thereon, "No bottom here, the shortest road to China."

... Wabash Avenue, between Adams and Jackson Streets, was regarded as out of town, where wolves were occasionally seen prowling about.[4]

The difficulty arose because Chicago was flat and low, being only about two feet above the river level. Moreover, the sewage that did drain off into the Chicago River flowed into Lake Michigan, the city's source of drinking water. The resulting epidemics of cholera, typhoid, and other diseases were not finally curtailed until the flow of the Chicago River was reversed in 1900. Before that, Chicago tried to lift itself from the quagmire by actually raising the elevation of the city. After the death of 1,424 people in 1854 from cholera, the city council, at the urging of community leaders including, particularly, a group of downtown businessmen and major industrialists in a power pattern repeated many times since, decreed that the streets should be elevated.

FIG. 3.11. Chicago slough, late 1880s. At the time of settlement, Chicago contained numerous sloughs, including this prominent one along South State Street. Chicago Historical Society.

FIG. 3.12. Clark Street, 1857. In 1855 the city council decided to raise the level of the streets and sidewalks to lift Chicago out of the mud. The project proceeded unevenly for several years, with the result that there were often several levels in the sidewalk in a single block. Engraving from A. T. Andreas, *History of Chicago: From the Earliest Period to the Present Time* (Chicago: A. T. Andreas, 1884–86); Chicago Historical Society.

Street levels were raised by piling fill several feet deep—sometimes the fill was obtained from the dredgings of the waterways.

In 1854 George M. Pullman demonstrated successfully, with the help of five hundred men and twenty-five hundred screwjacks, how even one of the largest of Chicago's buildings, the Tremont Hotel, could be lifted eight feet "without disturbing a guest or cracking a cup." The idea caught on in this spirited community of ardent boosters, and within two decades, several thousand acres had been raised three to five feet above their former level to allow for sewer pipes that were higher than the lake or river, thus improving drainage. For a time, however, Chicago exhibited a somewhat confusing pattern of disjointed sidewalks; some up and some down, depend-

ing on whether the owner had raised his property or not. And even today, especially in the inner city, one can find yards and homes below the raised street level—some with steps leading down to the first floor, and others with a small, bridge-like platform or steps leading from the sidewalk to what was formerly the second floor but is now the main entrance. In some of the areas, the street was paved on top of solid fill, but the sidewalk was raised over hollow spaces, or "vaults," and was held in place by a retaining wall on each side. For a while, the spaces under the sidewalks and bridgelike platforms were useful as places for outhouses or for the storage of coal; however, today, some of the vaulted sidewalks are in need of costly repairs.

Despite such problems, Chicago continued to grow and prosper. It was buoyed by the

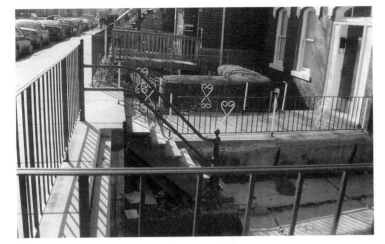

FIG. 3.14. Forks of the Chicago River, north from Randolph Street, before the 1871 fire. The North Branch flows from the top left and the South Branch from the lower right to form the main stem of the river. Two of the major businesses along the river are evident here: lumberyards and grain elevators. The open bridge on the right is at Lake Street; in the right background are Illinois and Michigan Canal barges tied up near Wolf Point, on the north side of the main stem of the river. Chicago Historical Society.

opening of the Illinois and Michigan Canal; heavy lake traffic (13,730 ships arrived in 1869); the coming of the railroads (thirteen were operating by 1870); the development of substantial industry, fueled somewhat by the Civil War; the further settling of its rich hinterland; and the accelerated influx of settlers. Chicago rapidly became the most important link between the industrial East and the rich agricultural lands to the west. Between 1850 and 1870, the population increased tenfold, from thirty thousand to about three hundred thousand. The disastrous Chicago Fire of 1871, however, cast a temporary pall on the growth of Chicago.

The Fire

Kogan and Cromie described the Chicago of that time as follows:

In the autumn of 1871, Chicago was a city of 334,000, partly a metropolis and partly a frontier town, six miles long and three miles wide. . . . It was known by various nicknames: Gem of the Prairie, Garden City, Queen City. And some considered it one of the wickedest cities in the land. No one thought to call it the Matchbox, with its thousands of wooden structures, wooden sidewalks and heavy streets paved with wooden blocks.

Chicago was divided into three divisions by its river, which was spanned by a dozen wooden bridges and which forked half a mile west of the lake, one branch running northwest and the other south. Nestling between the lake and the southern branch was the South Division, where the city's extremes of wealth and squalor were represented, the elegant houses along Michigan

Avenue contrasting with the hovels of Conley's Patch and Healy Slough and Kilgubbin, the principal business establishments balanced by ramshackle barns and storage sheds. Between the north branch and the lake was the North Division, primarily an area of upper-middle-class and wealthy homes, although along the river stood grain elevators, the Chicago and Northwestern Railroad depot, the McCormick Reaper Works, the wholesale meat market and laborers' dwellings. To the west of the river's fork was the West Division, comprising industrial plants, hundreds of frame houses occupied by workers' families and a small, handsome residential area around Union Park.[5]

After an unusually long period of drought, the city became tinder dry. The stage was set for the fire that broke out on October 8 in Mrs. O'Leary's barn at 558 De Koven Street (1100 S.), the site of the present Chicago Fire Academy. Fanned by a southwest wind, the fire spread rapidly. When it finally subsided two days later, it had thoroughly gutted about four square miles of the city. The fire took more than 250 lives, destroyed some seventeen thousand buildings, and left almost one hundred thousand people—about a third of the population—homeless.

The fire virtually consumed the entire area from approximately Twelfth Street (now Roosevelt Road) on the south to Fullerton Avenue (2400 N.) on the north, and westward nearly to Halsted Street (800 W.), including the entire downtown area. Only a handful of buildings were spared—including, ironically, the O'Leary house; of these, the Chicago Avenue Water Tower is the only remaining landmark. Indeed, the city's future appeared so bleak that a New Orleans newspaper

FIG. 3.15. People crowding west across the Randolph Street bridge to flee the approaching flames of the Chicago Fire of 1871. The Lake Street bridge is on the left. An important means of escape from the downtown area, especially after the bridges over the river had been destroyed by the flames, were tunnels under the river. They had been built to handle growing traffic and to circumvent the delays caused by the frequent opening of the bridges. The Washington Street Tunnel to the West Side was opened to traffic in 1868, and the La Salle Street Tunnel to the North Side was opened just three months before the fire started. From an engraving by Kellogg and Bulkeley in the October 28, 1871, issue of *Harper's Weekly;* Chicago Historical Society, ICHi-02961.

wrote, "Chicago will never be like the Carthage of old. Its glory will be of the past, not of the present, while its hopes, once so bright and cloudless will be to the end marred and blackened by the smoke of its fiery fate." Other editorialists, reflecting on Chicago's notorious reputation for gambling, saloons, and brothels, especially in its Levee district just south of downtown, felt this was proper retribution: "Again the fire of heaven has fallen on Sodom and Gomorrah!"

The positive faith of many in Chicago, however, was underscored the day after the fire. Joseph Medill's *Chicago Tribune,* printing from an improvised plant in the unburned area, editorialized,

CHEER UP!

In the midst of a calamity without parallel in the world's history, looking upon the ashes of thirty years' accumulations, the people of this once beautiful city have resolved that CHICAGO SHALL RISE AGAIN!

FIG. 3.16. Randolph Street, east from Market Street (now Wacker Drive), after the Chicago Fire of 1871. Prominently visible are the gutted remains of the courthouse and the city hall on the site of the present City Hall–County Building. Chicago Historical Society.

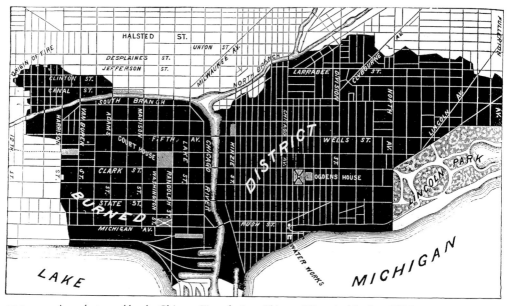

FIG. 3.17. Area destroyed by the Chicago Fire of 1871. Chicago Historical Society, ICHi-02870.

And Deacon Bross, one of Chicago's greatest boosters and a former lieutenant governor, declared,

I tell you, within five years Chicago's business houses will be rebuilt, and by the year 1900 the new Chicago will boast a population of a million souls. You ask me why? Because I know the Northwest and the vast resources of the broad acres. I know that the location of Chicago makes her the center of this wealthy region and the market for all its products.

What Chicago has been in the past, she must become in the future—and a hundredfold more! She has only to wait a few short years for the sure development of her manifest destiny!

Rebuilding and Further Expansion

Determined Chicagoans, who had already created a city on marshland, immediately turned to the task of rebuilding it. Five months after the fire, while some grain elevators and coal bins were still smoldering, Everett Chamberlain wrote in the *Lakeside Monthly* of April 1872,

Chicago has, on this 9th day of March, 1872,—five months from the date of that conflagration,—near twenty miles frontage of solid stone and brick buildings in progress, while the number of less permanent structures, from one to three stories high, already built, is counted by tens of thousands. When we take into consideration the fact that those five months have been winter months of unusual severity, the temperature having been, on an average far below the freezing point, we have illustrated, in a

single sentence, the extraordinary energy for which Chicago, as a type of the West, has become proverbial . . . the joke which was in everybody's mouth just after the fire—the joke wherein a citizen of some far-off town was represented as rushing with mad haste to the railway station, and refusing to brook any delay, because, as he said, he must reach Chicago on such a train, or they would have the whole town built up again before he could get a view of the ruins.

By 1875 little evidence of the catastrophe remained. The people's indomitable spirit and vitality, visions of a profitable future, and generous amounts of outside aid totaling over $5 million, including about $1 million from abroad, all contributed to building a new Chicago that was to emerge bigger and better than ever. Material contributions included fourteen thousand books donated by the British, with donors such as Queen Victoria, Carlyle, Ruskin, Tennyson, and others, many autographing their volumes.

The fire accelerated the movement of residential homes from the central business district. The new buildings in the downtown area were larger and higher, conforming to the new city ordinance that outlawed wooden buildings in the downtown area. In other parts of the city, thousands of homes were going up, many of brownstone and brick but also wooden homes, which were cheaper to build. The rebuilding activities attracted to Chicago thousands of laborers and numerous architects. In the 1880s many of them helped design and construct the world's first skyscrapers using the innovative steel skeleton, elevators, and, somewhat later, the floating foundation. The progenitor of the true skyscraper was probably William Le Baron Jenney's Home Insurance Building, built in 1885 with an iron and steel framework. It was situated on the northeast corner of La Salle (150 W.) and Adams (200 S.) streets where, today, the La Salle Bank Building stands.

Despite the fire, depressions, and sporadic violent labor strife, such as the 1877 Railroad Strike and the 1886 Haymarket Riot, Chicago continued to grow rapidly. Besides its commercial and transportation importance as a major handler of grain, cattle, and lumber, the city was increasingly distinguishing itself as a major center of diversified manufacturing.

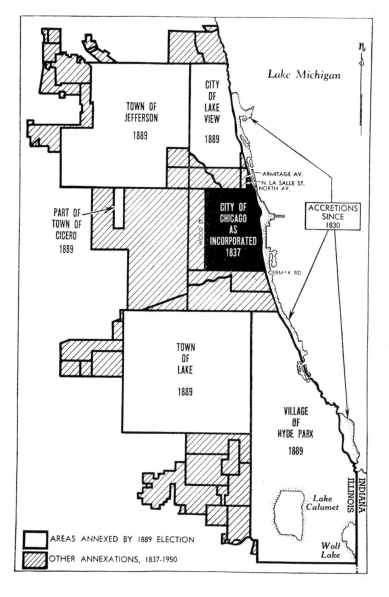

FIG. 3.18. Growth of Chicago, 1837–1950. In one year, 1889, Chicago increased its size about fourfold through a series of annexations. Since 1950 Chicago has annexed about fifteen additional square miles, accounted for largely by O'Hare International Airport, plus a few small pieces of land on the northwestern and southwestern fringes of the city. From Division of Curriculum Development, Chicago Board of Education, *Chicago* (Chicago: Chicago Board of Education–King Company, 1951), p. 44.

This industrial and commercial growth continued, despite decades of labor turbulence that followed the Civil War, and was abetted by a number of severe depressions, such as those in 1873 and 1893. Workers often felt that their bosses were getting wealthy at their expense—they toiled long hours for low wages, often in unsafe environments, under unsanitary working conditions, and with little job security. Momentum was growing for labor unions, espoused by highly vocal, often radical reformers, some of whom had their roots in European labor movements. In 1877 Chicago experienced a railroad strike that resulted in the temporary closing of many plants and climaxed in an altercation between workers and police, mainly at the railroad viaduct at Halsted (800 N.) near Sixteenth Street. It resulted in the killing of at least thirteen men and the wounding of scores of others.

Annexation by Chicago, in 1889, of four sizable but relatively sparsely populated communities—the towns of Jefferson and Lake, the city of Lake View, and the village of Hyde Park—increased its size from forty-three square miles to 168 square miles. By 1890, the city boasted a population of 1,099,850. In the preceding decade, the output of many of Chicago's major industries had more than doubled.

Protecting the People's Health

Chicago's rapidly increasing population and industrial growth created serious problems of waste disposal and protection of its water supply. Raw, untreated wastes from the Chicago area were being discharged into Lake Michigan through the Chicago River, thereby contaminating the city's own water supply. In the latter half of the nineteenth century, the Chicago area suffered extensively from waterborne diseases, such as cholera, typhoid fever, and dysentery. In 1889, in the wake of one such epidemic, the Chicago Sanitary District was created. It was later renamed the Metropolitan Water Reclamation District of Greater Chicago, as the district, in time, encompassed almost all of Cook County. It is an autonomous body, with elected officials and independent taxing authority.

The original purposes of the district were to protect the water supply and beaches of Lake Michigan from pollution, to collect and dispose of all domestic and industrial wastes, to provide a waterway that would carry runoff from storms, and to develop navigation links to the inland waterway system. To prevent the discharge of waste materials into the lake, the flow of both the Chicago and Calumet rivers was reversed, and an extensive, seventy-one-mile drainage and flushing waterway system was developed, consisting of rivers and fifty-two miles of constructed channels. These waterways include the Chicago Sanitary and Ship Canal, the North Shore Channel, and the Calumet Sag Channel. The building of the Chicago Sanitary and Ship Canal alone involved moving more earth than was dug in the construction of the Panama Canal.

The disposal of waste was based on the principle of dilution, by using enough fresh water, diverted from Lake Michigan and flowing through the waterways to the Illinois River, to allow natural purification processes to do the work. A court decision in 1930 later reduced the amount of water diversion from Lake Michigan, forcing the district to use seven major sewage treatment plants to treat the effluent sufficiently to ensure that it could safely be handled by the decreased amount of water. The largest plant, in Stickney, has

FIG. 3.19. Signs at Lake Forest Beach on Lake Michigan showing that pollution problems plague the wealthy as well as the poor. In recent years, some of the North Shore suburbs have had to close their beaches periodically, due to the discharge of pollutants into Lake Michigan by communities farther to the north. Steps are being taken to alleviate this problem. Photograph by Irving Cutler.

FIG. 3.20. World's largest sewage treatment plant at Stickney, Illinois, on the western border of Chicago. One of the many facilities operated by the Metropolitan Water Reclamation District of Greater Chicago, the plant treats up to 2 billion gallons of sewage and produces, at capacity, nine hundred tons of sludge daily. Some of the sludge was shipped by barge about two hundred miles southwest to Fulton County, Illinois, where it was used to reclaim strip-mined land and to boost agricultural production. Photograph courtesy of the Metropolitan Reclamation District of Greater Chicago.

the capacity to treat 1.2 billion gallons of wastewater each day. Overall, the district serves more than 5 million people in 125 municipalities in most of Cook County.

In recent years, a bold new plan has been developed by the district to alleviate the flooding and resulting pollution that often occurs after very heavy rains. When the existing largely combined sanitary and storm sewer system cannot handle all the storm runoff and sewage, the polluted excess flows untreated into basements and waterways, and sometimes backflows into Lake Michigan. Backflows occur when the gates of the North Shore Channel at Wilmette or those of the Chicago and Calumet rivers have to be opened to relieve the mounting water surplus. The plan envisions "bottling a rainstorm" by temporarily storing the contaminated storm water in a series of deep underground tunnels thirty-three feet in diameter, in chambers drilled in the solid rock at a depth of about three hundred feet. After the storm, the polluted water would be pumped to the surface, where it would be treated before being discharged back into the waterway.

This Tunnel and Reservoir Project (TARP), or "Deep Tunnel Project," is now well under way. When completed, it will be one of history's largest construction undertakings. However, the escalating cost of the total project, estimated in the billions of dollars, has made the project and its effectiveness controversial issues. Completion beyond the first phase, which alone includes 110 miles of tunnels, drop shafts, connecting structures, pumping stations, and a new treatment plant, will further enhance the system. When completed, the underground river will have four times the carrying capacity of the surface river system. The new, dirty downstairs river will

keep the upstairs river clean. The increasingly cleaner Chicago waterway system is making an important comeback as a recreational playground, providing sites for substantial residential and commercial development, especially in the central part of the city.

The Metropolitan Water Reclamation District has long lessened its disposal problems by using the treated waste to produce large quantities of fertilizer. One experiment of the district involved the recycling of solid sewage material into a treated sludge fertilizer, which was shipped by barge to Fulton County in downstate Illinois. There it was spread on land that had been spoiled by strip mining operations, thereby allowing the land to be put back into productive agriculture. The plan, however, was opposed by some of Fulton County's residents and has been discontinued.

Projects of the District have eliminated the incidence of serious disease related to polluted drinking water. In addition, two city-owned modern water filtration plants, on the lakefront, supply Chicago and about 120 of its suburbs with wholesome low-cost water. The filtration plant adjacent to Navy Pier is the world's largest.

The filtration plants obtain their water from intake cribs two to three miles offshore in Lake Michigan. The cribs are connected with the filtration plants by large water-supply tunnels under the lake bed. After the water is filtered and purified at the two plants, it is pumped, with the aid of eleven strategically located pumping stations, through more than forty-one hundred miles of mains, which supply water to about 40 percent of the people in Illinois.

While the problem of safe drinking water has been solved, the problem of garbage dis-

FIG. 3.21. Dunne–Sixty-eighth Street crib, two miles offshore in Lake Michigan, the source of water for the South Side of Chicago and numerous nearby suburbs for about a century. The crib is connected by ten- to twenty-foot-high tunnels—some seventy-five to two hundred feet below the surface of the lake—to the South Water Filtration Plant at Seventy-seventh Street and the lake. Photograph by Irving Cutler.

posal is becoming more serious as an affluent and growing society produces more and more garbage. The average Chicagoan is responsible for about half a ton of garbage each year. Chicago, however, with three large incinerators, is in a more favorable position than the suburban areas, which depend largely on sanitary landfills. The readily accessible landfills are rapidly becoming exhausted, resulting in the use of more distant and costly garbage hauling operations. Some thirty sanitary landfill sites in the Chicago metropolitan area accept municipal wastes, with the majority having an estimated site life of fewer than five years. Recycling operations, including the use of garbage as a supplemental fuel to generate electricity, are still largely in the experimental, high-cost stage. Unlike the operations of the Metropolitan Water Reclamation District, there is no area-wide garbage disposal agency, although a number of suburban communities have joint operations.

From Fair to Fair

In 1893, just twenty-two years after the fire had leveled the heart of the city, Chicago again attracted the attention of the world with its dazzling, classically styled World's Columbian Exposition. The 684-acre fair, with its Greek-, Romanesque-, and Renaissance-style architecture, displayed the accomplishments of the nineteenth century and suggested what lay ahead in the twentieth century. Among the famous contributors to this "White City" were Daniel H. Burnham, the chief of construction; Frederick Law Olmstead, who designed the landscaping; Louis Sullivan and Dankmar Adler, who designed the Transportation Building; and Daniel Chester French, Augustus Saint-Gaudens, and Lorado Taft, who contributed statuary. In contrast to the imposing orderliness of the fair proper was the amusement section, located westward along the Midway. It featured exotic displays and dancers, such as "Little Egypt," hosted entertainment from all over the world, and contained a giant Ferris wheel that could carry more than two thousand people at one time. In a man-made waterway, Venetian gondoliers even took passengers for a ride in their gondolas.

With its customary audacity, the city built the fair on what appeared to be an apparently impossible, sandy site along the lakefront, eight miles south of the river. It drew more than 27 million people, or more than 150,000 people a day. The fair sparked a feverish real estate boom on the South Side, especially in the Hyde Park–Woodlawn area around the Exposition grounds. As a legacy to the city, it left Jackson Park; the Midway; and the Museum of Science and Industry—the Fine Arts building of the fair—which, at the insistence of donors of very valuable artworks, was built as an especially sturdy and fireproof building, in contrast to the other buildings at the fair.

The many contrasting facets of Chicago in the 1890s were depicted by George W. Steevens, an English journalist, who wrote this sprightly portrayal of the city in 1896:

FIG. 3.22. World's Columbian Exposition, 1893. View is eastward from approximately Sixty-fifth Street. On the left is the Manufactures and Liberal Arts Building, and on the right is the Agricultural Building. In the six months the fair was open it attracted twenty-seven million visitors—the equivalent of almost half the population of the United States at that time. Photograph by C. D. Arnold; Chicago Historical Society, ICHi-02526.

FIG. 3.23. Century of Progress International Exposition, 1933, looking northward. The fair was on artificially created land along the lakeshore from Roosevelt Road to Thirty-seventh Street. In the upper right
are the two towers of the famous Skyride. Photograph by Aerial Survey Co.; Chicago Historical Society.

Chicago! Chicago, queen and guttersnipe of cities, cynosure and cesspool of the world! Not if I had a hundred tongues, everyone shouting a different language in a different key, could I do justice to her splendid chaos. The most beautiful and the most squalid, girdled with a twofold zone of parks and slums; where the keen air from lake and prairie is ever in the nostrils, and the stench of foul smoke is never out of the throat; the great port a thousand miles from the sea; the great mart which gathers up with one hand the corn and cattle of the West and deals out with the other the merchandise of the East; widely and generously planned with streets of twenty miles, where it is not safe to walk at night; where women ride straddlewise, and millionaires dine at midday on the Sabbath; the chosen seat of public spirit and municipal boodle, of cutthroat commerce and munificent patronage of art; the most American of American cities, and yet the most mongrel; the second American city of the globe . . . the first and only veritable Babel of the age; all of which twenty-five years ago next Friday was a heap of smoking ashes. Where in all the world can words be found for this miracle of paradox and incongruity?[6]

The growth of Chicago continued unabated during the first three decades of the twentieth century, despite periodic depressions, the turmoil of World War I, the curtailment of European immigration, and the gangster era of the Prohibition years, which created an image of lawlessness that the city's many accomplishments failed to overcome. The national and international notoriety of gangsters such as Al Capone was to reflect upon Chicago for many decades. Between 1900 and 1930, the population almost doubled, increasing from 1,698,575 in 1900 to 3,376,808 in 1930. By 1930 the entire city area, except for some small patches mainly on its fringes, had been occupied. In addition, especially since World War I, population was increasingly overflowing into the suburbs.

To celebrate a century of remarkable growth, Chicago staged the Century of Progress Exposition of 1933–34. The very colorful and modernistic structures of the World's Fair were erected on 427 acres of artificially created land along the lakeshore from Roosevelt Road (1200 S.) to Thirty-seventh Street. The fair emphasized the modern and futuristic in science, technology, industry, and architecture. Its most popular entertainment attractions included a complete automobile assembly plant, the towering Skyride, and Sally Rand's fan-dancing. An injunction to halt Sally Rand's fan-dancing was denied by Judge Joseph B. David, who stated that "lots of people in this country would like to put pants on horses. . . . If you ask me, they are just a lot of boobs come to see a woman wiggle with a fan or without fig leaves. But we have the boobs and we have a right to cater to them." For fifty cents admission, people could wander through over eight miles of exhibits, ranging from the highbrow to the obviously lowbrow.

Although the fair was held in the depth of the Great Depression, it attracted more than 39 million people and proved an unqualified financial success. More important, it showed the world how far the little, muddy portage town had come in one hundred years.

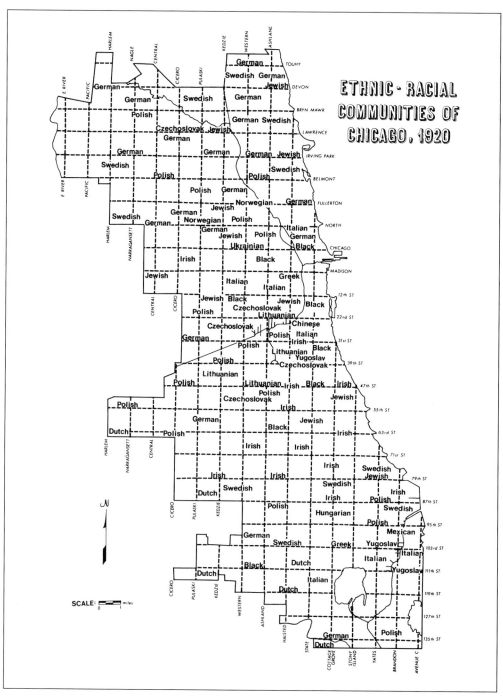

FIG. 4.1. Approximate locations of Chicago's ethnic and racial communities, 1920. None of the communities was totally homogeneous. For the ethnic and racial communities of 1980, see FIGURE 5.1. Map by Joseph Kubal based largely on U.S. Census, church, and Chicago Department of Planning data.

4 People and Settlement Patterns: The Europeans

Sources of Early Settlers

Chicago's unprecedented growth from a marshy wilderness to a city of nearly 3 million people in little more than a century and a half resulted largely from an almost constant flow of settlers into the area—settlers whose major points of origin, however, changed with the passing decades. At first, settlers came mainly from the eastern United States, then from northwestern Europe, later from eastern and southern Europe, and most recently, from the southern United States, the Caribbean, Mexico, and parts of Asia and Africa. In all, Chicago is an amalgam of almost one hundred identifiable ethnic and racial strains. Figure 4.1 shows the approximate location of the major ethnic and racial communities in 1920; Figure 5.1, in the following chapter, about more recent migration, shows the major ethnic and racial communities in 2000.

They came because opportunities in Chicago were much brighter than in their home areas, where they often had encountered economic, political, and religious difficulties. They came because jobs were available and because Chicago's network of waterways, roads, and rails made the city highly accessible. They contributed with brawn and brains to the development of the great mid-continent metropolis.

The first permanent settlers in the city and surrounding farmland came mainly from New England, the middle Atlantic states, and nearby Ohio and Indiana. Many were sons and daughters of pioneers who were emulating their parents. Unlike those who immigrated to southern Illinois, very few of Chicago's early settlers came from the South.

In the early decades of Chicago's growth, some of the settlers from the East became the city's political and economic leaders. Many lived in the fashionable areas along Michigan and Wabash avenues in what is now downtown. Although their role in the development of Chicago was important, it was probably never as great as that of the "native elite" in such cities as New York, Philadelphia, and Boston, whose roots in their cities sometimes went back two centuries or more. Chicago, especially in its early history, was largely a city of immigrants who came directly from overseas and who became a major force in the creation of the city.

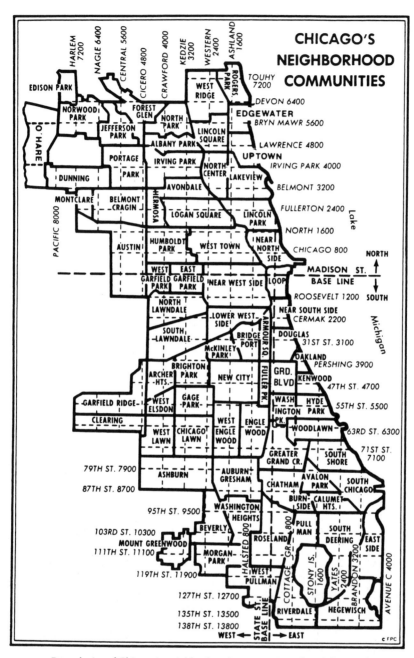

FIG. 4.2. Boundaries of Chicago's neighborhood communities, first delineated more than seventy years ago through the work of the Social Science Research Committee of the University of Chicago. Since then, perimeters have been refined only minimally, although an additional community, O'Hare, was created largely from land annexed in the 1950s for the airport. Later, the community of Edgewater was created from the northern part of Uptown, making a total of seventy-seven communities. Adapted from Margaret S. Rátz and Charles H. Wilson, *Exploring Chicago* (Chicago: Follett Publishing, 1958).

European Immigration

European immigration into Chicago started on a large scale in the 1840s. The first large group consisted of the Irish, who fled potato crop failures and the burden of absentee landlords. The Irish soon were followed by large numbers of Germans, especially after suppression of the democratic revolutions of the 1840s. Scandinavians also began to come in large numbers, together with smaller numbers of English, Welsh, and Scots. By 1860, more than half of Chicago's population of 112,172 was foreign born.

The movement of immigrants to Chicago had been spurred by the opening of the first rail connection between New York and Chicago in 1853, as well as by the organized solicitation of settlers and by the glowing reports of opportunities that the city's foreign settlers sent to their homelands. By 1890 about 79 percent of Chicago's 1 million people were either immigrants or the children of immigrants. Germans, Scandinavians, and Irish, in that order, were the three largest foreign-born groups in 1890. In 1900 Chicago had more Poles, Swedes, Czechs, Dutch, Danes, Norwegians, Croatians, Slovaks, Lithuanians, and Greeks than any other American city.

The flow of Europeans to Chicago continued unabated until the outbreak of World War I in 1914, but the geographic sources of immigration began to shift markedly about 1880. For about the next half century, until national immigration quotas were adopted in 1924, the majority of immigrants came from eastern and southern Europe. Poles, Italians, eastern European Jews, Czechs, Slovaks, Lithuanians, Ukrainians, Greeks, Croatians, Serbians, and Hungarians were among the largest groups, although there were newcomers from almost

FIG. 4.3. Chicago Avenue, with its streetcar tracks, brick paving, and wooden sidewalks, westward near Franklin Street, 1900. Chicago Historical Society.

every area in Europe. At the peak of immigration, Chicago was the largest Lithuanian city in the world, the second-largest Czech city, and the third-largest Irish, Swedish, Polish, and Jewish city. The concentrations of Irish, along with large groups from eastern and southern Europe, helped make Chicago the largest Roman Catholic archdiocese in the United States.

When immigration was sharply curtailed by the Immigration Act of 1924, European-born whites comprised about 27 percent of Chicago's total population. This figure fell to 20 percent in 1940, 15 percent in 1950, and 5 percent in 1980. The number of European-born (by major country of origin) in Chicago in 1920, in contrast to those in Chicago in 1980 and 2000, is shown in Table 4.1. The table demonstrates that the number of European-born is now comparatively small and that the proportion from northwestern Europe has declined markedly.

In 1970 the median age of European-born immigrants was sixty-two years, foreshadowing a further decline of the group that had, at one time, constituted a majority of the people of Chicago. Their decrease

TABLE 4.1.
European-Born in Chicago

Country of Origin	1920	1980	2000
Poland	137,611	43,338	89,501
Germany	112,288	16,075	6,878
Italy	59,215	18,593	6,128
Russia	102,095	17,497	4,643
Ireland	56,786	8,372	4,323
United Kingdom	37,932	5,589	3,892
Czechoslovakia	50,392	3,443	2,615
Austria	30,491	4,370	1,064
Sweden	58,568	2,155	563

Sources: Adapted from U.S. Census Bureau data; courtesy of Chicago Metropolis 2020

also marked the decline of one of Chicago's most colorful eras—a period when much of Chicago was a microcosm of Europe and when Chicago was probably the most ethnically rich city in the country. Enriched by many cultures and filled with the sounds of dozens of languages, Chicago sported a variety of colorful exotic dress and hosted myriad ethnic shops, schools, churches, synagogues, theaters, cafes, coffeehouses, and newspapers. The immigrants cherished the security of their own institutions in their own neighborhoods.

In his 1946 book *Midwest at Noon,* Graham Hutton described the variety of European immigrants at that time and the neighborhoods in which they lived.

Who are the Chicagoans? . . . [T]hey come from almost every race and people. . . . Germans form solid districts all over, but chiefly in the north and northwest, like the working-class quarters of Hamburg. Poles with their pseudo-baroque Catholic churches with green cupolas make whole areas look like Cracow or Lodz. Czechs and Slovaks keep their homes and little gardens more neatly and reproduce Brunn or Pilsen . . . . Lithuanians, Latvians, and Estonians have their homes out in the southwest, looking severe and North European in winter. There are Scandinavians of all kinds; Italians of all kinds, too, who keep their feast-days and market days as if in the old country and live in solid blocks of the city; Greeks, Yugoslavs, and Syrians mainly on the west side; Mexicans, Chinese, and Japanese, in their characteristic quarters; Hungarians down in the south and also on the north side, mixed in with the Czechs and Germans and Yugoslavs, whom in Europe they dislike; British, Dutch, Belgians, Spaniards, Portuguese, Russians,

FIG. 4.4. Foreign-language newspapers published in Chicago. Although the number and circulation of such newspapers have declined steadily through the years, Chicago still had about thirty in 2005. Changes in ethnic numbers have had their impact. Eighty years ago, there were four German-language newspapers but no Spanish newspapers. Today there are no German dailies but numerous Spanish-language newspapers. Most of the newspapers are tabloids put out by tiny two- and three-member staffs and sold in neighborhoods where there are heavy ethnic concentrations. *La Raza*, the Spanish newspaper, has the largest circulation. Collage by John Downs and Jack Bruza; photograph from the *Chicago Daily News*.

Ukrainians, and Armenians; and of course the Negroes. . . . Here is a potent source of variety and difference as well as vigor and restlessness.[1]

As the immigrants endeavored to work their way upward economically and socially, they occasionally encountered hostility from those who considered themselves "native Americans," many of whom were themselves the children or grandchildren of European immigrants.

An Ethnic Checkerboard
The newcomers generally worked at unskilled and menial jobs, with minimal remuneration. They usually found housing in congested, low-rent areas around the Loop, areas aban-

doned by earlier immigrant groups who had moved upward economically and outward geographically. The Near West Side has been the home of a succession of groups—Irish, Germans, Czechs, Jews, and later, African Americans and Hispanics.

The desire of the immigrants to be close to their countrymen and to establish in their new land the institutions that they had cherished in their homelands led to the formation of numerous ethnic neighborhoods. Some were even formed on the basis of subgroups, such as Venetian, Neapolitan, and Sicilian neighborhoods. A traverse in the vicinity of Halsted Street (800 W.) at the beginning of the twentieth century, from the North Side going south, would have taken one successively through Swedish, German, Polish, Greek, Italian, Jewish, Czech, Lithuanian, and Irish neighborhoods. Centrally located on Halsted Street was Jane Addams's Hull House, which catered to immigrants who were often needy, poorly educated, and bewildered by the unfamiliar setting.

Jane Addams described the conditions of the immigrant group as follows:

Between Halsted Street and the river live about ten thousand Italians. To the south on Twelfth Street are many Germans, and side streets are given over almost entirely to Polish and Russian Jews. Still farther south, these Jewish colonies merge into a huge Bohemian colony. To the northwest are many Canadian-French and to the north are Irish and first-generation Americans. The

FIG. 4.5. Hull House on South Halsted Street, 1910. The settlement house was founded by Jane Addams in 1889. Only two buildings of the thirteen-building complex were preserved when the campus of the University of Illinois at Chicago occupied the site in 1965. Chicago Historical Society, ICHi-20975.

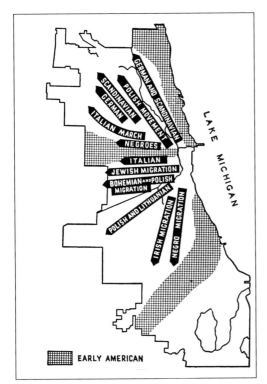

FIG. 4.6. Outward expansion of racial and ethnic groups in Chicago. Reprinted from Samuel C. Kincheloe, *The American City and Its Church* (New York: Friendship Press, 1938).

The immigrants helped each other find jobs and spouses and thus adapt to the new way of life. Intermarriage was shunned. In time, with some acculturation and economic success, the immigrant groups and especially their offspring moved outward from their crowded enclaves near the downtown area. These groups often migrated in an axial pattern, with many eventually settling in the suburbs. On weekends, some would return to the old neighborhood to visit their parents, attend church, and shop at a delicatessen or bakery. However, each migration outward was usually accompanied by a further loosening of Old World ties as each new generation became more assimilated, more geographically dispersed, and more active in its home community's civic and economic affairs.

Recent Population Trends

The 2000 U.S. Census showed major changes from previous decades. For the first time since the 1950 census, Chicago had an increase in population—4 percent in the 1990s—to a total of 2,896,016. Almost all the growth was due to immigration. Without immigration, the city would have lost more than a hundred thousand residents. Also of significance is the major change in racial composition. The figures show that there is no longer a

streets are inexpressibly dirty, the number of schools inadequate, sanitary legislation unenforced, the street lighting bad, the paving miserable and altogether lacking in alleys and smaller streets, and the stables foul beyond description. The older and richer inhabitants seem anxious to move away as rapidly as they can afford it. They make room for newly arrived immigrants who are densely ignorant of civic duties. Meanwhile, the wretched conditions persist until at least two generations of children have been born and reared in them.[2]

TABLE 4.2.
Foreign-Born in Chicago by Major Areas of Origin, 2000

Latin America	354,034
Europe	145,462
Asia	112,932
Africa	12,613
Canada	3,201

Source: Adapted from U.S. Census Bureau data, 2000

dominant majority group. While the white population continued its rather sharp decline in the 1990s, the black population also showed a slight decline. During the decade, the Hispanic population (80 percent Mexican) surged, while the Asian population continued its steady increase. Due to the large influx of these two groups, the foreign-born population increased sharply from previous decades and now constitutes 21.6 percent of the population. The largest group of new white, non-Hispanic immigrants came from eastern Europe, especially from Poland, after the collapse of communism in that region. However, the share of Chicago immigrants from Europe dropped from 88 percent to 26 percent between 1960 and 2000. Asians came from a variety of East Asia, South Asia, and Middle East countries, with immigrants from India being the most numerous, while the Japanese population in Chicago actually declined. The huge increase in the "other" category is due to the census bureau having placed into it for the first time all those who marked multiple races.

A breakdown of residents of European ancestry in the six-county metropolitan area shows that almost half of this group is from four European countries. In 2000 the U.S. Census no longer enumerated the category of those actually foreign born; instead, it used the much larger category of foreign ancestry.

TABLE 4.3

Chicago Residents Born in Large Numbers in Other States, 2000

Mississippi	118,808
Arkansas	31,888
Michigan	29,649
New York	29,164
Alabama	27,412
Indiana	26,400
California	23,634
Ohio	22,470
Tennessee	22,229
Texas	20,411
Wisconsin	19,445
Missouri	16,824
Pennsylvania	14,407
Louisiana	14,232
Georgia	12,303

Source: Adapted from U.S. Census Bureau data, 2000

TABLE 4.4

Chicago Racial and Ethnic Summary

Racial or Ethnic Group	1990	2000	Percentage of Change, 1990-2000	Percentage of Total, 2000
Black	1,074,471	1,053,739	−1.9	36.4
White	1,056,048	907,166	−14.1	31.3
Hispanic	545,852	753,644	38.0	26.0
Asian	98,777	125,409	27.0	4.3
Other	8,585	56,058	553.5	2.0
Total	2,783,726	2,896,016	4.0	100.0

Source: Adapted by U.S. Census Bureau data, 2000

TABLE 4.5

Percentages of European Ancestries Represented in Chicago's Six-County Metropolitan Area

German	15.8		Russian	1.4
Irish	12.9		Norwegian	1.3
Polish	10.1		Dutch	1.2
Italian	7.2		Greek	1.0
English	4.8		Scottish	1.0
Swedish	2.2		Lithuanian	0.9
Czech	1.6		Scotch-Irish	0.8
French	1.6			

Source: Adapted from U.S. Census Bureau data, 2000

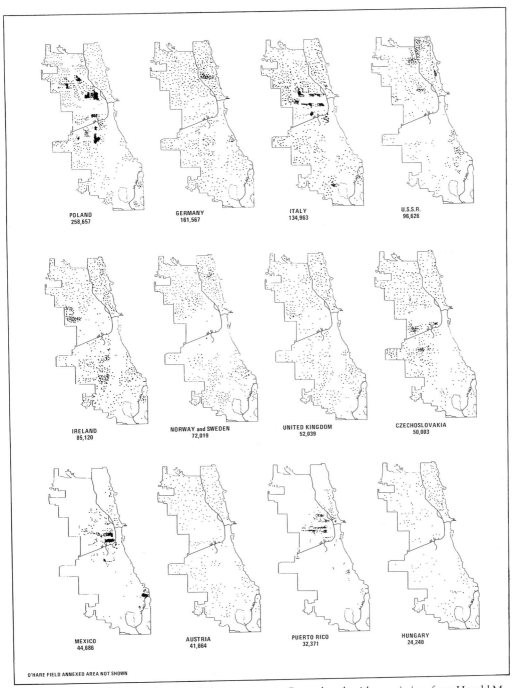

FIG. 4.7. Locational pattern of major ethnic groups, 1960. Reproduced, with permission, from Harold M. Mayer and Richard C. Wade, *Chicago: Growth of a Metropolis*, © 1969 by the University of Chicago.

The Irish

The Irish were the earliest European immigrants to come to Chicago in large numbers. In 1803 the builder and commander of Fort Dearborn was Irish-born Captain John Whistler. (He was also to become the grandfather of the famous painter James McNeill Whistler.) A small group of Irish pioneers lived in Chicago in 1833, when Chicago was first incorporated. That same year, they helped found Chicago's first Catholic church, St. Mary's, on the southwest corner of State and Lake streets. The cost of the little frame building was four hundred dollars. The first of the annual St. Patrick's Day parades was held ten years later, when Chicago had 773 residents of Irish birth. The marchers paraded from the "Saloon Building" on Lake and Clark streets to the new site of St. Mary's on Madison Street near Wabash Avenue.

The disastrous potato famines in Ireland between 1845 and 1860 and the perennial problems of overpopulation, political dissatisfaction, and an oppressive land system helped to greatly increase Irish migration to the United States. Many were unskilled or semi-skilled, unlike the earlier Irish immigrants, many of whom were craftsmen. In 1850 the Irish-born population in Chicago constituted 6,093 of Chicago's total population of 29,963, or about 20 percent, and they were the largest foreign-born group in Chicago. Although the Germans surpassed the Irish in numbers in the 1860s and succeeding census years, the Irish-born population continued to grow rapidly, reaching a peak of 73,913 in 1900. Today, Irish Americans still rank second only to Germans as the largest European ethnic group in the six-county area, and fewer than 2 percent are foreign born.

Numerous organizations were formed to aid the immigrants. They ranged in scope from nationalist groups to fraternal, cultural, and athletic organizations. Among the groups represented in the United Irish Societies were the Hibernian Benevolent Society, St. Patrick's Society, Irish American Club, and the Ancient Order of Hibernians. The Fenian Brotherhood, a nationalist organization, sent weapons, money, and men to Ireland to fight the British. Later, a nationalist group, Clan-na-Gael, was dedicated to the absolute independence of Ireland. Many of the very early Irish immigrants were Protestants who generally kept apart from their more numerous, poorer Irish Catholic countrymen.

The earliest Irish communities were largely situated along the Chicago River. The start of construction of the Illinois and Michigan Canal in 1836, which eventually employed thousands of Irish workers, resulted in a settlement along the South Fork of the South Branch of the Chicago River ("Bubbly Creek") in the "Hardscrabble" area. Somewhat later came settlement in the nearby "Canaryville" section of Canalport (later known as Bridgeport), close to the start of the canal route and employment. In 1847, while working on the canal, the Irish staged the first labor strike in the Chicago region but were unsuccessful in their demands for $1.25 a day in wages and a more agreeable foreman. The early Irish settlers grew cabbages for their dinner tables in the square block area at Thirtieth and Halsted, which is now part of McGuane Park. Until St. Bridget's Church was organized in 1850 as the city's first Irish parish to serve the needs of the growing Irish community around Archer Avenue, many of the Irish would row down the Chicago River on Sunday to attend mass at St. Patrick's Church, which originally was at Randolph Street (150 N.) and Des Plaines Street (700 W.).

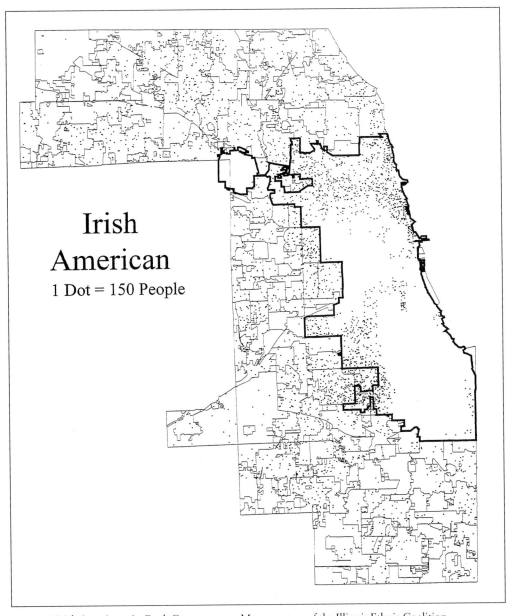

Irish
American

1 Dot = 150 People

FIG. 4.8. Irish Americans in Cook County, 1990. Map courtesy of the Illinois Ethnic Coalition.

St. Patrick's Church served the largest Irish community in the city. This settlement was in the present downtown area, mainly along the east bank of the South Branch of the Chicago River. In 1856 a new building for the church was completed at Des Plaines and Adams (200 S.). The building survived the Chicago Fire and today is the oldest church building in the city. It has been designated a Chicago landmark. In the vicinity of the church, around Adams and Franklin (300 W.), was "Conley's Patch," the birthplace of two colorful but corrupt politicians, Michael "Hinky Dink" Kenna and John "Bathhouse" Coughlin, who ruled the downtown First Ward for many years.

Toward the end of the 1850s, about a mile to the southwest of St. Patrick's at Twelfth Street near Morgan (1000 W.), another church was built that was to become a bastion of Irish culture. Holy Family Church rose out of the West Side prairie to a height of 246 feet, making it the fourth-largest church in North America at the time and Chicago's first skyscraper. A few years later, St. Ignatius College Preparatory School was established next to the church. Most Catholic parishes set up their own parochial schools to teach their religious views and to bypass the public schools of early Chicago, which were under Protestant domination. The local parish, with its various organizations and schools, was the most important Irish institution.[3]

Another area of early Irish settlement arose to the east of the North Branch of the Chicago River, in a shantytown section known as "Kilgubbin." It lay between Chicago Avenue (800 N.) and Division Street (1200 N.). This was an impoverished settlement of ramshackle houses, the premises of which often contained pigs, cows, chickens, and geese. An island in the area is thus named "Goose Island." Far to the south in South Chicago, amid the growing industrial area, a small Irish settlement started around mid-century.

The early Irish in Chicago, largely a rural people with limited education transplanted into an urban setting, worked mainly in unskilled occupations as canal diggers, teamsters, railroad builders, factory and stockyard workers, domestic servants, and washerwomen. In the predominantly Anglo-Saxon Protestant business environment of Chicago, they sometimes encountered "No Irish Need Apply" signs. But unlike most of the other immigrants, they knew the English language, understood the Anglo-Saxon political system, and showed a flare for public service that often helped link them to other Chicagoans. They overcame the initial discrimination and improved their lot. In time, many Irish became policemen, firemen, streetcar employees, teachers, priests, labor leaders, and politicians. Some advanced rapidly in these fields. In 1900, although comprising only 14 percent of the city's male labor force, an estimated 43 percent of the policemen and firemen were Irish, and many held high positions. Some became doctors, lawyers, professors, writers, and architects. In the last profession, Louis Sullivan is regarded as one of the fathers of modern American architecture and is particularly associated with the aesthetics of the skyscraper. Among his more famous Chicago buildings are the Auditorium (designed with Dankmar Adler, 1889), and the Carson Pirie Scott store (1899).

Among the early successful Chicago businessmen of Irish descent were Cyrus H. McCormick (farm machinery), John M. Smyth (furniture), Edward Hines (lumber), and Edward A. Cudahy (meatpacking). Charles A. Comiskey was the president of the

FIG. 4.9. St. Patrick's, Chicago's oldest church building. Built in 1856 at 718 West Adams Street, on the western fringe of downtown, the church and its school survived the Chicago Fire and once served the sizable Irish community of the area. Today the landmark church attracts downtown workers and visitors and remains the traditional starting point of the St. Patrick's Day Parade. In 1953 some of the church properties were razed for the Kennedy Expressway, but the congregation is now in the process of expanding its facilities and has a large and rapidly growing membership. Photograph by Irving Cutler.

Chicago White Sox baseball franchise from its founding until his death in 1931.

The Irish of Chicago were famously depicted in the writings of Finley Peter Dunne and James T. Farrell. Born of Irish-immigrant parents, Dunne (1867–1936) wrote a satirical Chicago newspaper column in which he commented on the affairs of the day with humor and insight through his legendary character, Mr. Dooley, a saloon keeper on "Archey Road" (Archer Avenue). Dunne lived when political corruption was rampant—such as in the First Ward—and where opium dens, clip joints, bordellos, and gambling were permitted by politicians such as "Bathhouse" John Coughlin and "Hinky Dink" Kenna, who operated on the principle "Chicago ain't no Sunday School."[4] As Lawrence J. McCaffrey explains, "Dooley poked fun at Irish vices such as clannishness, volubility, flamboyant American and ethnic patriotisms, the ability to condone political corruption, and their excessive thirst for beer and whiskey. But he also praised virtues like courage, generosity, sentimentality, a sense of humor, family solidarity, and hard work."[5] James T. Farrell (1904–79) is best known for his *Studs Lonigan* trilogy (1932–35), which fictionally depicted the life of working-class Irish Catholics in a neighborhood on the South Side where Farrell grew up. The setting was the vicinity of St. Anselm's Church (Michigan Avenue and Sixty-first Street). The Irish often retained their identity through the parish structure, rather than through the formation of strong ethnic communities.

As the Irish increased in numbers and moved upward financially—more rapidly than most European groups—they also began to disperse outward geographically. Many eventually settled in largely middle-class and upper-middle-class suburbs, where a good deal of their Irish identity has disappeared. From the Near North Side community they moved into the Lincoln Park, Lake View, and Uptown areas. Some moved to the Northwest Side, where a small number still live. But the greatest movement was to the south and west (see Fig. 4.1). From the Lower West Side and Bridgeport communities they moved southwest into McKinley Park, Brighton Park, and Chicago Lawn. Others moved south into New City, Kenwood, Hyde Park, Woodlawn, South Shore, West Englewood, Grand Crossing, Avalon Park, Chatham, Mount Greenwood, and Auburn Gresham. The wealthiest lived even farther south, in Beverly. Similarly, to the west, more affluence was evident as parish addresses advanced westward toward Austin and Oak Park: St. Malachy (2200 W.), Our Lady of Sorrows (3100 W.), Presentation (3900 W.), St. Mel (4300 W.), St. Thomas Aquinas (5100 W.), and St. Catherine of Siena on Austin Boulevard (6000 W.) in Oak Park, where the "lace curtain Irish" lived. Unlike many of the other ethnic groups, however, the Irish usually were a minority in the neighborhoods in which they lived.

Dispersal to the suburbs increased rapidly after World War II. Most Irish areas on the South Side and in Austin went through a rapid racial change. A 1975 survey showed that 110,000 Chicago residents considered themselves of Irish extraction, but there were almost twice as many (210,000) in the suburbs. Four suburbs in particular—Oak Park, River Forest, Oak Lawn, and Evergreen Park—had relatively high concentrations of Irish residents. Hardly any Irish neighborhoods are left in the metropolitan area. The Irish were the first European group to come to Chicago in large numbers, and having no language problem, they were one of the first

immigrant groups to melt into established
society. But several Irish social, fraternal, and
benevolent aid organizations and clubs are
still active, and there has been a recent revival
in such cultural activities as the Irish theater,
Irish dancing, and the new Irish American
Heritage Center.

The influence and leadership of the Irish are
great, especially in politics, education, and the
Catholic Church. Among the Chicago Irish,
65 percent of high school and 81 percent of elementary school students attended parochial
or private schools, compared with 27 percent
and 24 percent, respectively, of the total
student population. The Irish have been active
in building Loyola and De Paul universities,
and the Chicago Irish are ardent followers of
Notre Dame's Fighting Irish football team.

The bishops of the Catholic Church were,
from 1855 to 1915, with one exception, of
Irish descent. In 1906 the Irish claimed almost
half of the city's 173 parishes. This dominance
was resented by other Catholic groups, but
the establishment of national (ethnic) parishes
for non-English-speaking immigrants and
of territorial parishes that covered certain
geographic areas alleviated the tension somewhat. After about 1900 the high percentage of
Irish Catholics in the church declined with the
arrival of increasing numbers of immigrants
from eastern and southern Europe and from
Latin America.

Many of the notable members of the local
Catholic Church hierarchy have Irish lineage,
including Samuel Cardinal Stritch and
labor supporter Bishop Bernard J. Sheil, the
latter having been born in Chicago. Joseph
Meegan supported grassroots neighborhood
communities, such as the Back of the Yards
Neighborhood Council, and fought for
racial justice. In 1970, 16 percent of Irish
workers in Chicago held government jobs,

compared with 6 percent for the remainder
of the population. All of Chicago's mayors
from 1933 to 1976—Edward Kelly, Martin
Kennelly, and Richard J. Daley—were of Irish
descent, and all were born in the old Irish
community of Bridgeport. Richard J. Daley
served for a record twenty-one of these years

FIG. 4.10. Richard J. Daley, who grew up in the
Irish Bridgeport community of Chicago. A graduate
of De Paul University, he received his law degree in
1934 but never practiced law. However, he became
one of the most powerful political leaders in the
United States, "the last of the big-city bosses." After
serving in the Illinois House of Representatives
and the Illinois Senate, he was elected Democratic
mayor of Chicago in 1955 and won reelection five
times, usually by wide margins. Daley's tenure as
mayor lasted until 1976, when he died in office.
Photograph courtesy of the Office of the Mayor.

(1955–1976). His son, Richard M. Daley, also from Bridgeport, has served as mayor since 1989. Bridgeport is believed to have produced more priests and politicians than any other neighborhood in Chicago. In 1969 eleven of the top sixteen government offices in Chicago and Cook County were held by men of Irish descent. These posts included the positions of mayor, city collector, president of the Cook County Board, county clerk, sheriff, assessor, and state's attorney, as well as the heads of the Chicago police, fire, school, and park systems. For more than 125 years, the Irish have dominated much of the Catholic and political life of the city. Some of this history is depicted in the Irish American Heritage Center. The descendants of the laborers of early Chicago who lived in Kilgubbin, Conley's Patch, Canaryville, and Hardscrabble now occupy positions of power and prominence, and every St. Patrick's Day, when all of Chicago is said to be Irish, they are given their due recognition. There are parades and parties, and even the Chicago River is dyed green on that day. In addition to the downtown parade, the South Side Irish of Beverly, Mount Greenwood, and adjacent suburbs have their own large St. Patrick's Day parade on Western Avenue, between 103rd and 114th streets, past a number of Irish pubs.

The Germans

During the latter half of the nineteenth century and the first decade of the twentieth century, Germans were the largest foreign-born group in Chicago. In 1860 the percentage of foreign-born who were German was as high as 38.9 percent and, in 1890 it was still high at 35.7 percent. In this century the percentage of Germans in Chicago has steadily declined, due both to decreasing German immigration and to increased immigration from other areas.

TABLE 4.6.

Major Foreign-Born Groups as Percentage of Total Foreign-Born in Chicago

	Germans	Irish	Scandinavians	Eastern Europeans	Southern Europeans
1860	38.9	36.3	4.0	.25	.2
1890	35.7	15.5	16.0	12.5	1.8
1920	13.9	6.0	11.1	35.8	11.9

Source: Adapted from U.S. Census Bureau data

TABLE 4.7

Major Foreign-Born Groups as Percentage of Total Population of Chicago

	Germans	Irish	Scandinavians	Eastern Europeans	Southern Europeans
1860	19.4	18.2	2.0	.13	.10
1890	14.7	6.3	6.5	5.30	.62
1920	4.1	2.1	3.2	10.60	3.40

Source: Adapted from U.S. Census Bureau data

In 1980 Germans comprised only about 6 percent of the total foreign-born population, and the figure has declined since then. Over the years, however, far more Germans have come to Chicago than any other European group. The 2000 U.S. Census showed that 15.8 percent of the people in the metropolitan area were of German ancestry, the largest of any European ethnic group. Germans comprise the largest ethnic group in about 80 percent of the suburbs.

Table 4.6, based on U.S. Census data, shows the changes in the percentage of total foreign born of major foreign-born groups in Chicago by thirty-year intervals during the peak period of immigration. Table 4.7 shows the percentage of the total population in Chicago of the major foreign groups during the same years.

Germans first settled in Chicago in the 1830s, but it was not until 1848, when revolts in German states failed, that they started to arrive in large numbers. In 1845 there were only about a thousand Germans in Chicago; by 1850 the number had increased to 5,073; and by 1860 the number was 22,230, almost 20 percent of Chicago's entire population. The number of foreign-born Germans in Chicago reached a peak of 191,168 in 1914.

In general, the Germans who came in 1848 or soon thereafter—the "Forty-Eighters"—were articulate, well-educated, and reform-minded, with a small, vocal minority friendly to the socialist philosophy. Although their immediate reason for leaving Germany was political turmoil, their underlying motive, like that of later German immigrants, was largely economic. As a whole, however, they arrived much less destitute than did the Irish. The religious motive was unimportant to them.

Many Germans became active in antislavery movements, in founding radical political groups, and in organizing labor unions that were based partly on their experience with the guild system in Europe. Antiforeign feeling (fanned by the Know-Nothing movement) and cultural misunderstandings about such activities as keeping theaters and saloons open on Sunday brought the Germans into conflict with the city establishment on a number of occasions, including the "German Beer Riots" of 1855. In that year, Mayor Levi Boone ordered that all saloons and beer gardens be closed on Sundays. German workers, who had traditionally relaxed on Sunday with a stein of beer and the camaraderie of their countrymen, considered this an affront to their freedom. Two hundred German saloon keepers were arrested when they refused to obey the edict. Large numbers of Germans, some armed, marched to the courthouse downtown to protest. In a confrontation with the police, one German was killed, several were hurt, and many were arrested before peace and Sunday beer sales were restored.

A much graver event that attracted international attention was the Haymarket Riot of 1886. The preceding years had given rise to labor turbulence, such as the railroad strike of 1877 and a number of other strikes that were aimed primarily at bringing about an eight-hour workday and other improvements in poor working conditions and low wages. Some of the labor leaders were German socialists and anarchists. A number of the strikes were marked by violence, including one at the McCormick factory, where a clash involving strikers and police on May 3, 1886, resulted in two fatalities and a number of serious injuries. The following evening, a bomb was thrown into a group of policemen who were attempting to disperse a labor protest meeting

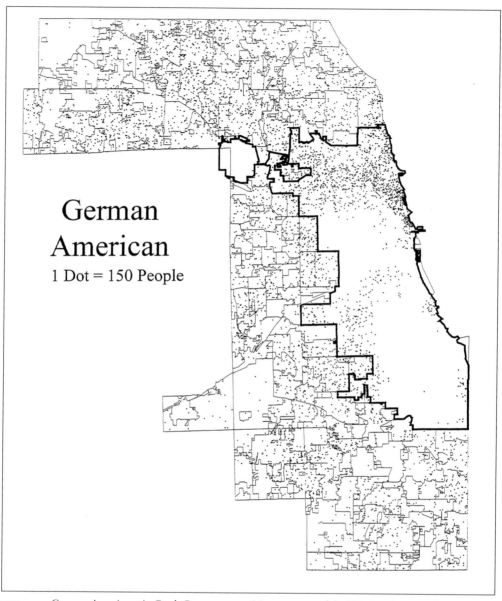

German
American

1 Dot = 150 People

FIG. 4.11. German Americans in Cook County, 1990. Map courtesy of the Illinois Ethnic Coalition.

being held outdoors in Haymarket Square, at Randolph Street (150 N.) and Des Plaines Street (700 W.). Many died, including eight policemen and ten civilians, in the resulting melee. The bomb thrower was never positively identified, but ten men characterized mainly as anarchist leaders were indicted. Eight of them were Germans.

Eight of the defendants in the Haymarket Riot were eventually convicted, more on the basis of their inflammatory rhetoric that incited murder than on any proven direct connection with the bomb throwing. Four of the convicted were hung, including Albert Spies, the fiery editor of an anarchist German-language newspaper, the *Arbeiter Zeitung,* and one committed suicide. In 1893 Governor John Altgeld pardoned the remaining three, stating that the defendants had not received a fair trial and had not been guilty of the crime as charged. This act of the very able, liberal, and first foreign-born (German) governor of Illinois ruined his promising political career.

Another result of the Haymarket Riot was the establishment of Fort Sheridan in 1887 on some six hundred acres of land along the shore of Lake Michigan, twenty-eight miles north of downtown Chicago. The land was donated to the federal government by the Commercial Club of Chicago, whose members evidently believed that the presence of federal troops nearby would help protect their interests against the further threat of violence. The radicalism and socialism of many German workers were tempered in the following decades as their standard of living rose; many attained high levels of achievement and moved into the middle class.

By 1890 the number of German-born who were living in Chicago had reached 161,039 and comprised almost 15 percent of the city's total population. At first there had been numerous small German settlements, such as those just north and west of the Chicago River and those to the south, running along both sides of the South Branch of the river between Twelfth and Twenty-second streets and spilling into the Bridgeport area. The greatest concentration by 1890, however, was on the North Side, from Clark Street westward to the North Branch of the Chicago River and from about Division Street northward, eventually extending into Lake View, Uptown, and Rogers Park. The area was filled with frugal Germans who owned their own homes and who made, first, North Avenue (1600 N.) and then Lincoln Avenue centers of their activities and settlement. Some worked as unskilled laborers in factories, but many were carpenters, shoemakers, barbers, butchers, cigar makers, coopers, furniture and wagon makers, and upholsterers.

For a number of decades, the most commonly heard language on North Avenue was German, and for a while, "Keep Off the Grass" signs in Lincoln Park were printed in both English and German. On Clark Street near North Avenue were the famous Red Star Inn and the Germania Club, built in 1888 on the fringe of what is today the Carl Sandburg Village complex. Farther south on Clark Street was the old Turner Hall, the home of several German and Swiss *Turnverein,* or physical fitness societies. Streets in the area bore such names as Goethe, Schiller, Lessing, Wieland, Germania, Siebens, and Beethoven.

North Avenue in the 1920s was largely a north European—mainly German—thoroughfare, though many of the wealthier Germans had moved farther north. In *The Gold Coast and the Slum,* Harvey Warren Zorbaugh describes the North Avenue neighborhood as it was in the late 1920s.

FIG. 4.12. Yondorf Block Building at the northeast corner of North Avenue and Halsted Street, 1963. Erected in 1887, the structure once housed numerous German organizations and included a theater and dance hall. Today the building is occupied by a bank. Photograph by Tom H. Long; Chicago Historical Society, ICHi-30422.

Its many German cafes—Wein Stube (with a bunch of huge gilded grapes over the door), Pilsner, Wurzn Sepp Family Resort, Komiker Sepp—give it a distinctive color .... The windows of the many delicatessen shops plainly proclaim Swiss, German, or Hungarian; and they have little tables about which men eat lunches of rye bread, sauerkraut, and pickles, perhaps with alpenkrauter, and talk in German.... At the corner of Larrabee and North Avenue is the Immigrant State Bank (with name in German, Hungarian, and Italian, as well as English).... To the east are building and loan associations and several steamship agencies. On Halsted, near North Avenue, are two German labor newspapers, and St. Michael's Bavarian Church. North Avenue has a few chain grocery stores, but most of its groceries are neighborhood stores.... The names along the street are nearly all northern European: Carl Bocker, Cigars and Tobacco; Stroup & Happel, Architects; A. Schlesinger, Schiffskarten.[6]

St. Michael's Church, erected in 1866 at Eugenie and Cleveland streets, became the largest German parish in the city and a major focal point of the Old Town community. Johnny Weismuller, a choirboy at the church, later became well known as a five-gold-medal Olympic swimming champion and even more famous as the portrayer of Tarzan in the *Tarzan of the Apes* movies.

Many of Chicago's approximately thirty breweries were in this area, most of them German-owned. (Chicago's first brewery had been established by Germans in a tenement building at the site of what is now Michigan and Chicago avenues). Some of the breweries even produced beer surreptitiously during the Prohibition era. In recent years they have closed down, partly because of a declining German population but mainly because of competition from large national brands. One of the last, the Sieben Brewery at 1470 North Larrabee Avenue (600 W.), with its extremely popular *Sieben Bierstude,* closed in 1967.

Although the largest German concentration was on the North Side, by 1920 Germans were scattered throughout most of the Northwest Side, with centers in such communities as Humboldt Park, Logan Square, Irving Park, Avondale, Lincoln Square, and Albany Park (see Fig. 4.1). There were also settlements west and southwest of the stockyards in Gage Park and in surrounding areas. And there were small communities to the southeast in Avalon Park and South Chicago.

A measure of the dispersion of the German population is revealed by the location of German churches. Curiously, the German churches were even more dispersed than the German population. Almost half of the ethnic churches erected in Chicago in the latter half of the nineteenth century were German.

FIG. 4.13. Beer tanks for sale, marking the end of Chicago's last large brewery, the Peter Hand Brewing Company, at 1000 West North Avenue, 1979. Photograph by Irving Cutler.

The peak building of German churches took place between about 1880 and 1900. After that, German church building, especially Catholic churches, slowed somewhat, as German immigration had started to taper off and German Catholics increasingly attended non-German Catholic churches. In 1900 there were 122 German churches of a variety of denominations within the city. Seventy-four of the churches could be classified as Lutheran or Evangelical, twenty-four were Catholic, thirteen Methodist, four Baptist, three Congregational, two Reformed, and two Adventist.[7] At that time, there were fifteen German churches in the suburbs, most of them Catholic.

Virtually all of the German churches had parochial schools, with instruction given in German. World War I, with its wartime anti-German hysteria, brought about a decline in the number of German parochial schools and the elimination of the German language from the public grade school curriculum. In 1920 a survey revealed that the churches were split nearly evenly between the North and Northwest sides and the South and Southwest sides, although the bulk of the German population lived to the north. Today there are about twenty predominantly German churches in the metropolitan area, few of which have some services in German. One of Chicago's most prominent religious leaders of German descent was George Cardinal Mundelein, the first cardinal of the Archdiocese of Chicago, who served in the area from 1915 until his death in 1939.

Germans were employed in virtually every type of occupation but were primarily skilled craftsmen, mechanics, technicians, and small shop owners, as one expert makes clear: "[In 1900, the Germans] formed over one-half of the bakers and butchers. More than one-third of the boot and shoemakers and repairers were German; also the masons. They made up about one-third of the iron and steel workers and the machinists and nearly one-third of the blacksmiths, painters, glaziers, varnishers, printers, lithographers, pressmen, and of the manufacturers and officials."[8] Like the Irish, though in smaller numbers, some had worked on the canal and some served in police work, fire prevention, and other public service capacities.

One of the largest present-day concerns that was founded by Germans is Oscar Mayer and Company, the meatpacker. Wieboldt department stores (now defunct) were also founded by Germans. Among the Germans in the field of planning and architecture were Charles H. Wacker and Ludwig Mies van der Rohe. Wacker, a second-generation German American who became wealthy in the brewing industry, was for seventeen years the chairman of the Chicago Plan Commission and a most vigorous proponent of the Burnham Plan of 1909. Mies van der Rohe was an internationally known architect who left Germany in 1937 and became the head of the school of architecture at the Illinois Institute of Technology. His work and that of his many students have helped alter the skyline of Chicago.

The Germans were always somewhat "group conscious," and this trait led to the early establishment of German churches, theaters, restaurants, unions, and stores that handled German goods. Their varied activities are perhaps best exemplified by their many clubs and organizations. In 1935, well past the peak of major German immigration, a German newspaper listed 452 active German clubs in the Chicago area. These associations included lodges and fraternal organizations,

FIG. 4.14. St. Paul's Catholic Church, founded in 1876 by Germans. Construction of the building, at 2127 West Twenty-second Place, began in 1897 and was completed a few years later with the help of parishioners who were craftsmen. Today most of the church membership is Mexican. St. Paul Federal Savings and Loan was started by the church. Photograph by Irving Cutler.

women's charitable groups, mutual and immigrant aid societies, soccer clubs, "turner" or gymnastic groups, veterans' organizations, and choral groups. They reflected such differing German backgrounds as Bavarian, Saxon, Rhenish, Prussian, and even some Danube Swabians who had come from southeastern Europe. Germans were especially active in music, and the founding of the Chicago Symphony Orchestra in 1891 was due largely to their enterprise. Initially, the ninety-member orchestra was predominantly German and was led by the famed German-born conductor Theodore Thomas. The orchestra performed in the Auditorium until it moved into its new home, Orchestra Hall, in 1904. Thomas's assistant director, Frederick Stock, also German born, became the conductor in 1905 and directed the distinguished orchestra for the next thirty-seven years. Also of cultural importance was Chicago's German-language theater, which produced a variety of plays, including classics by Goethe and Schiller, over some eighty years. The decline in German-born immigrants, the Great Depression of the 1930s, and the popularity of motion pictures led to its demise.[9]

Membership in many of the German organizations was adversely affected by the Americanization of the younger German generations and by the unpopularity of some of these organizations during the two world wars. The organizations were also hurt by the dispersal of the German population into the suburbs, where well over 80 percent of the people of German extraction lived in the 1990s. Today there are only about a hundred German organizations in the Chicago area. The major German-language newspaper, the *Abendpost*, founded in 1889, has ceased publication.

The German population in the area that surrounds Chicago has been significant for more than a century, although the greatest increase has taken place in the past few decades with the general movement of population to the suburbs. At one time, many German farmers on land around Chicago supplied the city and carried on a sizable trade in the city's markets. Some of the areas that now bear names of German origin include Schiller Park, Hanover Park, Bensenville, New Trier Township, Schaumburg, Hoffman Estates, Bremen Township, Bloom Township, and Frankfort. There were also early German settlements in such places as Addison, Arlington Heights, Blue Island, Chicago Heights, Crete, Country Club Hills, Des Plaines, Elmhurst, Flossmoor, Franklin Park, Hillside, Homewood, Itasca, Lincolnwood, Markham, Matteson, Morton Grove, Mount Prospect, Niles, Northbrook, Palos Heights, River Grove, Riverwoods, Sauk Village, Skokie, Thornton, Villa Park, Westmont, Wheeling, and Winnetka.

Today the German population in the metropolitan area is more evenly spread out than that of other ethnic groups, and there are few great concentrations of German stock in the larger suburbs. Several communities in the metropolitan area, however, have between five thousand and twenty-five thousand residents of German descent. These include Arlington Heights, Aurora, Des Plaines, Elgin, Elmhurst, Evanston, Homewood, Joliet, Oak Park, and Skokie.

In Chicago the approximately 190,000 people of German extraction live scattered mainly on the North and Northwest sides of the city, with smaller numbers on the Southwest Side. The main commercial concentration is along Lincoln Avenue—the diagonal street along which German farmers once hauled their produce from their northwest-area farms to Chicago markets. Although the highly concentrated German neighborhoods broke up about half a century ago, an influx of many post–World War II immigrants has helped to maintain some German commercial strips, especially along two stretches of Lincoln Avenue. One of these runs from Lincoln and Southport Avenue (1400 W.) northwest for a few blocks; the other runs along Lincoln from approximately Montrose (4400 N.) to Lawrence (4800 N.) avenues. In these areas are German delicatessens, bakeries, restaurants, music stores, meat markets, sport shops (featuring soccer equipment), import and gift stores, bars, meeting houses, travel bureaus, and the Davis Theater, where German-language movies are occasionally shown.

The Chicago communities with the greatest population of Germans are on the North and Northwest sides—Lake View, Uptown, Lincoln Square, North Center, Irving Park, and Portage Park. Chicago's German population is much older than the general Chicago population. The median age of 59.8 years for the German population contrasts with the 29.6-year median age for the general population, the latter reflecting a relatively large number of young African Americans and Hispanics. Politically, the present German population has changed drastically from that of a century ago, when many were socialists or anarchists. Surveys show that most of the people of German descent are now well-off and vote Republican. Despite their significant contributions to Chicago in culture, commerce, and industry and their large numbers, the Germans have kept a relatively low profile since the two world wars and, unlike smaller ethnic groups, do not even have a German museum.

The Scandinavians

Another sizable group of northern Europeans to settle relatively early in Chicago were Scandinavians. By 1870 they composed 9.5 percent of the city's large foreign-born population, and by 1890, 16.0 percent, surpassing the Irish in number. From 1850 to 1870, the largest group of Scandinavians came from Norway, but thereafter the Norwegians were outnumbered by Swedes. Danes constituted a small fraction of the Scandinavian immigrants. In 1890 there were 43,032 Swedes, 21,385 Norwegians, and 7,087 Danes in Chicago who were foreign born.

Many more thousands of Scandinavians fanned out from Chicago to settle elsewhere in Illinois and in Wisconsin, Minnesota, Iowa, and the Dakotas; some had first worked in Chicago temporarily to accumulate capital for the purchase of farmland. In Illinois, Norwegians settled in the lower Fox River valley in Kendall and La Salle counties, as well as adjacent areas. Farther west in Illinois, a Swedish religious community was established at Bishop Hill, near Kewanee. A sizable number of Danes settled north of Chicago in Racine, Wisconsin.

The earliest Scandinavians to settle in Chicago were two Norwegians who came in 1836. Even before their arrival, however, many of the Norwegian sailors on the Great Lakes had been familiar with Chicago. By 1860 there were 1,313 Norwegians in Chicago, and their numbers increased rapidly. In 1862 after a seventy-one-day trip, the schooner *Sleipner* arrived in Chicago with 107 passengers and 350 tons of cargo direct from Bergen, Norway, via the St. Lawrence River and the Great Lakes—the first such vessel to arrive directly from the mainland of Europe. (The trailblazing voyage of the *Sleipner* has been commemorated with a bronze plaque at the State Street Bridge, the site of the ship's first arrival). The trip was repeated in each of the next three years.

The first Norwegian settlement was established south of Chicago Avenue (800 N.), between Orleans (340 W.) and the lake.[10] In 1847, when their numbers were still small, the Norwegians joined with Swedes in establishing the first Scandinavian Lutheran Church, at Superior (732 N.) and La Salle streets (150 W.). In 1849 the Norwegian community was especially hard hit by a cholera epidemic. It was later discovered that all of the victims had used water from the same well into which the drainage of an outhouse had flowed.

As the Norwegians increased in number, they moved west of the river into an area bounded approximately by Milwaukee, Grand (520 N.), Halsted (800 W.), and Racine (1200 W.). A number of Norwegian churches were built in the area. Two of them, one Lutheran and the other Methodist, were founded in 1870 in the Grand and Sangamon (932 W.) area. The first Norwegian newspaper, *Skandinaven*, was begun in 1866 and survived until 1935. At its peak it had a circulation greater than that of any newspaper in Norway. In 1930 Chicago had the third-largest Norwegian population in the world, exceeded only by Oslo and Bergen.

Like their fellow Scandinavians, the Norwegians were a frugal, hardworking, law-abiding, and relatively well educated people. Many were skilled tradesmen. They found employment in the mills, railyards, and factories along the North Branch of the Chicago River. Some of the young girls worked as domestics in the homes of prosperous Chicagoans. In time many Norwegians set up their own shops, small manufacturing plants,

and professional offices. Chicago companies founded by men of Norwegian heritage include the Olson Rug Company, the Nester Johnson Skate Company, and the Gulbransen Company, which manufactured pianos. Many Norwegians also served aboard lake ships, some as captains. The Norwegians' continuing interest in sailors was evidenced by their sponsorship of seamen's missions, including one in the Lake Calumet area.

Before the beginning of the twentieth century, many Norwegians moved northwest into the newer, less crowded, attractive areas of Humboldt Park and Logan Square. The wealthier Norwegians, including doctors, lawyers, and businessmen, settled into beautiful homes in the Wicker Park area, around Damen Avenue (2000 W.) to the south of North Avenue. North Avenue, westward from Wicker Park to Humboldt Park and on to Pulaski Road (4000 W.), became the main Norwegian business street (see Fig. 4.1). There the chief languages spoken were Norwegian and Danish. Humboldt Park was an important center for gatherings, and in 1893 a statue of Leif Eriksson, the Norse discoverer, was erected there. Half a century ago, most of the twenty-six Norwegian churches in Chicago were in and around the Humboldt Park–Logan Square area.

Later many Norwegians moved farther northwest, especially into Irving Park, Portage Park, and Jefferson Park, with others in recent decades moving into the suburbs. At present, about fifteen thousand people of Norwegian ancestry live in Chicago. Many more live in the suburbs, and they compose 1.3 percent of the metropolitan population. Because of this outward migration and the rapid influx of Puerto Ricans, the Humboldt Park and Logan Square neighborhoods are now home to only a few Norwegian institutions and societies. They include the Norwegian-American Hospital and the Norwegian Memorial Lutheran Church, where some Sunday services are still conducted in the Norwegian language. An illustrious resident of the Logan Square area was Knute Rockne, the famous Notre Dame football coach. Other famous Chicagoans of Norwegian descent include Victor F. Lawson, for many years the publisher of the *Chicago Daily News*; Arthur E. Andersen, the founder of the nationally known accounting firm that bore his name; Ludwig Hektoen, the famous pathologist who is noted for his cancer research; and Thomas Pihfeldt, who between 1901 and 1941 supervised the building of more than fifty Chicago bridges.

The smaller Danish population's first Chicago settlement occurred north of the Chicago River, around La Salle (150 W.) and Kinzie (400 N.). Later, like the Norwegians, the Danes moved into the Northwest Side communities of Wicker Park; Humboldt Park, around the Trinity Danish Lutheran Church at Cortez (1032 N.) and Francisco (2900 W.) avenues; and adjacent Logan Square. The Dania Society of Chicago, originally just north of downtown, was founded in 1862 as the city's first Scandinavian club and the oldest Danish society anywhere outside Denmark. It was situated from 1912 until recent years on Kedzie Avenue, north of North Avenue. The Humboldt Park–Logan Square Danish area started changing after World War II, and now virtually no Danes live there. The three Danish Lutheran churches of the area have closed. A small pocket of Danes also existed on the Far South Side, around Eighty-fifth and Maryland (832 E.), where in 1875 Danish Lutherans opened St. Stephan's Lutheran Church.

Many of the Danes were artisans and journeymen who found employment in the building trades. Jens Jensen was a leading landscape designer who designed many of Chicago's parks and boulevards. A large Chicago contractor is the S. Nielsen Company. Some Danes opened little shops. A company that became nationally known is the market research firm of A. C. Nielsen. Chicagoans of Danish ancestry reached a peak of 28,695 in 1930 and then declined to about six thousand in 2000. Few new Danish immigrants come to Chicago, and like members of other ethnic groups, many Danes have moved to the suburbs. Because of their small numbers and dispersal, no strictly Danish churches are left in the Chicago area. Economic advancement and Americanization have virtually eliminated the vestiges of Danish culture that the immigrants brought to America.

By far the greatest number of Scandinavians to arrive in Chicago came from Sweden, and Chicago soon had the largest number of Swedes of any city in America. However, as Table 4.8 shows, Swedes initially lagged behind Norwegians in numbers. Early Swedish immigrants usually came from rural areas, whereas later arrivals came mainly from urban and industrial areas of southern Sweden.

The first "Swede Town" in Chicago was just north of the river to about Erie Street (658 N.), and from Wells Street (200 W.) west to the North Branch of the Chicago River. Danish and especially Norwegian settlers were also living in this area, which previously had been inhabited mainly by the Irish and was already assuming the characteristics of a slum. The building in 1850 of St. Ansgarius Swedish Episcopal Congregation on the

TABLE 4.8

Foreign-Born Scandinavians in Chicago

	Swedes	Norwegians	Danes
1860	816	1,313	150
1870	6,154	6,374	1,243
1900	48,836	22,011	10,166
1930	65,735	21,740	12,502
1970	7,005	3,094	1,708
2000	563	NA*	NA

Source: Adapted from U.S. Census Bureau data.
*NA, not available

corner of Franklin (300 W.) and Grand (520 N.) gave the Swedes their first communal center. The world-renowned singer Jenny Lind, "the Swedish Nightingale," assisted in construction with a donation of fifteen hundred dollars. This first Swedish church was followed in a few years and in the same general locale by a Lutheran and a Methodist church. The miserable shacks that housed the early Swedish immigrants in the area were gradually replaced with little wooden houses.

As immigration increased, Swede Town pushed northward to Division Street, while the earlier German inhabitants of the area moved on to the North Avenue area. By 1870 the Swedish Club at 1258 N. La Salle and the Immanuel Lutheran Congregation at Sedgwick, near Division, had become important centers of Swedish community life. Chicago Avenue, the main Swedish business street, was known as "Swedish Clodhoppers Lane."

Some of the Swedes of the area worked as maids, cooks, or gardeners for the rich to the east. Many of the men worked in construction as laborers and carpenters and eventually as engineers, architects, electricians, and contractors. The Gust K. Newberg Construction Company has become one of the largest in the Chicago area. It is estimated that Swedes may have been involved in the building of as many as half of the buildings in Chicago.

The Chicago Fire of 1871 destroyed much of the Swedish community, including four Swedish churches and as many Swedish newspapers.[11] With hard work, their great experience in construction, and outside financial aid (including some from Sweden), the Swedes quickly rebuilt their area.

Many Swedes soon began to move farther north, especially into Lake View, which by the turn of the century became the major Swedish community, with close to twenty thousand Swedes. The Lake View community centered on the intersection of Belmont Avenue (3200 N.) and Clark Street. Swedish businesses dominated the commercial stretch along Clark, and the area contained Swedish churches, meeting halls, cafes, singing clubs, the Swedish Engineers' Society of Chicago, and other facilities and organizations.

By the early 1900s, the once sizable Swede Town around Chicago and Division streets had given way to an influx of other immigrant groups, especially Sicilians. The Swedes kept moving farther north and northwest, beyond Lake View, where the Swedish population had declined to fourteen thousand by 1930. A very large Swedish community, Andersonville, had developed by 1900 in Uptown, around Clark and Foster (5200 N.). The Swedish also moved farther west into West Ridge, Lincoln Square, Albany Park, and North Park. In North Park, Swedish Covenant Hospital and Covenant Home, at California (2800 W.) and Foster avenues, began its operations in 1886 as a combination hospital, old people's home, and orphanage. In 1894 North Park College and Theological Seminary (now North Park University) was built at Kedzie (3200 W.) and

Foster by the Evangelical Covenant Church. Today the university is an important Swedish American cultural, research, and religious center. Between 1900 and 1920, encouraged by Swedish builders and by the opening of the Irving Park streetcar line, Swedes also moved into the communities of Irving Park, Portage Park, and Norwood Park.

Although the bulk of the Swedish population lived on the North and Northwest sides, there were also Swedish communities on the West and South sides of the city. These were areas of wooden houses that had been untouched by the Chicago Fire. By 1880 some twenty-five hundred Swedes lived in an enclave bounded by Kinzie (400 N.), Milwaukee, Division, and Ashland, a neighborhood where many Norwegians had already settled.[12] Some Swedes later settled farther west, in Austin.

The initial Swedish community on the South Side was in an area predominantly populated by Germans and Irish, and the

FIG. 4.15. Clark Street just north of Foster Avenue in Andersonville, once an important Swedish community in Chicago. Remaining are a number of Swedish stores, a Swedish museum, and the well-known Ann Sather Restaurant. Photograph by Irving Cutler.

FIG. 4.16. Swedish stores on Foster (5200 N.) and Spaulding (3300 W.) avenues in North Park, 2003. The area was once an important Chicago Swedish residential community and still contains the ever-expanding Swedish Covenant Hospital and North Park University, which was opened in 1894 and includes the Center for Scandinavian Studies. Photograph by Irving Cutler.

Swedes remained a minority there. In 1880 they were concentrated especially between Clark (100 W.) and Stewart (400 W.) and Twenty-first and Twenty-seventh streets. To serve the Swedes in this area, four denominations—Lutheran, Baptist, Methodist, and Evangelical Covenant, all of which had also been established among the North Side Swedes—started churches there. Physically, the area was similar to Swede Town, with generally ramshackle, wooden buildings.

As industry and the expanding black ghetto encroached on the area, some Swedes moved farther south, into the Armour Square area to the east of Bridgeport, and some moved into the "Stockholm" area near the McCormick reaper factories, which were around Western

(2400 N.) and Blue Island. Others settled near the industrial areas of South Chicago and Pullman. Swedes who had worked their way up economically also began to settle in other communities to the south, especially in Englewood, Greater Grand Crossing, South Shore, Chatham, Beverly, and Roseland.

The Swedes dispersed to the North, South, and West sides until there were about two dozen identifiable enclaves. So too did their numerous social, humanitarian, labor, and religious organizations. Early in the history of the Chicago Scandinavian community Swedes, Danes, and Norwegians had joined in various social causes and common organizations, including some of the early churches. However, as the size of each Scandinavian group increased, each nationality developed

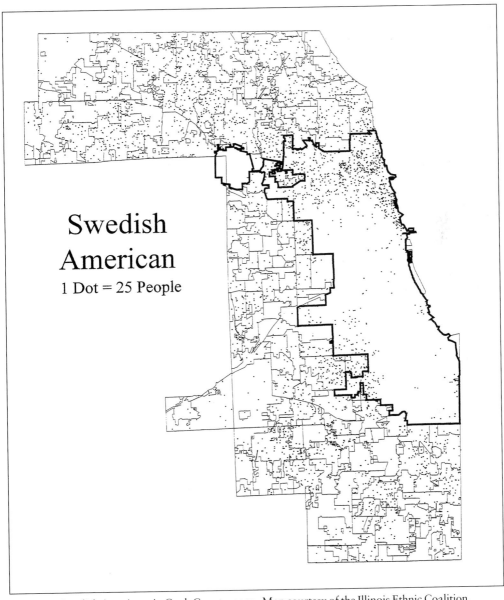

Swedish
American
1 Dot = 25 People

FIG. 4.17. Swedish Americans in Cook County, 1990. Map courtesy of the Illinois Ethnic Coalition.

its own facilities and organizations. The various Scandinavian nationalities were especially productive in the erection of hospitals and old people's homes to take care of their own.

The Swedes were also active in building churches throughout their communities. By 1905 the Chicago area contained forty-one Swedish Lutheran congregations, eighteen Swedish Methodist, eleven Swedish Baptist, and twelve Evangelical Covenant churches. Their combined membership was almost twenty-five thousand. Before World War I, most of these churches held their services in Swedish, but thereafter, services were increasingly held in English until the Swedish language was almost completely replaced. Today what were once Swedish Lutheran and other Swedish Protestant churches are increasingly becoming community churches, serving a variety of ethnic groups. Like the other Scandinavians, the Swedes had confidence in American secular education, but unlike other immigrant groups, they generally did not push the teaching of their native language in the schools.[13] However, by 1920, they had founded more than 130 secular clubs.

Now only an estimated twenty-five thousand people of Swedish descent live in Chicago, with many more in the suburbs. They comprise about 2.2 percent of the metropolitan area's total population. Immigration from prosperous Sweden is small. Many Swedish Americans now live in such suburbs as Evanston, Skokie, Morton Grove, Park Ridge, Geneva, Des Plaines, Wheaton, Glen Ellyn, Oak Lawn, and Homewood. In Chicago, the Swedes were easily assimilated and became scattered, so that today the only important Swedish

community left in the city is Andersonville, around Clark and Foster. Even there, the Swedish population is now small, mainly elderly, and intermixed with other groups, including a recent influx of Asians and Middle Easterners. Nevertheless, a few blocks on Clark Street, north of Foster Avenue, have been somewhat revitalized as a special Swedish commercial street. Bedecked with banners in the Swedish national colors of blue and yellow, the shops attract many who come to savor the smorgasbord of Nordic offerings. Traditionally, a bell was rung every Saturday to remind shopkeepers to clean their sidewalks. The merchants foster an annual parade.

Arrayed along the street are a few Swedish gift shops, restaurants, bakeries, delicatessens, fish stores, and grocery stores with Scandinavian delicacies. The famous Ann Sather Restaurant (now owned by an Irishman) is there, but missing are the offices of the *Swedish American Tribune*, one of seven Swedish newspapers that once existed in Chicago. Interspersed among the stores is a Swedish museum with a simulated log cabin exterior. Here one can learn about Polycarpus von Schneidau, the Swedish immigrant engineer who supervised construction of Chicago's first railroad, the Chicago and Galena; Charles R. Walgreen, who built the largest retail drug chain in the United States; Gloria Swanson, the movie star who was born in the Swedish community around Ashland Avenue; and, of course, Carl Sandburg, the Pulitzer Prize–winning historian, newspaperman, and poet who, in a famous poem, vividly portrayed Chicago as the "City of the Big Shoulders."

The Jews

Jews came to Chicago from almost every country in Europe. In Chicago they formed a kind of melting pot within the larger immigrant melting pot. Because of harsh discriminatory treatment in many European countries—sometimes culminating in outright massacres—the Jewish immigrants, despite some sentimental attachment to the old country, were less interested in returning to their homelands than were the members of any other immigrant group. Whereas the most affluent and educated members of other immigrant groups usually remained in their native land, where they occupied secure and respected positions, in most central and eastern European countries the Jews of all economic and educational levels welcomed the opportunity to settle in American communities. Although limited somewhat by occasional open anti-Semitism and by more frequent covert discrimination, especially in the earlier periods of their settlement, in Chicago the Jews were able to flourish when given the opportunity in a free land.

Jews who came to Chicago could be divided into two relatively distinct groups. The first group to arrive was one of German-speaking Jews from central Europe—from Bavaria, Prussia, Austria, Bohemia, and the German-occupied part of Poland. In general, these Jews were more secular, urbane, and affluent than the second group—the eastern European Jews who came in much larger numbers somewhat later. The latter spoke Yiddish and were mainly from Russia, Poland, Romania, and Lithuania, in which persecution was often especially severe and where there was little in the way of political or economic emancipation. They were a poor, deeply religious people, mostly from small towns and villages (shtetls) where they had frequently been con-fined to government-imposed ghettos. Despite their varied backgrounds and homelands, which resulted in occasional internal discord, the two groups, in time, achieved a degree of unity. For many decades, though, each had its own neighborhoods and institutions.

Among the earliest settlers in Chicago were small numbers of German Jews, mainly from Bavaria, who started trickling into the area in the late 1830s and early 1840s. In 1841 one of the settlers was Henry Horner, who became an organizer of the Chicago Board of Trade and helped found a major wholesale grocery company. His grandson of the same name was to serve as governor of Illinois from 1933 to 1940. By 1845 there were enough Jews to hold the first High Holy Day services and to purchase an acre of land for use as a Jewish cemetery in what is now Lincoln Park. In 1847, upstairs of a dry goods store owned by Rosenfeld and Rosenberg on the southwest corner of Lake (200 N.) and Wells (200 W.), a small group of about fifteen Jews agreed to form the first congregation, which they called Kehilath Anshe Mayriv (K.A.M., Congregation of the Men of the West). In 1851 the congregation erected a small frame synagogue on Clark Street, just south of Adams Street (200 S.).

The *Daily Democrat* of June 14, 1851, reported the dedication of the synagogue as follows:

The ceremonies at the dedication of the first Jewish synagogue in Illinois, yesterday, were very interesting indeed. An immense number had to go away, from inability to gain admittance. There were persons of all denominations present. We noticed several clergymen of different religious denominations.

No person that has made up his mind to be prejudiced against the Jews ought to hear such a sermon preached. It was very captivating and contained as much real religion as any sermon we ever heard preached. We never could have believed that one of those old Jews we heard denounced so much could have taught so much liberality towards other denominations.

The revolutionary movements that swept central Europe in 1848 increased Jewish immigration to the United States and, by 1860 there were about fifteen hundred Jews in Chicago. Most lived around Lake and Wells streets, where a few owned clothing and dry goods stores. Some of these store owners had started out as almost penniless backpacking peddlers. Later, large-scale retailers such as Mandel Brothers, Goldblatt Brothers, Maurice L. Rothschild, Maurice B. Sachs, Polk Brothers, Aldens, and Spiegel were to grow from similar modest beginnings, as were such manufacturers as Hart Schaffner and Marx, Kuppenheimer, Florsheim, Brunswick, and Inland Steel.

By 1870 the Jewish community had diffused somewhat, with the largest concentration residing between Van Buren (400 S.) and Polk (800 S.) streets, and between the river on the west and the lake on the east. There were enough Jews in the city to support seven synagogues scattered throughout what is today the central business district. One congregation was situated as far north as Superior Street (732 N.); today it is Temple Sholom on North Lake Shore Drive, the city's largest synagogue on the basis of membership. Another was located as far west as Des Plaines Street (700 W.); it is today's Oak Park Temple on Harlem Avenue (7200 W.).

The Fire of 1871 and another on the Near South Side in 1874 destroyed most of the Jewish community, including more than half of the synagogues.[14] The German Jews, increasing rapidly due to the continual influx of immigrants, moved out of the quickly spreading downtown business area. They settled mainly one or more miles south of downtown along such streets as Michigan, Wabash, and Indiana; later, in the Grand Boulevard, Washington Park, Kenwood, and Hyde Park communities; and eventually in South Shore. Large orphanages and homes for the aged were built, and in 1880 Michael Reese Hospital was founded at Twenty-ninth Street and Ellis Avenue (1000 E.). After World War I, Jews of eastern European descent also moved into these areas.

At their peak in the years after World War II, the communities of Hyde Park and South Shore each contained about a dozen synagogues; a few were Orthodox, but most were either Conservative or Reform. The Orthodox congregations adhered strictly to the traditional, fundamentalist Judaism. The newer Conservative and Reform movements conceived Judaism as more of a developmental religion that needed to adjust to contemporary conditions. The Conservative movement retained more of the traditional practices than did the Reform movement. Today only Hyde Park–Kenwood, with two synagogues, still has an active Jewish community on the South Side of Chicago, in the general vicinity of the University of Chicago.

In 1880 eastern European Jews comprised only a small fraction of Chicago's ten thousand Jews. But when Russia's especially brutal pogroms of 1881 were followed in 1882 by the very repressive so-called May Laws, which expelled many Jews from their homes and towns, a wave of Jewish emigration from

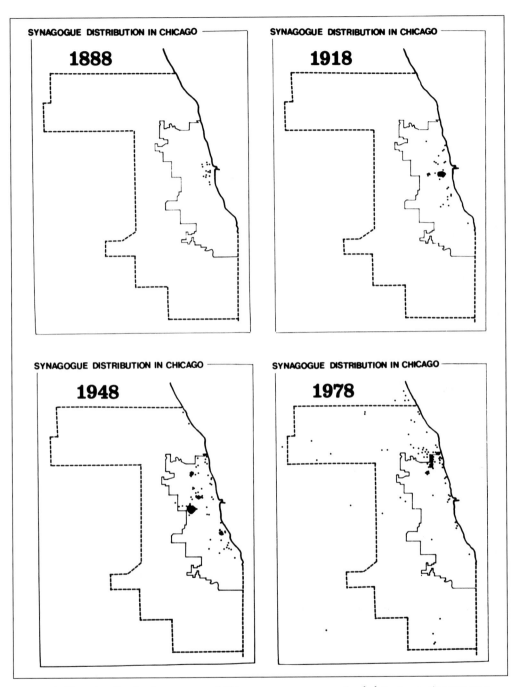

FIG. 4.18. Changing distribution patterns of Chicago-area synagogues *(each dot representing one syna-gogue)* by thirty-year periods, reflecting the changing residential locations of Jews in the area. There has been only slight change in synagogue locations since 1980. Today, about 70 percent of Chicago-area Jews live in the suburbs. Map by Irving Cutler and Joseph Kubal.

FIG. 4.19. Eastern European Jewish immigrant settlement around Twelfth and Jefferson streets in the Maxwell Street area, 1906. Chicago Historical Society.

eastern Europe was set off and lasted for almost half a century. In 1900 Chicago's Jewish population reached about eighty thousand, of whom an estimated fifty-two thousand were from eastern Europe, twenty thousand were from Germany and adjacent areas, and the remaining eight thousand were largely from northwestern Europe and the Middle East. By 1930 the Jewish population of the Chicago area was estimated at 275,000, of which more than 80 percent were of eastern European descent. They then comprised almost 9 percent of the city's population.

The Russian-Polish Jews crowded into the area southwest of downtown, a district formerly occupied by German, Bohemian, and Irish Christian communities. The Jews moved south along Canal (500 W.) and Jefferson (600 W.) streets and westward to Halsted, and then still farther west as new immigrants increased the congestion. By 1910 Jews were found in a ghetto that stretched approximately from Canal Street west to almost Damen Avenue (2000 W.), and from Polk Street (800 S.) south to about Fifteenth Street. Of the estimated fifty thousand immigrant Jews who arrived in Chicago during the last two decades of the nineteenth century, most settled in this Maxwell Street area.

Like other immigrant groups, the eastern European Jews initially found living in a big city quite difficult. In 1907 an article in the *Jewish Daily Courier* discussed the nostalgic feelings of these Jewish immigrants who had often fled persecution.

Why was it that something reminding the immigrant of the old home, like a pouch of tobacco, tea, or a European utensil brought forth a sigh and a tear? . . .

Furthermore how could one help but scoff at the longing of the immigrant for his old home when here in a city like Chicago he found himself in the center of a civilization that was prepared to offer him everything with a broad hand? The writer answered these questions in a typical Jewish manner. When one digs a little deeper, he said with a Talmudical flourish of his hand, he will see that there were certain values in the little town that are still lacking in the big city. In a small town everybody was friendly and knew everybody else. In the big city the houses are "cold" inside, no matter how much better built, and how superior in other ways they may be to the little cottages. Moreover, the social recognition given to men of learning and or honorable ancestry was lacking in the city.[15]

The main commercial arteries of the ghetto were north-south Halsted and Jefferson streets and east-west Twelfth and Maxwell (1330 S.) streets. Maxwell Street, especially, was well-known for its crowded, bustling, Old-World-style, open-market bazaar. The focal point of the community was around Halsted and Maxwell. In the blocks around this intersection, the population was about 90 percent Jewish. In many ways, the community resembled a teeming eastern European ghetto. It contained kosher meat markets and chicken stores, matzo bakeries and ones with bread and bagels, Yiddish newspaper offices, bookstores, cafes frequented by intellectuals, Yiddish theaters, Hebrew schools, literary organizations, tailor and seamstress shops, bathhouses, and peddlers' stables.

Conspicuously missing were the large number of saloons that could be found in other ethnic communities.

Louis Wirth offers the following contemporary description of the Maxwell Street market in the 1920s:

[The market was permeated with] . . . the smell of garlic and cheeses, the aroma of onions, apples and oranges, and the shouts and curses of sellers and buyers fill the air. Anything can be bought and sold on Maxwell Street. On one stand, piled high, are odd sizes of shoes long out of style; on another are copper kettles for brewing beer; on a third are second-hand pants; and one merchant even sells odd, broken pieces of spectacles, watches, and jewelry, together with pocket knives and household tools salvaged from the collections of junk peddlers. Everything has value on Maxwell Street, but the price is not fixed. It is the fixing of the price around which turns the whole plot of the drama enacted daily at the perpetual bazaar of Maxwell Street. . . . The sellers know how to ask ten times the amount that their wares will eventually sell for, and the buyers know how to offer a twentieth.[16]

Customers, hoping for bargains or merely curious, came from all over—from other ethnic neighborhoods as well as the Gold Coast. At one time Maxwell Street was the third-busiest retail shopping area in the city.

There were more than forty Orthodox synagogues. (For the Orthodox, the synagogue had to be within walking distance of the home.) These synagogues were usually small, with only a few having more than a hundred members, and were made up largely of immigrants who came from the same community

FIG. 4.20. Vendors in the Maxwell Street area about 1906, practicing a type of Old World retailing transplanted to America. After more than a century of existence, the market closed in 1994, the victim of redevelopment, expressway construction, a changing neighborhood, the expansion of the University of Illinois at Chicago, and changing shopping patterns. Photograph by Barnes-Crosby; Chicago Historical Society, ICHi-19155.

in Europe. Religiously, the eastern European Jews tried to cling to the old, whereas the German Jews espoused the new. There were also numerous Jewish educational, cultural, and fraternal organizations in the area, including the city's first large Jewish community center—the Chicago Hebrew Institute.

Even the dress was largely that of eastern European ghettos. One could speak Yiddish and wear a beard, a long black coat, and a Russian cap and boots without being ridiculed. But those who ventured into other neighborhoods often encountered scorn and even physical harassment.[17]

Ghetto life was hard and living conditions deplorable. The crowded wooden shanties and brick tenements of the area usually had

FIG. 4.21. Live goose for sale at a kosher butcher shop on Maxwell Street, about 1920. Marcy-Newberry Center Records (M-N neg. 152), Special Collections, The University Library, University of Illinois at Chicago.

insufficient light and few baths, and were surrounded by areas of poor drainage and piles of garbage. Despite the slum conditions, the crime rate was very low, and the death and disease rate was one of the lowest of the various immigrant groups.

To support themselves, the eastern European Jewish immigrants worked in the sweatshops of the clothing industry and in cigar-making factories. Many became peddlers, tailors, butchers, bakers, barbers, small merchants, and artisans. As they became more Americanized, they organized to fight for better working conditions. They composed about 80 percent of the forty-five thousand workers involved in the prolonged and successful garment strike of 1910, which resulted in the organization of the Amalgamated Clothing Workers of America under the leadership of Sidney Hillman. In 1910, 68.6 percent of the tailors in Chicago were Jewish, earning less than eight dollars a week and usually working twelve hours or more a day.[18]

The more affluent and established German Jews of the South Side "Golden Ghetto" were embarrassed by some of the Old World ways and beliefs of their eastern European Jewish brethren: the "poor, ignorant, ragged" peddlers of the Maxwell Street area who were tolerated mainly because they were Jews but who might bring about anti-Semitism, which the German Jews had hardly encountered in Chicago. They tried to aid in their Americanization by founding the Jewish Manual Training School, a settlement house, a dispensary, and other community facilities. Julius Rosenwald, who was of German-Jewish descent and the president of Sears, Roebuck and Company, contributed sizable sums to these institutions, as well to the University of Chicago, the Museum of Science and Industry, and other worthy causes, including housing and schools for African Americans. His brother-in-law, Max Adler, also a Sears executive, founded the Adler Planetarium. The proud Russian-Polish immigrants sometimes resented the paternalistic attitude of their more "aristocratic" German brethren but nevertheless accepted their help even though they often felt that the German Jews were trying to emulate the gentiles with their Reform Judaism.

Jews of the Maxwell Street area exhibited a physical and mental vitality that was sustained by a long tradition of hard work and learning. They strove for success, if not for themselves, then for their children. A surprising number of people with roots in this ghetto area became well known, as Ira Berkow notes in his book, *Maxwell Street:*

Joseph Goldberg was one of these immigrants. He came to America from Russia and eventually landed on Maxwell Street. He bought a blind horse, the only horse he could afford. He became a fruit-and-vegetable peddler; his son Arthur, would serve in President Kennedy's cabinet and became a Supreme Court Justice of the United States.

Samuel Paley became a cigar maker in America, as did Max Guzik. Samuel's son William, born in the back room of the modest family cigar store near Maxwell Street, is founder, president and chairman of the board of the Columbia Broadcasting System. Mr. Guzik's son, Jake, known as "Greasy Thumb," became the brains behind the Capone gang. . . .

Eastern European immigrants David Goodman and Abraham Rickover took jobs in Chicago as tailors. Their sons are Benny Goodman and Admiral Hyman C. Rickover.

Paul Muni's father owned a Yiddish theater near Maxwell Street. Jack Ruby's father was a carpenter there. John Keeshin, once the greatest trucking magnate in America, is the son of a man who owned a chicken store on Maxwell Street, as did the father of Jackie Fields, former welterweight champion of the world. The father of Federal Court Judge Abraham Lincoln Marovitz owned a candy store near Maxwell Street. Colonel Jacob Arvey, once a nationally prominent political power broker, is the son of a Maxwell Street area peddler.[19]

Other Jews who came from the area included movie mogul Barney Balaban, top professional boxers Barney Ross and "Kingfish" Levinsky, writer Meyer Levin, social activist Saul Alinsky, and gangsters "Yellow Kid" Weil and "Nails" Morton.

By 1910 improvements in economic status, the encroachment of industry and railroads, and an influx of African Americans impelled Jews to start moving out of the Maxwell Street area. By the 1930s only a small remnant of older Jewish residents remained in the area. But large Jewish-owned stores, such as L. Klein, Robinson, Gabels and Machevich, and hundreds of smaller vendors continued to do a good business until the riotous days of the late 1960s forced some businesses to pull out. However, the market continued to do business, especially on weekends, even though it was hurt through the years by the building of the Dan Ryan Expressway, which eliminated the eastern side of the market; the changing neighborhood; changing shopping patterns; urban redevelopment; and the expansion of the adjacent University of Illinois at Chicago.

Despite the strong efforts of many individuals and groups to save parts of the historic market, the city officially closed it in 1994. Soon, virtually the entire area was bulldozed, giving way to new student dormitories and a rapidly sprouting, gentrified, large, expensive "University Village" residential complex.

The city, however, did make one compromise in that they allowed for a new Maxwell Street market on Sundays only, one-half mile to the east along Canal Street. The busy new market's vending and merchandising somewhat resembles the original Maxwell Street market, except that Spanish instead of Yiddish is now the dominant language spoken there and the new market does not have the history, flavor, or smell of the old one.

The Jews of the Maxwell Street area dispersed in a number of directions. Some joined the German Jews on the South Side. A small number moved into the lakefront communities of Lake View, Uptown, and Rogers Park, joining Jews who had been moving northward from their small settlements on the Near North Side. A large number moved to the Northwest Side, where the nucleus of a Jewish community had been established in the late 1800s in the West Town area. There, many lived near their retail stores on Milwaukee Avenue and on Division Street (1200 N.). The first synagogues in the area were built in the 1890s, and eventually about twenty served a Jewish community that in time spread to the western side of Humboldt Park. Many of the Jews of this area were more inclined to emphasize Yiddish culture and somewhat radical philosophies rather than the religious orthodoxy of the Near West Side. Ideologically, the area was split among adherents of socialism, secularism, Zionism,

and orthodoxy. These differences declined markedly among their more-Americanized children.

The main commercial avenue was Division Street, with its numerous Jewish stores and the Deborah Boys Club. Although the Jews were a minority of the population, which included large numbers of Poles, Scandinavians, Ukrainians, and Russians, this area was the home of such well-known Jews as comedian Jackie Leonard (Fats Levitsky), movie impresario Michael Todd, columnist Sydney J. Harris, and Nobel prize–winning novelist Saul Bellow. Harris and Bellow were among a distinguished group of Chicago writers of Jewish descent, which also included Edna Ferber, Ben Hecht, Meyer Levin, Leo Rosten, Studs Terkel, and Louis Zara. Also well known were the popular columnists Ann Landers, Gene Siskel, and Irv Kupcinet.

Some Jews moved farther northwest into Logan Square and Albany Park, but most who were leaving the Near West Side leapfrogged over the railroad and industrial area and settled some three miles to the west, in the Lawndale–Douglas Park–Garfield Park area. This became the largest and most developed Jewish community that Chicago ever had. At its peak in 1930 this Greater Lawndale area contained an estimated 110,000 Jews of the city's Jewish population of about 275,000. Other areas with significant Jewish population in 1930 included the Lake View–Uptown–Rogers Park area (twenty-seven thousand), West Town–Humboldt Park–Logan Square (thirty-five thousand), Albany Park–North Park (twenty-seven thousand), and on the South Side, the Kenwood–Hyde Park–Woodlawn–South Shore area (twenty-eight thousand). Those in the South Side area had the highest economic status, followed by the North Side and Northwest Side communities. Smaller Jewish communities were found in Austin (seven thousand), Englewood–Greater Grand Crossing (four thousand), and Chatham–Avalon Park–South Chicago (three thousand). The Jewish population was served at that time by 105 synagogues, of which eighty-four were Orthodox, eight Conservative, and thirteen Reform. The Greater Lawndale area was a quieter residential area with comparatively spacious streets, yards, and parks. When German and Irish residents there initially refused to rent to them, the Jews bought a few of the one-story and numerous two-story homes in the area and built numerous three-story apartment buildings. By 1920 Greater Lawndale had become largely Jewish. The area stretched approximately from California Avenue (2800 W.) west to Tripp Street (4232 W.), and from Washington Street (100 N.) south to Eighteenth Street, although the greatest Jewish concentration was south of Roosevelt Road (Twelfth Street).[20] The Greater Lawndale area more than doubled in population between 1910 and 1930 to become one of the most densely populated communities in the city and the one with the greatest proportion of foreign-born—mainly Jews from Russia and Poland. By 1933, in

FIG. 4.22. Numerous Jewish institutions lining Douglas Boulevard (1400 S.). The Jewish People's Institute *(left),* on Douglas Boulevard and St. Louis Avenue (3400 W.), was a major cultural, social, and recreational center of Chicago Jewry from 1926 to 1955. It is now on the National Register of Historic Places. The Hebrew Theological College *(right)* was on Douglas Boulevard from 1922 to 1956; it is now in Skokie. The Jewish People's Institute building is now the home of the Lawndale Academy, a public elementary school, while the Hebrew Theological College building stands vacant. Photograph by Irving Cutler.

FIG. 4.23. Banquet at the Orthodox Jewish Home for the Aged, on Albany Avenue (3100 W.) near Eighteenth Street, about 1925. Most of the larger immigrant groups built facilities to care for their old, sick, and needy. Chicago Historical Society.

the central core of the area, Herzl, Penn, Howland, Bryant, and Lawson public schools each averaged around two thousand Jewish students, probably more than 90 percent of each school's enrollment.

The L-shaped parkway formed by Douglas Boulevard (1400 S.) and Independence Boulevard (3800 W.) was the heart of the area. Each boulevard extended for about a mile, with Douglas Park at the east end of Douglas Boulevard and Garfield Park at the north end of Independence Boulevard. Many of the major Jewish institutions of the community were located along these boulevards, including some dozen synagogues, most of imposing classical architecture and all but one Orthodox. Also there was a huge community center—the Jewish People's Institute, the Hebrew Theological College, a home for the Jewish blind, and a number of other religious, cultural, and Zionist organizations. Chicago had the first organized Zionist group in America, and a future prime minister of Israel, Golda Meir, lived in Lawndale for a while, working as a librarian in the local public library.

On the side streets were about four dozen more synagogues, all Orthodox, with many bearing the name of some community in Russia, Poland, Lithuania, or Romania, from which the founders had come. In 1944 about half of the city's synagogues were in this area. On Kedzie Avenue (3200 W.) were a Yiddish theater, the offices of the Workmen's Circle, and the building that housed a Jewish daily newspaper. On the east and west sides of Douglas Park—on California (2800 W.) and Albany (3100 W.) avenues—was an imposing array of social service institutions supported by the Jewish community. They included Mt. Sinai Hospital, a rehabilitation hospital, a convalescent home, a day and night nursery, a large orphanage, and a home for elderly Orthodox Jews.

The Greater Lawndale area was bisected by Roosevelt Road (1200 S.), the main commercial street. Jews came from all over the city to shop there. In the mile stretching from approximately Kedzie Avenue (3200

N.) to Crawford (Pulaski) Avenue (4000 W.) were half a dozen movie houses, Jewish bookstores and food stores, meeting halls, restaurants, and political organizations. The Twenty-fourth Ward was the top Democratic stronghold in the city, led for many years by Alderman Jacob Arvey. In the 1936 presidential election, the ward gave Roosevelt twenty-nine thousand votes to Landon's seven hundred, prompting President Roosevelt to call it "the number one ward in the entire Democratic Party." Although there have been many elected Jewish public officials, there has never been a Jewish mayor of Chicago.

Just as the area had changed from gentile to Jewish earlier in the century, a rapid, peaceful, and complete change from Jewish to African American occurred nearly as rapidly, from about 1946 to 1954. The Jews did not leave this area of second settlement because it had deteriorated. They left because they had attained relatively higher incomes and desired to raise their growing young families in homes of their own, rather than in apartments, and in areas with more amenities and higher status. There were few single-family homes in the area. The trend was aided by the improved mobility provided by the automobile. The younger, Americanized Jews, especially, were not interested in clinging to the magnificent institutional structures that their parents and grandparents had built. Some moved to Hyde Park and South Shore. Most moved to better and more prestigious areas on the North Side—some to Albany Park and Rogers Park, but more to West Rogers Park (West Ridge)—and to parts of the northern suburbs, especially, initially, to Skokie and Lincolnwood. A much smaller number went to the western and southern suburbs.

Jews started moving into Albany Park a few years after the completion of the Ravenswood elevated line in 1907, with its terminal at Lawrence (4800 N.) and Kimball (3400 W.) avenues. By 1930, Albany Park contained about twenty-three thousand Jews, almost half the population of the community. Many came from the older and less affluent Jewish areas of the West and Northwest sides. They viewed Albany Park as a more Americanized community. In religious matters, it was a transitional community between the Orthodoxy of the West Side and the Reform Judaism of the South Side. Orthodox, Conservative, and Reform synagogues, as well as other Jewish institutional facilities, dotted the area, with a strong concentration around Kimball Avenue. The main business street, Lawrence Avenue, was somewhat similar in character to Lawndale's Roosevelt Road.

During the post–World War II exodus from Lawndale, many Jewish families, including some of the most Orthodox groups, still settled in Albany Park, while some of the more affluent earlier Jewish settlers of Albany Park moved farther north. The Jewish movement out of Albany Park accelerated during the 1960s, and by 1975, only an estimated five thousand Jews remained, most of them elderly and of limited means. Today, fewer than two thousand Jews live there.

Until the northward extension of an elevated line to Howard Street (7600 N.) in 1909, Chicago's most northeasterly community, Rogers Park, had been largely an area of single-family frame houses. The community started to grow rapidly with the improvement of transportation, and numerous large apartment buildings and apartment hotels were built, especially in the eastern portion adjacent to Sheridan Road and the lake. Jews began to move into the area after

FIG. 4.24. Devon Avenue (6400 N.) looking east from Richmond Avenue (2932 W.), 2003, showing a variety of Jewish stores. The largest Jewish retail shopping area left in Chicago, it has declined in length to about a half mile. An Indian-Pakistani retail area has taken over the former Jewish shopping area on Devon Avenue east of California Avenue (2800 W.). Photograph by Irving Cutler.

1910, and by 1930 about ten thousand lived there. After World War II the area contained about twenty thousand Jews, who constituted about one-third of the community's population. Thereafter the Jewish population in the area gradually declined to an estimated thirteen thousand in 1980. Most of the remaining Jews are elderly, and there are few Jewish children. The average age of the Jewish population in Rogers Park is about sixty.

Since World War II, the most significant intracity movement of the Jews who have left their former communities on the South, West, and Northwest sides has been into West Ridge. This area, popularly referred to as West Rogers Park, lies between Rogers Park and the Albany Park–North Park area.

There were fewer than two thousand Jews in West Rogers Park in 1930; by 1950 there were about eleven thousand. Then, in the 1950s, the Jewish population quadrupled, and in 1960 it reached an estimated forty-eight thousand, or about three-fourths of the community's total population. Most were Jews of Russian-Polish descent. They had come from Lawndale and Albany Park and had purchased new single-family homes in the northern part of the community. Today, West Rogers Park is the largest Jewish community in Chicago. There are about ten synagogues, many of which were founded almost a century ago in the Maxwell Street area and reached

West Rogers Park via the Lawndale area. Most of the synagogues are Orthodox. Many are aligned along California Avenue, between Peterson (6000 N.) and Touhy (7200 N.) avenues, in a manner slightly reminiscent of Douglas Boulevard in the Lawndale area. Devon Avenue (6400 N.), the main business street, houses many merchants who were once located on Roosevelt Road or on Lawrence Avenue. In West Rogers Park, the rhythm of Orthodox Jewish life is still evident—ranging from the daily synagogue prayer service to the closing of many stores on the Sabbath. On California Avenue (2800 W.), from Peterson Avenue (6000 N.) to Howard Street (7600 N.), are some fifteen Jewish institutions, including eight synagogues.

Compared with the rest of the city's population, the Jewish population of West Rogers Park is older and has a higher median income and educational level. But, like the population of the city as a whole, it has been declining in numbers. At present, there are about thirty-five thousand Jewish residents. Young Orthodox Jewish families continue to maintain their strength and institutions in the community. But, increasingly, Indians, Pakistanis, Slavs, Greeks, and others have been moving into the community. Devon Avenue is becoming a street of many nations. Commercially, the Jews are now situated to the west of California Avenue, and the Indians and Pakistanis to the east.

After World War II, certain prevalent restrictions on Jews in employment, college admissions, and places to live were largely lifted, and since then, the major movement of Jews has been out of Chicago into the north and northwest suburbs. Small numbers of

Jews, mainly descendants of the early German immigrants, including Julius Rosenwald, moved into such unrestricted North Shore suburbs as Glencoe and Highland Park before World War I. But by 1950 only about 5 percent of Chicago-area Jews were living in the suburbs. By the early 1960s, however, some 40 percent of the Jewish people were living in the suburbs; today, the proportion is about 70 percent. It is estimated that more than 80 percent of the Jews in the entire metropolitan area now live north of Lawrence Avenue. (See Fig. 4.18). The bulk of the remainder resides in the high-rise complexes along Chicago's lakeshore, south to the Near North Side. Some Jews also live in Hyde Park; a few are scattered in other Chicago communities. And there are small numbers of Jews in most western and southern suburbs, with some concentration to the west in Oak Park, River Forest, Oak Brook, Westchester, and Naperville; and to the south in Homewood, Flossmoor, Olympia Fields, and Park Forest.

The first major north suburban move was into Skokie and adjacent Lincolnwood, mainly after World War II. These communities were near the Jewish concentrations in Rogers Park, West Ridge, Albany Park, and North Park. By the 1960s Skokie and Lincolnwood were estimated to be about half Jewish. In 2000 these two suburbs contained about a dozen synagogues, mainly Orthodox or Conservative, in contrast to the greater concentration of Orthodox synagogues in West Rogers Park and the preponderance of Reform temples in the more distant suburbs. Skokie is also home to the Hebrew Theological College and the Holocaust Museum.

In place of the previous divisions of the city into North, South, and West side Jewish communities, today's Chicago-area Jewish community is being concentrated increasingly in the northern suburbs and is moving outward over a wide geographic area. Based on survey data compiled in the mid-1970s by the Jewish Federation of Metropolitan Chicago, the northern suburbs of Niles, Evanston, Wilmette, Winnetka, Morton Grove, Northfield, and Deerfield are estimated to be from 10 percent to more than 20 percent Jewish. Glencoe and Highland Park are about 50 percent Jewish. Some of the Jews moving into these suburbs continue to come from Chicago; some, however, come from other suburbs, especially from Skokie, where Jewish population has declined some 25 percent in recent years.

The latest settlement pattern has been for young Jewish families to move to outlying suburbs to the northwest, where there is still vacant land and more reasonably priced housing. Serving these newer Jewish communities are synagogues in Hanover Park, Schaumburg, Hoffman Estates, Des Plaines, Buffalo Grove, and Vernon Hills. The Buffalo Grove area, some twenty-nine miles northwest of the Loop, with a rapidly growing Jewish population, now has eight synagogues, some for each major branch of Judaism. There are also two synagogues as far out as McHenry County.

A survey by the Jewish Federation in 2000–2001 showed that, buoyed somewhat by Russian Jewish immigration, the area's Jewish population has increased 4 percent in the last decade to 270,500. Another noted growing trend was that suburban Jews, mainly empty-nesters and young people, are moving into the city. More rapid growth has been held down by a low birth rate, movement to the Sunbelt states, intermarriage, and decreasing immigration from overseas. Jews now comprise about 4 percent of the total metropolitan population.

With some exceptions, the Jewish community today is relatively prosperous, comprising many successful professional and business people. It remains a strong supporter of Israel and its continued existence; is worried about the growing rate of intermarriage and the preservation of a strong Jewish identity, especially among the young; is concerned about growing world anti-Semitism; and assists the Jews of the area who live below the poverty level.

The abandoned Jewish institutions in the city have been replaced by new ones, scattered mainly in the northern fringes of the city and in the suburban areas where Jews live. Major active Jewish community centers serve the people in eight places. They are under the sponsorship of the Jewish Federation of Metropolitan Chicago, an umbrella-type community organization. From the contributions of many thousands to the Jewish United Fund, the Jewish Federation supports dozens of community, social welfare, cultural, religious, and educational services and organizations.

In 2004 the Jewish Federation raised about $72 million to support these activities and to help other Jewish communities throughout the world.

With the passing of the original immigrants from the scene, there has been a sharp decline in the hundreds of *landsmanshaften* fraternal organizations and synagogues, which encouraged Jews from the same towns in Europe to band together to assist Jews in their homeland and to provide support for other Jewish causes. They have been replaced by numerous local, regional, and even national institutions and organizations. There now is a greater diversity in religious beliefs, though religious convictions are no longer always the motivation for joining a particular congregation. In 2003 there were approximately 140 synagogues in the metropolitan area—up from 125 in 1980. About sixty were Orthodox or Traditional, thirty-five Conservative, thirty-six Reform, and the remainder essentially independent. The Conservative and Reform congregations usually have larger memberships than the Orthodox congregations; consequently, it is estimated that of the religiously affiliated Jews, 30 percent are Orthodox, 35 percent are Reform, and 35 percent are Conservative.

The children of the European immigrant parents often lived in two worlds, sharing the values and traditions of both—those of their immigrant parents and those of America. The grandchildren became even more acculturated. They pursued American cultural and leisure activities, intermarried more, and followed the white middle-class movement out of the old neighborhoods toward the suburbs. The descendants had more education and economic security than their forebears, and they produced eight Nobel Prize winners from the area. Yet, despite the generational changes, there usually lingered in most an ingrained Jewish feeling that manifested itself in many ways—in support of Israel and in religion, diet, humor, attitudes, and friends.

The once sharp division between the German and eastern European Jews has largely disappeared. The transition from European *shtetls* to Chicago suburbs took less than a century and was accompanied by much success and many contributions to society, but

as with other immigrant groups, it required much hardship, toil, and perseverance.

The Czechs and Slovaks

The first group of Czech immigrants from Bohemia and Moravia started filtering into Chicago in 1851 and 1852, shortly after the suppression by the Austrians of the 1848 Czech revolution. Their kinsmen to their east, the Slovaks, started coming to Chicago several decades later, in about 1890.

The earliest Czechs were squatters on what is now the southern part of Lincoln Park in an area called "The Sands."

After being evicted in 1855, they moved temporarily into the area around Van Buren (400 S.) and Clark (100 W.) streets. By 1860 they had moved into an area bounded approximately by Canal (500 W.), Halsted (800 W.), Harrison (600 S.), and Twelfth streets. By 1870 this community, known as Praha (Prague), contained some ten thousand Czechs and a number of Czech institutions. The first Czech Catholic church in Chicago, St. Wenceslaus, was founded in 1863 at De Koven (1100 S.) and Des Plaines (700 W.) streets. The first Czech daily newspaper in America, *Svornost,* began publication in 1875 on Canal Street. The first Bohemian Sokol (Falcon) was established in 1868 at Canal and Taylor (1000 S.) streets. Its major purpose was to develop physical fitness through gymnastics, and its organization was paramilitary, but it also fostered cultural development and served as a social and national unifying force, as well as a free-thought school.

After the Chicago Fire, which started in Praha about a block from St. Wenceslaus Church, the Czechs started to move southwest. Meanwhile, newer immigrant groups, such as eastern European Jews and later Italians and Greeks, moved into Praha. The area into which the Czechs moved became known as Pilsen, named after the local "Pilsen" tavern, which, in turn, had been named after Bohemia's second largest city. By 1895, the Pilsen area, bounded approximately by Sixteenth, Twenty-second, Halsted, and Western, contained about sixty thousand Czechs and was the center of their culture.

A focal point of the Pilsen community was the vicinity of Eighteenth and Allport (1234 W.). On one corner stood the stately St. Procopius Church with its green copper tower. The church was organized in 1876 and soon attained prominence as a great religious, educational, and cultural complex. It even included a Benedictine abbey. In the 1880s, Sunday church attendance averaged about six thousand parishioners. The first Bohemian Catholic Literary Society of Chicago was organized there. Its boys' high school was the forerunner of Benedictine University, now located in Lisle, Illinois. Associated with the church were vocational and commercial classes, and a Catholic Bohemian press aimed at counteracting the large number of Bohemians who were antireligious free thinkers or secularists—people who had often resented the Catholic Church's close ties with the politically oppressive Austrian regime in their homeland.

Across the street from St. Procopius Church was Thalia Hall, which housed a theater, meeting rooms, and offices for Czech organizations, many of which were destined to play an important role in exerting pressure for the creation of an independent Czechoslovakia after World War I. Further west, at Eighteenth Place and Paulina (1700 W.), was St. Vitus Church, founded in 1888 by the Bohemian Benedictine Fathers. Near the church was the Leader Store, a famous ethnic-type department store where thousands of immigrants had their *perinys* (Czech feather comforters) made annually. Nearby, on Blue Island Avenue, was Pilsen Auditorium, and on Ashland Avenue, was the Pilsen Sokol Hall. Pilsen also has an Antonin Dvorak Park named after the Czech composer.

By 1900 about seventy-five thousand first- or second-generation Czechs lived in Chicago. There were then six Czech Catholic parishes and one Slovak Catholic parish in the city. By 1910 there were about 110,000 Czechs in Chicago. Chicago was sometimes referred to as "Czechago" because it contained more Czechs than any other city in the United States. It soon would be the second-largest Czech city in the world, after Prague. The Czech immigrants were not as poor as many of the other immigrant groups. Their illiteracy rate was low, only about 2 percent, compared with an illiteracy rate of 24 percent for all immigrants. By the 1920s, at the height of Czech culture in the city, Chicago had four Czech daily newspapers representing the divergent views of Catholics, Free Thinkers, Socialists, and the unaffiliated and business community. In addition, there were a number of Czech periodicals. One common denominator among the rival presses was their fight for the liberation and preservation of the original homeland, Bohemia and Moravia. In an effort to preserve their heritage, classes were held throughout the community on Saturdays for thousands of children, teaching them the Czech language, culture, and history.

Many of the Czechs were skilled workers, such as carpenters, tailors, butchers, musicians, weavers, and smiths. Some worked in lumber and grain facilities along the Chicago River, while others worked in furniture factories, the Peter Schoenhofen Brewery

FIG. 4.25. Thalia Hall on the southeast corner of Eighteenth Street and Allport Avenue (1234 W.), 1963. The building had been a major institutional center for the Czech Pilsen community, housing a Czech theater, meeting rooms, and the offices of numerous Czech organizations. Photograph by Sigmund J. Osty; Chicago Historical Society.

on Eighteenth Street, the nearby Burlington Railroad yards, and in garment shops. Many worked at the huge McCormick Works or the Western Electric plant farther west. Some worked in offices or owned stores, shops, or saloons. In 1900, 1,521 such facilities were Czech owned.[21] The second generation often tended to prefer office work or professional careers.

The Czechs were noted for their reliability, hard work, and thrift and thus were readily hired as workers. They usually took advantage of overtime, and their job stability built seniority. Many became foremen in factories. Even at the prevailing low wages, many Czechs were able to prosper, as shown by the following account written in 1895.

Often good artisans were compelled to work for low wages, even $1.25 a day; still, out of this meager remuneration they managed to lay a little aside for that longed-for possession—a house and lot that they could call their own. When that was paid for, then the house received an additional story, and that was rented so that it began earning money. When more was saved, the house was pushed in the rear, the garden was sacrificed, and in its place an imposing brick or stone building was erected, containing frequently a store, or more rooms for tenants. The landlord, who had till then lived in some unpleasant rear rooms, moved into the best part of the house; the bare but well-scrubbed floors were covered with Brussels carpets, the wooden chairs replaced by upholstered ones, and the best room received the added luxury of a piano or violin.

In those early days rent was high and flour ten dollars a barrel, but they bought cheap meat at four cents a pound, coffee at twelve cents; and thus by dint of great economy many were able to lay aside money each year, and some of those early settlers now own property ranging in value from fifty thousand to two hundred thousand dollars.[22]

The Czechs were especially prominent in building and loan associations. In 1910 ninety-four of 197 such associations in Chicago were Czech owned. A zeal for saving enabled Czechs to become homeowners and to move westward into some of the city's better residential areas, settling eventually in the western suburbs.

Sickness and death benefits were provided by many of the five hundred Czech lodges and clubs that existed in the 1920s in Chicago. These organizations were usually formed by people from the same Czech village or town. In the 1920s there were also some twenty Czech soccer clubs in the city.

As early as 1880 Czechs began moving into what was to become the largest Czech community in Chicago. Known as "Czech California," it derived its name from California Avenue (2800 W.). The settlement encompassed mainly the community of South Lawndale and was bounded approximately by Rockwell (2600 W.) to the east, the community of Cicero to the west, Fourteenth Street to the north, and Thirty-third Street to the south. By 1910 Czechs owned about 80 percent of the dwellings in Czech California. The major artery of this community was Twenty-sixth Street, which was lined with Czech facilities, especially between Rockwell and Pulaski (4000 W.). At Lawndale Avenue (3700 W.) was the three-story Sokol Havlicek-Tyrs, which contained a large hall that doubled as a gymnasium. At Albany Avenue (3100 W.), adjoining the Pilsen Brewery, was Pilsen Park, where, for more than half a century, many Czechoslovakian organizations held picnics, dances, festivals, and political rallies—especially rallies for the independence of Czechoslovakia. A number of Czech churches were established in the area, including Catholic St. Ludmila at Twenty-fourth Street and Albany Avenue, Blessed Agnes at Twenty-sixth Street and Central Park (3600 W.), and Protestant John Hus Church at Twenty-fourth Street and Sawyer Avenue (3232 W.).

Partly due to differing views on religion among the Czechs, somewhat competing and duplicating facilities were often erected. In 1916 the Czech Free Thinkers of Chicago completed the Juhn Hus Memorial Hall on Twenty-second Street near Keeler Avenue (4200 W.). The Bohemian Free Thinkers also helped organize the Bohemian National Cemetery at Foster Avenue (5200 N.) and Pulaski Road. In 1893 they helped found the nearby Bohemian Old People's Home and Orphanage, now a Korean facility. The Free Thinkers were generally secular and opposed to Roman Catholic clericalism.

Czech influence permeated Czech California. The Czech language was taught

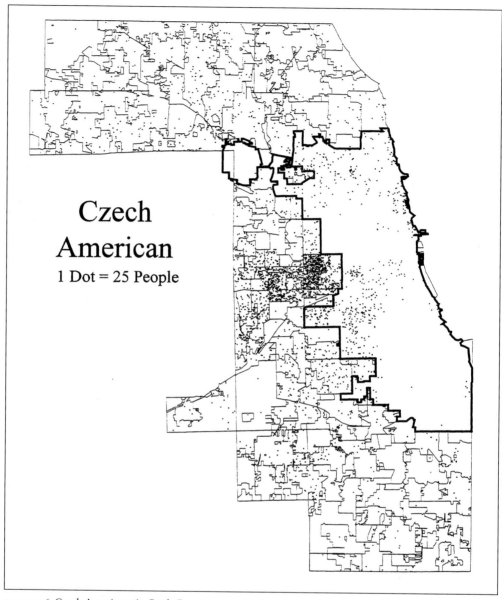

FIG. 4.26. Czech Americans in Cook County, 1990. Map courtesy of the Illinois Ethnic Coalition.

FIG. 4.27. Cermak Road in Cicero, or "downtown Bohemia," with its Bohemian restaurants, bakeries, food shops, and numerous savings and loan associations, 1986. Photograph by Irving Cutler.

at Farragut and Harrison high schools, and streets in the area, such as Kostner, Karlov, and Komensky, were named for prominent Czechs. Twenty-second Street was changed to Cermak Road to honor Chicago's only foreign-born mayor, Anton J. Cermak, a resident of the area who was killed in 1933 during the attempted assassination of President-elect Franklin D. Roosevelt. The Douglas Park elevated line, which traversed both Pilsen and Czech California, was dubbed the "Bohemian Zephyr."

On the periphery of the community, located in 1912 at 3659 Douglas Boulevard (1400 S.), was the prestigious Bohemian Club ("Ceska Beseda"), whose members were the leaders of the arts, professions, and commerce in Chicago's Czech community. The club's programs included concerts, plays, lectures, dances, and social receptions. The club hosted Thomas G. Masaryk, the first president of

Czechoslovakia, and his son, Jan Masaryk, who later became the Czech foreign minister. Mayor Cermak, Judge Otto Kerner, and his son, Otto, who served as governor of Illinois, were members of the club. The composer Rudolph H. Friml, who lived in Chicago for several years, also visited the club. Other well-know Chicago-area Czechs include George Halas, the founder and owner of the Chicago Bears football team, and the American astronaut Eugene Cernan, who landed on the moon in 1972.

The Czechs were very active politically. Between 1890 and 1920, for example, they elected some eighty public officials, ranging from city aldermen to state legislators to U.S. congressmen.

In addition to the three major Czech settlements of Chicago—Praha, Pilsen, and Czech California—there were smaller settlements in other parts of the city. One such settlement was south of the stockyards, around Sts. Cyril and Methodius Church, which was established in 1891 at Fiftieth Street and Hermitage Avenue (1732 W.). Some Czechs lived in the Bridgeport area, some near the steel mills in South Chicago, some in the "Merigold" area around Our Lady of Lourdes Church at Fifteenth Street and Keeler Avenue, and a small early settlement was established on the Northwest Side around Milwaukee and Foster avenues, not too far from the Bohemian National Cemetery. By 1940, there were about a dozen Czech parishes in Chicago, all with parochial schools. There were also about two dozen Free Thought schools, which met in the afternoon or on the weekends to teach Czech children the language, literature, and history of Czechoslovakia. After World War I there were also several Czech Protestant churches and missions, and some of the Czech Free Thinkers joined them.

Before World War II the Czechs began to move into the western suburbs. First they moved into Cicero and Berwyn, and then generally following Cermak Road, Ogden Avenue, and the Burlington Railroad, they moved into Riverside, North Riverside, Westchester, Lyons, Brookfield, La Grange, La Grange Park, Hinsdale, Downers Grove, Naperville, and even out to Aurora. Generally, the more affluent lived farther out. There is a Czechoslovak museum in Oak Brook.

By 1930 more than one third of the combined population of Cicero and Berwyn, or 113,629, was of Czechoslovak descent and represented the greatest concentration of Czechs in the metropolitan area.

The main commercial street of Cicero and Berwyn is Cermak Road. At the Chicago boundary with Cicero, where the African American residential population ends abruptly, once stood the huge Hawthorne Works complex of the Western Electric Company, Cicero's largest employer at the time. Large numbers of Czechs and Slovaks had once been employed there. Nearby, on Cermak Road just west of Cicero Avenue (4800 W.), stood the hotel where the gangster Al Capone had his headquarters in the 1920s. Capone terrorized Cicero and controlled its gambling, bootlegging, and even some of its elections and public officials. In recent years Cicero has been plagued with corrupt government officials.

Farther west on Cermak Road lies "downtown Bohemia," with numerous store signs bearing Czech names, babushka-wearing women, bakeries displaying Bohemian pastries, and restaurants such as Klas, with its multicolored Old World exterior. Because of its numerous savings and loan associations—often spaced only a block or two apart and sometimes even on adjoining corners—Cermak Road had often been referred to as the "Bohemian Wall Street" but now has a growing Hispanic presence. Next to almost every savings and loan association was a real estate office with pictures of modest bungalows and two-flats in the window. The penchant for thrift was reflected in a *Cicero Life* newspaper survey in the 1960s, which showed that "18 out of every 19 Bohemians in the two communities paid cash for their cars—either 100 percent down immediately or within 90 days of purchase." Off the main street are rows of similar two-story red or brown brick houses, many of which are modest bungalows, neat and well-kept, on twenty-five-foot or thirty-foot lots, and usually debt free. In recent decades, the Czech population in these communities declined sharply as numerous Hispanics moved in. More than half of the population of Cicero is now Hispanic. Many of the Czechs and their numerous organizations have moved out—mainly westward. The famous International Houby Festival—a folk festival honoring the fabled mushroom, which is sacred in Czech cuisine—has been held every autumn since 1969 along Cermak Road in Cicero.

Today the majority of people of Czech descent in the Chicago area live in the suburbs. Unlike the suburban population of many other groups, the Czech suburban population is not widely dispersed, being largely concentrated in a few western suburbs. The rapid and continuing movement to the suburbs, however, has largely depleted the old Czech neighborhoods of the city. Praha, on the southwestern fringe of the Loop, has long been an industrial area. Pilsen is now almost wholly Mexican, and St. Procopius is now a Mexican church. The Czech movement out of Czech California has been more recent and is now virtually complete. Here, too, Mexicans now occupy most of the area. Most Czech institutions have faded from the scene. Pilsen Park, the great Czech gathering place, has been replaced by a steel-and-glass shopping center with a large parking lot.

While Praha, Pilsen, and Czech California have become legends to many of the descendants of the people who came from Bohemia and Moravia, there are other communities in Chicago in which Czechs still reside. These are mainly small communities on the Southwest Side, such as Garfield Ridge, Clearing, and Ashburn, and to the north, in Lake View, Portage Park, and West Town.

Some of the Czechs in these communities and in the suburbs are refugees and political exiles who came as a result of the Nazi or communist takeover of their country. But, despite this more recent infusion, the tempo of Czech ethnic life in the Chicago area has slowed considerably as the processes of Americanization, ethnic intermarriage, and assimilation continue unabated. In 2000, 1.6 percent of the metropolitan area's population was of Czech ancestry.

It is estimated that fewer than one-third as many Slovaks as Czechs live in the Chicago area. The Slovaks started arriving in Chicago after 1890. Because the Slovaks and Czechs had some language, cultural, and historical differences, the Slovaks generally formed their own separate organizations in the United States. Coming from a more rugged, rural, and isolated part of Europe, most Slovaks lacked the educational opportunities of the Czechs.

Many Slovak immigrants settled and worked in the coal mining and steel mill areas of Pennsylvania and Ohio. Of those who settled in Chicago, many also worked in the steel mills. Some settled in the heavily industrialized part of northwestern Indiana—in Hammond, Whiting, East Chicago, and Gary. Some worked in the Chicago stockyards; others worked as carpenters, masons, and cabinet makers; and some found jobs in a field in which they excelled—that of wireworkers who either mended pots and pans or produced new wire products.

Unlike most of the Czechs, the Slovak men frequently came to America alone. They came with the idea of making some money, which they could take back home or use to bring

FIG. 4.28. Steelworkers' homes in South Chicago in the early 1900s. Photograph by R. R. Earle; Chicago Historical Society.

their families to the United States. Most of them remained, however, built churches, and soon owned their own homes with the aid of their savings and loan associations. Each of their communities and parishes soon had fraternal, charitable, social, dramatic, and athletic clubs. Being predominantly Catholic, there were fewer divisions among the Slovaks than among the Czechs, who had sizable Free Thinker and secular groups.

Many Slovaks settled in or near the Czech communities, but they were generally more widely dispersed and in smaller concentrations. In the early days, Slovaks from the same section of Slovakia often settled close to one another.

The first Slovak church, St. Michael Archangel, was organized in 1898, and a church building was erected near the stockyards at Forty-eighth and Winchester (1932 W.). It contained a large parochial school. Until St. Simon's was built in 1926 at Fifty-second and California, St. Michael Archangel was the largest Slovak Catholic parish in America. St. Joseph was built in Pilsen near the Czech St. Procopius Church. Slovak churches were also established in Bridgeport, South Chicago, Roseland, South Lawndale, and on the Northwest Side in the West Town and Humboldt Park communities. In time, as the Slovaks moved upward economically, they moved into the same western suburbs as the Czechs, especially into Cicero and Berwyn. Today's Slovaks, like the Czechs, can be found in the Chicago communities of Garfield Ridge, Clearing, and Lake View. Most of the Slovak churches in the old working-class neighborhoods have closed as their members have moved outward in the city and into the suburbs. At the start of the twenty-first century, St. Simon the Apostle of Fifty-second and California was the only Catholic church that continued to offer Mass in the Slovak language.

The Poles

Although the Poles were the last of the major European immigrant groups to arrive in Chicago in large numbers, they now constitute the largest European ethnic group in Chicago. With more than 1 million people of Polish descent currently in the area, or 10.1 percent of the total population, Chicago has become the fourth-largest Polish city in the world.

Until the end of World War I, Poland had been partitioned among Germany, Austria, and Russia; consequently, precise figures of Polish immigration are somewhat difficult to obtain inasmuch as immigrants were listed in some censuses by country of origin. Supplementary data, however, indicate that there were relatively few Poles in Chicago before the late 1860s and only about two thousand in 1870, or less than 1 percent of the city population. Thereafter, until 1930, more Poles than any other ethnic group arrived in Chicago. Most of them were landless, poorly educated, rural people fleeing poverty, military conscription, and foreign domination.

The first major Polish community in Chicago started to develop in the 1860s around Division (1200 N.) and Noble (1400 W.) streets, about two miles northwest of the city's business center and just west of the North Branch of the Chicago River. Here,

St. Stanislaus Kostka, the first Polish Roman Catholic parish in Chicago was organized in 1867, and in 1877 the construction of its massive, baroque-style, cathedral-like church, with twin green cupolas, commenced at Noble and Bradley (now Potomac, 1300 N.). The St. Stanislaus district, or "Stanislawowo" (sometimes called "Old Polonia" or the "Polish Downtown"), expanded rapidly, with some of the precincts around the church having been composed of more than 90 percent Polish. This highly congested area consisted mainly of streets lined with two-story wood or wood-brick bungalows and tall, narrow three-story brick tenements, usually built on twenty-five-foot lots and often containing shoddy wooden shacks on the rear of the lot. Usually, at the corner, but often also in the middle of the block, were small stores on the ground level of residential buildings. These might house a "ma and pa" grocery, a bakery, a butcher shop, or the local tavern.

The "Main Street" of the community was Noble Street, lined with small shops and stores of all kinds, as well as with religious and other institutional facilities. The business hub became the nearby triangle bounded by Milwaukee, Ashland (1600 W.), and Division streets. It was in this area that many of the growing number of Polish fraternal, religious, financial, and commercial organizations opened their offices, among them an increasing number of Polish newspapers and some of the largest Polish national organizations.

In the 1890s the parish of St. Stanislaus Kostka had about forty thousand parishioners, distinguishing it as one of the largest Roman Catholic parishes in the world. In 1893 more than two thousand baptisms, almost four hundred weddings, and about one

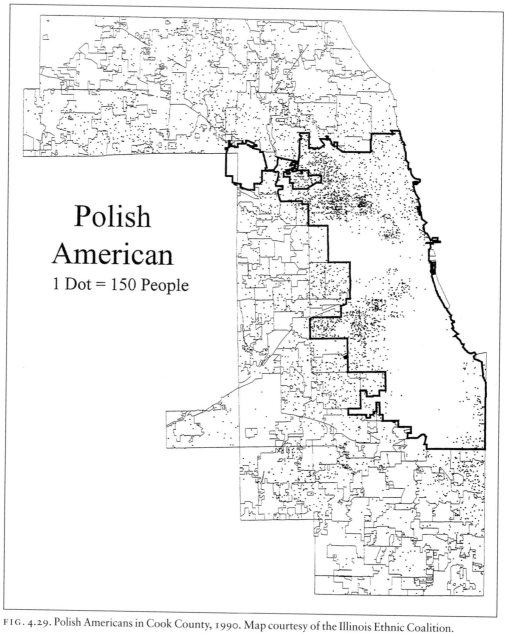

Polish
American

1 Dot = 150 People

FIG. 4.29. Polish Americans in Cook County, 1990. Map courtesy of the Illinois Ethnic Coalition.

thousand funerals were held in the church. The church complex eventually contained a rectory, convent, parish school (which enrolled some four thousand students at its peak), huge auditorium, and parish hall, which accommodated various activities ranging from Polish singers to political meetings. The parish also had its own savings and loan association. Much of the church's growth took place under the direction of a vigorous immigrant pastor, Father Vincent Barzynski. He also played a role in organizing some twenty-five other parishes in Chicago.[23]

Although St. Stanislaus Kostka remained the parent church of the Polish Roman Catholic churches in Chicago, other churches were soon built nearby to handle the burgeoning Polish population. Holy Trinity, organized in 1873 as a mission of overcrowded St. Stanislaus Kostka, was just two blocks to the south. Within a mile of St. Stanislaus Kostka were St. John Cantius (1893), St. Mary of the Angels (1899), and Holy Innocents (1905). The architecture of these large churches was also essentially baroque, with large green domes dominating the landscape.

The Poles were more church-oriented than most of the other immigrant groups, and nearly all of them were Roman Catholic. The fusion of religion with culture was part of their way of life. The churches were landmarks that reflected the Old World and were constructed as if the people intended to remain in the neighborhood forever. Polish parishes channeled more of their revenue into church buildings than did almost any other ethnic group.

By 1910 the Polish community had expanded to include the area bounded approximately by the river on the east, California Avenue (2800 W.) on the west, Fullerton Avenue

(2400 N.) on the north, and Chicago Avenue (800 N.) on the south. Many Poles worked in the factories in the river area, including the many tanneries. Of the two hundred thousand people then residing in the area, about half were Polish. These hundred thousand Poles represented 40 percent of the quarter million Poles who lived in the city in 1910.

The Poles kept moving northwest on both sides of Milwaukee Avenue—the Polish commercial corridor. Early in this century, aided by improving public transportation along Milwaukee Avenue, some Polish families leaped over German and Scandinavian settlements in the Logan Square area to settle farther out in such areas as Avondale, Irving Park, and Portage Park.

Most of the other Poles in Chicago lived in a few other sizable Polish communities on the West or South sides. A large church was the focal point of each community. Each community was near numerous factories. Lack of industrial experience (80 percent of the Polish immigrants had been farmers or farm laborers), as well as the language barrier, forced Poles to accept unskilled, low-paying jobs that were usually strenuous and often dangerous. A survey in 1911 showed that a foreign-born Pole earned about one third less than a foreign-born German.

One such Polish community developed around St. Adalbert's Church at Seventeenth and Paulina (1700 W.), organized in 1874. Jobs were available in nearby quarries and breweries, as well as in the many factories along the Burlington Railroad and the ship canal. By 1910 there were about fifteen thousand Poles in the area. On the other side of the waterway, around the bad-smelling stockyards, were the Bridgeport and Back of the Yards areas, with a 1910 Polish population of almost thirty thousand. This

FIG. 4.30. St. Stanislaus Kostka Church. The first Polish Roman Catholic parish in Chicago was organized in 1867, and construction of the church building, at Noble and Bradley (now Potomac) streets, was started in 1877. In the 1890s the parish was one of the largest Polish congregations in the world. Today its membership is a mixture of Hispanics, Poles, and some African Americans. Separate masses are celebrated in Spanish, Polish, and English. One of the twin green cupolas was damaged by lightning and never replaced. Photograph by Irving Cutler.

FIG. 4.31. Cottage in a Polish immigrant area on the Near North Side, 1880s. Adjustment had to be made to the home because the grade of the street and sidewalk was raised. Chicago Historical Society.

area contained five Polish-language Catholic churches, the oldest in Bridgeport being St. Mary of Perpetual Help (1883) and the oldest in the Back of the Yards area being St. Joseph (1887). Five Holy Martyrs Church, organized in 1908 and located at Forty-third and Richmond (2932 W.), was visited by Pope John Paul II during his visit to Chicago in 1979.

A dozen or more miles southeast of the Loop, in an area stretching from South Chicago to Hegewisch, there lived some eighteen thousand Poles in 1910. Church steeples and factory smokestacks dominated the skyline there. Although remote and isolated from the main Polish communities, this heavily industrialized, smoke-filled steel area offered many employment opportunities. Immaculate Conception Parish was organized there in 1882, and a church was built at Eighty-eighth Street and Commercial Avenue (3000 E.), a few blocks from the steel mills.[24]

In none of these communities, however, was the population density or the percentage of Poles as high as it was in the Stanislawowo area. Instead of tenements, most of the people lived in frame cottages, which often housed two or more immigrant families, plus boarders. In none of the areas other than Stanislawowo did the Poles comprise much more than a quarter of the population. Their neighbors usually included Germans, Czechs, and Lithuanians, and frequently Irish and Italians. From 1910 to 1930, however, while the Stanislawowo area's Polish population remained relatively static, the Polish populations in the St. Adalbert, Bridgeport–Back of the Yards, and South Chicago–Hegewisch areas were each increasing about 50 percent, and in the newer Brighton Park–McKinley Park area on the Southwest Side, it rose sharply to some twenty-five thousand Poles. The Polish community on the Far Northwest Side grew even more rapidly until, in 1930, it contained some ninety thousand Poles.

As the Polish population grew, so too did the number of their organizations, which at their peak probably numbered more than four thousand. These included religious, educational, immigrant aid, cultural, fraternal, financial, veteran, social, and athletic organizations. Today the two largest organizations, both with national headquarters in Chicago, are the Polish Roman Catholic Union, founded in 1873, and the larger Polish National Alliance, founded in 1880. The Polish Museum of America at 984 North Milwaukee Avenue is maintained by the former organization. Although the aim of both organizations was to promote the welfare of Polish Americans through insurance and social and cultural programs, the approach of the rival organizations differed. The Polish Roman Catholic Union, a Catholic fraternal order, was organized along parish lines and

was dominated by the clergy. The Polish National Alliance, more of a nationalistic fraternal order, implemented its programs through local secular institutions and laymen. Other major national organizations headquartered in the Chicago area include the Polish Women's Alliance, the Polish Alma Mater (youth work), and the Polish American Congress. The last is a nationwide "umbrella" of Polish organizations. The Copernicus Center, opened in the early 1980s on the Northwest Side, is a major Polish entertainment facility.

With its large Polish immigrant population, Chicago supported a flourishing Polish-language press. In 1920 there were five Polish daily newspapers, but with the subsequent decline in immigration, the press gradually dwindled until, today, only three Polish dailies remain, the *Polish Daily News* being the oldest.

The larger social welfare agencies operated by the Polish community included St. Mary of Nazareth Hospital, Guardian Angel Day Care Center, St. Joseph Home for the Aged, St. Vincent's and St. Hedwig's orphanages, and the Polish Welfare Association. Over one hundred building and loan associations were Polish owned, and in time, about two-thirds of the Polish families owned their own homes—about double the city average. Poles found it difficult to acquire land ownership in the old country; in Chicago, hard work and thriftiness could achieve the security, status, and neighborhood stability that came with home ownership.

Integral to many of the Polish organizations were the Polish-language Roman Catholic churches, of which there were eventually forty-three in the city. The church, however, was not without its dissenters. Around the turn of the century, a splinter group broke off from the Roman Catholic Church and formed the Polish National Church, which today has some ten thousand to fifteen thousand members and a small number of congregations in the city. Conflict within the church frequently centered on the efforts of Poles to establish more Polish parishes and separate Polish dioceses, as opposed to territorial parishes; to maintain the use of the Polish language and religious traditions; to obtain financial control of church property; to achieve national autonomy within the American Roman Catholic Church; and to end the underrepresentation of the Poles in the Roman Catholic hierarchy. The Roman Catholic Church hierarchy in Chicago was dominated largely by two earlier immigrant groups, the Irish and the Germans, although at one time the Poles comprised between one third and one half of the Catholic parish membership, and about one sixth of the parishes. Alfred L. Abramowicz, of Polish descent, was an auxiliary bishop of the Roman Catholic Archdiocese in Chicago.

The Poles have also been underrepresented in political office, considering that people of Polish descent have made up 12 to 18 percent of the city's population in past decades. Poles have never held some of the highest offices, such as that of mayor. Among the more prominent Polish officeholders have been judges La Buy and Jarecki, state treasurer John Smulski, state's attorney Adamowski, and congressmen Kluczynski, Derwinski, Pucinski, and Rostenkowski.

In proportion to their numbers, Poles have also lagged in commerce and industry. In the last few decades they have fared somewhat better in the business, professional, and educational worlds, although they are still more likely to be employed as laborers, mechanics, and craftsmen than is the general population.

Poles have been active through the years in the labor movement and have participated in a number of major strikes. They have been especially active among the packinghouse workers and the steelworkers. Ed Sadlowski, in the 1970s and 1980s, led a reform movement in the United Steelworkers union.

Poles are proud that their unemployment rate has been consistently below the city average, that their median income has been about 20 percent above the city average, and that the number of Poles on welfare has been far below the city average. They have been far more likely to attend private and parochial elementary schools than the average city resident (52 percent versus 24 percent in 1970), but they have had somewhat less total schooling than that of the general city white population. In 1970 only 30 percent of all Polish adults in Chicago had completed high school, compared with 44 percent for all Chicagoans. However, this past disparity was due in part to the lesser educational attainments by the older generations of rural Poles.[25]

The World War II period brought a temporary renewal of Polish immigration to the Chicago area, mainly of refugees. Most were younger, better educated, more articulate, and more aggressive than the rural Polish immigrants who came earlier in the century. Many were professionals, and their attitude toward the established institutions and organizations often conflicted with that of older Polish generations. Because of the solidarity crackdown in Poland from 1981 to 1983 and, in recent years, because Poland is no longer a communist country, Polish immigration to the United States has increased markedly.

A bigger change in the Chicago Polish community started even before World War II.

This was the tendency of second- and third-generation Poles to move out of the once-stable Polish communities into much more mixed areas, although the Poles generally remained in their old neighborhoods longer than most ethnic groups. Higher incomes, changing lifestyles, the desire for better surroundings, improved transportation, and pressure from expanding minority groups all helped to accelerate the geographic dispersion of the Poles, especially after World War II. In the desire to become more Americanized, the younger generations of Poles lost some of their tenuous attachment to the established Polish communities and institutions. Through the years, as with other ethnic groups, there has been a declining interest among Poles in their language, newspapers, and radio programs. There has also been a tendency of some to Americanize their names. Since the 1970s, however, there has been a renewed interest on the part of the young of various ethnic groups to learn more about their heritage. A few Chicago public high schools offer Polish language classes. The Poles, in particular, were interested in upgrading their image and combating the disparaging effects of Polish jokes.

The outward movement and scattering of Poles has been mainly to the southwest and northwest parts of the city and into the suburbs. Archer Avenue leading to the southwest and, especially, Milwaukee Avenue leading to the northwest, have been the main commercial corridors of this movement. The 2000 census revealed that in addition to the old Polish concentrations in the Chicago communities of West Town and Logan Square, Poles reside in large numbers in communities farther to the northwest, generally along the Milwaukee Avenue corridor in communities such as Belmont Cragin, Dunning, Avondale, Irving Park, Portage Park, Jefferson Park, and Norwood Park. To the south and southwest, Poles live in Hegewisch, Clearing, Bridgeport, Brighton Park, Gage Park, Archer Heights, Garfield Ridge, McKinley Park, and West Lawn. The Poles now comprise 7.5 percent of the city's population and are the largest white ethnic group.

Sizable numbers of Poles live in such suburbs as Berwyn, Elmwood Park, Hoffman Estates, Joliet, Naperville, Orland Park, Palatine, Schaumburg, Oak Forest, Mt. Prospect, Wheaton, Tinley Park, Downers Grove, Elk Grove Village, Arlington Heights, Des Plaines, Park Ridge, Niles, Lansing, and Oak Lawn. They also reside in the industrial suburbs of the Calumet steel area of north-western Indiana. The suburban area now contains about three quarters of the people of Polish descent in metropolitan Chicago, and ethnic Polish commercial facilities are increasingly found throughout the area, with many coming from Polish areas in Chicago. The suburbanites are far less likely to be officially affiliated with the ethnic-oriented churches, although some retain a sentimental or "weekend" attachment to certain parishes.

The old Polonia district is undergoing rapid change, due especially to an influx of African Americans and Puerto Ricans. On both Milwaukee Avenue and Division Street, signs in Polish and newer signs in Spanish are seen side by side. One drugstore carries a sign that reads "Mowimy po Polsku. Se hablo Espanol. We also speak English." Noble Street, where it still exists, is no longer a Polish "Main Street."

The parent church, St. Stanislaus Kostka, still stands across from Pulaski Park as a landmark of the original Polish settlement in Chicago. It successfully withstood an effort to demolish it to make way for the Kennedy

FIG. 4.32. Polish group in front of the headquarters of Kosciuszko Guards at the southeast corner of Division (1200 N.) and Noble (1400 W.) streets, 1890. Chicago Historical Society.

Expressway—a project which helped in the disruption of the old community—as did Noble Square, a major urban renewal project. The once large membership of the church is now down and is divided among Hispanics, African Americans, and Poles, the latter often older people. Nearby, the spacious Polish Museum of America still remains, as do the headquarters of a number of Polish institutions, including the Polish Roman Catholic Union. However, the move of the Polish National Alliance headquarters and the *Polish Daily Zgoda* from the Division-Milwaukee-Ashland triangle to the northwest fringe of the city symbolizes the outward migration of the Polish population. The numerous prominent Polish churches, which can be seen on a drive northwestward along the Kennedy Expressway, are striking evidence of a century of outward Polish migration from the original cradle on Noble Street near Division Street. The Polish Milwaukee Avenue corridor between Kedzie Avenue (3200 W.) and Pulaski Road (4000 W.) is now becoming increasingly Hispanic. But nearby St. Hyacinth Church, founded in 1894, still has a weekly attendance at mass of about eight thousand. And where Milwaukee Avenue enters the suburb of Niles, opposite the large Polish St. Adalbert Cemetery, is the huge Przyblos' White Eagle Restaurant and banquet hall, where the Pope and presidents have dined.

The Lithuanians

Chicago's Lithuanian community is the largest outside Lithuania. And probably due to the occupation of their homeland by the Soviet Union until 1991, the Lithuanians of the Chicago area are one of the most determined of the ethnic groups to retain their identity, culture, and customs. Chicago has become a focal point of Lithuanian culture, where the language is being preserved and where there is a strong nationalistic spirit.

Almost one hundred thousand people of Lithuanian descent live in the Chicago area today, about twenty thousand in the city itself. It is a small number in comparison with such groups as the Irish, Poles, Italians, and Germans but a large number for a people whose homeland contains only about 3½ million people. Proportionately, the emigration from Lithuania was larger than that from most European countries, exceeded perhaps only by the emigration from Ireland. During the last decades of the nineteenth century and those in the beginning of the twentieth century, some 20 percent of the Lithuanian population migrated from their homeland, the greatest number of Lithuanians coming to America. Czarist oppression of Lithuania, the inability of urban industry to absorb Lithuania's landless peasants, and periods of famine spurred the migration to America. Today, about 0.9 percent of the area's total population is of Lithuanian descent.

The first Lithuanians to appear in Chicago were a group of eighteen men who came to help lay railroad tracks. Finding no Lithuanians with whom to live, many of them boarded with Polish families in the growing Polish community around Division and Noble streets. Although, historically, there had been some conflict in Europe between Poles and Lithuanians, in Chicago the Polish culture was the closest to that of the Lithuanians, and some Lithuanians understood the Polish language from their contacts with the Poles in the Old World. As a result, the Lithuanians initially used some of the facilities of the

FIG. 4.33. Intersection of Division, Milwaukee, and Ashland, once the crossroads of the Polish community, 1980. The changing neighborhood is reflected by the juxtaposition of a Hispanic food store and the former home of the *Polish Daily Zgoda*. The newspaper later moved to the northwest fringe of Chicago, following the Polish people. The Chopin Theater is still at the intersection. Photograph by Irving Cutler.

Polish churches and organizations, although there was occasional friction between the groups. Many Lithuanians attended services at St. Stanislaus Kostka, the first of the Polish churches in the city. The only Lithuanian Catholic church on the North Side, St. Michael, was established in 1904 at 1644 West Wabansia (1700 N.). Although a small Lithuanian community existed in this area for many years, by far the largest Lithuanian communities developed on the South and Southwest sides. However, the Lithuanian population in these three areas has declined sharply in recent decades.

The largest early Lithuanian communities were in the vicinity of the stockyards—in Bridgeport to the northeast of the stockyards and in the Back of the Yards area to the west. Because most of the early immigrants were peasants with little education and no particular skills for working in the big city,

they worked mainly as common laborers in freight yards, breweries, brickyards, factories, foundries, and especially the stockyards. During the little more than a century of the stockyards' existence, approximately one hundred thousand Lithuanians worked there. Before World War I, they were second only to Poles in numbers of workers employed by the stockyards.[26] Thus it was not accidental that the main character of Upton Sinclair's novel *The Jungle* (1906), depicting the inhuman conditions of the stockyards, was a Lithuanian. Some of the early immigrants worked hard, thinking of making some money and returning home.

By 1910, because very few Lithuanian immigrants had any experience in business, only a very small percentage of the Lithuanians were self-employed. However, as their communities developed, Lithuanians began

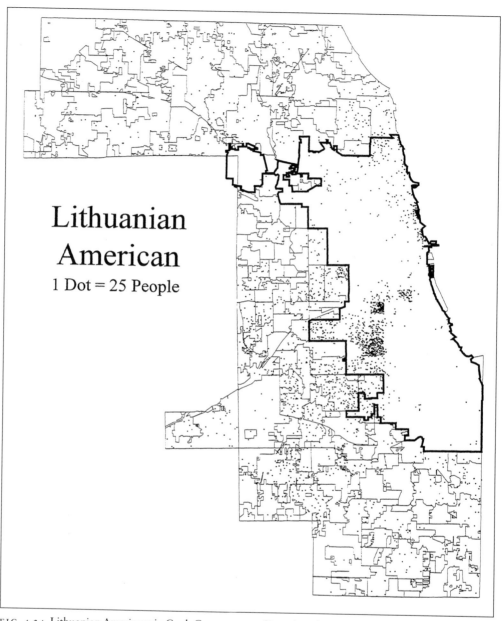

FIG. 4.34. Lithuanian Americans in Cook County, 1990. Since then there has been a major movement of Lithuanians out of the Southwest Side communities of Chicago Lawn and Gage Park. Map courtesy of the Illinois Ethnic Coalition.

to own grocery stores, saloons, barbershops, restaurants, and even savings and loan associations and banks. Ultimately Lithuanians became numerous in many professions and, among the various ethnic groups, came to have one of the higher proportions of graduate school training.

The first Lithuanians moved into the Bridgeport area in the 1880s. In 1892 they established St. George's Catholic Church on the corner of Thirty-third Street and Auburn Avenue (now Lituanica Avenue, 900 W.). In 1896 this small wooden church was replaced by a tall, spired, beautiful church, which was then probably the largest Lithuanian church in America. Affiliated with the church was a parochial school where courses in the Lithuanian language were taught, along with the major part of the public school curriculum. The church was torn down a number of years ago. Lithuanian-owned stores and facilities of various types soon stretched along Halsted Street near the church, especially between Thirty-first and Thirty-fifth streets. Antanas Olsauskas, who came to America in 1889, opened Chicago's first Lithuanian bank in 1896 in Bridgeport. He also founded a Lithuanian newspaper and published about 130 Lithuanian books. In addition, he bought and built numerous buildings in Bridgeport.

To the west of the stockyards, Lithuanians settled in the communities of New City and Brighton Park, in what had been the Town of Lake. Holy Cross Parish was organized in 1904 at Forty-sixth and Wood (1800 W.), and a new church was consecrated there in 1915. In 1914, about a mile to the west at Forty-fourth and Fairfield (2732 W.), Immaculate Conception Parish was organized and a church was soon completed. Its membership later reached about one thousand.

A small Lithuanian community existed near the Providence of God Church, built in 1915 at Eighteenth and Union (700 W.). The church is now used by the surrounding Mexican community and was visited by Pope John Paul II in 1979. The area no longer contains the office of *Naujienos* (News), founded in 1914 as a socialist newspaper. The Chicago area now has three remaining Lithuanian newspapers, with *Draugus* being the largest. Almost two miles to the west, another small Lithuanian community existed around Our Lady of Vilna Church, 2323 West Twenty-third Place, which was organized in 1904, and around the Lithuanian Zion Evangelical Lutheran Parish, organized in 1903. The latter had a church at Bell Avenue (2232 W.) and Cermak Road (2200 S.). Some of the members of the congregations worked at the nearby International Harvester and Crane plants.

Other Lithuanian communities developed around the South Chicago steel mills. In some iron and steel plants, the workers spoke only Polish or Lithuanian. In 1900 St. Joseph Church was established in this area at 8801 South Saginaw Avenue (2638 E.). In the Roseland-Pullman area, All Saints Church was founded in 1906. Like those of the Polish communities, the Lithuanian churches were mainly Roman Catholic. From the end of the nineteenth century until the late 1920s—the peak period of their church building—the Lithuanians established eleven Roman Catholic parishes and one Lutheran parish. Later, two more Protestant churches were built. Many of their churches were large, graced by unique steeples decorated with the ancient Lithuanian sun cross.

The churches offered numerous services to their members, including the establishment of St. Casimir Lithuanian Cemetery in 1903 by nine Lithuanian churches. It is located

FIG. 4.35. Office of *Naujienos,* the *Lithuanian Daily News,* on Halsted Street near Eighteenth Street in the 1980s. The area contained a small Lithuanian enclave but in recent years has become mainly Mexican. Photograph by Irving Cutler.

FIG. 4.36. Lithuanian-Polish butcher at 3355 West Thirty-eighth Street, 1913. The taller man is Stanley Balzekas. His son, Stanley Balzekas Jr., founded the Balzekas Museum of Lithuanian Culture in 1966 in Brighton Park. It is now at 6500 South Pulaski Road. Chicago Historical Society, ICHi-13831.

on 111th Street between Pulaski Road and Cicero Avenue, in extreme southwestern Chicago. In 1912 the denominational Lutheran National Cemetery was located in Justice, Illinois.

In time there was some conflict between the Lithuanians and the Catholic church hierarchy concerning use of the Lithuanian language in the liturgy. As among the Poles, there was also some conflict between the ardent nationalists and the religionists, although Lithuanians were almost unanimous in their strong desire for an independent Lithuania.

Living standards were low in the various early Lithuanian communities. Houses were often simple wooden structures, and few Lithuanians owned their own homes. In time, however, aided by their savings and loan associations, an extremely high percentage of Lithuanians owned their own homes and the houses were improved and well kept. Lithuanian neighborhoods had increasing numbers of Lithuanian-owned stores. On some streets, such as Ashland Avenue near the stockyards, taverns were so numerous that, according to the Lithuanian newspaper *Draugas,* they were literally "cropping up like mushrooms after the rain."

The Lithuanian population in Chicago increased rapidly after the turn of the century. In 1900 an estimated fourteen thousand people of Lithuanian descent lived in Chicago; by 1910 there were some fifty thousand; and in 1924 about eighty thousand. During World War I, Lithuanian immigration largely ceased. Then, after Lithuania achieved independence in 1918, in a burst of patriotism for their newly independent homeland, there was actually a short period when Lithuanians left the United States and returned home.

In 1940, however, Lithuania was forced to become part of the Soviet Union. This action resulted in many thousands of Lithuanian

refugees coming to Chicago after World War II. Many settled in the Marquette Park area of the community of Chicago Lawn. They helped to enhance the Lithuanian cultural life in Chicago and to perpetuate the intense, nationalistic, anti-Soviet spirit. Many were white-collar workers and professionals; some had been among Lithuania's foremost intellectuals. The Marquette Park area contained a larger percentage of such people and of skilled workers and mechanics than did the older Lithuanian neighborhoods.

The largest concentration of Lithuanians in Chicago, and perhaps in the United States, was in the Marquette Park area. There, more than thirty thousand people of Lithuanian descent (of a total community population of about forty-five thousand) lived and maintained major Lithuanian institutions. This area was bounded approximately by California Avenue (2800 W.) and Marquette Park on the west, Western Avenue (2400 W.) on the east, Sixty-third Street on the north, and Seventy-first Street on the south. The heart of the area—between Marquette Road (6700 S.), Sixty-ninth Street, Rockwell Avenue (2600 W.), and California Avenue— has been given the honorary designation of "Lithuanian Plaza" by the city of Chicago.

In 1911 the Sisters of St. Casimir, a Lithuanian Catholic order led by Mother Marija, built a convent, part of which was used as a girls' academy. It was built on land between Sixty-seventh and Sixty-eighth streets, and between Washtenaw (2700 W.) and Talman (2623 W.) avenues. Although the site was then somewhat marshy and largely unsettled, it was close to the many Lithuanian parishes on the South Side. The convent became the nucleus for a number of major Lithuanian institutions located in a couple of

FIG. 4.37. Interior of the residence of an immigrant, probably a Lithuanian bachelor, about 1920. Balzekas Museum of Lithuanian Culture and Chicago Historical Society, ICHi-39086.

square blocks in the heart of the Marquette Park area and for a neighborhood of numerous brick homes, mainly one-story, which were built by the Lithuanians after World War I. The institutions built by the Lithuanians included Holy Cross Hospital, Nativity BVM Church, and Maria High School. The latter, a girls' preparatory school for the Lithuanians, was also attended by Poles, members of other eastern European groups, and now also by minority groups. Nativity BVM Church has the distinction of being the largest and wealthiest Lithuanian church in Chicago. A new building was erected in 1957 to handle the increased membership. The parish also has a parochial school.

Three-hundred-acre Marquette Park, on the western edge of the community, is the site of numerous Lithuanian meetings, outings, and soccer games. At the northeast corner of the park is a monument to Darius and Girenas, two Lithuanian American flyers who in 1933 attempted to fly nonstop from the United States to Kaunas, Lithuania, in a plane named *Lituanica*. They died when their plane crashed in Germany, just short of their goal.

Lithuanian-owned facilities in the Marquette Park area once included a Lithuanian bookstore, real estate offices, overseas parcel-shipping services, savings and loan associations, florist shops, grocery stores, restaurants, bakeries, delicatessens, and taverns. The main commercial street was Sixty-ninth Street and, to a lesser extent, Seventy-first Street. Along Sixty-ninth Street from Western to Washtenaw were about a dozen taverns, many catering to different Lithuanian clientele such as soccer players, artists, intellectuals, young people, and older people. But most of these facilities are now gone. Lithuanians moved out of the neighborhood and were replaced by African Americans, who started moving west of Western Avenue in the 1970s, and to a lesser extent by Hispanics and Arabs. For a while, the changing neighborhood was punctuated by racial tension and violence.

Surrounding areas also still contain Lithuanian facilities. At 4545 West Sixty-third Street is the modern plant of *Draugas*, a daily Lithuanian newspaper founded in 1916, which serves not only the Chicago Lithuanian community but also national, Canadian, and Latin American Lithuanian communities. As elderly immigrants continue to pass from the scene, the circulation of the paper has dropped to about five thousand from more than double that number in the 1960s. Leonard Simutis (1892–1975), a leading Lithuanian spokesman in the United States, was the editor of *Draugas* from 1927 until his retirement in 1968.

About a mile to the northeast of the Marquette Park area is the Lithuanian Jesuit Youth Center, built in 1957–58 at Fifty-sixth Street and Claremont Avenue (2333 W.). Although geographically in Gage Park, culturally it is part of Marquette Park, for it is a major focal point of Lithuanian culture. Plays, vocal and instrumental recitals, and art exhibits are held in its auditorium. The center has a Saturday high school and an Institute of Lithuanistics, hosts numerous secular and religious clubs and societies, and maintains extensive archives. It is part of a vigorous effort, together with family upbringing, to keep ethnic vitality alive among young Lithuanian Americans by teaching them the language, history, literature, and folkways of their parents and grandparents. Generally, the effort has been successful, as Lithuanians still usually marry Lithuanians and, even if they move to the suburbs, still bring their children to the city every Saturday for Lithuanian cultural instruction. To the southwest, at 6500 South Pulaski Road (4000 W.), is the Balzekas Museum of Lithuanian Culture, the only such museum in North America.

The Lithuanian community of the Chicago area supports numerous cultural, fraternal, and political organizations, most of which were once in the Marquette Park area. There are numerous Lithuanian choral, dance, art, and literary groups and radio and television programs. There is even a Lithuanian Opera Company, which annually performs an opera in Lithuanian, some of the operas being original. In 1940 a Lithuanian newspaper discerningly discussed the importance of transmitting the Lithuanian cultural heritage to the second generation of immigrants to America.

[W]hen people speak of new immigrant groups, they refer not only to the foreign born, but to their children. There is probably no group in our population that is making a more distinguished contribution to American life than the sons and daughters of immigrant parents.

There is no group, also, which is so much a "lost generation" as many of these native-born Americans. They are without roots, many of them, either in the new world or the old.

They may learn in our schools about the Pilgrim Fathers and the farmers who stood at Lexington, but whose historic events and traditions find no echo in their personal or home life.

Their vital American background is Ellis Island, the immigrant steerage, city slums, the mine and sweatshop.

On the other hand, their parents, too often, have not the background or education to give them a sense of the cultural heritage they have brought from the old country—a heritage, which, if they were able to share it, would help to give these young people a new dignity and self-reliance and to make them more effective Americans.[27]

The Lithuanian population has declined in most of the older neighborhoods. Hispanics have moved into the Lower West Side and some of the Back of the Yards area. African Americans have moved into the Roseland area on the Far South Side. Sizable but generally declining numbers of Lithuanians still live in the Chicago communities of Bridgeport, Garfield Ridge, Beverly, Mount Greenwood and especially Brighton Park and Chicago Lawn. Some live in the peripheral Southwest Side communities of Ashburn and Garfield Ridge, and some in such western and south-western suburbs as Burbank, Naperville, Oak Lawn, Orland Park, Darien, Tinley Park, Oak Forest, and Palos Hills. Farther out, Lemont has become the newest hub of Lithuanians in suburbia, with a large retirement-church complex and the Lithuanian World Center. Cicero contains an old, established, declining community of Lithuanians, many of whom once worked at Western Electric. St. Anthony's Church was established in Cicero in 1911 and now has many Hispanic members.

Politically, because of their relatively small numbers, Lithuanians have not had many major officeholders. There are Lithuanian judges, state senator John Shimkus, and U.S. senator Dick Durbin, whose mother is of Lithuanian descent. Also from Chicago is the president of Lithuania, Valdas Adamkus, who headed a five-state U.S. government environmental agency.

The past few decades have seen major demographic changes in the Lithuanian population. Massive numbers of Lithuanians have left Marquette Park and other Lithuanian communities in Chicago and moved farther southwest in the city and into the suburbs. Many of the younger Lithuanian Americans, whose ethnic ties may not be as strong as those of their parents, have joined the exodus to the suburbs. But the bulk of Lithuanians seem determined to retain their major institutions and as much of their culture and tradition as possible. Since Lithuanian independence, a small trickle of nostalgic and nationalistic Lithuanians returned to Lithuania, where they can live well on their American savings. Lithuanian Americans are concerned for their homeland's freedom and welfare and, as with other ethnic groups, generously send money, food, clothing, and equipment to Lithuania to bolster its security and economy.

The Italians

In the 1680s, the Italian explorer Henri de Tonti, the lieutenant of La Salle, became one of the first white men to pass through the Chicago area. Two centuries later, in 1880, when Chicago's population was already over half a million, there were only 1,357 foreign-born Italians in the city. Even so, the number was a huge increase from a mere four in 1850. In contrast, the German-born population in 1880 numbered 75,205, and the Irish-born 44,411. Thereafter, Italian immigration increased rapidly as part of the last great wave of European immigration, which came largely from eastern and southern Europe. The peak period of Italian immigration was from 1899 to 1924. Chicago's Italian population increased almost tenfold from thirteen thousand in 1890 to 124,000 in 1920. Today, the Chicago area is home to over half a million people of Italian descent, a number exceeded among European ethnic groups only by the Polish and German communities. Until the 1880s, the bulk of Italian immigrants came from relatively prosperous northern Italy—from the regions of Tuscany, Genoa, Lombardy, Piedmont, and Venetia.

They generally came as family units. Some of the men worked at skilled or semiskilled jobs, some in the service and trade fields, and some became street vendors and small retailers.[28]

The first Italian settlements were in the heart of what is now the downtown area, along the south branch of the Chicago River and around Clark (100 W.), Plymouth Court (31 W.), Harrison (600 S.), and Polk (800 S.). Another settlement, predominantly Genoese, was just north of the river around Wells (200 W.) and Illinois (500 N.) in the angle formed by the river and its North Branch. Here, in 1880, construction started on the Assumption of the Blessed Virgin Mary Church. It was completed in 1886. Resembling an Italian village church in design, the building still stands at 313 West Illinois Street, amid multistory commercial and new residential buildings in the shadow of the Merchandise Mart.

The great influx of Italian immigrants started in the 1880s. More than 75 percent of these immigrants came from the poor rural districts and small towns of southern Italy—the Mezzogiorno. This area lying south of Rome included the provinces of Lucania, Apulia, Campania, Abruzzi, Calabria, and Sicily. About a quarter of the immigrants came from Sicily. Between 1899 and 1910, one-fifth of all the immigrants to the United States were southern Italians. Most of them were struggling financially, being in debt and heavily taxed, and had little or no education. They were extremely oriented to village and family, with strong and expressive feelings and pride. Sometimes almost an entire village came to the United States, occasionally bringing the village priest with them. A majority of these Italians settled along the eastern seaboard, but many came to Chicago. In Chicago, they usually moved into neighborhoods where friends and relatives from their town or province

already lived. These were neighborhoods that had previously been populated and then abandoned by German, Irish, and Swedish immigrants who first resisted the Italian intrusion. Many of the southern Italians were single males who moved in with their friends and relatives as roomers. Some came to make money and return home, but most wanted to bring over their families or perhaps a girlfriend.

To obtain employment, the southern Italians frequently turned to the padrone, a labor agent or boss. The padrone, often an earlier arrival from the same home province, spoke some English and understood Old World traditions, as well as New World business operations. He had established contacts with American businessmen who needed unskilled laborers, so he was usually able to provide the newly arrived immigrants with jobs, especially in construction or with the railroads. Chicago became a major padrone operations center, partly because of its geographic location and partly because it was the country's greatest railroad center. The city served as a clearinghouse for seasonal railroad and construction jobs throughout the Midwest and much of the rest of the United States. The workers would return to Chicago during the winter season, often as boarders.

Although many of the eastern and southern European immigrants had some type of labor boss system, the influence of the padrone on workers from southern Italy was especially strong. Around the beginning of the twentieth century, many of these immigrant workers were beholden to the padrone for not only their jobs but in some cases even their passage tickets from Italy, although the total probably never approached half of the workforce.[29] The padrone system became notorious

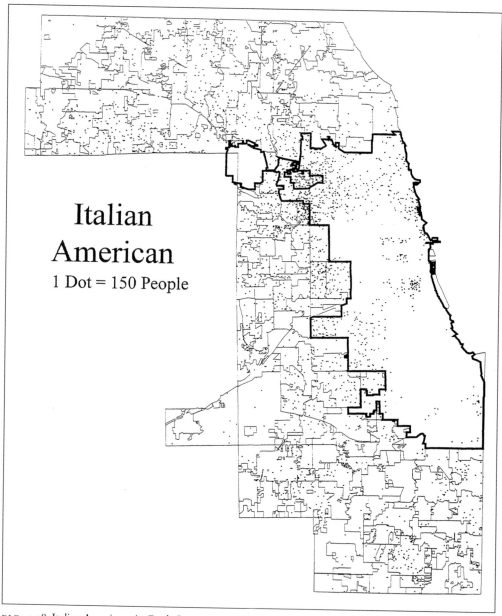

FIG. 4.38. Italian Americans in Cook County, 1990. Map courtesy of the Illinois Ethnic Coalition.

because of the abuses of some unscrupulous padrones. They took exorbitant commissions, overcharged for inferior food and lodging at railroad and construction camps, secretly pocketed some of the money provided by employers for the workers, and exploited the workers in numerous other ways. The system started to decline rapidly about 1900, after revelations of fraud by a number of social agencies and governmental investigative commissions resulted in new labor legislation. Pressure applied to the railroad and construction officials caused them to change their labor practices. In addition, as the immigrants became familiar with the English language and with American labor practices, as the Italian community became better established, and as more and more immigrants had relatives who could help them find jobs, there was less need for an intermediary to obtain employment. The immigrants no longer were easy prey for the padrone.

In time, Italian Americans branched out into a wide range of economic activities. In 1916 almost 50 percent were still common laborers, by 1931 that number had decreased to 30 percent, and in 1950 only 11 percent worked as such.[30] The railroads decreased in importance as a source of employment for Italians. They became stonecutters, masons, hod carriers, and the like. Many obtained jobs in public service, becoming garbage collectors, street sweepers, streetcar employees, and policemen. Increasing numbers worked in factories—about a third of the garment workers in Chicago were Italian, usually women, some of whom worked at home. Although as new immigrants the Italians had sometimes been used as strikebreakers, they later became active in a number of unions, including the garment workers' union.

Many Italians opened small businesses of their own. They were grocers, fruit merchants, bakers, barbers, painters, carpenters, tailors, musicians, candy store owners, street vendors, restaurant owners, saloon keepers, and small factory owners. John F. Cuneo, whose grandparents came from Genoa in 1847, built one of the nation's largest printing concerns—Cuneo Press. Anthony J. Paterno rose from owner of a small grocery store in the vicinity of Grand and Western avenues to become one of the largest wine distributors in the country and a prominent civic leader in the Italian community. The Gonella Bread Company has been supplying bread for over a century. A number of Italians became wealthy in the real estate business. During Prohibition a few became financially successful by organizing gangs to control the distribution of illegal beverages to a thirsty public. The highly publicized operations of these gangs reflected unfavorably on the image of an immigrant group whose crime rate was not significantly different from the national average.[31] A proud highlight in the history of the Chicago Italian community was the 1933 flight of twenty-four Italian seaplanes to the Century of Progress Fair on Chicago's lakefront. The feat brought some respect to the Italian community, which had been stigmatized by constant stereotyped references to Italian gangsters such as Al Capone.

Two Italian immigrants to Chicago became world renowned. Enrico Fermi (1901–54), a distinguished Nobel Prize–winning physicist, came to Chicago in the 1930s as a refugee from Mussolini's Italy. He led the team of eminent scientists at the University of Chicago who achieved the first human-controlled nuclear reaction. Mother Frances Cabrini

(1850–1917) founded the Missionary Sisters of the Sacred Heart and did social work among the poor Italian immigrants in Chicago. Her order established hospitals, orphanages, and schools for the immigrants. In 1946 the Roman Catholic Church canonized her, the first American citizen to have been raised to sainthood.

On the basis of the 1970 U.S. Census figures, "Italians in the Chicago area were more likely to be employed as operatives and laborers (31 percent) and as craftsmen (17 percent) than the general employed population (26 percent and 13 percent, respectively), less likely to be professionals and managers (12 percent versus 18 percent) or sales and clerical workers (27 percent versus 30 percent), and just as likely to be service workers (13 percent)."[32] Forty percent of employed Italians worked in manufacturing, compared with 32 percent of the general employed population. However, by 2000, their income level was above average and they were well represented in medicine, law, and business. Because they arrived late, the number of Italians who have held church or political office is relatively small, compared with the size of the Italian population. However, in recent years a number of well-known Italians have served in legislative bodies, including alderman Vito Marzullo, state representatives Victor Arrigo and Anthony Scariano, and congressmen Frank Annunzio and Martin Russo. Especially prominent in the academic world is John Rettaliata, who served for many years as the president of the Illinois Institute of Technology.

As the Italian population increased from less than 1 percent of the foreign-born in Chicago in 1870 to over 8 percent in 1970, many worked their way upward financially;

besides working as laborers, they were also carpenters, tailors, shoemakers, grocers, and restaurant owners and employees. They began to move outward from the downtown area. Sometimes they were pushed outward by expanding industry. The Italian enclave in the area around Plymouth Court and Polk Street near the Dearborn Street railroad station (where some of the immigrants disembarked from the trains that brought them from the East) gradually began to expand westward between Harrison and Twelfth streets. They spread out first to the South Branch of the Chicago River, then to Canal Street (500 W.), later to Halsted (800 W.) and in 1905 into the area between Morgan (1000 W.) and Racine (1200 W.). The Italians lived there in crowded, often squalid tenements and, for over three decades, much of the area was controlled by corrupt, unscrupulous Irish alderman Johnny Powers, who often acted like a feudal lord. To the north was a Greek community and to the south was the eastern European Jewish community. After 1910 the Italians began to move westward from Racine to Western Avenue (2400 N.), then to Cicero Avenue (4800 W.) and beyond, into the Austin area in the 1920s.

"Little Italy," situated on the Near West Side, was the largest Italian concentration in Chicago. The percentage of Italians in the total population of this area was especially high in the vicinity of Halsted and Taylor (1000 S.), but it decreased as one went farther west. Unlike many other Chicago Italian communities, this one was a melting pot of all the regional subcultures of Italy—combining Venetians, Neapolitans, Sicilians, Tuscans, and others. Some of the regional groups, often from the same Italian village, clustered on certain blocks within the community. In the early 1920s, the West Side area, encompassed by the Chicago River west to Paulina Street and from Van Buren Street south to Twelfth Street, contained perhaps half of Chicago's Italian population and included two large Italian parishes.[33]

The first Italian church in the area was Guardian Angel, founded in 1899 at 717 West Arthington (900 S.), just east of Halsted. It had been preceded by the Guardian Angel School, which was just a block west of Hull House. As the Italian population west of Halsted Street grew, the Guardian Angel parish was divided. Consequently, Our Lady of Pompeii Church, staffed by the Scalabrini Fathers, was erected in 1910 at Lexington (732 S.) and Racine (1200 N.). Feast days and festivals were important, colorful religious events among the Italians of the area. Despite Italian church expansion through the years, there were some conflicts with the Irish-oriented Catholic Church hierarchy and some regional and religious antagonisms among the Italians themselves. However, by 1927 the Italians had twelve parishes.

After reaching a peak in the 1920s, the population of the Near West Side Italian community gradually declined. In the 1960s the community's existence was threatened by the intrusion of the campus of the University of Illinois at Chicago, which was built despite the vehement protests of the community, led especially by Florence Scala. But unlike the former Greek community to the north, a small Italian residential community has survived in the area between the university campus to the east and the giant medical complex to the west. The institutional influence has greatly increased land value in the area and has brought about much redevelopment, new construction, and demographic diversity. Nevertheless, glimpses of Little Italy are still visible, for example, along stretches of Taylor Street and around Arrigo Park (formerly

Vernon Park), with its Italian churches and the former Mother Cabrini Hospital, which is now residential. Arrigo Park has a statue of Columbus, which had originally been exhibited at the Italian Pavilion during the 1893 World Columbian Exposition. Along Taylor Street remain Italian bakeries, groceries, and many restaurants, such as Rosebud, Gennaros, Tuscany, Al's Italian Beef, and the ever-popular Mario's Lemonade Stand. Recently, an Italian sports museum has opened there, directly across the street from a small public plaza that displays a statue of Joe DiMaggio.

Probably the second-largest Italian area extended westward from the river along Grand Avenue (520 N.) and adjacent streets, in the vicinity of the Chicago Commons Settlement House, which was at Grand Avenue and Morgan Street. This had been first an Irish, and then a Swedish, area. In the 1890s sizable numbers of northern Italians moved into the area and were followed by others from southern Italy and Sicily. In 1899 the Swedish Lutheran Church at Grand Avenue and Peoria Street (900 W.) was purchased and converted into an Italian Catholic church, Santa Maria Addolorata. In 1904, almost two miles to the west, Holy Rosary Church was established at 612 North Western Avenue. The community later moved farther west, paralleling Grand and Chicago avenues to Kedzie Avenue, and then out toward Cicero Avenue (4800 W.). Some Italian Americans still live in this Northwest Side area.

On the Near North Side was an area, settled chiefly by Sicilians, to the east of the North Branch of the Chicago River, less than a mile west of the lakefront Gold Coast apartments. It was in the vicinity of Division (1200 N.), Oak (1000 N.), Cambridge (528 W.), and

FIG. 4.39. Taylor Street, shown here in 2000. Once the commercial heart of the large West Side Italian community, the street still retains a number of Italian facilities, such as bakeries, grocery stores, and restaurants. Photograph by Irving Cutler.

diagonal Clybourn. This "Little Sicily" had previously been known as "Little Hell" because of blight and the lawlessness of its previous residents, a pattern of behavior that did not readily change with the coming of newer residents who included the "Black Hand" gangsters. In 1910 more than eight thousand Italians (almost all from Sicily) lived in Little Sicily. In 1929 the area was described as follows:

Little Hell, or Little Sicily, is a world to itself. Dirty and narrow streets, alleys piled with refuse and alive with dogs and rats, goats hitched to carts, bleak tenements, the smoke of industry hanging in a haze, the market along the curb, foreign names on shops and foreign faces on the streets, the dissonant cry of the huckster and peddler, the clanging and rattling of railroad and the elevated, the pealing of the bells of the great Catholic churches, the music of marching bands and the crackling of fireworks on feast days, the occasional dull boom of a bomb or the bark of a revolver, the shouts of children at play in the street, a strange staccato speech . . . on every hand one is met by sights and sounds and smells that are peculiar to this area, that are "foreign" and of the slum.

Two generations ago this district was an Irish shanty town called Kilgubbin. A generation ago it was almost equally Irish and Swedish. Then the "dark people" began to come. At first they came slowly, meeting no little resistance. . . .

But the Sicilians pushed slowly into the district. Industry was demanding cheap labor. Sicilians came in great numbers, especially in 1903–4, the tremendous Italian immigration year. In this river district of the Near North Side they found cheap living quarters. It was the old story of a competition of standards of living, colored somewhat by national antagonisms. The Irish and Swedish, more prosperous, moved out of the district and northward. And by 1910 Kilgubbin and Swede Town had become Little Sicily. . . .

The colony centers about the church of St. Philip Benizi. . . . West Division Street, the colony's principal street, is lined with Italian businesses and shops; numerous grocery stores and markets, florist shops, the Sicilian pharmacy, undertaking establishments, cobbler's shops, macaroni factories, cheap restaurants, pool rooms and soft drink parlors which are the lounging places of the second generation, and the barber shops which have replaced the saloon as the center of gossip for the older people. On the corner of Elm [1142 N.] and Larrabee [600 W.] is a curb market. Along Oak Street are numerous stalls where fruit, vegetables,

coal and wood, and oysters on the half-shell are sold. The shingles of the doctor and the midwife are frequently seen. The vicinity of Oak and Townsend is the center of the colony's population. Many of the influential Sicilians live along Sedgwick [400 W.], however, the colony's eastern boundary and more prosperous and fashionable street.

Because of its isolated situation, due to poor transportation and the barrier of river and industry, Little Hell remained until the war relatively untouched by American custom, a transplantation of Sicilian village life in the heart of a hurrying American city. . . .

During the last four years there has been a great change; the colony is slowly disintegrating; old customs are giving way. Contacts with the outside world, through work and school, have given boys and girls a vision of freedom and new opportunity. They are going to night school and making their friends outside the old circle. They are out of patience with the petty interests and quarrels of the older group, and refuse to have their lives ordered by their parents, whom they know to be ignorant and inexperienced. Families are not being broken up; the deep affections still persist; and though the old folks have misgivings, in their indulgent way they are letting the new generation take the lead and are proud of their progressive sons and daughters.

Young married couples are making their homes north of the old district, within easy reach of their parents, but away from the old associations. Evidences of refinement are seen in their homes and in their manner, and their children are dressed and fed according to most modern standards.[34]

FIG. 4.40. Italian religious festival at Cambridge Avenue and Oak Street in front of St. Philip Benizi Church, 1947. The area later contained the Cabrini-Green Homes, low-income high-rise public housing, now being demolished. Photograph by James D. McMahon; Chicago Historical Society, ICHi-20953.

In recent decades the Italians in the community have been replaced by African Americans, many of whom live in the large Cabrini-Green public housing complex, a name that still partially reflects the former Italian character of the area. The public housing complex is now being demolished.

In addition to the three large Italian communities, there were perhaps another twenty smaller Italian communities scattered throughout the city. These included a group of Italians who were mainly from Tuscany. They resided around Twenty-fifth Street and Oakley Avenue (2300 W.), near the large International Harvester plant. In this community, St. Michael's Church was established in 1903 at Twenty-fourth Place and Western Avenue. It closed a century later, in 2003. Another Italian community was situated in the Roseland, Pullman, and Kensington areas on the Far South Side and consisted of immigrants largely from Venetia and Lombardy. There the church of St. Anthony of Padua was established in 1904 at 216 Kensington Street (11552 S.). Italians also settled south, along Clark and Wentworth (200 W.), into Armour Square, and into part of the Bridgeport area. Santa Maria Incoronata Church was founded in 1899 at Clark and Eighteenth streets. In 1914 the church was moved to Wentworth and Alexander streets (2246 S.). This community had many Neapolitans, as well as some northern Italians, but is today a Chinese community.

Some of these Italian communities declined significantly in population as African Americans or Hispanics moved into the areas. One Italian community that remains is the small Italian enclave around Twenty-fifth Street and Oakley Avenue. It is noted citywide for its numerous Italian restaurants, although a number have recently closed. The alderman of this area who served six terms in office was the colorful, Sicilian-born Vito Marzullo.

With the decline in Italian population, Italian membership in the local churches also declined. In addition, many more mobile and affluent second- and third-generation Italians turned away from Italian-dominated churches toward Americanized churches. With the decline of the Italian-born population and with the concomitant development of government social welfare programs, most of the hundreds of Italian mutual aid societies—often started by immigrants from the same home region—ceased to exist. Recent years have seen little immigration from Italy. However, Chicago still has the third-largest Italian population of any city in the United States.

In 2000 the largest concentrations of Italian Americans in Chicago resided on the West, North, and Northwest sides of the city in such communities as Portage Park, Dunning, Norwood Park, Lake View,

Lincoln Park, and West Town. Italian Americans also resided in Bridgeport, to the south. Chicago now has approximately 102,000 people of Italian ancestry, who comprise 7.2 percent of the metropolitan area population. But most of the Italian Americans, mainly second- and third-generation, now live in the suburbs. With the exception of Chicago Heights to the south and Highwood to the north, the suburbs with a significant percentage of residents of Italian American descent are to the west and northwest. These suburbs include Melrose Park, Elmwood Park, Downers Grove, and Northlake. Harlem Avenue (7200 W.), between North Avenue (1600 N.) and Irving Park Road (4000 N.), now is home to many Italian stores, which also serve those living in the western suburbs.

Today important Italian-sponsored organizations and activities continue to exist in Chicago, but many others are now in the suburbs. Among the latter is the Scalabrini Fathers senior citizens' home in Northlake: Villa Scalabrini was the dream of Father Armando Pierini. Stone Park has an Italian cultural center. Arlington Heights has the Italo-American Soccer Club. There are also a number of Italian civic organizations, such as the Joint Civic Committee of Italian-Americans in Stone Park. That organization serves as a type of umbrella organization for other Italian groups. Although most of the major Italian folk and religious "fests" are celebrated in Chicago, including the annual Columbus Day parade, a few take place in those suburbs having large Italian populations. For many suburbanites, the nostalgia for the old closely knit Chicago Italian neighborhoods remains strong.

The Greeks

Greek immigration to Chicago began slowly and relatively late. Small numbers of Greeks began arriving during the 1880s and 1890s. The number increased rapidly during the first few decades of the twentieth century, reaching a peak from 1900 to 1920. In 1890 there were only 245 people of Greek birth in Chicago; in 1900 there were 1,493; by 1920 the number had risen to 11,546. Since World War II, partly because of internal strife in Greece, Greeks have been among the most numerous of the European groups to arrive in the city. By the late 1970s the Chicago metropolitan area contained an estimated 125,000 people of Greek ancestry, making it the city with the largest Greek population in the world outside Greece. The U.S. 2000 Census listed about seventeen thousand people of Greek ancestry living in Chicago, 1 percent of the total population of the metropolitan area.

The Greeks came from a small, scenic country with a glorious history and proud traditions, but it was largely a nation of peasants, poverty, and frequent wars. The first immigrants came primarily from southern Greece, or Peloponnesus, initially from the area around Sparta in the province of Laconia, and later from the province of Arcadia. As time went on, they started arriving from almost all parts of Greece.

About 95 percent of the early immigrants were male, mainly young peasants. They were often poor and minimally educated. In some cases, whole villages were virtually emptied of men. The Greek immigrants came to Chicago primarily for economic betterment, often with the idea of making money and then returning home. An estimated 40 percent of the earlier immigrants did return home, but many remained and, in the tradition of other immigrant groups, used their savings to help support relatives in Greece or to help finance their passage to America.[35] Others returned to Greece to marry and then came back to Chicago with their wives.

Although most of the early Greek immigrants had been peasants in their home country, in America they preferred to settle in big cities like Chicago, even though they sometimes encountered hostility from "native Americans." There employment was readily available, wages were paid weekly, and they could share the companionship of their fellow countrymen. Later the better-educated Greeks, including merchants and those trained in the professions, joined the movement to Chicago.

Around the turn of the century, small Greek concentrations were in three areas. The earliest were on the Near North Side around Clark and Kinzie (400 N.), around Sixty-first and Michigan (100 E.) in Washington Park, and on the Near West Side in what was known as the "Delta," the triangle formed by Harrison (600 S.), Halsted (800 W.), Blue Island, and Polk (800 S.). There the first permanent Greek Orthodox church, Holy Trinity, was established in 1897.[36] For more than half a century, the Delta area was the site of the main Greek community in Chicago, attaining at its height a Greek population of about thirty thousand.

The Delta was essentially a self-contained Greek community. The main streets of this "Greek Town" were Blue Island and Halsted. For several blocks these streets were lined with groceries, newspaper offices, barbershops, bookstores, labor agencies, travel agencies, and coffeehouses, the windows of which contained signs in Greek letters. The community had its church, school, and numerous fraternal organizations. A large office building on the corner of Blue Island and

Harrison housed the offices of Greek doctors, dentists, lawyers, and businessmen.[37]

Coffeehouses, a familiar institution in Greece, sprang up across the Delta and provided a familiar gathering place for many lonely immigrant men. There, for the price of a cup of thick black Turkish coffee, men—and men only—could sit at a table, smoke, read Greek newspapers, play cards, gamble, reminisce about Greece, and discuss politics with great animation while sitting beneath the framed picture of the Parthenon on the Athenian Acropolis. The coffeehouse also often functioned as an informal post office, as Ernest Poole noted in *Everybody's Magazine* in October 1910.

Here many come to seek news from home. On the wall at one spot were pinned some score of letters, the addresses in strange Greek scrawl. When the postman came in with the evening mail, a half dozen rose and crowded around him, but came back disgusted; except for one chubby-faced man who took a blue letter—also chubby—back to his corner table, and sat complacently smiling down, lighting a fresh cigarette before beginning to read. Stories cluster thick round this rough, simple post office, but of these you can get only hints. There was a boy of eighteen who walked in every night for over six months, never asking for letters, but simply glancing up at the place on the wall—for the missive which never came. On the wall are some envelopes dingy with months of waiting for readers, the stories still hidden inside. And here one night an anxious group of big workmen sat breathing hard over a letter to be sent to a mother in Greece, to say that her son had

lost his leg, in a tunnel explosion, that by passing the hat in the café for the past five evenings they had collected enough for his passage, and that he would soon start for home.

Greek Town lay in the very shadow of Jane Addams's social settlement complex at 800 South Halsted Street. Addams had begun her pioneering social reform movement there in 1889 and, over the years, had fought to improve the condition of the succession of peoples in the area by helping to educate and Americanize them. Just as she had with other groups, Addams opened the doors of Hull House to the Greeks, befriended them, and attempted to help them adjust. Hull House became a second home to thousands of young Greek immigrants, and many of their numerous Greek organizations met there. The first Greek play in Chicago, *The Return of Odysseus*, was performed at the Hull House Theater in 1899. When Jane Addams died in 1935, Greek businesses closed for her funeral. A major event for the Greeks of the area occurred in 1910 at Hull House when President Theodore Roosevelt addressed the Greek community, urging it to perpetuate its "incomparable Greek heritage" while becoming American.[38]

The Greek Town of the Delta area was displaced in the early 1960s by the newly constructed campus of the University of Illinois at Chicago, although Greek Town had begun to decline some years earlier. Holy Trinity Church is now gone, as are many other Greek institutions. Still remaining, however, is a thriving Greek commercial strip consisting of a few blocks, mainly along Halsted Street between Adams (200 S.) and Van Buren (400 S.) streets. This strip contains a concentration of Greek restaurants, some of which feature entertainment, and a number of Greek groceries, bakeries, import stores, and other business establishments. Greeks from throughout the metropolitan area come to shop and dine in this area, where many have their roots. Yet many of the diners are non-Greeks, commonly Loop workers who lunch at the profusion of fine Greek restaurants or others desirous of an evening of Zorban entertainment.

Today, Greek Americans are found in every profession and type of business, although they are best known for their great success in the restaurant business and related food enterprises. Some individuals started as street pushcart food venders but ran into periodic opposition from established grocery store and restaurant owners and eventually opened their own storefronts. As far back as 1919, the Greeks were believed to own one of every three restaurants in Chicago, including a large number of those in the Loop.[39] At one time John Raklios owned or operated thirty-two restaurants in the Chicago area. Today Greeks run some of that area's most famous restaurants. Successful Greek-owned restaurants, including many that do not specialize in Greek cuisine, are common throughout the metropolitan area.

One possible explanation for the heavy Greek concentration in the restaurant business is that the early Greek immigrants, almost all male, arrived alone and poor.

FIG. 4.41. Old Greek Town on South Halsted Street, between Jackson Boulevard and Van Buren Street, 1976. Although the commercial strip still contains a number of Greek restaurants, bakeries, grocery stores, and import stores, the once-sizable Greek residential community was displaced by the construction of the Eisenhower Expressway and the campus of the University of Illinois at Chicago. Photograph by Irving Cutler.

They arranged to live in groups, cooking for themselves in community kitchens. In this way, some of them became expert cooks and, upon realizing that they could make money selling meals to the public, they eventually opened their own restaurants. Moreover, little financial investment was required to do so.

In numerous cases, newly arrived Greek immigrants were hired by Greek-owned restaurants. In time, through frugality and hard work, they too became restaurant owners. A number of immigrants owned chains of restaurants. Immigrants and their descendants from one village in Greece, Nestani, now own or control nearly one hundred restaurants in the Chicago area.

Many Greeks started out as street peddlers selling candy, flowers, fruit, and sandwiches from pushcarts and lunch wagons. Some Greeks worked as busboys, dishwashers, cooks, and countermen. A large percentage of Greeks were self-employed, and a very small percentage worked in factories. Few Greek women entered the labor market. When they had saved enough money, the immigrants often went into the retail business by opening a candy store, ice cream parlor, floral shop, restaurant, grocery, or fruit and vegetable store. In the 1920s, they operated an estimated ten thousand stores. From grocery and fruit and vegetable retailing, many eventually moved into the wholesale produce business, where Greeks comprised almost one-third of the merchants in the South Water and Randolph Street produce market districts. Greeks were also active in the entertainment field. They owned theaters, nightclubs, and ballrooms—including the famed Aragon and Trianon ballrooms, both of which were owned by the Karzas brothers.[40] Their dominance, however, was most pronounced in the restaurant industry. Over the years, the Greeks often competed with the Italians for land on the Near West Side and for employment in the food industry as street venders, food store owners, produce and grocery wholesalers, and restaurant owners.

The economic success of the Greeks was due in large part to their willingness to work hard for many hours a day. Success, in turn, allowed them to assist the second generation's rise into the professions and to extend a helping hand to their relatives in Greece. Second-generation Greek Americans ranked high in educational achievement.

With the continuing influx of immigrants, the Greeks grew in number and prospered. Many joined Greek national organizations such as the American Hellenic Educational and Progressive Association (AHEPA), which focused on Americanization and adaptation. Others joined the rival Greek American Progressive Association (GAPA), which emphasized the preservation of the Greek language, church, and traditions.

As new Greek communities were established, the population began to disperse. On the South Side, Saints Constantine and Helen Church, established in 1909 at Sixty-first Street and Michigan Avenue, became one of the largest Greek Orthodox parishes. In 1946 it moved to 7351 South Stony Island. When the neighborhood changed racially, the building was sold to Black Muslims, and in 1972 the church moved to suburban Palos Hills.

A Near North Side Greek settlement established Annunciation Church in 1910 at 1017 North La Salle Street. It became the Cathedral for the diocese. After 1920, as other Greek settlements developed, many Greek Orthodox parishes arose throughout the city and the suburbs. In Chicago small Greek communities developed around Clark and Diversey (2800 N.), Harrison and Central (5600 W.), and Diversey and Austin (6000 W.). As some of the Greek population dispersed, churches were built in a number of suburbs, including Des Plaines, Mt. Prospect, Park Ridge, Arlington Heights, Orland Park, Naperville, Justice, Glenview, Oak Lawn, and Palos Hills. The Greek community also established a number of elementary day and afternoon schools, the chief objective of which included the transmission of the Greek language and cultural heritage. The schools bore such revered names as Socrates, Plato, Solon, Aristotle, Pythagoras, and Archimedes. The first Greek school in the United States, Socrates Elementary School, was established in Chicago in 1908.

At present, the largest concentration of Greeks in Chicago reside in the Lincoln Square community, which fans out from the Lincoln-Western-Lawrence-avenues area into adjacent communities, such as West Ridge, North Park, and Albany Park. Today, an estimated five thousand Greek Americans live in this declining Greek Town North. Like the former Delta area, the main streets still have a few Greek establishments, including restaurants, bakeries, and grocery stores.

Although Greeks have been in the Lincoln Square area since the 1920s, the surge of Greeks into what was once a predominantly German community took place mainly after World War II. Greeks were attracted by both the community's residential possibilities and the presence of the imposing St. Demetrios Church, at 2727 West Winona Avenue (5132 N.). The church has been in the area for over half a century. Also there is a library community center and the Solon Greek Afternoon School. The area is now becoming a mixed community of Asians, Germans, and Irish, as many Greeks move to suburbia.

Like other ethnic groups, the Greek community has experienced conflicts regarding church language and ritual; conflicts within and between Greek organizations; conflicts between recent immigrants and second- and third-generation Greek Americans; conflicts in regard to education policy; and conflicts over assimilation. But perhaps to an even greater degree than other ethnic groups, the Greeks have made a determined effort to preserve some of their native culture, and they continue to evidence a deep interest in their Greek homeland. There is a steady infusion of Greek culture from the homeland, with people traveling back and forth and some even resettling in Greece. Although today's Greek American community comprises one of the smaller ethnic groups and is a relative latecomer to Chicago, it is active, highly organized, prosperous, well educated, and now numbering about a hundred thousand in the metropolitan area, with about one-third foreign-born owing to late immigration patterns. Its history in Chicago has been beautifully depicted in the novels and short stories of one of its renowned sons, author Harry Mark Petrakis.

The Ukrainians

Although Ukraine has ethnic and national traditions going back more than a millennium, in later centuries it was often conquered and occupied by outsiders. The last occupiers were the Russians, ruling much of the area from the eighteenth century until 1991, when Ukraine became an independent country. Some Ukrainian immigrants also came from eastern Galicia and Subcarpathia, regions of the former Austro-Hungarian Empire.

Stalwart in maintaining their Christian beliefs, in the nineteenth century the Ukrainians also became adamant in their nationalism, fueled by literature, music, history, and nostalgia. Unable to practice their heritage freely under foreign rule and plagued by poverty, many came to the United States determined to uphold and preserve their traditions. Hence the Ukrainians belong to one of the longest-lasting, institutionalized European communities in Chicago.

In the 1870s the first Ukrainians started coming to Chicago from Russian-occupied Ukraine and to a lesser extent from the Austro-Hungarian Empire. They came in a number of waves. One wave of Ukrainians arrived during the period from the late 1800s to World War I, one arrived after World War I into the 1920s, one arrived after World War II into the 1950s, and one arrived more recently, after Ukraine became independent. The new arrivals were hard-working, self-reliant, and thrifty, while maintaining a great deal of their Ukrainian heritage. The 2000 U.S. Census stated that 43,324 individuals of Ukrainian ancestry lived in the six-county Chicago metropolitan area, of which 13,579 lived in the city proper.

The first Ukrainian community was established west of the Loop. It gradually moved northwest into West Town, which maintains by far the largest Ukrainian community in Chicago: 3,349 people of Ukrainian heritage were listed by the census in 2000. Other smaller Ukrainian communities existed mainly near South Side industrial areas, where work was readily available. One such community developed near the steel mills in Burnside, where the Ukrainian Catholic church, Saints Peter and Paul, was opened in 1909 at Ninety-second Street and Avalon (1232 E.).

In 1917 a group of parishioners who disagreed with some of the church's religious practices broke away and organized their own parish, St. Michael's, in West Pullman on Chicago's Far South Side. Another small working-class community was established in the Back of the Yards area near the stockyards, where many of the Ukrainian immigrants worked. Nativity of the Blessed Virgin Mary Church was established in the area at Forty-ninth and Paulina (1700 W.).

In these communities, the Ukrainians established churches of various denominations (Orthodox, Catholic, Catholics of Eastern Rite, and Protestant), as well as schools and organizations. Besides some religious disputes, there were also political disputes as to the future direction of Ukraine. During the 1920s and 1930s, three ideological groups competed for the favor of the important Chicago Ukrainian community—the Communists, the Monarchists, and the Nationalists, with the last eventually emerging victorious after World War II.

The South Side Ukrainian communities have declined in size or even vanished in recent years, while some of the Ukrainian population has moved to the northwestern fringes of the city and into the suburbs. In 1977 St. Joseph's Ukrainian Catholic Church, a striking edifice that combines traditional and modern architecture, was built on the Far Northwest Side at Cumberland Road (8400 W.), near Lawrence Avenue (4800 N.). In the suburbs, Ukrainian parishes exist now in such communities as Palatine, Niles, Roselle, Addison, Palos Park, and Joliet. There are also five parishes in heavily industrialized Lake County, Indiana.

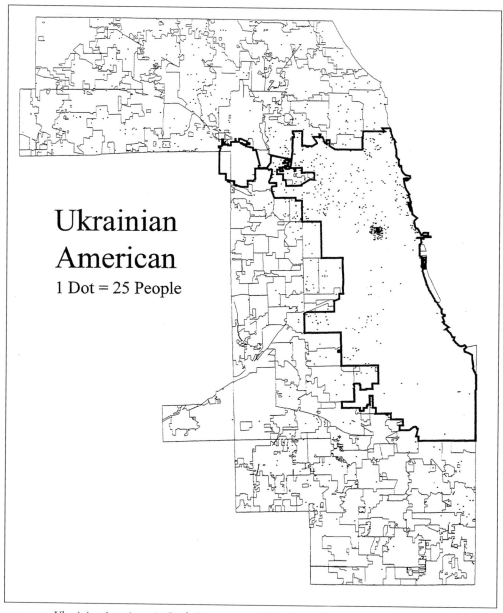

FIG. 4.42. Ukrainian Americans in Cook County, 1990. Map shows the concentration in Ukrainian Village, centered on Chicago and Oakley avenues. Courtesy of the Illinois Ethnic Coalition.

FIG. 4.43. Looking west along Chicago Avenue from Leavitt Street (2200 W.) at some of the stores of the main commercial street of Ukrainian Village, 1994. Photograph by Irving Cutler.

The largest Ukrainian community in Chicago is in West Town and occupies about a square mile, centered on Chicago Avenue (800 N.) and Oakley Boulevard (2300 W.). This is the famous Ukrainian Village, which still maintains well-preserved housing and tree-lined streets. Ukrainians have lived there for almost a century. It is just to the south of the gentrifying, bustling Wicker Park, where wealthy non-WASP Europeans once lived. In 2003 the Ukrainian Village was declared a Chicago landmark.

Chicago Avenue is the locale of many well-known Ukrainian establishments, such as Ann's Bakery, Ukrainian Village Grocery, a number of restaurants, a publishing company, an import store, a youth center, the Ukrainian Village Cultural Center, and the Ukrainian Institute of Modern Art. Along Oakley Boulevard, in a stretch of about half a mile, are three large Ukrainian churches and the Ukrainian National Museum. The northernmost of the three churches, St. Vladimir Ukrainian Orthodox Church, has been at the corner of Cortez (1032 N.) and Oakley

Boulevard since 1945. The largest is the thirteen-dome St. Nicholas Ukrainian Catholic Cathedral, at the corner of Rice Street (832 N.). It was completed in 1915 and ordained a cathedral in 1960. The church has a parochial school of several hundred children.

A few blocks to the south, at the corner of Superior Street (732 N.), is the relatively new gold-domed Sts. Volodymyr and Olha Ukrainian Eastern-Rite Catholic Church, dedicated in 1973. It was organized by a splinter group of parishioners from neighboring St. Nicholas who became upset when the traditional calendar and rituals were altered. Built at a cost of more than $2 million, the members of the new church also showed dedication and confidence in their ethnic community—qualities that have often been lacking among the city's other European communities, many of which have disappeared. More recently the church built a large, adjacent cultural center. With the improvements and gentrification of the surrounding

FIG. 4.44. Gold-domed Sts. Volodymyr and Olha Ukrainian Catholic Church, at 739 North Oakley Boulevard. The building, constructed in the shape of a Byzantine cross, was dedicated in 1973. The congregation was organized by a splinter group from nearby St. Nicholas Ukrainian Cathedral *(left, background)* who had objected to changes in the traditional calendar and ritual. St. Nicholas, with its thirteen green domes, was completed in 1915. Photograph by Irving Cutler.

neighborhoods, some suburban Ukrainians began resettling in the old neighborhood.

Ukrainian organizational and cultural life has been extensive. Almost one hundred Ukrainian organizations of various types are now in the Chicago area. They include religious, social, political, women's, educational, and nationalistic groups. Culturally, choral groups are especially numerous, but there are also dance, drama, band, and orchestra groups. A cultural highlight of the Ukrainian community, although without their own country at the time, was sponsorship of a large, interesting pavilion at the Century of Progress Chicago's World's Fair in 1933–34 that attracted about 1.8 million people.

The Ukrainians today are generally prosperous and supportive of their vibrant community but remain concerned about the fate of their homeland and about growing assimilation in Chicago. For nearly a century now, they have been determined not only to keep their culture and religion alive in their Chicago enclave but to help in freeing their homeland—a task that was finally accomplished on August 24, 1991, amid joyful celebration.

Other European Groups

Numerous other European groups came to Chicago in smaller numbers: French and French Canadians were among the earliest explorers and settlers of the Chicago area. Although their numbers were never large, there were a few small French settlements. One was in the Halsted-Congress (500 S.) area around Notre Dame Church, established in 1864, and another was in Brighton Park in the parish of St. Joseph and St. Anne Church, founded in 1889. The National Shrine of St. Anne, in the church at Thirty-eighth Place and California Avenue (2800 W.), was also an important center for French religious life in the United States. There are about 160,000 people of French or French Canadian descent in the metropolitan area, with about 20 percent living in Chicago.

The English and Scots were important to the early settlement of Chicago. In the 1890 Census, they both ranked among the ten largest foreign-born groups in Chicago. Unencumbered by language barriers, neither the English nor the Scots developed the type of ethnic neighborhoods that characterized most of the other European groups, but there was a

FIG. 4.45. Notre Dame Church, 1335 West Harrison Street (600 S.) on the Near West Side. Built in 1889 by French Catholics, including French Canadians, who lived in the area, the church is now multiethnic, with a predominance of Italian and Hispanic members. Photograph by Irving Cutler.

Scottish concentration near the Presbyterian McCormick Theological Seminary in the Lincoln Park area. Emigration from England and Scotland slowed during the twentieth century when their workers' labor costs were higher for American industry than the cheaper labor coming in large numbers from eastern and southern Europe. In addition, within the vast British Empire, the English and Scots had alternate places to settle. The Chicago metropolitan area has over one-half million people of English and Scot descent, but only about 15 percent, or about eighty-three thousand, live in Chicago. Like other early settlers, they were among the first groups, and in the highest proportions, to move to the suburbs.

Dutch settlers started immigrating to Chicago in the 1840s. The peak number of Dutch foreign-born in Chicago was reached in 1900, when they numbered almost twenty thousand. Most arrived as families. Many of the Dutch in the Chicago area were truck farmers who lived in the south and southwest areas of the city and Cook County, especially in the South Holland–Lansing–East Chicago Heights area and, to a lesser extent, in Riverdale, Alsip, Evergreen Park, Oak Lawn, and Summit. In areas that later became part of Chicago, the Dutch were concentrated especially in Roseland, in the adjacent West Pullman community, and to a lesser extent, in Mount Greenwood and Englewood. Many in the suburban area were truck farmers until the last decades of the twentieth century, when the gradual disappearance of the Dutch farming communities began. Small numbers worked for the railroad and in the great industrial plants around Roseland such as International Harvester, Sherwin-Williams, and Pullman. Some worked in the Illinois Central yards and others worked in the steel mills—facilities

FIG. 4.46. Scottish home for the elderly in Riverside, Illinois, with a woman dancing. Photograph from the *Chicago Daily News*.

whose establishment helped change the character of the area. Still others worked in the building trades, and many entered private businesses of various kinds.

A Dutch community that at one time numbered almost two thousand people was on the Near West Side around Fourteenth Street and Ashland Avenue. It lasted well into the twentieth century. Because many of the Dutch in this community had teams of horses, they drifted into garbage collecting for the Loop area and other parts of the city.[41] Waste Management, Incorporated, one of the largest waste service companies in the United States, evolved from a small family operation that began in this community. The Reformed Church was well established in this and other major Dutch communities. In 1950 it helped establish Trinity Christian College in suburban Palos Heights. The largest of the Dutch communities, in Roseland, continued to exist until recent decades, when the population of the neighborhood became predominantly African American. There are now about twelve thousand of Dutch descent living in the city of Chicago and about one hundred thousand living in the entire metropolitan area, with large numbers living to the south, in Will County.

The Belgians and Luxembourgers in Chicago were never as numerous as their European neighbors, the Dutch. At their peak in 1930, there were over four thousand Belgians, mainly Flemish-speaking, and almost two thousand Luxembourgers of foreign birth in Chicago. The Luxembourgers arrived early in Chicago. Many became truck farmers in the vicinity of the first St. Henry's Church, which they built in 1851 at Devon and Ridge avenues. Luxembourgers were also commonly greenhouse operators and were among the earliest settlers of what were later

to become the suburbs of Lincolnwood and Skokie. The Belgians were somewhat more scattered than the Luxembourgers, but a small colony resided around St. John Berchman's Church at 2517 West Logan Boulevard (2600 N.) in Logan Square. The Logan Square area was organized in 1903 as a national parish for Belgian Catholics. In 1916 the church was opened to all nationalities. A Belgian community center was also in the neighborhood, on Fullerton Avenue. Many Belgians worked in building maintenance.

Austrians and Hungarians from the Austro-Hungarian Empire began arriving in Chicago in large numbers in the 1880s. They reached their greatest population in Chicago in 1920, when there were thirty thousand foreign-born Austrians and twenty-six thousand foreign-born Hungarians living in the city. They were scattered throughout the city, with the Austrians often living in close proximity to, or intermingled with, the German population. There are now approximately forty thousand residents of Austrian ancestry in the Chicagoland area. Many come from the eastern Austrian area of Burgoland, while others come from the multicultural area that comprised the Austro-Hungarian Empire. Their dominant language was German. Although small in number, the Austrians have continued to maintain a number of cultural institutions and frequently interact with other central European ethnic communities. Some Hungarians also settled around the older German community on the North Side—they organized St. Stephen King of Hungary Church at 2015 West Augusta (1000 N.). A major Hungarian colony developed in the Burnside area, around Ninety-fifth Street

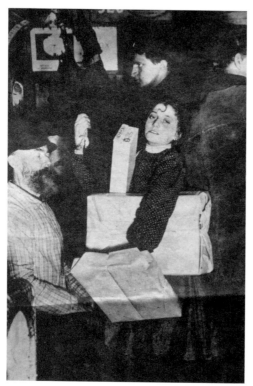

FIG. 4.47. Immigrant woman returning home from work on a streetcar in 1933, carrying bundles of cloth to work on at night to help support her family. Photograph courtesy of Harold M. Mayer.

Chicago's most southeasterly community; others moved into such south and southwest communities as Lansing, Naperville, Downers Grove, Joliet, and Aurora; and still others moved to the northern communities of Niles, Skokie, and Northbrook. Today the only Hungarian church left in the city is St. Stephen King of Hungary. Some of its members are refugees—often professionals—from the aborted Hungarian uprising in 1956, which was crushed by the Russians. There are now approximately thirteen thousand people of Hungarian descent in the city and about fifty thousand in the metropolitan area.

Croatians, Serbians, and Slovenes started coming to Chicago in the 1880s. Their homeland became Yugoslavia after World War I, but their old nationalistic feelings and religious differences generally continued to survive. The Serbs are mainly Orthodox, while the Croatians and Slovenes are principally Catholic. Most immigrants settled on the South Side, where they worked in the stockyards and steel mills. In the steel mills, they generally replaced the original workmen from northwestern Europe—the British, Irish, Germans, and Scandinavians. Some of the immigrants worked in the oil refineries in nearby Whiting, Indiana. Many initially lived as lodgers and were delayed in bringing their families over from Europe by the Balkan Wars of 1912 and 1913, and by World War I.

More often in the past than in the present, many eastern European immigrants lived in the area between the Calumet River and Lake Calumet, on the Far Southeast Side of the city. Although much of the area was originally swampland, it later contained numerous waste disposal sites and much of Chicago's heavy industry, especially steel plants. In recent decades, the area has declined

and Cottage Grove Avenue, with many immigrants finding work in the nearby railroad yards and steel mills. A number of Hungarian stores and restaurants opened in the area. Our Lady of Hungary Church was established in the area in 1904, and the Hungarian Center was built in 1927. Hungarians also spread into the nearby communities of South Chicago, West Pullman, and Roseland. As these communities started changing racially, most of the Hungarians relocated. Some moved to Hegewisch, economically, resulting in many abandoned rust-belt plants, increased unemployment, and fiscal hardship. It was in this area that many of these groups lived in close proximity, albeit with some friction, especially between the Eastern Orthodox Serbs and the Catholic Croatians—a carryover from the Old World, where there were often bitter clashes between the two groups. Many had their bungalows in the Tenth Ward, once ruled by the powerful but controversial alderman Edward Vrdolyak, whose parents had owned one of the many neighborhood taverns.

There were a number of sizable South Side Croatian settlements, each served by a Croatian-founded Roman Catholic church. The largest church, St. Jerome's, was founded in 1912 in the Bridgeport area at Twenty-eighth Street and Princeton Avenue (300 W.). Former Chicago mayor Michael A. Bilandic, of Croatian descent, was a member of this church. In 1914 two other churches were founded by the Croatians. One was Holy Trinity, in the Pilsen area on Throop Street (1300 W.) near Eighteenth Street, an area that is now largely Mexican; the other, Sacred Heart, was in the South Deering steel mill area at Ninety-sixth Street, near Exchange Avenue. Croatians also live in the adjacent

Southeast Side communities of Hegewisch and East Side. There were also Croatian churches at Fiftieth and Throop (1300 W.) and at Twenty-eighth and Central Park (3600 W.). Many Croatians now live north in Rogers Park and West Ridge, and some live farther north in Skokie, Morton Grove, and Northbrook. In the 1970s, the large Croatian Cultural Center of Chicago was established at 2845 West Devon Avenue in the middle of Jewish and Indian neighborhoods. To the east, on Devon and Ridge avenues, is Angel Guardian Croatian Catholic Church. Also serving to perpetuate Croatian customs and culture are some twenty Chicago lodges of the National Croatian Fraternal Union and a dozen more of the Croatian Catholic Union. Today Chicago is the fourth-largest Croatian city in the world.

The Serbians also established a church in the steel mill area at 9805 South Commercial Avenue (3000 E.). This was the Serbian Eastern Orthodox church of St. Michael the Archangel. More recently in the area, a Serbian church, St. Simeon, was built at 3737 E. 114th Street. It bears a striking resemblance to a beautiful Serbian monastery built in the

FIG. 4.48. Croatian cultural center, opened during the 1970s in a converted supermarket building at 2845 West Devon Avenue (6400 N.), in the middle of Indian and Jewish communities. Photograph by Irving Cutler.

Middle Ages. Many of the Serbs worked in the steel mills of the Calumet region, Gary, and Joliet. The Serbians also had small settlements on the Northwest Side, including one on Clybourn Avenue near Fullerton Avenue (2400 N.) and another in the Wicker Park area in the vicinity of Damen (2000 W.) and Evergreen (1332 N.) streets. In recent decades the Serbs have moved from the Wicker Park area, and many have also left the Calumet region. A new Serbian Orthodox Cathedral,

Holy Resurrection, was built in 1973 near O'Hare Field. A prolonged and bitter conflict in the Serbian community erupted between the Belgrade wing of the Serbian Orthodox Church and the anticommunist Free Serbian Orthodox Diocese. It involved the ownership of the beautiful $2 million-dollar Serbian monastery, church, cemetery, and children's camp—St. Sava—founded in 1923 near Libertyville, Illinois. In 1979 the Free Serbian

FIG. 4.49. Serbian Orthodox church, St. Simeon, at 3737 E. 114th Street in Chicago. The building closely resembles a beautiful Serbian monastery built during the Middle Ages. The church is almost directly behind the sizable home of Croatian American Ed Vrdolyak, for many years the alderman and political boss of the area. Photograph by Irving Cutler.

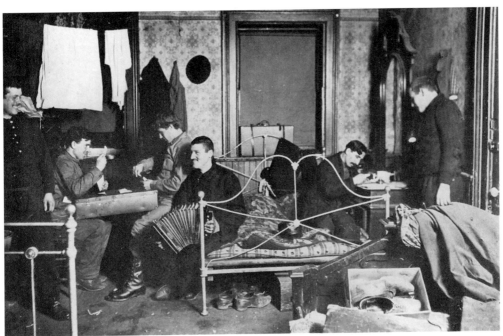

FIG. 4.50. Bulgarian lodging group on the West Side of Chicago in the early 1900s. Nine men occupied two rooms. Photograph by R. R. Earle; Chicago Historical Society.

group began construction of "Grachanitsa," a rival facility nearby, at Third Lake. It was situated on sixty acres and cost $4.5 million. The church at Grachanitsa resembles one in Kosovo, Serbia, that was built in 1321. Most Serbs now live scattered among numerous suburbs, especially those to the north and southwest of Chicago. The present governor of Illinois, Rod Blagojevich, is of Serbian descent.

The Slovenes, the smallest of the Yugoslav groups in Chicago, also had one of their most important settlements in the steel mill district in south Chicago. Some two thousand to four thousand Slovenes lived around St. George's Slovenian Church (now mainly Mexican) on Ewing Avenue near Ninety-sixth Street. A number of Slovenes have moved to the southwest suburbs, where they have a cultural center in Lemont. Many also live in Joliet. A perennial conflict among the Slovenes existed between those who favored the Catholic Church and those who were Free Thinkers, some of whom were socialists.

Today the people of Serbian, Croatian, and Slovene descent number several hundred thousand in the metropolitan area, with the Serbians comprising the largest group. All have campaigned vigorously for their homelands, and in the 1990s, with the turbulent breakup of Yugoslavia, Croatia and Slovenia finally achieved independence.

The Bulgarians were another small Balkan group. Like the Serbians, Croatians, and Slovenes, the Bulgarians lived near the steel mills of the South Chicago area. They also established a small colony around Halsted

FIG. 4.51. Holy Trinity Orthodox Cathedral, 1121 North Leavitt Street. Built in 1903 by the Russian community in the area, the church received some financial aid from the czar of Russia. The architect was Louis Sullivan, and the stuccoed church is now an official Chicago landmark. In the tradition of the homeland, the church contains no pews and the congregants (except those handicapped) stand during the services. Worship services, now in English, are well attended, attracting people from a wide area, including the revitalized Wicker Park area. Photograph by Irving Cutler.

FIG. 4.52. Last of Chicago's public bath-houses, 1998. On Division Street in an area settled mainly by Russians, Poles, and Ukrainians, this facility was like many others throughout the city before most residences had bathtubs and showers. Photograph by Irving Cutler.

and Adams streets (200 S.). It contained Bulgarian coffeehouses, food stores, and lodging houses for the numerous nonfamily men. Employment agencies in the area often shipped the Bulgarians out to work on the railroads, to lay pipes, or to pave roads. Many of the Bulgarians in this colony returned to their homelands in order to fight in the

Balkan Wars. In the 1990s, after the fall of state socialism in their homeland, thousands of young, well-educated Bulgarians (unlike their predecessors, who were largely peasants or unskilled laborers) arrived in Chicago. In 1996 St. John of Rila Bulgarian Church was established on the Northwest Side at 5944 West Cullom Avenue (4300 N.). The last census counted 5,683 people of Bulgarian ancestry in the Chicago metropolitan area, although community estimates are much higher.

Although the reported number of Russians who came to Chicago through the years is relatively high, many of the immigrants have actually been not Russians but members of such national groups as Ukrainians, Poles, Lithuanians, and Belorussians, who were under Russian rule. Many of the immigrants from Russia were Jews. The "true" Russians were found in small numbers in just a few parts of the city. These included the Calumet steel area on the Southeast Side, as well as the Northwest Side West Town community, where two Russian Orthodox churches stand. These are St. George Belorussian, at 1500 N. Maplewood (2532 W.), and Louis Sullivan's landmark Holy Trinity Orthodox Cathedral, at 1121 North Leavitt (2200 W.). The latter was completed in 1903, after receipt of a four-thousand-dollar donation from the czar of Russia.

The Romanians, like the Bulgarians, were small in number. But like most ethnic groups, they had their churches, food stores, social centers, and restaurants—the most famous of which was Little Bucharest in Lake View. Most of the Romanians live on the North and Northwest sides of the city, in proximity to about a dozen churches. Around one-third of the Romanians live in the suburbs, mainly to the north.[42] Many of the Romanian men worked in greenhouse farming and construction, while the women often worked in the garment industry. The 2000 U.S. Census showed that 25,050 residents of the Chicago metropolitan area are of Romanian ancestry, 11,871 of whom are immigrants.

Chicago's European Neighborhoods

The European ethnic neighborhoods of Chicago, though distinct culturally from one another in many ways, have exhibited certain common characteristics and problems. Each newly arrived ethnic group usually met hostility in varying amounts from the established groups until it mastered the prevailing customs and thereby acquired a degree of tolerance and acceptance. The various ethnic groups generally developed a similar mix of religious, cultural, and social service institutions. These were usually based on Old World patterns, with religious institutions wielding the most influence. Bickering and fractionalization occurred within almost all of the ethnic groups, often over religious differences, such as the secular versus the nonsecular, but also sometimes over economic and political issues. In addition, different immigrant groups often did not relate well to each other.

Virtually all of the immigrant groups were originally situated in the central part of the city, where they established major ethnic neighborhoods, and also in smaller, scattered ethnic clusters. In time, these areas were taken over by newer, poorer immigrant groups as the earlier arrivals prospered and dispersed outward geographically. The earliest ethnic groups have also generally moved the farthest outward. Many of the later-arriving ethnic groups reached suburbia only in recent decades. Over forty suburbs now have a higher percentage of first- and second-generation ethnics than does the city itself. Meanwhile, the percentage of such European ethnic families still residing in Chicago has continued to decline sharply from its peak earlier in the last century. As the European roots of the younger generations of Chicago's ethnic groups become more distant and obscure, ties with the Old Country and Old World

FIG. 4.53. Changing neighborhood, as shown by the Polish-founded St. Mary of Nazareth Hospital *(left)*, in the vicinity of 2200 West Division Street for almost a century, and the Roberto Clemente Public High School *(right)*, opened in the 1970s with a largely Puerto Rican student body. Photograph by Irving Cutler.

ways become increasingly tenuous and less important. Among every ethnic group, it is the older generation that is most concerned about marriage outside the group, about the too-rapid assimilation of their young, and about the status of their homeland.

Some immigrants approved of the weakening of ties with the Old World, which they felt often fostered clannishness, occasionally fanned nationalistic prides and prejudices, and sometimes made Americans suspicious of one another. Others, however, felt that one of America's greatest strengths has been the diversity of backgrounds and cultures of its various peoples, each of which has contributed in its own way to the remarkable vitality and success of the nation.

Mike Royko, in his book on the late Mayor Richard J. Daley, depicted the characteristics and significance of Chicago's ethnic neighborhoods and the feelings of their people with his characteristic humor and insight.

Chicago, until as late as the 1950s, was a place where people stayed put for a while, creating tightly knit neighborhoods, as small-townish as any village in the wheat fields.

The neighborhood-towns were part of large ethnic states. To the north of the Loop was Germany. To the northwest was Poland. To the west were Italy and Israel. To the southwest were Bohemia and Lithuania. And to the south was Ireland.

It wasn't perfectly defined because the borders shifted as newcomers moved in on the older settlers, sending them fleeing in terror and disgust. Here and there were outlying colonies, with Poles also on the South Side, and Irish up north.

But you could always tell, even with your eyes closed, which state you were in by the odors of the food stores and the open kitchen windows, the sound of the foreign or familiar language, and by whether a stranger hit you in the head with a rock.

In every neighborhood could be found all the ingredients of the small town; the local tavern, the funeral parlor, the bakery, the vegetable store, the butcher shop, the drugstore, the neighborhood war hero, the neighborhood police station, the neighborhood team, the neighborhood sports star, the ball field, the barber shop, the pool hall, the clubs, and the main street.

With everything right there, why go anywhere else? If you went somewhere else, you couldn't get credit, you'd have to waste a nickel on the streetcar, and when you finally got there, they might not speak the language.

Some people had to leave the neighborhood to work, but many didn't, because the houses were interlaced with industry.

On Sunday, people might ride a streetcar to visit a relative, but they usually remained within the ethnic state, unless there had been an unfortunate marriage in the family.

The borders of neighborhoods were the main streets, railroad tracks, branches of the Chicago River, branches of the branches, strips of industry, parks, and anything else that could be glared across.

The ethnic states got along just about as pleasantly as did the nations of Europe. With their tote bags, the immigrants brought along all their old prejudices, and immediately picked up some new ones. An Irishman who came here hating only the Englishmen and Irish Protestants soon hated Poles, Italians, and blacks. A Pole who was free arrived hating only Jews and

Russians, but soon learned to hate the Irish, the Italians and the blacks.[43]

According to Royko, another good reason for staying close to home and your own ethnic neighborhood was that you could never tell what would happen if you entered the territory of another ethnic group.

[But in your own neighborhood] . . . you were safe. At least if you did not cross beyond, say, to the other side of the school. While it might be part of your ethnic state,

it was still the edge of another neighborhood, and their gang was just as mean as your gang.

So, for a variety of reasons, ranging from convenience to fear to economics, people stayed in their own neighborhood, loving it, enjoying the closeness, the friendliness, the familiarity, and trying to save enough money to move out.[44]

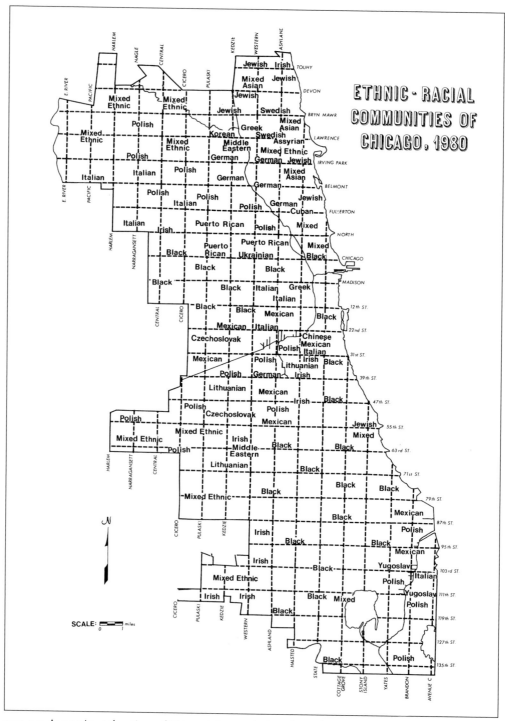

FIG. 5.1. Approximate locations of Chicago's larger ethnic and racial communities, 1980. Almost none of the communities was completely homogeneous. For the ethnic and racial communities in 1920, see Figure 4.1. Map by Joseph Kubal based largely on data from U.S. Census, churches, and Chicago Department of Planning.

5 People and Settlement Patterns: Recent Migration and Trends

Population Changes

The 2000 Census figures for the city of Chicago indicated a population of 2,896,016—up slightly from the 1990 population of 2,783,726. The 2000 Census also showed that substantial changes had taken place in the population diversity of Chicago. The changes resulted from two factors. One was the continued exodus of white families to the suburbs. The other was the substantial increase in the population of Asians and, especially, Hispanics. Since the 1970 Census, Chicago's African American population has remained relatively stable, while the white population has been about halved. But the Hispanic population has been greatly bolstered, especially by Mexicans and, to a lesser extent, by Puerto Ricans, smaller numbers of Cubans, and other Latin Americans. The Hispanic population in the city increased from 247,343 in 1970 to 753,644 in 2000. Asians coming to Chicago from such countries as South Korea, India, Pakistan, the Philippines, Thailand, South Vietnam, Cambodia, Taiwan, Laos, and China, and from Middle Eastern countries, increased from fewer than a hundred thousand in 1970 to more than 125,000 in 2000. The Asian population has

also grown rapidly in the suburbs, where an even larger number reside. Native American numbers in Chicago have remained stable at less than ten thousand. Since 1970 Chicago's population density has declined from 14,823 people per square mile to 12,680 in 2000. Table 5.1 shows the top ten immigrant countries for the entire Chicago metropolitan area by foreign-born in 2000. The majority of these countries continue to be non-European. Recent migration to Chicago by these groups

TABLE 5.1.

Foreign-Born in the Chicago Metropolitan Area from the Top Ten Immigrant-Sending Countries, 2000

Country	Total
Mexico	567,488
Poland	130,496
India	70,315
Philippines	60,294
China	43,361
Korea	32,730
Italy	24,588
Germany	24,064
Guatemala	18,946
Ukraine	18,633

Sources: Adapted from U.S. Census data; courtesy of Chicago Metropolis 2020

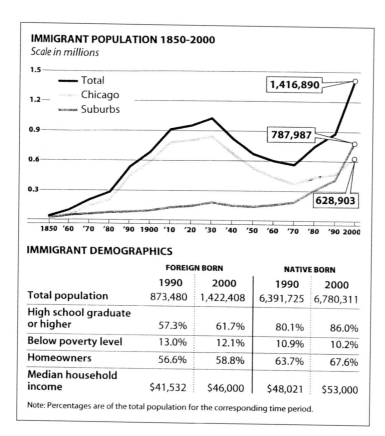

IMMIGRANT POPULATION 1850–2000
Scale in millions

Total
Chicago
Suburbs

1,416,890

787,987

628,903

1850 '60 '70 '80 '90 1900 '10 '20 '30 '40 '50 '60 '70 '80 '90 2000

IMMIGRANT DEMOGRAPHICS

	FOREIGN BORN		NATIVE BORN	
	1990	2000	1990	2000
Total population	873,480	1,422,408	6,391,725	6,780,311
High school graduate or higher	57.3%	61.7%	80.1%	86.0%
Below poverty level	13.0%	12.1%	10.9%	10.2%
Homeowners	56.6%	58.8%	63.7%	67.6%
Median household income	$41,532	$46,000	$48,021	$53,000

Note: Percentages are of the total population for the corresponding time period.

FIG. 5.2. Immigrant population and demographics. The number of immigrants in the Chicago area has reached a record high. Suburban Chicago has had a dramatic growth in immigrant population, with the number of foreign-born living there now greater than that of those living in the city proper. *Chicago Tribune* graphic. All rights reserved. Used with permission. Adapted from Rob Paral, Michael Norkewicz, *The Metro Chicago Immigration Fact Book* (Chicago: Institute for Metropolitan Affairs, Roosevelt University, 2003).

was spurred by the continuing demand for labor, especially during World War II and the boom years that followed. As the twenty-first century started, the mainly European ethnic checkerboard, which had characterized Chicago for well over a century, had largely given way to a tripartite division of the city into black, white, and Hispanic areas.

The African Americans

African Americans have lived in Chicago since its earliest days. Jean Baptiste Point du Sable built his cabin in the late 1770s near the mouth of the Chicago River and was referred to by the Potawatomi tribe as "the Negro who was the first settler of Chicago."

After Chicago was incorporated as a city in 1837, its African American population increased slowly but steadily. Some African Americans came via the Underground Railroad for fugitive slaves, which had a number of stops in the Chicago area, including one at what is now 9955 South Beverly Avenue in Chicago, and another at the Old Grau Mill in what is now Oak Brook. Chicago was once labeled by the editor of the *Cairo (IL) Weekly Times* as "a sinkhole of abolition."

Just prior to the Civil War, the 1860 census listed 955 African Americans, or slightly less than 1 percent of the city's total population of 112,172. A half century later, in 1910, the census listed 44,130 African Americans, but this still constituted only 2 percent of the city's quickly growing population, which had passed 2 million persons as a result of the rapid influx of various European groups.

The first significant African American settlement developed generally along the South Branch of the Chicago River during the 1840s and was composed of both free African Americans and fugitive slaves. To serve the community, a number of small African American churches, mainly Baptist and Methodist, were established. They also often served as stations on the Underground Railroad. The first African American church, Quinn Chapel, was officially organized in 1847 in the downtown area with about fifty members. Since 1891, Quinn Chapel of the African Methodist Episcopal Church has been at 2401 South Wabash Avenue (45 E.). One of the church's most illustrious leaders, Archibald J. Carey, became its pastor in 1898. He gained renown as an accomplished speaker and as a powerful African American political figure. His well-known son Archibold J. Carey Jr. also served as pastor of this church and as a city alderman and county judge.

A few years after the founding of Quinn Chapel, both Olivet Baptist Church and Bethel African Methodist Episcopal Church were established. By 1910 there were almost two dozen African American churches in Chicago. At least initially, most of the African American Baptist churches were offshoots of Olivet, the city's oldest and largest African American Baptist church, while the African Methodist Episcopal churches were generally founded by dissident parishioners from Quinn Chapel and Bethel Church.[1]

During the latter half of the nineteenth century, Chicago's African American population was small and attracted little attention. Although there was some prejudice and discrimination, many of the city's whites openly fought and disobeyed both the federal Fugitive Slave Acts and Illinois' oppressive Black Code laws. With the ending of the Civil War, the Black Code laws were repealed, thus officially—although not always in reality—banning school segregation and discrimination in public accommodations and granting African Americans such civil rights as the right to vote, to serve on juries, and to testify against whites. But even with these legal rights, as well as the advantages of native birth, a common language, and religious beliefs generally similar to those of the native whites, the African Americans still occupied a social and economic position inferior to European immigrants streaming into Chicago. Although African Americans comprised only 1.3 percent of Chicago's population in 1890, they represented 37.7 percent of the city's male servants and 43.3 percent of the female servants.

Instrumental in repealing the Illinois Black Code laws was one of Chicago's first civil rights leaders and an early leader of Chicago's African Americans, John Jones (1816–79). Of mixed white and free African American parentage, Jones came to Chicago from North Carolina in 1845 and opened a downtown tailoring shop that soon became successful. His home became a frequent meeting place for such fellow abolitionists as John Brown, Frederick Douglass, and Wendell Phillips. His pamphlet *The Black Laws of Illinois and a Few Reasons Why They Should Be Repealed,* was published in 1864 and helped influence the vote of the state legislature. In 1871, with white support, he was elected to the Cook County Board of Commissioners, the first African American to hold public office in the county.

FIG. 5.3. Quinn Chapel of the African Methodist Episcopal Church, 1980. Officially organized in 1847 in downtown Chicago as the city's first African American church, Quinn Chapel has occupied its present site at 2401 South Wabash Avenue since 1891 and is a city landmark. Those who have spoken from its pulpit include the educator Booker T. Washington, poet Paul Lawrence Dunbar, Dr. Martin Luther King Jr., and presidents William McKinley and Theodore Roosevelt. Photograph by Irving Cutler.

Another prominent African American civil rights activist was Ida B. Wells (1869–1931). Born in Mississippi, she became a crusading journalist and lecturer who tried to arouse public opinion against the horror of lynching. She first came to Chicago in 1893, soon marrying Ferdinand L. Barnett, a journalist, who in 1878 founded the *Conservator,* the first African American newspaper in Chicago. She helped start many African American organizations, became the first African American woman adult probation officer in Chicago, and was the first African American woman admitted to the bar in Illinois. She wrote for both the *Conservator* and for the *Chicago Defender,* which had been founded by Robert S. Abbott (1870–1940) in 1905 and was to become one of the largest and most successful of African American newspapers. At its peak it had a circulation of 250,000 but was down to just 17,500 in 2003. In 1940 a South Side public housing project, built by the Works Progress Administration (WPA) in the vicinity of what is presently Martin Luther King Drive (400 E.) and Pershing Road (3900 S.), was named for Ida B. Wells.

As Chicago grew, the number of its African Americans remained relatively small. Much of the African American population of the late 1800s lived in scattered small groups, interspersed with the white population, mainly on the Near South Side. They often lived in poor areas on the fringes of wealthy white residential districts, where many African Americans worked as domestics. One such small, isolated enclave existed farther south on Lake Park Avenue, near Fifty-fifth Street in Hyde Park, until it dwindled in the early 1900s, due partly to pressure from some elements of the surrounding white community.

When the African American population started increasing rapidly after the turn of the century, as is shown in Table 5.2, the

TABLE 5.2.
African American Population of Chicago, 1840–2000

Year	Total Population	African American Population	Percentage of Total Population
1840	4,470	53	1.2
1850	29,963	323	1.1
1860	112,172	955	0.9
1870	298,977	3,691	1.2
1880	503,185	6,480	1.3
1890	1,099,850	14,271	1.3
1900	1,698,575	30,150	1.8
1910	2,185,283	44,103	2.0
1920	2,701,705	109,458	4.1
1930	3,376,438	233,903	6.9
1940	3,396,808	277,731	8.2
1950	3,620,962	492,265	13.6
1960	3,550,404	812,637	22.9
1970	3,369,359	1,102,620	32.7
1980	3,005,072	1,197,000	39.8
1990	2,783,726	1,074,471	38.6
2000	2,896,016	1,053,739	36.4

Source: Adapted from U.S. Census Bureau data

African Americans became concentrated and segregated in older neighborhoods of the inner city that had been abandoned by earlier immigrant groups. Some of the European immigrant colonies tended to break up with the passage of time, but the African American areas became increasingly crowded because the residents had nowhere to move. Especially congested was a strip three miles long and barely one-fourth mile wide that ran from south of downtown to Thirty-ninth Street, and was bounded by the Rock Island Railroad on the west and the South Side elevated on the east.

The African American population in the city increased 148 percent in the World War I decade (1910–20), especially after 1915, when many African Americans started coming from the South. They were lured by jobs that became available in Chicago when immigration from Europe was virtually cut off by the war. The African Americans also fled the South at this time because their traditional poverty was intensified by low cotton prices, the damage to cotton plants by the boll weevil, a series of disastrous floods, and racial discrimination. Chicago offered hope of escape from poverty and oppression. Southern African Americans were urged to go north, not only by some northern industrialists but by African American newspapers, especially the *Chicago Defender,* which was often distributed by Pullman porters at southern railroad stops.

Thousands of African Americans sometimes arrived in a single week, usually at the Twelfth Street Illinois Central Station or, during the Great Migration in later years, at the Sixty-third and Stony Island Avenue (1600 E.) bus station. They came mainly from such southern states as Mississippi, Louisiana,

Georgia, Alabama, and Arkansas. Previously, the largest numbers of African Americans had come from such upper southern states as Kentucky, Tennessee, and Missouri. In 1915 the Chicago Urban League was established specifically to help resettle the migrants. It collaborated with the National Association for the Advancement of Colored People (NAACP), whose first Chicago chapter was organized in 1911. The NAACP was devoted primarily to legal and legislative action dealing with equal rights and integration, while the Chicago Urban League concerned itself more with housing and employment.

With the huge increase in Chicago's African American population around the time of World War I, the relatively benign equilibrium that had existed between the African Americans and whites began to change drastically. African Americans, who had previously been employed chiefly as hotel and restaurant employees, as domestic servants in private homes, as janitors in large buildings, and as porters on trains, now began to compete with white immigrant workers for factory jobs. In 1910 more than 51 percent of the male African American labor force was employed in domestic or personal service jobs; yet by 1920 this figure had dropped to 28 percent. Barred from membership in most unions, the African Americans had been used as scabs in a number of strikes, including those of the meatpackers and teamsters. This created further ill will between African Americans and whites, although the African Americans were usually fired after the strike.

Competition for housing, which was in short supply during the war period, caused the most tension between the races. Bombings and other forms of violence occurred as the rapidly increasing African American population attempted to move beyond the confines of the crowded black ghetto. On a scorching Sunday in July 1919, a stone-throwing melee between African Americans and whites broke out on the beach at Twenty-ninth Street, near the unofficial line of racial segregation. This incident resulted in the drowning of a fourteen-year-old African American youth which, in turn, touched off Chicago's most violent race riot. It lasted six days before order was restored by the state militia. The final toll included twenty-three African Americans and fifteen whites dead, with 537 injured.

The race riot dealt a severe blow to whatever hope remained for a more integrated city. It did, however, for the first time, focus serious attention on the African Americans and their problems, especially with regard to housing. Until then, the African American community typically had been neglected by social reformers.

The increased racial tension also brought to light the resentment of some Old Settler African Americans against the more recent, less-educated African American migrants from the rural south. The Old Settler African Americans looked back nostalgically and perhaps somewhat unrealistically to the days before the Great Migration from the South, as the following passage from Drake and Cayton's *Black Metropolis* makes clear:

The southern migrants reacted enthusiastically to the economic opportunities and the freer atmosphere of the North. But the Old Settlers were far from enthusiastic over the migrants, despite the fact that many of them were eventually to profit by the organization of the expanding Negro market and the black electorate. The Riot, to them, marked a turning point in the history of Chicago. Even today, as they reconstruct the past,

they look back on an era before that shattering event when all Negroes who wanted to work had jobs, when a premium was placed on refinement and gentility, and when there was no prejudice to mar the relations between Negroes and whites. As they see it, the newcomers disturbed the balance of relationships within the Negro community and with the white community. From their point of view, the migrants were people who knew nothing of the city's traditions, were unaware of the role which Negroes had played in the political and economic life of Chicago, and did not appreciate the "sacrifices of the pioneers."[2]

Some African American leaders believed, however, that it was the self-help, "accommodationist" attitude of some of the Old Settlers, rather than the militant protest of the newcomers, that brought about the segregation of the African Americans into the black ghetto.

The Great Migration from the South during the World War I period also greatly affected the religious tenor of the African American community, in whose life religion played an extremely important role. It was observed that the African Americans had more churches in relation to their population than did any other ethnic community. In *Black Chicago: The Making of a Negro Ghetto, 1890–1920*, Spear explains the effects of the Great Migration on African American religion.

Before the war, the large middle-class Baptist and Methodist churches had dominated Negro religious life in Chicago. Although they had not completely discarded the emotionalism of traditional Negro religion, these churches had moved toward a more decorous order of worship and a program of broad social concern. The migration, however, brought into the city thousands of Negroes accustomed to the informal, demonstrative, preacher-oriented churches of the rural South. Alienated by the formality of the middle-class churches, many of the newcomers organized small congregations that met in stores and houses and that maintained the old-time shouting religion. Often affiliated with the more exotic fringe sects, Holiness or Spiritualist, these storefront churches became a permanent force in the Chicago Negro community and secured a powerful hold on thousands of working-class Negroes.[3]

As the tensions of the race riot period began gradually to subside, a new and increased wave of more than 120,000 African Americans came to Chicago from the southern states during the 1920s. Among these migrants were some of the best educated and most skilled African Americans of the South. Drake and Cayton explain that the decade was a relatively prosperous one.

The five years from 1924 to 1929 were no doubt the most prosperous ones the Negro community in Chicago had ever experienced. A professional and business class arose upon the broad base of over seventy-five thousand colored wage-earners and was able for a brief period to enjoy the fruits of its training and investment. Throughout the Twenties, additional migrants from the rural South swelled the size of the Black Belt market. The Fat Years were at hand.

The Negroes spread along the once fashionable South Parkway and Michigan Boulevard, closing up the pocket which

existed in 1920, taking over the stonefront houses and the apartments, buying the large church edifices and opening smaller churches in houses and stores, establishing businesses, and building a political machine as they went. By 1925 the Black Belt business center had shifted two miles southward, and those who could afford to do so were trying to move from the slums into more stable residential areas. The masses flowed along persistently as the Black Belt lengthened.[4]

However, the 1920s were characterized not only by such signs of progress but also by restrictions on the activities of Chicago's African Americans, as Drake and Cayton observe.

There were stores and restaurants that didn't like to serve Negroes. To walk into certain downtown hotspots was unthinkable. To run for any state office higher than Senator from the Black Belt just wasn't done. To hope for a managerial or highly skilled job in industry was ridiculous. To buy or rent a house out of the Black Belt precipitated a storm. But after all, Chicago was in America, not in France or Brazil. It was certainly different from slavery sixty years ago, or from the South today. Negroes like Midwest Metropolis.

There were evidences of every hand that "the Race was progressing." Here were colored policemen, firemen, aldermen, and precinct captains, state representatives, doctors, lawyers, and teachers. Colored children were attending the public schools and the city's junior colleges. There were fine churches in the Negro areas, and beautiful boulevards. It seemed reasonable to assume that this development would continue with more and more Negroes getting ahead and becoming educated. There were prophets of doom in the Twenties, but a general air of optimism pervaded the Black Belt, as it did the whole city.[5]

By 1930 the African Americans lived in seven densely populated concentrations. Six of these were small enclaves, although the seventh was larger than the other six combined. Some of these areas had been occupied by African Americans for decades, and none of them was even close to the far North Side. Of the small enclaves, the one farthest north was around Division Street (1200 N.) and Larrabee Avenue (600 W.) in what had been a Sicilian area until after World War I. A survey of the 1930s revealed that about 90 percent of the African Americans in this area had been born in rural parts of the South. One settlement straddled Lake Street (200 N.), from about Ashland Avenue (1600 W.) to west of Western Avenue (2400 W.). This was an older African American community that had started in the 1880s. Another was south of Roosevelt Road in the Maxwell Street area, which had previously been occupied by eastern European Jews. There was also a small community in Englewood, around Sixty-first Street between Racine (1200 W.) and Loomis (1400 W.) avenues. African Americans had lived in Englewood since 1870, when the area was a railroad center. Farther south was a small settlement in Lillydale, around Ninety-fifth and State streets, and one in Morgan Park, within an area bounded approximately by 107th and 119th streets and by Halsted Street and Ashland Avenue. Many of these small areas were bounded by transportation corridors, especially railroads.

The major Black Belt was a narrow strip of land that started south of downtown, wedged between railroad yards, factories, the ethnic communities west of Wentworth Avenue, and the fashionable homes east of Wabash Avenue. By 1900, this largely self-contained Black Belt ("Bronzeville") stretched south beyond Thirty-ninth Street; by 1930 it had reached approximately Sixty-third Street. It had also expanded eastward to Cottage Grove Avenue, except for the area immediately south of Washington Park to Sixty-third Street.

The first African American settlement in an area was usually established on side streets; later it expanded to include the better homes along the boulevards. Increasing immigration from the South, coupled with only limited opportunity for expansion, kept increasing the population density.

More than 80 percent of Chicago's African Americans lived in the major Black Belt. Unlike the various European ethnic groups, even the African Americans of wealth and education usually found it impossible to move out of the Black Belt into higher-status areas. Higher rents, restrictive real estate practices, threats, and even violence were used to keep African Americans out of parts of such adjacent communities as Hyde Park and Woodlawn. A total of fifty-eight racially motivated bombings occurred between 1917 and 1921. The result was an economic stratification within the Black Belt. As was generally the case with white settlement patterns, the quality of neighborhoods and homes, educational level, and job status within the Black Belt tended to improve as one proceeded outward from downtown. Differences in economic and social status within all the African American areas were often reflected in the quality and types of stores, the number of storefront churches, and the frequency of gambling establishments.

The 1920s also focused attention on the strides some African Americans were making in business, the professions, and politics. Efforts were made by African American groups to encourage African Americans to patronize African American–owned businesses. There were two African American banks, seven African American insurance companies, and numerous, small African American–owned businesses. These included groceries, beauty parlors, barber shops, restaurants, wood and coal dealerships, and funeral establishments. From small beginnings, some large, African American–owned Chicago firms arose and became prominent, among them John J. Johnson's Johnson Publishing (*Ebony, Ebony Junior, Black Star,* and *Jet*); George Johnson's Johnson Products Company, a cosmetics firm; and J. H. Parker's Parker House Sausage Company. Jesse Binga, an ex–Pullman porter, opened a bank at Thirty-fifth and State Street and owned valuable real estate. Anthony Overton, an ex-slave, owned a chain of businesses that included a bank, newspaper, insurance firm, and manufacturing plant. The South Side saw the development of such entertainment places as Club De Lisa, the Regal Theater, Dreamland, the Royal Gardens, and the Savoy Ballroom. They attracted some of the best African American talent in the country, including Louis Armstrong, King Oliver, Duke Ellington, Count Basie, Sam Cooke, and Nat King Cole. The nightclubs became a mecca of jazz and blues, and the Black and Tan clubs attracted many white people. The New Regal Theater was opened in 1987 in the former home of the Moorish-style Avalon movie palace at Seventy-ninth and Stony Island Avenue (1600 E.) but has had financial difficulties and is up for sale.

Among prominent African American professionals was Dr. Daniel Hale Williams (1858–1931) who helped found Provident Hospital on the South Side in 1891, a facility that gave young African Americans a place to train as nurses and doctors. In 1893 Dr. Williams was the first physician to close a heart wound successfully. Percy Julian (1899–1975), a distinguished research chemist with more than fifty patents to his credit, founded the firm of Julian Laboratories. Despite his accomplishments, Dr. Julian initially was harassed when in 1951 he purchased a home in the Chicago suburb of Oak Park. Theodore Lawless (1893–1971) was a nationally known dermatologist who attracted patients from throughout the Chicago area, regardless of race. A South Side housing development is named after him.

Other prominent African Americans from Chicago include writer Richard Wright, one of the first well-known African American novelists to protest the white treatment of African Americans; Gwendolyn Brooks, the first African American poet to win a Pulitzer Prize; and Mahalia Jackson, a long-time Chicago resident who gained national fame for her gospel singing. Many of her most popular gospel songs were written by Thomas Dorsey, the "father of gospel music," who for many years was associated with the Pilgrim Baptist Church in Chicago. For years Oprah Winfrey has hosted one of the nation's most popular television programs. Among the many outstanding African American athletes associated with Chicago are Jesse Owens, Ernie Banks, Walter Payton, and Michael Jordan.

There are numerous African American cultural institutions and festivals, ranging from the Du Sable Museum of African American History founded by Margaret Burroughs in 1966 to African American theaters, numerous art galleries, music fests, and the annual Bud Billiken Day Parade, a South Side lavish back-to-school parade that ranks as the third-largest parade in the country. In 2004 a newly built Harold Washington Cultural Center was opened at 4701 South Martin Luther King Drive.

Some African Americans became wealthy in "protected businesses," notably the numbers or policy racket that usually operated under the benevolent patronage of the city hall machine. In politics, Oscar De Priest (1871–1951), a prominent African American Republican political figure and real estate dealer, was elected in 1915 as Chicago's first African American alderman. In 1928 he became the first African American to be elected to the U.S. House of Representatives from a northern state. He represented his South Side district until 1935. Thereafter the number of African Americans who held public office increased steadily, although not in proportion to their total population. Until the 1930s and Franklin D. Roosevelt's New Deal, African Americans traditionally voted Republican, identifying themselves with the party of Abraham Lincoln.

African American politics generally was similar to the prevalent ethnic political context of Chicago. There were rewards for party loyalty, although usually not proportionate to those received by other groups. Some African American political figures had strong commitments to African American civil liberties and social and economic advancement. Another powerful African American politician was William Levi Dawson. Starting as a Republican alderman in the city council in the 1920s, he later became a Democratic machine politician with a large patronage army. He

served in the U.S. House of Representatives for fourteen consecutive terms—from 1942 until his death at age eighty-four in 1970.

The Depression years of the 1930s hit the African American community of Chicago especially hard. African Americans, who often were the last to be hired by white-owned companies, were the first to be fired. And African American businesses had few reserves to fall back on. Angered by their rising unemployment, African Americans boycotted and picketed those white-owned stores in African American neighborhoods that hired few or no African American workers. And they vigorously protested the eviction of African Americans from their homes and apartments. The same policy of eviction was also applied against thousands of Chicago's poor white families who also could not meet their rent or mortgage payments during the Depression.

Despite the dire economic conditions that prevailed in the city during the 1930s, more than forty-three thousand African Americans from the South migrated to Chicago during that decade. Even with its problems, Chicago looked better to them than the South, where they suffered from the collapse of cotton tenancy and from the discriminatory distribution of relief and emergency employment. In Chicago, however, as the policies of the New Deal began to take effect, relief and work in the form of such federally funded programs as the WPA began to alleviate the economic situation of the African Americans somewhat. In addition, toward the end of the 1930s and into the 1940s, the war-stimulated economy greatly improved the employment opportunities for African Americans.

Between 1940 and 1970, a period of general economic prosperity in the city, the African American population in Chicago almost quadrupled, increasing from 277,731 to 1,102,620. Similarly, the percentage of African Americans in the population increased from 8.2 percent in 1940 to 32.7 percent in 1970. At the start of 2000, the percentage of African Americans was 36.4 percent, and Chicago had become the second-largest African American city in the country, exceeded only by New York. African American Chicagoans had a high birth rate and, on the average, were much younger than non-African Americans.

The large African American migration to Chicago during and after World War II taxed the inferior recreational facilities and the overcrowded schools of the African American areas and built up a strong demand for housing. The artificial ghetto boundaries, such as Cottage Grove, Stony Island, and Ashland avenues, began to give way. Today, the main segment of the African American residential area has reached south to the city limits. The other major segment reached the western city

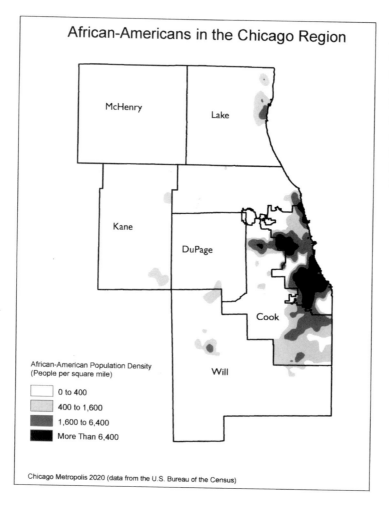

FIG. 5.4. African American population density in the six-county metropolitan area, 2000. African Americans are highly concentrated on the South and West sides of Chicago, as well as in the southern suburbs. Map courtesy of Chicago Metropolis 2020.

FIG. 5.5. Alley between Ellis and Cottage Grove avenues, south of Thirty-fifth Street, 1950. Recent redevelopment in the area has resulted in a variety of greatly improved housing. Photograph by Mildred Mead; Chicago Historical Society, ICHi-00825.

limits as the African American population moved into North Lawndale, East and West Garfield Park, and finally, Austin.

The expansion of the African American areas has almost always been on a block-by-block basis outward from the edges of the established ghetto. That expansion has often been into adjacent ethnic communities that resisted the arrival of the African Americans with resultant friction and even occasional violence. But once a number of African American families had established themselves, the whites moved out. Their departure was often hastened by unscrupulous panic-peddling real estate dealers who bought houses from the whites at extremely low prices and then sold the houses to incoming African Americans at much higher prices. In certain communities, such as Washington Park, North Lawndale, and East and West Garfield Park, the change from white to African American took barely a decade.

Along with the growth of the African American population and the expansion of the African American residential areas came an increasing number of public housing projects. By 1980 the Chicago Housing Authority had constructed about forty-five thousand low-rent public housing units, mainly in ghetto areas, in which more than 135,000 people lived. African Americans now occupied about 85 percent of the units. The high-rise complexes tended to be isolated, segregated, unsafe, crowded, noisy, and unsuitable and inadequate for the large number of children who lived in them. The complexes had the basic ingredients, in many cases, to become instant ghettos.

Some buildings became havens of drugs and crime, including murders. One of the complexes—the twenty-eight identical sixteen-story Robert Taylor Homes that were completed in 1963 along the Dan Ryan

FIG. 5.6. Cabrini-Green Homes on the Near North Side of Chicago, 1959. This high-rise housing project for low-income families is one of a number of such developments operated by the Chicago Housing Authority. The projects have generally tended to be isolated, segregated, crowded, noisy, and unsafe and to offer only limited facilities for the large number of children who reside there. This complex, now being demolished, contained twenty-three high-rise buildings and fifty-five row houses on seventy acres, providing homes to almost fourteen thousand people. Photograph by Betty Hulett; Chicago Historical Society, ICHi-35772.

Expressway—was the world's largest public housing complex. It contained 4,415 apartments and housed twenty-seven thousand people. In recent years, the Chicago Housing Authority has embarked on a program to tear down most of these high-rise buildings and to refurbish a few. Some of the evicted residents have moved into newly built, more suitable low-rise public housing, while others have been given government stipends to live in scattered private housing. However, those who move still usually end up living in ghettos, often in largely African American suburbs to the south. Besides the Robert Taylor Homes, the four other large, high-rise public housing projects in the nearly five-mile-long Dan Ryan–State Street public housing corridor are also being torn down. The plan is to replace much of the land with mixed-income, low-rise rental or public housing, where some of those who are displaced may live.

Efforts to build new, usually low-rise public housing in the city outside the ghettos have usually been blocked by legal and political maneuvering that often reflects racial prejudice. Sizable but greatly diminished parts of Chicago still have no or very few African American residents; some parts of the city remain highly segregated. Ironically, well-intentioned urban renewal programs have often had the effect of reducing the amount of low-cost housing available for African Americans by pushing up rents beyond their means to pay. African Americans still spend a much higher percentage of their income on housing than do whites, even though much of the city's substandard housing is in African American neighborhoods. Overall, the City of Chicago Housing Assistance Plan of 1979 estimated that 281,300, or 24.9 percent, of the city's 1,128,000 dwelling units were substandard. It is estimated that in recent decades, the African

American areas of the West and South sides have lost almost a third of their housing stock. Both North Lawndale on the West Side and Englewood on the South Side have lost well over half of their population since 1960.

The 1960s was a turbulent decade that gave rise to many civil rights demonstrations for open housing, greater employment opportunities for African Americans, and the elimination of school segregation. Many of the demonstrations were led by Dr. Martin Luther King Jr., who came to Chicago to try to work with Major Richard J. Daley to improve conditions for African Americans in the city. His assassination in Memphis in the summer of 1968 brought on two days of rioting, arson, and looting in Chicago's depressed West Side ghetto. The intervention of the National Guard and federal troops was required to restore order. Whole blocks of businesses and housing along some streets—especially Roosevelt Road and Madison Street—were burned out. Many of these areas still have not been fully restored. For a number of decades, fires and abandoned buildings were a continuing problem in many parts of the West Side and in Woodlawn on the South Side.

Mayer and Wade, in 1969, summarized living conditions for the African Americans as follows:

> Staggering congestion resulted. Blocks virtually burst at the seams; the deterioration of already substandard buildings accelerated. In its train came the long list of social ills that afflict blighted areas—poor health, inferior education, unskilled jobs or none at all, fragile family life, delinquency, and much more. The old became discouraged; the young despaired; hopelessness pervaded the ghetto. Finding a footing in the city had

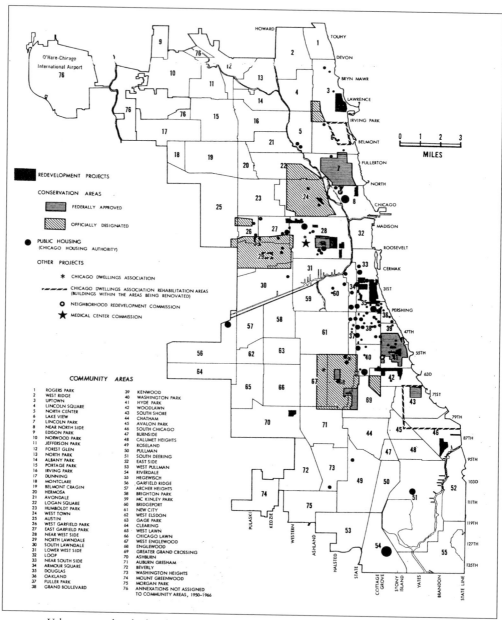

FIG. 5.7. Urban renewal and related activities near their peak in Chicago, 1967. Most public housing was built in areas occupied by African Americans. Much of it for the poor, especially the high-rise buildings, is being demolished. In its place frequently are more suitable low-rise public housing. Many tenants are given vouchers to rent nonpublic residences scattered throughout the area. Reproduced, with permission, from Harold M. Mayer and Richard C. Wade, *Chicago: Growth of a Metropolis*, © 1969 by the University of Chicago.

never been easy for any group; discrimination based on color added another high hurdle; for some it made advancement impossible.

Despite all the obstacles, increasing numbers of Negroes managed to hold family and careers together, and began the long trek out of the worst areas. By 1968 over a third of Chicago's nonwhite population was listed by the social statisticians as "middle class." This achievement often involved dependence on more than one breadwinner in the family, but it made possible a more satisfying, hopeful life. Some moved into good neighborhoods recently vacated by the whites at the edge of the ghettos. Middle class blacks kept moving further south in the Black Belt. Other successful Negroes found housing on a non-discriminatory basis in Lake Meadows, Prairie Shores, Sandburg Village, Beverly or Hyde-Park-Kenwood. Chatham on the South Side became an all black solidly middle-class neighborhood whose fine housing attracted some black millionaires.

Yet the numbers who escaped the ghetto were still small. The Negro's confinement continued, increasing the bitterness of those who were successful and sought a housing market free of discrimination, and reinforcing the despair of those who seemed hopelessly caught in the teeming tenements of the South and West sides. A few Negro families moved into white suburbs without incident; others clustered in the isolated ghettos within other suburban communities. Fair housing ordinances in the city and in a number of the smaller surrounding communities indicated a growing official determination to end this demeaning practice. But sporadic outbreaks of violence on the West Side and civil rights marches into

outlying neighborhoods in 1966 and large scale rioting in 1968 were grim reminders of the distance Chicago had still to travel before it became an open metropolis.[6]

The Civil Rights movement continued to gain momentum, led by such African American activists as Al Raby, Ralph Metcalfe, and Jesse Jackson. In 1983 Harold Washington, a Democratic Party liberal who had broken with the machine and who had served in the state legislature and in the U.S. House of Representatives, was elected as Chicago's first African American mayor. After a tumultuous first term, he was reelected in 1987 with the support of African Americans and numerous white liberals but died shortly thereafter.

Partly because of the Civil Rights movement, more and better opportunities have been made available for Chicago African Americans in housing, employment, education, and politics. Because of increasing economic opportunities, there has been a marked increase in African American home ownership and movement into good neighborhoods that were previously segregated. However, the movement of inner-city African Americans into the outer ethnic ring sometimes still causes racial friction. In 1946 African Americans owned only about 5 percent of the dwellings they occupied in the city; by 1960 the figure had reached 15 percent; and by 2000 it had reached 37 percent, compared with 52 percent of white home ownership in the city. In the entire six-county metropolitan area the figures are 42.4 percent for African Americans and 74.5 percent for whites.

The rapid expansion of African American areas in the post–World War II years precipitated a merging into the large Black Belt

FIG. 5.8. Harold Washington (1922–87), elected Chicago's first African American mayor in 1983. A graduate of the Northwestern School of Law in 1952, he later served in the Illinois house of representatives, the Illinois senate, and the U.S. House of Representatives. Washington died in 1987, shortly after reelection to a second term as mayor. Photograph courtesy of the Office of the Mayor.

of previously isolated African American enclaves, such as those in Englewood, Lillydale, and Morgan Park. Attractive new African American communities were established in such areas as Avalon Park, Chatham, Calumet Heights, Auburn-Gresham, Washington Heights, Roseland, and South Shore. Most of the African Americans still live in highly segregated communities. The exceptions to segregation are Hyde Park (where the University of Chicago is located), Kenwood,

Beverly, areas around the Loop, and the north lakefront communities of Lincoln Park, Lake View, Uptown, Edgewater, and Rogers Park, where there has been an increasing but scattered African American population. Despite these changes, Chicago is still rated as one of the most segregated cities in the country. Integration has often been the period between the time that the first African American family moves in and the last white family moves out. In 2001, two decades after Chicago agreed to integrate its public schools, only 9.6 percent of students in these schools were white; forty-eight percent of the white students in the city attended private schools.

At the time of the 2000 U.S. Census, five of the city's seventy-seven community areas had virtually no African Americans, while twenty-two community areas were more than ninety-five percent African American. The patterns of segregation, however, seem to be less rigid than in the past. Some African Americans now live in most parts of the city, the major exceptions being much of the Northwest and Southwest sides. The recent movement of small but increasing numbers of African Americans into the North Side lakefront communities has been without any noticeable incidents. Also, some residential intergroup mixing seems to have occurred in recent years in communities with a sizable Hispanic population such as Uptown, West Town, Rogers Park, Lake View, South Deering, New City, Chicago Lawn, Edgewater, Humboldt Park, and South Chicago. In some cases, whites have been moving into certain well-located African American neighborhoods, particularly around the downtown area, raising the fear among some African Americans that the low- and moderate-income African American residents of these areas will be displaced.

In recent decades, further expansion of African American residential areas on the South Side continued in Roseland, West Pullman, South Deering, West Englewood, Auburn Gresham, South Chicago, Burnside, Calumet Heights, and into Chicago Lawn in the Marquette area. The West Side African American area expanded westward in Humboldt Park and Austin to the city limits. Bronzeville in the communities of Douglas and Grand Boulevard, once the heart of the Black Belt, is now reviving after decades of decay, with parts being gentrified for more-prosperous African Americans. An effort is being made to preserve some of its historic sites.

In recent years, African Americans have been facing increasing job competition, especially from the growing number of Hispanics in the area. In addition, the complete shut-down or movement of manufacturing jobs out of Chicago and into the suburbs has especially hurt the large numbers of unskilled or semi-skilled city-dwelling African Americans who had been dependent on those factory jobs. For example, in 1970, 53 percent of Chicago's African Americans occupied blue-collar jobs, compared with 34 percent of non-African Americans. Reaching suburban jobs from the city's African American areas is often financially unfeasible for African Americans, as opposed to whites, because the median household income of an African American family in the Chicago area is only about 50 percent of the median household income of a white family. This is true despite African American incomes having increased 18.9 percent in the 1990s, versus an increase of 14.9 percent for white households. Moreover, some tacit forms of housing discrimination are still practiced in some suburban areas. The decline in blue-collar jobs in the city has led to social problems,

including the increase in frustration, crime, and the single-parent family.

Although most of the suburbs have enacted open housing laws and the number of African Americans in the suburbs keeps increasing, the percentage of the total metropolitan-area African American population living in the suburbs has increased only moderately. African Americans now comprise 9.3 percent of the six-county suburban population, up from 6 percent in 1980. Some of the suburbs still house no African Americans at all, and a few have merely token integration. Fairly sizable African American populations in predominantly white suburbs are found in some communities, including Evanston, Zion, Summit, Bolingbrook, Oak Park, South Holland, Justice, Glenwood, and Park Forest. African Americans now comprise a majority of the population of Calumet Park, University Park, Phoenix, Broadview, Bellwood, Country Club Hills, Calumet City, Dolton, Hazel Crest, Matteson, Riverdale, Maywood, Markham, Harvey, and Dixmoor. However, about two-thirds of the suburban African Americans still live in older industrial satellites such as Gary, East Chicago, Chicago Heights, Waukegan, North Chicago, Aurora, Elgin, and Joliet or in such African American ghetto suburbs as Robbins, Phoenix, and Ford Heights. Most of the largely all-white suburbs have steadfastly resisted the construction of any public housing, at least partially because of the fear that it would attract low-income African American residents.

In recent decades, a declining birthrate, dwindling migration from the South, and some reverse migration to the South, coupled with continuing expansion of African Americans into formerly white neighbor-hoods, took pressure off some of the crowded

African American ghettos, although there has been some immigration from African countries, such as Nigeria and Ethiopia. In recent years, the expansion of African American residential areas within Chicago has been much more rapid than the growth of the African American population. Though much still needs to be accomplished, in recent decades the African Americans of the Chicago area, as a whole, have achieved significant gains in housing, employment, education, and political power. But, while the expanding African American middle class has made substantial progress, a sizable number of African Americans continue to live in poverty.

The Hispanics

From 1980 to 2000, Chicago's Hispanic population increased by 78 percent, from 422,061 to 753,644. Hispanics now comprise 26 percent of Chicago's population. These figures generally do not include illegal aliens, mostly Mexicans, who may number as many as several hundred thousand, according to U.S. Immigration and Naturalization Service data. The Spanish-speaking community is now the second-largest minority group after the African Americans, and in recent years, it has been by far the most rapidly growing segment of Chicago's population. Chicago now ranks third nationally in the number of its Hispanic residents, trailing only New York and Los Angeles.

Chicago is the only major city in the United States that has a sizable representation of each of the nation's three major Spanish-speaking groups—Mexicans, Puerto Ricans, and Cubans. It has the largest Mexican population in the United States outside Los Angeles

and the largest Puerto Rican population in the country outside New York. In addition, smaller numbers of immigrants (some of whom are well-educated professionals) from more than a dozen other Latin American countries have settled in various parts of Chicago. It is estimated that of the Hispanics in the city, 70 percent are Mexican, about 15 percent are Puerto Rican, 1 percent are Cuban, and the remainder are from other Latin American countries.

Although the Hispanic groups have come from different geographic backgrounds, they have certain characteristics in common, in addition to their common language. They are relatively recent arrivals in Chicago, but like their European predecessors, they came mainly for the economic opportunities and, to a lesser extent, for the political and social freedom. Because many generally lack sufficient education and urban job skills, and because some cultural and racial discrimination persists, most find themselves competing for the poorer-paying, often menial jobs of the unskilled laborer. Many do not have regular or full-time employment. Some live in the decaying older areas that have been abandoned by previous immigrant groups.

Many Hispanic immigrants to Chicago lack an adequate knowledge of the English language. Indeed, Spanish is the second language of the city, with public telephone, transit, and emergency directions usually written in the two languages. The lack of adequate knowledge of English hinders the Hispanics both economically and politically. They are also handicapped by their relative newness to Chicago, the frequent lack of cooperation among the various Hispanic groups, and the fact that many Hispanics, especially Mexicans, cannot vote because they are not citizens. The Mexicans are the least assimilated of the major Hispanic groups and tend to drop out of school at a high rate. These handicaps, plus skillful gerrymandering by the entrenched political machine, prevented Hispanics from obtaining their fair share of political representation, despite their occupation of large contiguous areas. However, their rapid population growth in recent years has greatly increased their political clout, representation, and public employment. Many have succeeded in business ventures, often catering to their own groups.

The Hispanic immigrants who came to the United States included skilled professionals, some political refugees, and especially, poor peasants and those from small villages. Although they have much in common, each of the major Hispanic groups has its own history of development and settlement in the city and each group generally lives in its own separate and distinct community.

The major groups are sometimes at odds with each other. The Cubans are generally conservative white-collar professionals interested in the overthrow of Cuba's communist government. They are also interested in immigration, as are the Mexicans, who are, however, mainly blue-collar laborers and generally liberal. The Puerto Ricans also tend to be liberal, but unlike the other two groups, they do not have immigration problems because they are U.S. citizens. However, their average income is the lowest of the groups, ranking even below that of African Americans, despite their probable status as the most Americanized of the Hispanic groups.

The Mexicans

Mexicans were the earliest Hispanic migrants to Chicago and remain the largest segment of the Spanish-speaking community. They began to arrive in Chicago after the start of the Mexican Revolution in 1910. Many came from rural areas. The migration accelerated greatly around the time of World War I, when the demand for labor was great, especially by the steel mills but also by the railroads and the stockyards. Migration accelerated again during World War II and the ensuing years of industrial prosperity.

In many ways, the Mexicans who settled in Chicago followed the same patterns and encountered the same problems as other immigrant groups, such as prejudice toward a different culture, fear of invasion by large and growing numbers, and fear of job competition, although they are a reliable and hard-working group, fulfilling many of our nation's job needs. The Reverend Patrick J. McPolin traced the history of Mexican immigrants in 1975 with a speech titled "Mexicans in Chicago":

> [T]he slow trickle of Mexican laborers crossing the border in 1911 rapidly enlarged to the proportions, first of a river, then a flood. Letters began to make their way back into the homes of those families whose relatives or friends had gone to the United States, and they told of a land of peace and plenty, where men in those times were paid $3.00 to $6.00 a day in wages. Often the marvelous character of the story grew as it was repeated and people came in ever-increasing numbers. First the single men, followed by those family men who could arrange to leave their families behind until growing wealth would justify bringing them into a new home in Chicago. Lastly came the family groups who moved North as units. This immigrant flood began in 1922 and continued through the twenties . . . all moving here for one basic reason—in

search of a life better both economically and socially than the one they had known. In brief, the roads they traveled were these:

1. As workers in maintenance gangs of railroads, where they transferred from point to point until they reached a railroad workers' camp in the outlying section of Chicago.

2. Employment agents of the steel mills hired them and brought them there.

3. They themselves came directly to Chicago to find work on the representations of friends who were already working here.

4. And at the close of the various harvest seasons in Michigan and Minnesota, they came to Chicago rather than return south.

In the beginning there were difficulties—many difficulties. The Chicagoans in the '20s and '30s, in general, made little effort to integrate the Mexicans into their society. We find the Mexicans live in the shabbiest quarters in the city, not from choice but from economic necessity. And thus, it was mostly in the manufacturing and commercial quarters that the Mexicans found welcome.

Once started within a given neighborhood, the colony grew by ties of race, and the bewildered newcomer naturally seeks out a place to live among his own. He finds within the colony a strong spirit of group cohesion and an element of group consciousness exercising a governing control over the entire colony through the force of public opinion.... [A]lso in the field of industry, the Mexican soon found that he was welcome only as an unskilled laborer at jobs which were the dirtiest and most uncomfortable.

The first areas they came into were the railroad neighborhoods of Clyde-Cicero and around the McCormick and Crane Works. There were also hundreds who lived in boxcars in the shadow of what is now the Merchandise Mart. They moved from these temporary quarters to areas like Lake Street, Polk Street, and finally Roosevelt Road. This latter group was the beginning of the largest Mexican colony—the West Side colony. In addition to this area the Mexicans moved into the South Chicago steel mill area, and into the stockyards district....

Along came World War II. It was a great leveler.... The first generation of Mexicans began to move away from the barrio into neighborhoods where previously Mexicans were unwelcome. Even the traditional Mexican neighborhoods changed—and we find the shift from 12th Street to 18th Street ... and now to the Lawndale Area.

In 1910 the U.S. Census listed only 102 foreign-born Mexicans in Chicago; by 1920 the number had increased to 1,224; and by 1930 it had swelled to 14,733, but Mexicans still comprised only about 0.4 percent of the city's population. During these prosperous decades, Mexicans were hired because they were hard-working, reliable laborers who accepted lower wages than did the incoming European immigrants. As their numbers increased, they clustered in colonies near their work. Because many Mexicans hoped to return eventually to their homeland, they initially adhered strongly to their own traditions instead of integrating into American cultural patterns. However, the Mexican birth rate is very high and the average age is low, with the young population having fewer ties to the Old Country.

FIG. 5.9. Mexican workers in Willow Springs, twenty-one miles southwest of Chicago, 1917. Photograph by *Chicago Daily News*; Chicago Historical Society, DN-0068516.

The oldest Mexican settlement is in South Chicago. There, in 1925, a Catholic chapel was constructed; it later became Our Lady of Guadalupe at 3100 East Ninety-first Street. Because Mexicans are traditionally a religious people, it was just one of numerous Catholic churches gracing their neighborhoods. Most of the Mexicans in this settlement lived near the U.S. Steel plant in the Mill Gate and Bush areas, or around the Wisconsin Steel plant at 106th Street and Torrance Avenue (2634 E.). Their main shopping area was, and continues to be, around Ninety-second Street and Commercial Avenue (3000 E.). At present, mostly second- and third-generation Mexicans live in this area, as do increasing numbers of African Americans and some Puerto Ricans. In 2000, Mexicans comprised about one-third of the population of South

Chicago and, in adjacent South Deering, much of the Mexican housing was owned by other immigrant groups who charged high rentals, often forcing Mexicans to crowd more people into their apartments to help defray the cost.

Some Mexicans lived in the ethnically diverse Back of the Yards area of the New City community as a result of having worked in the stockyards during World War I. A larger Mexican community, one that has all but disappeared, once thrived in the very poor Hull House–Halsted Street area near the railway yards. The Mexicans in this area numbered seven thousand to eight thousand and were aligned sporadically along Halsted Street from Harrison Street (600 S.) to Fifteenth Street. The area contained a number of Mexican churches, the most important being St. Francis of Assisi at 813 West Roosevelt Road. This community diminished in numbers during the Depression years of the 1930s, when many Mexicans returned home. It then grew somewhat during World War II, when employment was high. At that time, some fifteen thousand Mexican contract laborers (braceros) were brought in temporarily under international treaty, joining an influx of Mexican Americans from Texas. The neighborhood was largely demolished, however, during the 1960s with the construction of the campus of the University of Illinois at Chicago. U.S. immigration policy has been, and continues to be, a persistent issue for the Mexican community.

In recent decades a major Mexican settlement developed in the Pilsen area and then spread farther west to the La Villa Chiquita (Little Village) area. Both of these areas had been predominantly Czech and Polish until after World War II, when Mexicans from the Halsted–Hull House area began moving in, along with large numbers of new arrivals from Mexico, many of whom came illegally. The large influx of immigrants created a need for larger Mexican communities and slowed the dreams of assimilation of earlier Mexican Americans. Today the illegal status of many of the newcomers also means that they are willing to work for low wages at jobs that other groups have refused. These wages, however, are still much better than what they could earn in Mexico. Although they often work as dishwashers, waiters, busboys, bellhops, janitors, transit drivers, gardeners, and factory workers, many have become successful small entrepreneurs, usually catering to the Hispanic population. Relatively few Mexicans are on public welfare. There

are also many helpful Mexican community organizations, some of which are Mexican hometown associations.

Pilsen, a port of entry for many immigrants, has been transformed into a vibrant Mexican community. Signs and banners in Spanish are everywhere, as are colorful patriotic, religious, and political wall murals. Mexico's Independence Day and Cinco de Mayo are marked with parades and bands. Barbershops have become barberias, groceries have become supermercados, and hot dog stands are now taco stands. Churches founded by the Czechs, such as St. Procopius at Eighteenth and Allport (1234 W.) and St. Vitus at Eighteenth Place and Paulina (1700 W.), are now utilized chiefly by the Mexicans as Hispanic Catholic churches. Hispanic Protestant churches are uncommon. The main business streets of the Pilsen community include Eighteenth Street from Halsted to Western, Blue Island from Eighteenth Street to Cermak Road, and Ashland from Sixteenth Street to Cermak Road. At the intersection of Blue Island, Cermak, and Ashland, Benito Juarez High School, the first public school constructed in the area in the twentieth century, was opened. It offers bilingual instruction. Pilsen contains some of the oldest housing in the city, but architecturally it has some of the most interesting and varied buildings. Much of the housing in the area is rental. Pilsen is the highest-density Hispanic community in Chicago. One of the numerous cultural institutions in Pilsen is the recently enlarged Mexican Fine Arts Museum at 1852 West Nineteenth Street. It was founded in 1982 and has a significant permanent collection of Mexican art, in addition to many special exhibits.

In the 1950s the Mexicans started to overflow to the west, mainly into South Lawndale. They replaced the Czechs, who

FIG. 5.10. Blue Island Avenue near Eighteenth Street, looking southwest, 2005. The street is one of the main business thoroughfares of the growing Mexican community in the Pilsen area of Chicago. The community once consisted largely of people of Czech and Polish descent. Photograph by Irving Cutler.

FIG. 5.11. Casa Aztlan, a Mexican community center at 1831 S. Racine Avenue in the Pilsen neighborhood, 2005. The building previously had served as a Czech community center. Photograph by Irving Cutler.

FIG. 5.12. One of many street vendors along Twenty-sixth Street in the Mexican Little Village neighborhood, 2005. Photograph by Irving Cutler.

were moving into the western suburbs. The Mexicans who moved into this area, La Villa Chiquita, were generally wealthier than their Pilsen counterparts. Many were second- or third-generation Mexican Americans, and many owned their own homes and shops. If Pilsen resembles a poor, crowded Mexican barrio, La Villa Chiquita resembles a Mexican "suburb." About four square miles in size, its main shopping streets are Cermak Road, from about Western Avenue to Kedzie Avenue; and Twenty-sixth Street, from about Albany Avenue (3100 W.) to the city limits at Cicero Avenue (4800 W.). Few Czechs or other Slavs remain in the area, and those who do are typically elderly. Eighty-three percent, or 75,613, of the people of South Lawndale are now of Mexican descent. This area, with its "south of

the border" atmosphere, is hoping to attract tourists to its many restaurants, bakeries, interesting stores, and outdoor vendors.

Recently Mexicans have moved to the south of Pilsen and South Lawndale. For example, the 2000 census data revealed that the late Mayor Richard J. Daley's Irish Bridgeport community was about 25 percent Mexican. Similarly, there are sizable and growing numbers of Mexicans in McKinley Park and New City—about 50 percent each—and in Brighton Park, where about 70 percent, or 31,218, of a total community population of 44,912 are Mexican.

In recent decades, some of the more affluent Mexicans have left the old, crowded, often drug- and crime-infested Hispanic communities in Chicago for the suburbs in Cook, Lake, Kane, and Du Page counties—especially

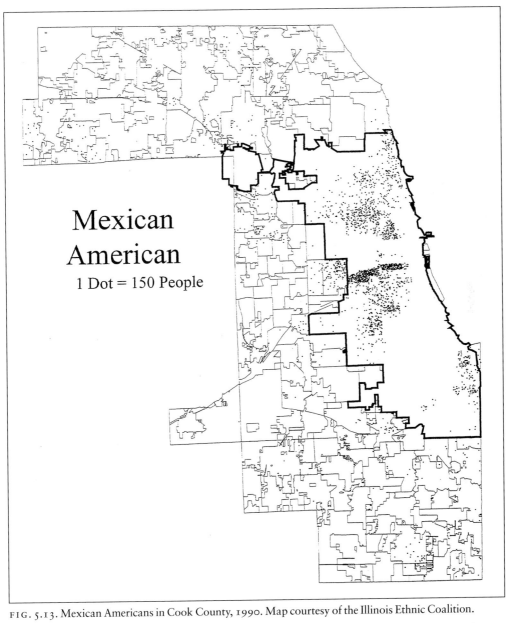

Mexican
American
1 Dot = 150 People

FIG. 5.13. Mexican Americans in Cook County, 1990. Map courtesy of the Illinois Ethnic Coalition.

FIG. 5.14. Former Serbian church, now Hispanic, 1994. Until the early 1980s a small Serbian community lived in the vicinity of Schiller (1400 N.) and Wicker Park (1800 W.) avenues. Photograph by Irving Cutler.

those cities with job opportunities, such as Joliet, Waukegan, Elgin, Aurora, Berwyn, Melrose Park, West Chicago, Blue Island, and Cicero. Among Cicero's population of 85,616, 58,542 are Mexican. About 54 percent of the Mexicans of the six-county metropolitan area now live outside Chicago. There are also Mexicans in parts of industrial northwest Indiana, especially in East Chicago. Some Mexicans who arrived decades ago as migrant workers for farms and nurseries in the urban-rural fringe areas were among the first Mexican suburbanites, never having lived in Chicago.

The Puerto Ricans

Puerto Ricans are the second-largest Hispanic group in Chicago, numbering about 113,000 in the city and about seventeen thousand in the suburbs. The relatively small numbers of Puerto Ricans in the suburbs, like the Mexicans, live largely in industrial communities. They are relative newcomers to Chicago even though they have been citizens of the United States since 1917. The Census Bureau first enumerated Chicago's Puerto Ricans as a separate classification in 1960. They entered the Chicago area mainly after World War II, some via New York City, where the job market became saturated in the 1960s. Also, after 1960, low-cost direct air service was established between Chicago and San Juan. As American citizens, Puerto Ricans can move freely between the United States mainland and their sunny but relatively poor and crowded island. Many move back and forth between Chicago and Puerto Rico, shifting between two cultures and never establishing deep roots in Chicago. Their movement frequently depends on the respective economic conditions of the two areas. Some of the movement, however, is due to homesickness, and a small amount is seasonal, with some Puerto Ricans returning home during the middle-latitude winter.

At times, migration of Puerto Ricans out of Chicago has been greater than migration into Chicago. Many Puerto Ricans have returned to their island because of unemployment in Chicago or the low pay for unskilled jobs. Others have left because of difficulties with language, overcrowded housing, and a desire to remove their youth from areas with gang, drug, and crime problems. At present, the Puerto Ricans have the lowest average income and the least amount of schooling of any minority group in Chicago. Many work in restaurants, hotels, and hospitals; some work in factories. Like other Hispanic groups they are young, with an average age of twenty-one.

Despite improving economic conditions in Puerto Rico, many still find conditions in Chicago more favorable. Their continuing migration to Chicago, together with their large families, accounts for the increase of Puerto Ricans in Chicago. They, like most Hispanics, have strong family ties.

Some of the earlier Puerto Rican settlers lived in scattered areas, including the South Side communities of Woodlawn and South Chicago. Some lived near established Mexican communities and, initially, still others lived near African American communities. The Puerto Ricans sometimes had a stronger racial association with the African Americans than did the Mexicans. Unlike the African Americans, however, comparatively few Hispanics lived in public housing.[7]

Most Puerto Ricans, however, soon concentrated on the North and Northwest sides, miles north of the major Mexican communities. Today the major Puerto Rican community is concentrated in West Town, Logan Square, and Humboldt Park and is continuing to expand northward into Hermosa, Belmont Cragin, Avondale, and Albany Park. Puerto Ricans now comprise a third of the population in Humboldt Park and a fourth in Logan Square. Division Street (1200 N.) is the area's main business street, with two huge, fifty-ton metal Puerto Rican flags along its main route. On Division at Western is the Roberto Clemente High School, built in the 1970s and named after a star Puerto Rican Major League baseball player who died in an air crash. Puerto Rican population growth has slowed in West Town, parts of which are being gentrified. Puerto Rican migration to the continental United States has slowed considerably in recent years.

A number of churches dot the Puerto Rican community, but their influence is not as great as in the Mexican community. Puerto Ricans have few of their own clergy. Only in the past few years have Puerto Ricans elected a few political representatives. Ideological differences and a certain degree of disunity among the various Hispanic groups have hampered their political efforts, although they are generally united in their desire to secure more jobs, better housing, and some bilingual education. Poverty, overcrowding, and a lack of political power have probably contributed to a number of Northwest Side riots that resulted from prior confrontations between the police and some Puerto Ricans—mainly youths—some

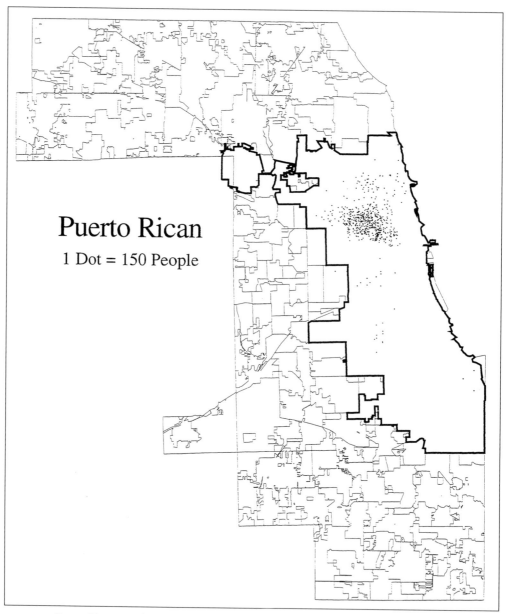

Puerto Rican

1 Dot = 150 People

FIG. 5.15. Puerto Rican population in Cook County, 1990. Most Puerto Ricans live on the Northwest Side of Chicago; relatively few live in the suburbs. Map courtesy of the Illinois Ethnic Coalition.

FIG. 5.16. Division Street near Damen Avenue looking east, 1975. The street is one of the main business thoroughfares of the Puerto Rican community on the Northwest Side of Chicago. In the background is the San Juan Theater, which featured Spanish-language films. The population of the neighborhood was once predominantly of Polish descent. In recent years, part of the area was being gentrified, forcing some of the Puerto Ricans to move out. Photograph by Irving Cutler.

FIG. 5.17. Changing neighborhood, depicted by the different ethnic stores at the intersection of Division, Milwaukee, and Ashland in the 1970s. At that time, the Polish population in the area was being replaced by Hispanics, mainly Puerto Ricans. Photograph by Irving Cutler.

of whom were agitating for Puerto Rican independence.

The Puerto Ricans have been the only Hispanics involved in major riots. Most are black or mulatto and are more vulnerable to racial discrimination than the other Hispanic groups. They have the highest rates of unemployment and welfare among Hispanics, and about 30 percent of households are headed by women. For years gang killings were most numerous in areas of high Puerto Rican concentrations. Because of their relatively low income, only about 15 percent of Puerto Ricans now live in the suburbs, compared with 54 percent of Mexicans. Puerto Ricans live primarily in those suburban communities with manufacturing jobs, such as Waukegan, Aurora, and Joliet.

Since the Puerto Rican riots of 1966 and 1977, conditions have improved with the increase of official attention paid to their problems. Numerous social agencies, such as Casa Central, help the Puerto Ricans. In 1993 the Pedro Albizu Campos Museum of Puerto Rican History and Culture was established at 1457 N. California Avenue (2800 W.). Every June since 1966 has seen a huge Puerto Rican parade with up to 150 floats. Joining it are such dignitaries as the mayor of Chicago, as well as City Treasurer Maria Santos, and Congressman Luis Guttierez, both Puerto Ricans.

The Cubans

There were few Cubans in Chicago until Castro took over Cuba in 1959. Then Cubans started fleeing their country in large numbers. The largest number settled in Florida, but many came to Chicago. They essentially came in three waves. The first wave of Cuban immigrants arrived in 1960 and consisted of political refugees. Many of them were white professionals, including doctors, teachers, engineers, and accountants; skilled workers; and entrepreneurs who had lost almost everything in the Cuban Revolution. The second wave came in the 1970s and consisted of people from more rural areas who were poor peasants or laborers with little education, many of them blacks or mulattos looking for better economic conditions. Some came to reunite with their families in the United States. The third wave occurred in 1980 and was composed of the Mariel boat-lift people: prisoners and malcontents disgorged by Castro into the United States.

Because the number of Cubans in Chicago is small, consisting of less than 1 percent of the Hispanic population, and is not growing, there are no concentrated Cuban settlements comparable to those of the Mexicans or Puerto Ricans. Most Cubans live dispersed on the North and Northwest sides of the city in communities of reasonable quality that have considerable ethnic and racial mixture. Small communities, each less than a thousand, are found in Logan Square, Edgewater, Uptown, Lakeview, West Ridge, Albany Park, and Portage Park.

Compared with other Hispanic groups in Chicago, the Cubans have tended to be older (their average age is thirty-four), have smaller households, are better educated, and possess greater employment skills, especially those of the first wave. Some are business owners of food markets and jewelry or retail clothing stores. Others are often employed in construction, real estate, and insurance. Some Cubans are factory workers. Only a small percentage of Cubans are unemployed, however. Their income is higher than that of other Hispanic groups, and the percentage who receive welfare is much lower. Forty-five percent

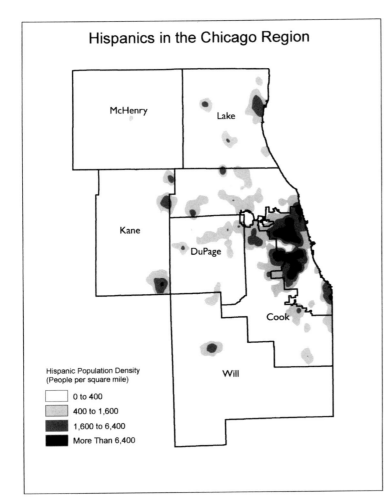

FIG. 5.18. Population density of Hispanics, mainly Mexicans and Puerto Ricans but some Cubans and others from Central and South America, residing in the six-county metropolitan area, 2000. The large Hispanic concentrations in Chicago exist especially on the Northwest and Southwest sides. Map courtesy of Chicago Metropolis 2020.

are home owners. Sixty-eight percent are foreign born. Cubans are sometimes resented by the other Hispanic groups because they were the last to come, yet are now the best off and tend to live among the white ethnics, having become the most assimilated. About 35 percent of the Cubans in the metropolitan area live in the suburbs, especially in northern communities such as Skokie and western suburbs such as Oak Park. The movement to the suburbs has helped to decrease Chicago's Cuban population from 11,513 in 1980 to

8,084 in 2000, although some Cubans have moved to Miami, where the climate is more like that of their homeland and where there is a larger concentration of their fellow countrymen. Unlike the Puerto Ricans and Mexicans, the Cubans cannot readily go back and forth to their homeland. Although Cubans remain interested in Cuba and are still mainly anti-Castro, with the passing years, their hope and desire to return to Cuba have diminished as they become increasingly well established in the United States. But, like other immigrant groups, they continue to send money to their families in Cuba to help improve their standard of living.

The Asians

Since the late 1960s, there has been a large influx of people from East and South Asia, as well as from the Middle East—Filipinos, Chinese, Koreans, Indonesians, Indians, Pakistanis, Thais, Vietnamese, Cambodians, Iranians, and Arabs. Their coming had been especially spurred by the turmoil in Southeast Asia and by the relaxation of immigration restrictions. By 2000, combining the various U.S. Census classifications for that area, there were about 125,000 people of Asian descent in Chicago, or 4.3 percent of the city's population, and about 380,000 in the metropolitan area, or 4.7 percent of the total population. Their growing number of small shops, restaurants, and religious and cultural facilities has added significantly to the cosmopolitan atmosphere of Chicago.

Many of the Asian immigrants were initially handicapped in their adjustment to life in Chicago by language and cultural differences, climatic differences, and some lingering employment and housing discrimination. However, with characteristic hard work and self-reliance, and because many of them were professionals, business people, or skilled craftsmen, most were able to overcome the obstacles they initially encountered. The largest concentration of Asians in Chicago is in about ten wards on the North and Northwest sides and in Chinatown on the South Side.

The Asians value education highly, and Asian students often rank highest in their classes in academic achievement. Although generally newcomers to the area, their 1999 median family household income is equivalent to the white population's income and is much higher than that of the Hispanics or African Americans. Because of their higher income, thousands have been able to move into attractive suburbs. It is estimated that about a third of the physicians in the Chicagoland area are now Asians.

In contrast to the generally well-off Asians in Chicago is the group of more recent arrivals from Southeast Asia. They fled that turbulent area under the most harrowing and perilous of conditions, which included long stays in refugee camps and attacks by pirates on their overcrowded vessels. Most are Vietnamese, with small numbers being from Cambodia and Laos. Many were helped by special U.S. government resettlement programs and by various other organizations. They are concentrated especially in poorer parts of Uptown, with smaller numbers in adjacent Edgewater and in somewhat more distant Albany Park and West Ridge. Many have language problems and encounter some difficulty in trying to pass their culture on to their youth.

About ten thousand of the fifteen thousand Vietnamese in the six-county metropolitan area live in Chicago. Their colorful and busy Vietnamese commercial strip of small businesses stretches for three blocks along Argyle Avenue (5000 N.) between Broadway and Sheridan Road in Uptown. In the 1970s this stretch of Argyle was envisioned as a Chinatown North by Jimmy Wong and other Chinese entrepreneurs who bought a number of buildings on the street. But Vietnamese soon started pouring into the area, and the street rapidly became more Vietnamese than Chinese. The numerous grocery stores,

FIG. 5.19. Looking east from Broadway along Argyle Avenue (5000 N.), at the predominantly Vietnamese shopping strip that extends some three blocks to Sheridan Road in Uptown, 2004. Photograph by Irving Cutler.

restaurants, gift shops, bakeries, and other shops draw customers (especially Asians) and curiosity seekers from all over the metropolitan area who are attracted by the variety of generally low-priced and exotic products. The late Charlie Soo, the "unofficial mayor" of Argyle Avenue and head of the local businessmen's association for many years, helped to improve and promote the street. He succeeded in having the Chicago Transit Authority (CTA) remodel its elevated station into one of Oriental design and art, including a colorful Oriental pagoda-style roof over the passenger platform.

Occupying the same areas of Chicago as the Vietnamese and Laotians are a few thousand Cambodians. They are among the poorest of ethnic groups, still recovering from the vicious killings by the Khmer Rouge in their homeland in the 1970s. They are mainly Buddhists and utilize the many Buddhist temples that have opened in recent years. The Cambodian Association in Uptown is trying to help the refugees, most from rural areas, who settled in Chicago mainly during 1979–85. A number have worked their way up economically and have moved into the suburbs.

A few hundred Japanese lived in Chicago prior to World War II, mainly in the Woodlawn–Hyde Park–Kenwood area. During the war, there was relatively little discrimination against them, unlike that encountered on the West Coast. Many were

FIG. 5.20. Japanese children attending Saturday morning classes at Loyola University to learn about their culture, 1977. Photograph by Irving Cutler.

students or graduates of the University of Chicago. After the war, their numbers increased as West Coast Japanese released from internment camps sought haven and jobs in Chicago, although some later returned to the West Coast. A small Japanese community, "Little Tokyo," was established around Clark and Division streets until it fell victim to such urban renewal as the large Sandburg Village development. The magnificent Midwest Buddhist Temple, built in 1972, is just to the north at 435 West Menomonee (1800 N.). About 60 percent of the Japanese of the Chicago area work in white-collar and professional occupations.

The Japanese community in the city today is largely scattered in North Side lakefront communities, especially in Edgewater, Lake View, Uptown, West Ridge, and the Near North Side. In recent years there has been little immigration from relatively prosperous Japan,

and the Japanese population has not increased significantly. The recent census showed fifty-five hundred people of Japanese descent living in the city, and another 17,500, especially the younger generation, living in such suburbs as Evanston, Hoffman Estates, Skokie, Arlington Heights, and Lincolnwood. The Japanese have assimilated rapidly and have a high rate of interracial marriage. Additionally, several thousand Japanese, representing Japanese business concerns, commonly reside temporarily in Chicago.

People from Thailand first started trickling into Chicago in the early 1950s and were composed largely of college students. In the last fifteen years the Thai population has increased markedly until, today, an estimated ten thousand live scattered across the North and Northwest sides and in the suburbs, especially Bridgeview. More than half of those employed work in the health field, many as doctors and nurses. Medical personnel found it easy to obtain visas when there was a shortage of health professionals in the United States. The Thai have established the Thai Buddhist Temple in Bridgeview to serve as both a religious and cultural center and as a service center for the immigrants adjusting to the new land. It is the largest of five Thai temples in the area, three of which are in the southwest suburbs. The Thai also help support about a dozen Thai groceries. Thai restaurants are increasingly popular with the general public, and there are now about two hundred scattered throughout the metropolitan area, with a number concentrated around the Lakeview-Uptown-Edgewater communities, as well as on the Near North Side. Because of the difficulty of adapting to an American diet, some produce was initially flown in from Bangkok to accommodate the Thai population. Now much of that type of produce is grown in the United States.

Filipinos first came to Chicago in the 1920s when their homeland was still an American possession and immigration was initially unhampered. Most were men who came alone. But William Howard Taft's "little brown brothers" found discrimination in employment and were confined largely to subordinate positions in the post office, to menial work for Pullman, and to labor in hotels and restaurants. By 1930 there were about two thousand Filipinos in the city. They formed a small colony on the Near South Side. The Filipino population remained small until the immigration laws were liberalized in 1965. By the year 2000 the ensuing wave of immigration increased their numbers to about twenty-nine thousand in the city and eighty-one thousand in the metropolitan area. They lived in such cities as Skokie, Waukegan,

Glendale Heights, Morton Grove, and North Chicago. The Filipinos had an advantage over other Asians in that they had been introduced to American culture, government, and language during the more than four decades that the United States ruled their homeland. The Filipinos are now probably the fourth-largest group currently immigrating to the Chicago area, after the Mexicans, Poles, and Indians.[8]

The Filipinos who have arrived in recent years have been generally well educated, with many professionals among them, including, like the Thai, many in the medical field, particularly nurses. Most live on the North Side (especially in Uptown, Lakeview, and Edgewater) and on the Northwest Side (Albany Park, West Ridge, Irving Park, and Lincoln Square), often near the hospitals where they work or near the CTA elevated lines. They are not as concentrated in clusters as other Asian groups, who are less familiar with American ways. They are relatively well-off economically. The 2000 census showed that their annual median household income, at $55,164, was the highest of any Asian group. Like most of the other Asian peoples, they keep a low profile. Because the Filipinos usually take care of their own, they have few public welfare cases. They also have relatively few delinquency problems, and their crime rate is exceptionally low. The Filipino-American Council of Chicago, an umbrella organization in the Rizal Memorial Center at 1332 West Irving Park Road (4000 N.), numbers dozens of member organizations that represent different homeland provincial groups, as well as various cultural and professional groups. It was founded in 1948. The facility is also used by other Asian groups of the area.

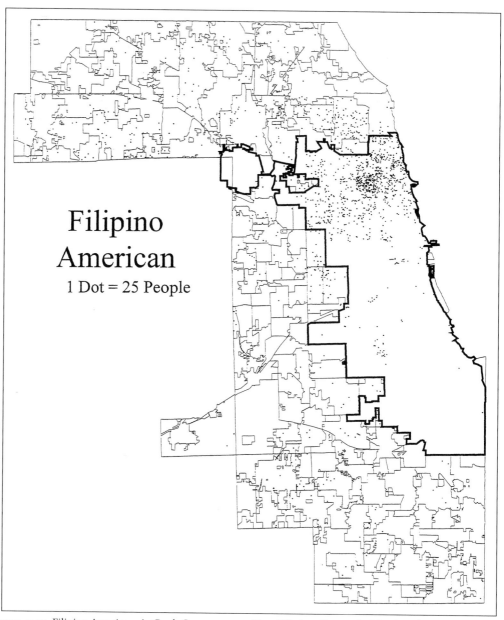

FIG. 5.21. Filipino Americans in Cook County, 1990. Most Filipinos live on the North and Northwest sides of the city and in the northern suburbs. Map courtesy of the Illinois Ethnic Coalition.

The Korean (South) population in metropolitan Chicago has grown from a few dozen families in the late 1950s to forty-five thousand in the 2000 census, with thirteen thousand living in Chicago. Some came as students and war brides after the Korean War, and many more came after immigration restrictions were eased in 1965. Like the recent Thai and Filipino immigrants, the Koreans are well educated, with many holding college degrees. Their number also includes many engineers, physicians, and nurses. Many Koreans settled first in Lakeview and Uptown, and Korean commercial establishments were opened along Clark Street. In recent years, as they have become established economically, the Koreans have moved outward geographically, some into the suburbs; but their greatest concentration is now found in the former largely Jewish community of Albany Park and nearby communities, such as North Park and West Ridge. The mile stretch of Lawrence Avenue between Kedzie Avenue (3200 W.) and Pulaski Road (4000 W.) now has many Korean-owned commercial establishments and has honorary Seoul Drive street signs. There are now more than thirty Korean restaurants in the city. Almost two hundred Korean churches are scattered throughout the various neighborhoods where Koreans live. Most of the churches are of the Christian faith, partly reflecting the intensive work of American missionaries in Korea. Since about 1990, many of the Korean churches have adopted English-language services for the younger generation, while keeping Korean-language services for their immigrant parents. The several Korean language newspapers, the largest being the *Korean Times*, boast a circulation of about fifteen thousand. Koreans live in such northern and northwest suburbs as Skokie, Glenview, Niles, Morton Grove, Mt. Prospect, Schaumburg, and Northbrook. In recent years, immigration has declined sharply as South Korea has become a prosperous nation. Some Koreans have returned home.

About 30 percent of working Koreans are self-employed as entrepreneurs—the highest percentage of the Asian groups. There are more than two thousand Korean laundry and dry cleaning stores and about a thousand Korean-owned grocery, restaurant, martial art, import trade, clothing, wig, and other facilities. The Korean median household income in 2000 for the metropolitan area was more than forty thousand dollars. Many stores were opened not only in Korean neighborhoods but also in African American neighborhoods, where there were many vacant stores but often high crime and insurance rates. There have been a number of episodes of friction between the African American residents and the Korean merchants. The African Americans have charged that they are often not treated in a fair manner and that the merchants do not contribute adequately to the community by employing local residents or by patronizing African American–owned banks. In recent years there has been an effort to improve customer relations and to overcome racial animosities. Another problem that Koreans, as well as other immigrant groups, face is dealing with the division between first- and second-generation Korean Americans.

Among the smaller Asian and Middle East groups in Chicago are the Assyrians, Armenians, Syrians, Indonesians, Iranians, and Arabs. The Assyrians, who in biblical times controlled a large empire in the Middle East, opened their first church in Chicago on the Near North Side in 1917. They are now mainly Christians. They gradually moved northward into Uptown, Edgewater, Rogers

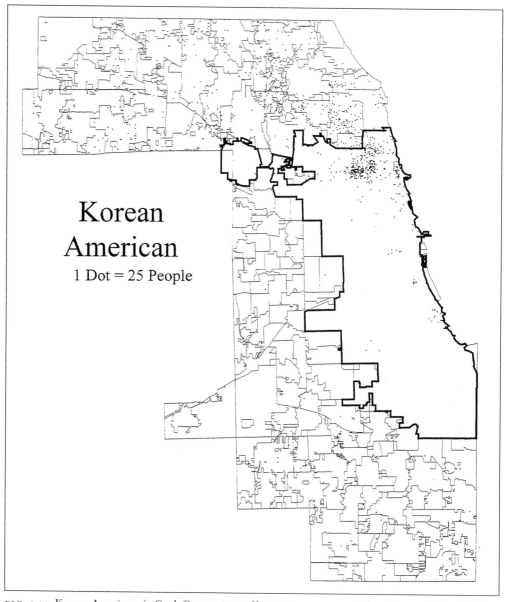

FIG. 5.22. Korean Americans in Cook County, 1990. Koreans are concentrated mainly on the North Side of Chicago and in northern suburbs, especially Skokie. Map courtesy of the Illinois Ethnic Coalition.

FIG. 5.23. Korean commercial strip in the 3300 block of West Lawrence Avenue (4800 N.), 1980. Many such stores are on Lawrence Avenue between Kedzie Avenue (3200 W.) and Pulaski Road (4000 W.). Photograph by Irving Cutler.

FIG. 5.24. Lawrence Avenue (4800 N.) in Albany Park, 2004, with an honorary "Seoul Drive" street sign. Also shown are a Korean restaurant and two Korean newspaper vending machines. Photograph by Irving Cutler.

FIG. 5.25. Changing ownership—from Jewish to Korean—of an institutional facility in the 4900 block of North Kimball Avenue (3400 W.), evidence of a population shift in the Albany Park community in the late 1970s. Photograph by Irving Cutler.

Park, and Albany Park and into such suburbs as Skokie, Niles, Roselle, and Morton Grove. They established five churches and other institutions, including a number on Devon Avenue in Rogers Park and a new one in Skokie in 2003. Their church services are in Aramaic, their ancient language. Chicago is believed to have the largest Assyrian population in the country: 15,683, according to the 2000 census. Many recent immigrants have come from Iraq after Saddam Hussein seized control there. They have also come from other hostile Middle Eastern countries. Their organizations try to help those left behind. Many are small shop owners or skilled workers. Many own North Side video rental stores, and others operate dollar-store franchises.

The first Syrians in Chicago arrived in 1893 as merchants, hoping to sell their products at the World's Columbian Exposition. However, by the outbreak of World War II only about thirty Syrian families lived in the city. Their population gradually increased after the Six-Day War in 1967. Many of them initially worked as street peddlers and later opened dry-goods retail and wholesale stores. Some catered to luxury tastes in linens and carpets.

The Armenians come from one of the oldest Christian countries in the world—an area that, for centuries, had been under Turkish or Russian rule. Some came in the early 1900s due to severe persecution in Turkey. Many initially lived in the Far South Side community of West Pullman. For a while, they were divided between pro-Soviet and proindependence groups. After gaining independence from the Russians in 1990, many left Armenia to join the small community in Chicago, which is mainly on the northwest fringe of the city and in the suburbs. Waukegan has a fairly sizable Armenian population and, for a number of years, had a mayor of Armenian descent. Armenians in the Chicago area tend to be businessmen, and they dominate the imported rug market.

There are only about six thousand Iranians in Chicago and perhaps as many as twenty-five thousand in the metropolitan area. Many came immediately before or just after the overthrow of their monarch in 1979. They represent a number of ethnic and religious groups, including Azeri, Turks, Kurds, Persian-speaking Muslims, Iranians, Lurs, and Bahá'í. The Bahá'í Temple in Wilmette is their religion's headquarters in the country. Some work as cab drivers, some are in the professions, and some opened small retail

stores and restaurants. Many live in or near Uptown, the location of one of their most famous restaurants, Reza's.

There are a growing number of Arabs, about eighty-five thousand in the metropolitan area, most of them of Palestinian origin but also immigrants from other Middle Eastern countries. Many came after a series of unsuccessful wars with Israel. The Palestinian Arabs live in two main areas of Chicago, one being Chicago Lawn on the Southwest Side, in the vicinity of Sixty-third Street between California Avenue (2800 W.) and Pulaski Road (4000 W.). They gradually moved farther west as African Americans and Hispanics moved in from the east. A number of Arab stores and institutions are along Sixty-third Street. As with the Korean retailers, there have been periods of tension between the Arab retailers and their African American customers. Another area

FIG. 5.26. Assyrian American Association at 1618 West Devon Avenue, established in 1917 and pictured here in 2004. Assyrians were among the first Middle Easterners to settle in Chicago. Two blocks to the west, at 1748 West Devon Avenue, is an Assyrian Pentecostal Church. Photograph by Irving Cutler.

FIG. 5.27. Arab facilities on the Southwest Side of Chicago at Sixty-third Street and Kedzie Avenue, 2003. The neighborhood also has Hispanic, Lithuanian, and African American residents. Photograph by Irving Cutler.

FIG. 5.28. Muslim women on Devon Avenue in the Indian-Pakistani shopping area, 2001. Photograph by Irving Cutler.

where Arabs, some of whom are Christian, are found is in Albany Park, along Kedzie Avenue (3200 W.) between Lawrence (4800 N.) and Montrose (4400 N.) avenues. There, a mixture of Palestinian, Lebanese, Iraqi, and Syrian, as well as Indian-owned stores, coexist. Some Arabs have moved into southwest suburbs, such as Bridgeview, Oak Lawn, and Hickory Hills.

There are only a small number of Indonesians from South Asia in the Chicago area, as many of them have opted for their former colonizer, the Netherlands. Even so,

the number of Indonesian restaurants in Chicago is increasing. In 2000 fewer than one thousand Indonesians were scattered throughout the metropolitan area.

Indians and Pakistanis

It is the groups from mainland South Asia that are growing very rapidly—people from India and Pakistan. Indians and Pakistanis come from two of the most populated, poorest countries in the world, where opportunities are often limited for even those with the best qualifications. Many highly educated Indians and, to a lesser extent, Pakistanis flocked to the United States after the immigration laws were changed in 1965. Some originally came as university students. Doctors, engineers, scientists, and college professors made up the first wave of these immigrants. With their professional skills and knowledge of the English language, they did well economically and moved quickly from such communities as Uptown into affluent suburban neighborhoods. More recent arrivals, however, are poorer immigrants who generally lack professional skills and struggle to move up the economic ladder. They often start as cab drivers, janitors, and office workers. The Indian and Pakistani population in the Chicago area has increased rapidly in recent decades. They now comprise about 30 percent of the Asian Americans in Chicagoland. Indians number about 114,000 in the Chicago metropolitan area, more than six times the Pakistani population. Only New York City has more Indians and Pakistanis.

The Indians and Pakistanis are dispersed throughout the metropolitan area, with sizable numbers residing in Skokie, Naperville, Schaumburg, Mount Prospect, Hoffman Estates, Hanover Park, Oak Brook, Glendale Heights, Downers Grove, Des Plaines, and Palatine. The commercial focal point of the Indian-Pakistani community is a stretch of Devon Avenue (6400 N.) in Chicago, from California Avenue (2800 W.) to about Damen Avenue (2000 W.), formerly a Jewish commercial strip. The change began in 1973 when an Indian sari company opened a store in Chicago; finding Loop rents too high, it settled for a vacant store on Devon Avenue. Other Indian and Pakistani merchants opened stores nearby, and the street soon became known as "Little India," a bustling, colorful marketplace for Indians, Pakistanis,

various Asian groups, and others who sometimes come from many miles away to shop. Aligned along the street are numerous sari, jewelry, electronic, grocery, butcher, gift, video, book, and other facilities. There are numerous vegetarian and other restaurants. A street-corner kiosk even sells regional language publications from the homelands, as well as English-language publications.

The street is crowded, particularly on weekends, with women dressed in their colorful saris. Merchandise from India is sold there, but much American merchandise is also for sale and is frequently purchased by more affluent members of the community to take along on family visits to India and Pakistan. At the intersection of California and Devon avenues is an honorary brown street sign on a west corner. It bears the name "Golda Meir," in reference to the Jewish commercial stretch that still exists west of California Avenue. On an east corner is another honorary brown street sign with the name "Ghandi Marq." East of Western Avenue are "Ali Jinnah" signs that honor the founder of modern Pakistan.

Indians and Pakistanis also operate retail stores in some of the suburbs. And scattered throughout the Chicago metropolitan area are numerous Dunkin Donuts franchises run by Indians or Pakistanis.

There are many regional linguistic groupings among the Indians. Each linguistic group has its own associations, and the older Indian generations usually associate with their own. There are about seventy non-Muslim Indian associations in Chicago. At times there has been friction between the different groups. However, the younger generations are essentially not involved in these regional groupings.

The Indians are one of the most economically successful ethnic groups in the Chicago

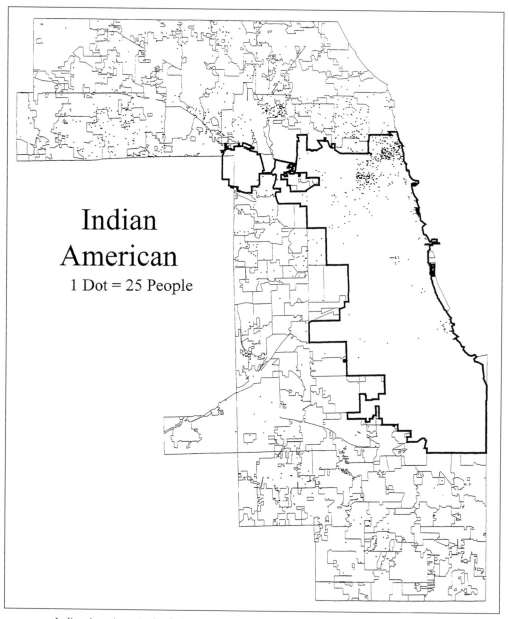

FIG. 5.29. Indian Americans in Cook County, 1990. Most live on the North Side, where their colorful, bustling commercial street is Devon Avenue (6400 N.). Map courtesy of the Illinois Ethnic Coalition.

FIG. 5.30. Indian sari dress stores on the 2600 block of West Devon Avenue in Chicago, 2003. Photograph by Irving Cutler.

FIG. 5.31. "United Nations" on Devon Avenue. Just east of California Avenue (2800 W.), an Israeli restaurant, a Russian bookstore, and a Muslim food store coexist in close proximity, 2001. Photograph by Irving Cutler.

area, and they are the third-largest immigrant group currently arriving in the area.

About 80 percent of the Indians of the area are Hindu, 7 percent are Muslim, and 5 percent are Sikh. The Hindus have a number of temples, including major ones in Aurora, Lemont, and a new one in Bartlett. The Hindu Temple of Greater Chicago in Lemont, dedicated in 1986, is situated on a twenty-acre site on a bluff above the Des Plaines River valley. It has an eighty-foot-high white front tower decorated with religious figures. The temple continues to expand through the years. Other religious Indian faiths have their own facilities. Caste considerations are usually ignored, except when it comes to marriage.[9]

The Pakistanis also have their own, mainly Muslim religious facilities. They also have their own educational and social facilities. They generally keep separate from the

Indians, although the two groups often live in close proximity and have had similar experiences, including some discrimination. Both groups, like other immigrant groups, worry whether the younger generations will preserve their Old World traditions. Both follow events in their homelands closely, but in Chicago their relations are more peaceful than those on the Indian subcontinent.

The Chinese

The city's oldest, most distinct, and most compact Asian community is the Chinese neighborhood, "Chinatown," about two miles south of the Loop. Today's prominent Chinatown community was preceded by the city's first Chinese community, which started in the late 1880s in downtown Chicago, along Clark Street (100 W.) south of Van Buren (400 S.). Most of the early Chinese were men who had come from the Canton area via San Francisco and had worked on the construction of the western railroads. Because of the Chinese Exclusion Act of 1882 and some local hostility, there were only 1,179 Chinese in Chicago in 1900.

In Chicago, many Chinese could initially find work only as cheap laborers in restaurants and as laundrymen, but through hard work and long hours they were soon able to establish their own restaurant and laundry facilities throughout Chicago.

FIG. 5.32. Looking north in Chinatown on Wentworth Avenue near Cermak Road, 1952. The original area of Chinese settlement was downtown, on South Clark Street. Photograph by J. Sherwin Murphy; Chicago Historical Society, ICHi-04881.

FIG. 5.33. Part of the new addition to Chinatown, 2003. Chinatown Square now occupies a large tract of land formerly owned by the Santa Fe Railroad. The development contains hundreds of new residential units, commercial facilities, and a twelve-acre park centered on a pagoda-style structure along the South Branch of the Chicago River. Photograph by Irving Cutler.

Around 1910, because the community was being compressed by the expanding downtown business community and because of some racial prejudice, Chinese businessmen purchased property and started Chicago's present Chinatown, around Cermak Road (2200 S.) and Wentworth Avenue (200 W.). It was an area where Italians and Croatians had been living and where real estate and rentals were cheap—partly due to the neighborhood being on the fringe of Chicago's notorious red-light "Levee" vice district. However, a small segment of the original downtown Chinatown remained until 1975, when the area was cleared to build the Metropolitan Correctional Center. The new Chinatown was concentrated in a few square blocks encompassed by railroads and later by two expressways. In that limited, crowded area

the Chinese developed a commercial district with a variety of stores that serve local needs. Numerous gift shops and, especially, restaurants attract many curious outsiders who come to shop and to enjoy the inexpensive, tasty Chinese food offered there. Celebrations such as the Chinese New Year and the Chinese Summer Fair, with its parades, entertainment, and cultural events, attract throngs of outsiders to the community. The imposing Chinatown Gate, completed in 1975; the many pagoda-style buildings; the red and green colors that symbolize luck and wealth; and the street signs in the Chinese language contribute to the ambience of the area.

Chinatown is largely a self-contained community, with many of its residents, especially the elderly, speaking only Chinese and rarely venturing outside the community. Although the neighborhood had a type of self-governance, it also encountered its share of problems. A major problem was the huge population imbalance that initially existed between Chinese men and women. Due to the exclusion laws and to China's reluctance, until recent decades, to allow women to leave their country, the men far outnumbered the women. This lopsidedness led to significant amounts of prostitution and gambling, with resultant gangs and fraud, which ultimately were prosecuted successfully by the government.

The Chinese population in Chicago increased significantly after World War II, when the Chinese exclusion laws were eliminated. The Chinese generally arrived in three waves: first, after the Chinese mainland became communist; second, during the Vietnamese War, when many Chinese fled Southeast Asia; and, more recently, after the United States and China established relations in the 1970s. The 2000 census listed 67,425 Chinese in the six-county Chicago metropolitan area, with 31,813 living in Chicago, especially in the Chinatown area. Smaller numbers reside in Uptown, around the new Chinatown North on Argyle Avenue, an area that now also has many Vietnamese.

The Chinese are becoming a more heterogeneous community, with Taiwanese, Indo-Chinese, American-born, racially mixed, and mainland Chinese. The mainland Chinese are the largest, most recent immigrant group and are primarily Mandarin, who are generally from a more-educated, higher social class than the earlier Cantonese immigrants. The

FIG. 5.34. Ping Tom Park at Eighteenth Street and the South Branch of the Chicago River in the Chinatown area, 2005. Photograph by Irving Cutler.

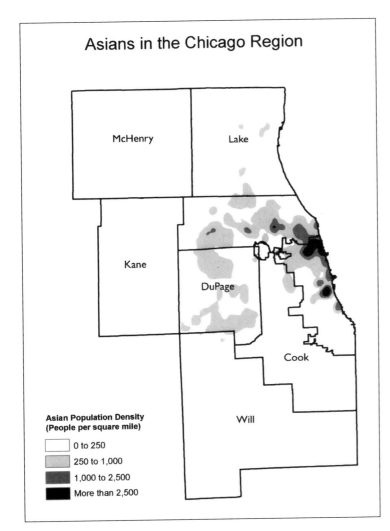

FIG. 5.35. Population density of Asians in the six-county metropolitan area, 2000. In the city, Asians live mainly on the North Side and in Chinatown, which is on the Near South Side. Relatively better-off economically than other immigrant or minority groups, most Asians now live in the suburbs, almost entirely those to the north and west. Map courtesy of Chicago Metropolis 2020.

immigrants, especially, keep a close watch on events in China, Taiwan, and Hong Kong.

Many Chinese are now college graduates and hold responsible jobs as professionals in such fields as medicine, engineering, and computers, where they are especially valued for their work ethic and are readily accepted by the broader community. The Chinese are especially strong in the restaurant industry. The Chicago metropolitan area has an estimated eight hundred to nine hundred

Chinese restaurants. However, Chinese laundries, of which there were about eight hundred in 1930, mainly in small, steamy storefronts, have largely disappeared because of the availability of washing machines and the ubiquitous laundromat. The second and third Chinese American generations are not as interested in Chinese mainland events as were their parents, who had vehemently protested the Japanese and communist takeover in

China. They still have strong family ties and, like other immigrant groups, have strong interests in education, housing, and social services that were previously supplied by the numerous Chinese organizations but are now increasingly provided by government agencies.

Major changes have recently taken place in Chinatown. The community has a Chinese Gate with the inscription in Chinese, "The world is for all"; a few new buildings, including a nine-story senior citizen home; a branch of the Chicago Public Library that has the largest branch circulation in the city for its size; a Chinese Christian church; and a Catholic elementary school. However, the surrounding area has undergone greater changes.

Due to the influx of recent Chinese immigrants, Chinatown was becoming increasingly crowded and, in recent decades, has surged beyond its old boundaries. To the north of Cermak Road is a new Chinese-style two-level commercial strip known as "Chinatown Square." Built in Chinese-style architecture are numerous store facilities, doctors' offices, and restaurants, as well as a Walgreens Drug Store with a large sign in Chinese. Behind this new commercial strip is the Santa Fe Garden project, which consists of a large tract of land once owned by the Santa Fe Railroad that now contains about four hundred housing units—condos, townhouses, and single-family houses. Also there are a new Chinese community and service center and, along the south branch of the Chicago River, the beautiful, new twelve-acre Ping Tom Memorial Park, with its pagoda-style facility. To the south, the Chinese have moved in large numbers into the Irish-founded Bridgeport community. Of the eighteen thousand Chinese who live in the greater Chinatown area, ten thousand now live in Bridgeport and eight thousand live in Chinatown. With the overall improvement in conditions in Chinatown, plus higher-quality, readily available housing, many Chinese professionals and retirees who had spread out through the years into other parts of Chicago and into such suburbs as Skokie, Morton Grove, Lincolnwood, and Naperville, are now returning to their old neighborhood.

The Native Americans

Native Americans lived and passed through Chicago many centuries before the coming of the white man. The tribes included the Potawatomi, Miami, and Illinois. About twenty-one thousand Native Americans now live in the Chicago metropolitan area; about half live in the city itself. They originate from over forty tribes and represent diverse cultures and geographical areas. They are especially concentrated in the Uptown area, where an American Indian Center at 1630 West Wilson Avenue (4600 N.) offers meeting facilities and a great variety of social services, senior citizen and youth programs, and cultural enrichment opportunities. Its exclusively Native American board of directors comes from a variety of tribes. Founded in 1952, it is the oldest urban Native American center in the United States.

The Native Americans found it difficult, initially, to make the transition from their tribal, rural lifestyle to the complicated life of the big city. They often have more problems than those who come from foreign lands. Compared with the general population, Native Americans are more likely to be poverty-stricken, to have more female-headed households, and to be mobile within the metropolitan area, often jumping back and forth between their tribal reservations and the city.

Some Native Americans are professionals, but many work as laborers or household workers.

Socioeconomic Patterns

The Chicago metropolitan area consists of several hundred communities. Seventy-seven are recognized as neighborhood community areas in Chicago, with the remainder being suburban municipalities (see Fig. 4.2). These seventy-seven communities display a great range of socioeconomic conditions. This range is indicative of the diverse racial, ethnic, and educational backgrounds of their inhabitants, and of the substantial variation in the opportunities available to them. The median annual household income in Chicago in 1999 was $38,625, ranging from $10,739 for the South Side community of Oakland to $68,269 for the Far Northwest Side community of Forest Glen. In general, the lowest income levels are found in the crowded inner-city African American areas on the South and West sides. Chicago's average household income is highest near the lake but also increases to the north, northwest, and southwest. It is also high in the later-settled peripheral communities of the city, such as Beverly, Mount Greenwood, Forest Glen, and Edison Park. However, average household income reaches its peak in the suburbs.

Just as there is marked variation in the economic status of the communities in Chicago, there is also great variation among the suburbs. Of the twenty-five wealthiest suburbs, fifteen lie to the north, six to the west, and four to the south of Chicago. The North Shore suburbs have such natural amenities as Lake Michigan and an interesting topography, as well as good commuter transportation to the Loop and extensive areas free of polluting industries. The poorest suburbs virtually all lie to the south of the city, with the largest African American suburbs of Robbins, Phoenix, and Ford Heights reporting some of the lowest incomes. Ford Heights has a median annual household income of $17,500, whereas Kenilworth, on the North Shore, has a median annual household income of more than $200,000. The median annual income for the six-county Chicago metropolitan area is $51,995.

Many of the economic elite of early Chicago once lived on the Near West Side, along fashionable Washington (100 N.), Ashland (1600 W.), and Jackson (300 S.) boulevards and on some of the adjacent streets, including the Union Park area. In the 1880s Potter Palmer led the way northward in settling along the "Gold Coast" of the lakeshore (just as in the 1860s his actions had established State Street as the retail heart of the city). This very-high-income axial development eventually reached the North Shore suburbs, including Wilmette, Kenilworth, Winnetka, Glencoe, Highland Park, and Lake Forest. The eastern part of Chicago's north lakefront area, including the Near North Side, Lincoln Park, and Lakeview, has the top socioeconomic ranking within the city. An almost solid array of expensive high-rise apartments and condominiums overlook Lake Michigan and line most of North Lake Shore Drive. They are occupied largely by young professionals, empty nesters, and affluent retirees; relatively few children live there. Until 1960 the western part of the Near North Side had been near the bottom in socioeconomic ranking, but by 2000, with substantial redevelopment and new buildings, especially condominiums, it has moved up substantially.

By the 1880s, high-grade housing to the south had spread from its location on Wabash

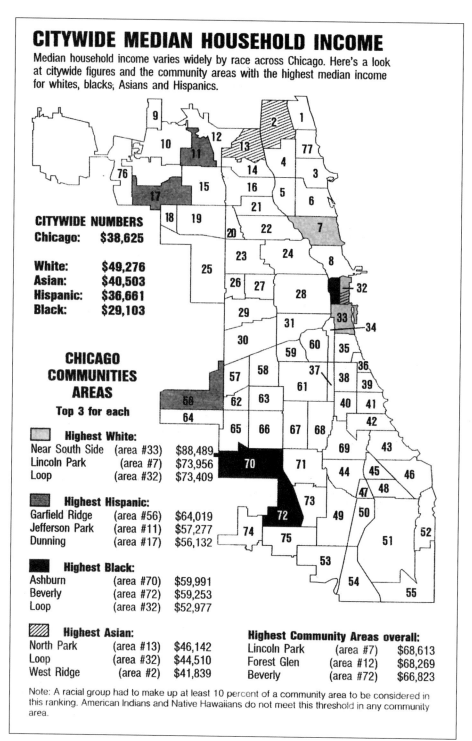

CITYWIDE MEDIAN HOUSEHOLD INCOME

Median household income varies widely by race across Chicago. Here's a look at citywide figures and the community areas with the highest median income for whites, blacks, Asians and Hispanics.

CITYWIDE NUMBERS

Chicago: $38,625

White: $49,276
Asian: $40,503
Hispanic: $36,661
Black: $29,103

CHICAGO COMMUNITIES AREAS

Top 3 for each

Highest White:
Near South Side	(area #33)	$88,489
Lincoln Park	(area #7)	$73,956
Loop	(area #32)	$73,409

Highest Hispanic:
Garfield Ridge	(area #56)	$64,019
Jefferson Park	(area #11)	$57,277
Dunning	(area #17)	$56,132

Highest Black:
Ashburn	(area #70)	$59,991
Beverly	(area #72)	$59,253
Loop	(area #32)	$52,977

Highest Asian:
North Park	(area #13)	$46,142
Loop	(area #32)	$44,510
West Ridge	(area #2)	$41,839

Highest Community Areas overall:
Lincoln Park	(area #7)	$68,613
Forest Glen	(area #12)	$68,269
Beverly	(area #72)	$66,823

Note: A racial group had to make up at least 10 percent of a community area to be considered in this ranking. American Indians and Native Hawaiians do not meet this threshold in any community area.

FIG. 5.36. Citywide and highest median household incomes by race and Chicago communities, 1999. As published in the *Chicago Sun-Times*. Copyright 2002 by Chicago Sun-Times, Inc. Reprinted with permission.

FIG. 5.37. Residences along North Dearborn Parkway (36 W.) in the Near North Side "Gold Coast" area near Lincoln Park, 2005. Many of the interiors retain memories of bygone Victorian elegance, although high-rise condominiums have encroached on the area. Photograph by Irving Cutler.

(45 E.) and Michigan (100 E.) avenues within the confines of today's downtown, southward along Indiana (200 E.), Prairie (300 E.), and Calumet (344 E.) avenues to about Twenty-sixth Street. On Prairie Avenue near Eighteenth Street, the location of the 1812 Fort Dearborn Massacre, there stood in the 1880s the mansions of some of the social and economic leaders of Chicago—Pullman, Armour, Glessner, Kimball, Buckingham, and

Field. This area was recently restored as an historic landmark. In time, with the spread of industry and immigrant groups in the area, and the threat of the growing Levee vice area to the west, many of the economic elite moved north to Lake Shore Drive or the northern suburbs. Some moved farther south, along Grand Boulevard (now Dr. Martin Luther King Jr. Drive; 400 E.) and Drexel Boulevard

FIG. 5.38. 700 North Green Street, 1949. Before the development of zoning laws, homes and industry were crowded together. Photograph by Mildred Mead; Chicago Historical Society.

(900 E.) into Kenwood and Hyde Park. Later they and others moved into South Shore, Beverly, and, bypassing the older Calumet industrial satellites, into suburban Homewood, Flossmoor, and Olympia Fields. A trend was developing for many of the higher-income and better-educated people—those who would ordinarily form a solid tax and leadership base for the city—to move to the suburbs.

In time, some of the older, high-income parts of the city deteriorated into the city's worst slums, as the rich and the middle class left and their homes were subdivided to accommodate the poorer migrants, especially African Americans and Hispanics. However, in recent decades, some of these areas, such as Prairie Avenue, have undergone massive urban renewal and redevelopment, reemerging as highly desirable residential locations. The major changes were fostered and aided by various government bodies, civic

FIG. 5.39. Looking north on Michigan Avenue from Eighth Street, about 1911. The twenty-two-story Blackstone Hotel had just been completed in 1909. The site of the homes was later to be occupied by one of the world's largest hotels, the Stevens (Conrad Hilton and Towers). Chicago Historical Society.

FIG. 5.40. Fashionable South Side residential area, 1893. The view is looking north on Prairie Avenue (300 E.) from about Twenty-First Street, 1893. Chicago Historical Society.

FIG. 5.41. New $1 million to $2 million single-family homes on the 1800 block of South Prairie Avenue, 2005. Built where the wealthy of Chicago lived more than a century ago, the new homes resemble in architectural style the nineteenth-century homes that once stood there. Photograph by Daniel Cutler.

groups, financial and real estate companies, and institutions such as large hospitals and universities.

While urban redevelopment, generally radiating outward from the downtown area, has been upgrading the older inner-city areas with much more expensive housing and some new commercial developments, the poor who once lived in these areas have been pushed outward. Once again, they have crowded into what were once stable neighborhoods, often creating new slums.

The redevelopment to the north, south, and west of downtown Chicago has been impressive in its scope, while in the downtown area itself, some twenty-six thousand new residential units were built in the 1990s. In recent years, the rapid sales of these residential units seem to reflect the desire of people to live not only close to where they work but also close to museums, theaters, concert venues, restaurants, nightclubs, parks, beaches, and other recreational attractions. Sales were aided for years by a strong economy, two-income families, and low interest rates.

Just north of downtown lies the River North area, which stretches westward to the North Branch of the Chicago River. The area has changed from a declining factory and warehouse area to one of Chicago's choice bustling communities, filled with restaurants, nightclubs, art galleries, and health clubs. It is the site of new high-rise buildings, as well as older buildings converted into upscale residential facilities, such as the huge former complex of Montgomery Ward and Company.

Farther north, stretching for almost a half mile and situated roughly between Division Street (1200 N.) and North Avenue (1600 N.), is Sandburg Village, completed in 1966 and containing nearly two thousand apartments (now condominiums) in an alignment of high-rise and low-rise buildings. This complex helped initiate the transformation of that rather run-down neighborhood and attracted mainly young white men and women.

Essentially to the west of Sandburg Village rests the city landmark Old Town area. It was a major German area after the Chicago Fire of 1871 until about World War II. North Avenue, its main commercial street, was sometimes referred to as "German Broadway." During and after World War II a housing shortage precipitated the subdivision of homes into rooming houses, a change that started deterioration of the area. In the 1960s Wells Street in Old Town became a commercial and entertainment street that attracted many tourists. At that time the neighborhood began attracting mainly young professionals who were drawn to the area's prime location, history, and low real estate prices, thus starting a boom in the renovation of old buildings and in the construction of new homes, some of which now sell for more than a million dollars.

Following in the footsteps of Old Town, communities farther to the west and northwest, such as the De Paul area, Wrigleyville, Wicker Park, and, more recently, Bucktown and Logan Square, are undergoing some renovation. Wicker Park, which radiates out from North (1600 W.) and Damen (2000 W.) avenues, where there is an El stop, has particularly undergone a major change. It was originally settled by wealthy Germans and some Scandinavians and was later occupied by Poles, some Jews, and, after World War II, many Hispanics. Starting in the 1970s, some young professionals began buying the once-stately mansions at low prices and renovating them. Others followed, and today the

FIG. 5.42. View east from the Ogden Avenue viaduct north of Division Street (1200 N.), 1954, showing part of the Near North Side that Harvey Zorbaugh described in his 1929 book *The Gold Coast and the Slums*. The Gold Coast consists of the luxury high-rise apartment buildings along the lakefront, barely visible in the background. Photograph by Lillian Ettinger; Chicago Historical Society.

area is largely trendy and gentrified. Real estate prices have skyrocketed, and restaurants, places of entertainment, art galleries, and even a used bookstore for the newcomers have spread throughout the area, which also boasts an annual art fair. Expensive new homes and condominiums have also been built. German, Polish, and Norwegian-founded hospitals reflect the diverse history of the area, as do the variety of churches. These include three Ukrainian churches in the Ukrainian Village, just to the south of Wicker Park, and the land-

mark, picturesque Holy Trinity Orthodox Cathedral, designed by Louis Sullivan in 1903 for Russian immigrants.

Among prominent businessmen who lived in the Wicker Park area were W. A. Wieboldt, A. N. Pritzker, Henry Crown, and some owners of the Schlitz brewing company. Michael Todd, the movie impresario, lived in the area, as did Nelson Algren, the writer whose novels depicted the area at one of its low points.

Of all of the residential growth in and around the downtown area, the greatest changes occurred to the west. The old skid

FIG. 5.43. Lake Meadows apartment community *(center)* looking northwest from Thirty-fifth Street, with the Illinois Central Railroad tracks at the lower right. Many of the apartments were later converted into condominiums. This predominantly African American community was developed by the New York Life Insurance Company as part of an urban renewal program in what had been one of the worst slums of the city. The development contains a shopping center, a public park, and a community center, as well as an elementary school and an office building. The high-rise complex to the right in the background is the adjoining Prairie Shores development, also predominantly African American. More than a century ago, much of this land was owned by Senator Stephen A. Douglas, who lies buried in the small park *(lower right)* just west of the tracks. A tall pillar, topped by a statue of the man, caps his tomb. Photograph courtesy of the Department of Urban Renewal, City of Chicago.

row that developed around Madison Street, from just west of the Loop to beyond Ashland Boulevard (1600 W.), has undergone a massive change from the days when it was lined with numerous flophouses, dozens of taverns, cheap restaurants, a half-dozen missions, and Salvation Army facilities, all catering to thousands of derelict men, each struggling with his own story and problems. In their place, starting at Clinton (540 W.) and Madison streets, are the four new beige high-rise Presidential Towers. They contain twenty-three hundred residential units. The redevelopment stretches almost two miles west, to the new United

Center (the stadium that Michael Jordan helped build) on a well-landscaped street lined with multistory, mid-rise condominiums and rentals.

More than twelve thousand new units have been built in the old skid row area within the last five years, and cranes continue to dot the skyline. Prices generally range from two hundred thousand dollars to eight hundred thousand dollars, with a few units set aside and priced at $150,000, due to governmental pressure for affordable housing. With the explosion in the area's population have come new retail establishments such as Starbucks, Blockbuster, and Dominick's. A flourishing

FIG. 5.44. Skid row in the shadow of downtown, 1974. The men are lined up to obtain a free meal from the Helping Hand Mission, 848 West Madison Street. Photograph by Irving Cutler.

FIG. 5.45. Madison Street looking west from Peoria Street (900 W.), 2004. Once a skid row with cheap flophouses, taverns, and eateries and numerous missions aimed at helping the destitute, the area has been transformed in recent years into a trendy residential area with upscale restaurants, Starbucks coffeeshops, and a landscaped median strip. Photograph by Irving Cutler.

restaurant row now exists on Randolph Street (150 N.), in the midst of the historic Randolph Street food market. Today it is not unusual to see a young woman walking a dog or riding a bicycle at dusk—something unheard of just a few years ago. Many of the residents are young urban professionals drawn by the area's great location and its opportunities for enjoying city life.

Largely missing from this area now, besides skid row, are the large, colorful ethnic communities to the south, such as the Italian neighborhood and Greektown. They were like small towns in the heart of the city, providing all necessities within walking distance. Now prominent in the area are, instead, the expanding University of Illinois at Chicago, opened in 1965; the huge Illinois Medical Center with the new Stroger Cook County Hospital; the Whitney Young Magnet School; the Chicago Police Training Academy; the Oprah Winfrey Studio; and a new thirty-nine-story residential high-rise ("Sky Bridge") on the corner of Madison and Halsted Streets.

The land south of downtown was, until about 1910, home to some of the wealthiest people in Chicago. Later, it became one of the worst slum, vice, and crime areas of the city, interspersed with expanding industry and huge railway facilities. It has also recently undergone tremendous change. The redevelopment stretches as far south as Thirty-fifth Street and even beyond. About two-thirds of the land available for development around the downtown area is to the south, where land is cheaper than that north of downtown.

The first major redevelopment was in the South Loop (now named Burnham Park) area, in Printer's Row. Aligned here, between Congress Street (500 S.) and Polk Street (800 S.), and standing along Dearborn Street (36 W.) and Plymouth Court (31 W.), were old, underused multistory buildings that formerly housed mainly printing and bindery establishments. In the 1970s developers took a chance and converted some of the buildings into rentals or condominiums, including artists' lofts and retail facilities. Their success not only revitalized the South Loop but also stimulated similar developments farther south, such as Draper and Kramer's Dearborn Park, a development of new townhouses and apartments south to Roosevelt Road and, later, farther south.

Large unit blocks of low-cost and underused land on the Near South Side, south of Roosevelt Road, were soon being developed at a rapid pace by different developers who were generally supported through the years by such area institutions as the Illinois Institute of Technology, Michael Reese Hospital, and Mercy Hospital. On the former site of the Illinois Central Railroad station there is now a huge residential development, the area's largest, called Central Station. It includes a number of tall buildings that already house a few thousand residents. This location is

desirable due to its proximity to the lake, Grant Park, the museums, and the downtown area. One of its residents is Mayor Richard M. Daley.

The southern end of the Central Station development also covers the Prairie Avenue Historic District, which is rapidly losing some of its historic luster as costly condominiums, town houses, single-family homes, and a new small park take over most of the area. The asking price of a new single-family four-story home on Prairie Avenue (300 E.), near Eighteenth Street is $1.8 million. Ultimately, Central Station is expected to house more than seven thousand families and will be the largest real estate development in Chicago history, measured by the number of buildings, acreage, new real estate taxes, and dollar value.

About a mile to the west, south of Roosevelt Road and along both sides of Halsted Street in what until the 1990s was the Maxwell Street market area, a whole new community is being built—University Village. The project is being fostered by the University of Illinois at Chicago, which lies directly to the north. Plans call for the sixty-eight-acre site to be developed with a mix of mid-rise residences, townhouses, two student dormitories, academic buildings, and shops and parks. There are about a thousand housing units, ranging in price from approximately $150,000 to $700,000. Further expansion will take place in the direction of the nearby South Water Produce Market, which is being phased out and its buildings converted into 824 condominiums. New, expensive homes are also being built on Halsted Street south of Fourteenth Street. To the south of University Village is the Mexican Pilsen community, where some residents fear that eventual

FIG. 5.46. Part of the new University Village of about one thousand residential units, which replaced the old Maxwell Street Market, 2003. The market was closed by the city in 1994 and demolished after more than a century of existence. Photograph by Irving Cutler.

FIG. 5.47. Sunday-only "Maxwell Street" Market, which stretches along Canal Street (500 W.) from Taylor Street (1000 S.) to Fifteenth Street, about a half mile east of the old market. The new market bears some resemblance to the original one, although Spanish, instead of Yiddish, is now the predominant language on the street, 2003. Photograph by Irving Cutler.

encroachment and gentrification will force the poorer Mexicans to leave.

In line with these ventures, the area to the south, Bronzeville—the heart of the African American community until its deterioration—is also being improved. On a seventy-acre tract of land once owned and developed by Senator Stephen A. Douglas (during the Civil War there was an army Camp Douglas situated there), redevelopment started in the 1950s and 1960s with the building of three major private high-rise housing developments—Prairie Shores, Lake Meadows, and South Commons. Once substantially integrated, they now house mainly African Americans. As the area continues to improve, many middle-class and professional African Americans are moving into the area.

Just to the west of Bronzeville, centered around Thirty-third and State streets, is the campus of the Illinois Institute of Technology (IIT), which is undergoing major expansion in housing and academic facilities. A new addition to the famous campus buildings designed by Mies van der Rohe is a new 550-foot-long dormitory designed by a well-known IIT alumnus, Helmut Jahn. Another improvement on the South Side involves the renovation or demolition of the troubled public housing projects, such as Ida B. Wells, Stateway Gardens, Dearborn Homes, and the Robert Taylor Homes.

Most of the city's redevelopment has taken place in and around the downtown area, often on the site of poor areas that had problems in the way of housing, crime, schools, drugs, and numerous vacant lots. Also visible, though often slight, are improvements in such communities as Uptown, Rogers Park, West Town, Humboldt Park, Kenwood, and

Woodlawn. One of the poorest communities, North Lawndale, now has a new large middle-class development called Homan Square, built on land that once mainly contained the large Sears, Roebuck and Company headquarters complex. It is partially subsidized by both the company and the city.

Theoretical Internal Arrangement of Chicago

Approximately eighty years ago, Professor Ernest Burgess of the highly respected Chicago school of urban sociology, proposed his concentric zone theory of the internal arrangement of cities. This theoretical model of urban structure, based largely on his studies of Chicago, postulated that the modern city consists of a pattern of five concentric zones or circles, with each zone having certain distinguishing characteristics. Figure 5.48 shows the model as applied to the Chicago of the early 1920s, semicircular because of the presence of Lake Michigan.

Zone I, the center and the original core of the city, consists of the downtown area, or the Loop. This core is surrounded by Zone II, an area in transition, which contains principally wholesale and light manufacturing activities, interspersed with areas of cheap hotels, rooming houses, and some tenements. This zone has deteriorating and neglected facilities that are often held for speculative purposes on the assumption that the downtown area will expand outward, increasing land values. Next come a series of residential zones whose economic status improves as one moves away from the older, inner core of the city to the newer commuters' or suburban zones. Planned social change and the dispersal of various groups and facilities have affected

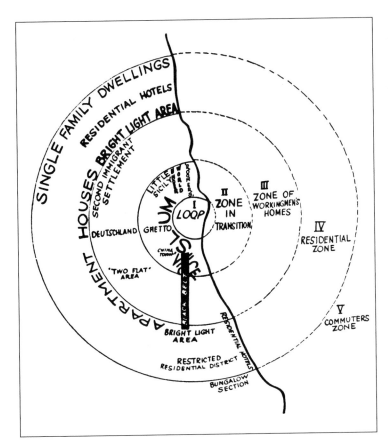

FIG. 5.48. Burgess's concentric zone theory of the internal arrangement of cities, as applied to the Chicago of the 1920s. This theoretical model suggests that a city expands radially from its center to form a series of five concentric zones, each having certain distinguishing characteristics. The Chicago model is semicircular because of the presence of Lake Michigan. From Robert E. Park, Ernest W. Burgess, and Roderick D. McKenzie, *The City* (Chicago: University of Chicago Press, 1925).

the pattern postulated by this theory, but in general the idealized pattern, as applied to Chicago, can still be detected.

Other theoretical models have also been advanced to help explain the internal arrangement of cities. One such model, the sector theory of internal growth, assumes that a city develops largely in a series of sectors or wedges radiating from the downtown area, and that each sector is dominated by a certain type of land use. Figure 5.49 shows a combination of the concentric circle and the sector theories. In Chicago such sectors are evident in the expensive apartments that line the lakeshore from the Loop northward, in

the industrial wedges along many of the rivers and railroads, and in the African American belts that radiate south and west of the Loop.

Chicago's internal arrangement also reflects the multiple nuclei theory, which postulates that a city is made up of a number of cells or nuclei having basically similar functions. For example, one cell contains the University of Chicago complex. Other cells include numerous types of residential cells of varying economic, ethnic, and racial composition. And there are entertainment district cells, a steel area cell, an airport complex, and so on. The

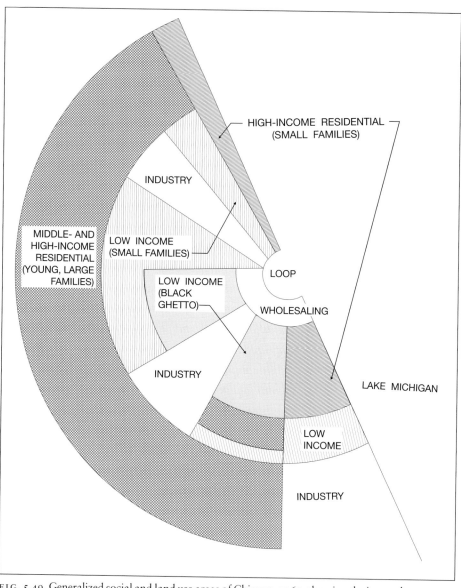

FIG. 5.49. Generalized social and land use areas of Chicago, 1960, showing the internal arrangement theories. Adapted from Philip Rees, "The Factorial Ecology of Metropolitan Chicago, 1960" (master's thesis, Department of Geography, University of Chicago, 1968).

formation of cells is based on the tendency of like activities and people to cluster together. This sometimes occurs in response to zoning laws and sometimes because certain groups and activities profit by being near each other.

Chicago reflects, in many ways, characteristics of all three of these theories. However, since they were first postulated, the city's structure has changed in important ways. These modifications are due to changing neighborhood ethnic populations, the construction of the expressways and, especially, in Burgess's zone of transition around the downtown area, a major metamorphosis into an area that is largely gentrified. Whatever theory is used to describe and explain the internal arrangement of Chicago's settlement and population patterns, the city's patterns are the result of more than a century and a half of immigration, internal growth and development, and continuous change.

FIG. 6.1. McCormick Reaper Works, 1906, on the West Side along the South Branch of the Chicago River. The huge plant, as part of International Harvester, continued operations for about half a century after this photograph was taken. Chicago Historical Society.

6 The Economy of Chicago

Early Industry

On one of the great buildings at the World's Columbian Exposition of 1893 in Chicago was inscribed a statement by Lord Francis Bacon, that three things make an area "great and prosperous: a fertile soil, busy workshops, and easy transportation for men and goods from place to place." Chicago fits this description admirably.

Less than two centuries ago, Chicago was a small trading and military post. Buoyed by its excellent geographic location in a growing area, it soon evolved into a bustling lake and river port, then into a canal terminal and railroad center, and finally into a major commercial and distribution center. The city's industries developed more slowly at first but generally paralleled its commercial development. In only a century and a half, Chicago grew from a small manufacturing city to the nation's second-largest industrial center. Today, the Chicago area is the nation's leading producer of a variety of items, ranging from snuff to steel. Moreover, Chicago's location is such that within a five-hundred-mile radius of the Loop are found about 33 percent of the nation's wholesale and retail trade, 35 percent of its manufacturing, and 25 percent of its population.

The earliest industries of Chicago—milling, meatpacking, tanning, and woodworking—were closely related to the products of the surrounding fields and forests. Other industries arose in response to the need of the area's growing population for printed matter, household utensils, clothing, wagons, boat supplies, building materials, and quarry products.

From early on, Chicago developed a lucrative symbiotic relationship with its rich hinterland. It received, processed, and distributed the products of the farms; it also produced and sent back to the farms clothing, furniture, and agricultural machinery and implements.

One of Chicago's earliest major industries was the farm machinery company (the forerunner of International Harvester) established by Cyrus McCormick in 1847 on the north bank of the Chicago River, on what is the present site of the Equitable Building. After the Chicago Fire of 1871, an enlarged McCormick Reaper Works was built on the West Side, near Blue Island and Western (2400 W.) avenues, where it flourished for almost a century. It closed in 1961, having been supplanted by International Harvester plants in the suburbs, in other parts of the country, and indeed, throughout the world. Today the company is known as Navistar International.

Business directories show that in Chicago in 1856, the largest group of related firms—some eighty-six—were engaged in food processing, meatpacking, and industries that used animal by-products to produce goods, such as leather. The printing industry ranked second, with sixty-five firms; next, with more than fifty firms each, came the textile-garment-millinery industry and the building trades industry. The latter included brickyards, planing mills, lumberyards, and door and sash factories.

Certain industrial location patterns were already apparent. The area north of the river contained the fewest factories. Those located there included the McCormick Reaper Works and a number of breweries, which clustered in the area because of a large German population. The present downtown area, south and east of the river, contained the printing industry and numerous handicraft industries, such as dressmaking, shoemaking, tailoring, and cigar manufacturing. West of the river, on the Near West Side, were numerous metal-using and metal-manufacturing firms.

Many of the early industries congregated along transportation routes—first along the waterways and later along the railroads. Lumber, grain, and tannery facilities were concentrated along the Chicago River. More than five hundred acres of land between Halsted Street and Western Avenue, along the South Branch of the Chicago River, became the largest lumber distribution center in the world. The lumberyards, stocked from Wisconsin, Michigan, and Canadian forests,

supplied the booming home building and furniture industries of the city, as well as the needs of the prairie farmers. Today a residual maze of tracks, lumber slips, and a Lumber Avenue still occupy the area, but there are few lumberyards, and Chicago's importance as a furniture mart has declined.

In 1867 manufacturing in the Chicago area was described as follows:

At first Chicago began to make on a small scale the rough and heavy implements of husbandry. That great factory, for example, which now produces an excellent farm wagon every seven minutes of every working day, was founded twenty-three years ago by its proprietor investing all his capital in the slow construction of one wagon. At the present time, almost every article of much bulk used upon railroads, in farming, in warming houses, in building houses, or in cooking, is made in Chicago. Three thousand persons are now employed there in manufacturing coarse boots and shoes. The prairie world is mowed and reaped by machines made in Chicago, whose people are feeling their way, too, into making woolen and cotton goods. Four or five miles out on the prairie, where until last May the ground had never been broken since the creation, there now stands the village of Austin, which consists of three large factory buildings, forty or fifty nice cottages for workmen and two thousand young trees. This is the seat of the Chicago Clock Factory. . . . A few miles farther back on the prairies, at Elgin, there is the establishment of the National Watch Company, which expects soon to produce fifty watches a day . . . . They are beginning to make pianos at Chicago, besides selling a hundred a week of those made in the East; and the great music house of Root and Cady are now engraving and printing all the music they publish. Melodeons are made in Chicago on a great scale.[1]

The Union Stock Yards

Probably the most famous of Chicago's older industries were the stockyards. Originally, a number of small stockyards were scattered throughout the city. Arising with these stockyards were small handicraft shops, dependent on by-products from meatpacking, which produced shoes, gloves, saddles, soap, candles, and glue. Some of the tanneries that grew in conjunction with nearby meatpacking were on the North Branch of the Chicago River, around Goose Island.

By the 1860s the scattered stockyards were too small and inefficient to handle the increasing numbers of animals shipped to Chicago, with its growing market and unexcelled means of distribution. Furthermore, as the city grew, the stockyards became an undesirable source of odor and sanitation problems within the city proper.

The scattered stockyards were consolidated in 1865 when a consortium of nine railroads joined with packing interests to establish the Union Stock Yards. At the time, the

FIG. 6.2. Union Stock Yards, looking west on Exchange Avenue, with sheep being driven to the slaughter pens, about 1905. After more than a century of operation, the yards closed in 1971. Photograph by Barnes-Crosby; Chicago Historical Society, ICHi-19106.

FIG. 6.3. Immigrant worker loading meat at a stockyards slaughterhouse, 1904. Irving Cutler collection.

huge yards were outside the Chicago city limits, south of Thirty-ninth Street and west of Halsted Street. They eventually occupied about a square mile of land, with numerous related companies developing on the periphery.

Almost from the start, the stockyards were the largest and busiest in the world, and Chicago became the meat capital of the world. Peak capacity was reached in the years soon after World War I, when the yards employed over thirty thousand people and received nearly 19 million head of livestock annually.

The Union Stock Yards in itself was almost a city, with its own newspaper, bank, "Board of Trade," electric plant, water wells, post office, inn, office building, fire department, amphitheater, and canal. But the yards consisted mainly of thousands of pens in the eastern section and the large packing plants in the western Packingtown section—Armour, Swift, Wilson, Cudahy, and Libby, McNeil and Libby. The yards were interlaced with dozens of miles of railroad tracks for trains that delivered the animals, miles of overhead ramps for the circulation of animals within the yards, and a branch of the city's elevated line to transport the workers. The yards also had a large arena, the International Amphitheatre, built originally for livestock shows but that also served as the site of boxing, basketball, circus, and music events. It also was the site of a number of national political conventions, including the infamous Democratic Convention of 1968.

The stockyards, in one way, were a model of efficiency, for it was claimed that only the squeal of the hog was wasted. As "Mr. Dooley," the famed fictional character created by Chicago's Finley Peter Dunne, aptly observed in the *Chicago Evening Post,* "A cow goes lowin' softly into Armour's an' comes out gelatin, fertylizer, celooloid, joolry, sofy cushions, hair restorer, washin'sody, soap, lithrachoor an' bed springs so quick that while aft she's still cow, for'ard she may be anything fr'm buttons to pannyma hats."

For years, the Union Stock Yards was the city's greatest employer. Hundreds of thousands of European immigrants and, later, African Americans from the South found employment there. A number of future mayors worked there also. But the stockyards also, at one time, contained horrifyingly unsanitary working conditions, which were exposed by Upton Sinclair in *The Jungle,* and they were surrounded by shoddy, often stench-filled

FIG. 6.4. Smoking Union Stock Yards' meatpacking plants, about 1912, looking eastward across a cabbage field near Ashland Avenue. Upton Sinclair exposed the deplorable unsanitary conditions in the stockyards in his book *The Jungle*, published in 1906. Chicago Historical Society, ICHi-01869.

FIG. 6.5. Stockyards workers protesting low wages and poor working conditions, circa 1921. Irving Cutler collection.

FIG. 6.6. Long-abandoned slaughter-houses of major meat-packers in the western part of the Union Stock Yards, about 1985. Photograph by Irving Cutler.

neighborhoods, such as the old Back of the Yards area.

The stockyards declined rapidly after World War II. By then they were in the geographic center of Chicago, with its congestion and high taxes. There were labor problems, and a trend toward the decentralization of the packing industry was discernible. Furthermore, the yards' facilities had become obsolete, since they had been designed to be served by railroads and most animals were now being shipped by truck. In 1971, after 106 years of service, the Union Stock Yards closed, although a few small meat-product plants remain on the periphery of the former stockyards. In recent years, the city and industrial developers have greatly improved the street network on the land previously occupied by the yards. Today, the land is occupied by numerous new one-story plants engaged in a variety of endeavors, but virtually none of those is related to meatpacking. Employment in the new facilities is about one-fourth that of the old stockyards.

Pullman

Until the 1860s, Chicago industry supplied primarily the local market and the surrounding farm areas. The requirements of the Civil War, however, helped propel Chicago into the larger national market. After the Civil War, the city's industrial expansion continued unabated through an era of great technological advances and industrial consolidation. Manufacturing rapidly surpassed commerce in importance to the city's economy and soon became the dominant source of employment.

A variety of new industries developed in Chicago, one of the most important being the manufacture of railway equipment. Chicago provided many attractions for this industry; it not only was the railroad center of the nation but also offered a growing steel industry and a central location.

Foremost among the numerous railroad equipment manufacturers was the company founded by George Pullman, the inventor of the sleeping car. Its operations were unique, not only because of their size but also because they were centered in a privately constructed "total community" erected in the early 1880s on the west shore of Lake Calumet, a dozen miles south of downtown Chicago. The bold and original new model town, designed by the architect Solon S. Beman, occupied more than thirty-five hundred acres of once swampy land and housed the factories of the Pullman Palace Car Company, as well as its workers. Pullman was a company town, but it was one of the first to be totally planned—exceptionally well planned for its time—and gained for the community an international reputation.

Utilizing some of the mass production techniques that made his railroad car company a prosperous giant in its field, Pullman erected fourteen hundred residential units and all the facilities of a self-contained community, including a shopping center, church, theater, library, firehouse, school, hotel, and bank. The houses, each constructed of brick and featuring indoor plumbing, fell within three categories for the various levels of employees: fine, single-family homes for the executives and row houses and block houses (tenements)

for the bulk of the workers. In 1884 some eight thousand people resided in that community, which was largely concentrated in the area now bounded by 103rd and 115th streets and by Lake Calumet and Cottage Grove Avenue.

The factories were located apart from the residences, and the community was beautifully landscaped with gardens, parks, and even a small artificial lake. Many of these features were forerunners of modern suburban developments. Maximizing efficiency was the goal of all planning. Bricks for the Pullman community were baked from clay dredged from the bottom of adjacent Lake Calumet. Steam from the plants heated some of the homes. And the sewage from the community was converted into fertilizer and then pumped to a company farm just south of Pullman. This 175-acre farm provided vegetables for the town market.

George Pullman designed his community to be clean, decent, beautiful, and modestly

FIG. 6.7. Community of Pullman in the 1880s, looking eastward. In the distance is Lake Calumet. Some of the prominent landmarks, such as the water tower *(left)*, the small lake *(center)*, and the Arcade *(right)*, no longer exist, and the Illinois Central tracks have been raised. But many other prominent features, such as the Florence Hotel and Greenstone Church *(both right of center)*, still stand. Printed by Western Manufacturer; Chicago Historical Society, ICHi-01918.

FIG. 6.8. Historic Florence Hotel, now owned by the state of Illinois. Built in the 1880s as part of the model town of Pullman, it was used by visiting salesmen and executives. George Pullman had a suite on the second floor. The hotel contained the town's only tavern, whose use was limited mainly to managers. Image by Wernher Krutein; by permission of Photovault.

priced but simultaneously profitable in all aspects. He tried to promote sobriety and godliness in his workers by banning all taverns, except for one in the Florence Hotel that could be used only by executives. He purchased the surrounding land and kept it vacant as a buffer against the encroachment of the surrounding society's vices. For a while, his brother was the minister of the only church permitted in the community. Such a community, Pullman believed, would attract the finest craftsmen of Europe. He believed also that its advantages and surroundings would make

"better workmen by removing from them the feelings of discontent and desire for change that so generally characterizes the American workman, thus protecting the employer from the loss of time and money consequent upon intemperance, labor strikes, and dissatisfaction which generally result from poverty and uncongenial home surroundings."

Pullman's paternalism, however, created resentment in some workers. As one worker quipped, "We were born in a Pullman house, fed from a Pullman shop, taught in a Pullman school, catechized in the Pullman church, and when we die we shall be buried in the Pullman cemetery and go to a Pullman hell!" When the depression of 1893 curtailed railway car orders, Pullman severely cut the pay of his workers but failed to lower their rent or food prices. The following year, the bitterness of the workers culminated in a prolonged and violent strike that curtailed railroad operations nationally. The strike ended only after President Cleveland sent in federal troops to move the mail.

The Pullman town was never the same after the strike. Annexation a few years earlier, in 1889, by the city of Chicago precipitated a change in the private character of the town. Then, in 1898, an Illinois Supreme Court order forced the Pullman Palace Car Company to sell the town because it was "opposed to good public policy and incompatible with the theories and spirits of our constitution." Most of the homes were sold to the Pullman workers. George Pullman died in 1897 and was buried in the Graceland Cemetery, with his body encased in a cement block covered with steel rails to protect it from possible vandalism by some of his embittered workers.

Today the basic pattern and homes of the more-than-a-century-old, sturdily built Pullman community remain largely intact, although time has wrought certain changes. The population has dropped to about half of what it was at its peak, the operations of the Pullman Company have long ceased, and many of its facilities are now utilized by other companies. A few new structures are evident, but some of the community's famous landmarks, such as the lake, the water tower, and the Arcade, are gone. However, more than 90 percent of the residences are still there, as is the Greenstone Church and the Florence Hotel. And they will undoubtedly remain, as Pullman has been declared a National Historic Landmark. Active civic and historic organizations are working hard to preserve and restore the community. Some of the historic buildings are now owned by the State of Illinois, which is helping finance their restoration, including the administrative clock tower building that was badly damaged by fire in 1998. To further enhance the area as a major tourist attraction, there is a proposal that one of the factory buildings be made into a transportation museum complex.

FIG. 6.9. Abandoned Pullman factory buildings along 111th Street, 2005. The Pullman Car Works produced its last railroad car in 1981. Photograph by Irving Cutler.

Present Industry

In the last century and a half, the Chicago area's industrial growth has been so rapid that it now ranks third among the nation's metropolitan areas in the number of people it employs. In 1980 the six-county Chicago metropolitan area had about 3.5 million workers; in 2002 the number reached over 5 million. Of these, 638,000 were engaged in manufacturing; 1,028,000 were involved in wholesale and retail trade; 1,762,000 in service; 540,000 in government; 526,000 in finance, insurance, and real estate; 300,000 in transportation, communications, and public utilities; 252,000 in construction; and the remainder in a variety of other occupations. Service-producing, white-collar employment has shown the greatest gains in the last twenty-five years, more than doubling, while employment in manufacturing has declined about 30 percent. There are, however, decided yearly fluctuations due to changing economic conditions.

During the past century, the location, facilities, and products of Chicago's industry have changed greatly. The leading products before World War I—meatpacking, steel, men's apparel, furniture, agricultural implements, and railway equipment—have declined in relative importance. At the same time, Chicago's industrial base has undergone widespread and healthy diversification. Today it includes almost every kind of industry, enhanced by excellent location, good living conditions, and a strong set of universities. In addition to industrial diversification, its strong commercial, transportation, service, and government-employment components provide the area with one of the most diversified and best-balanced economies in the nation, rendering it less vulnerable to recessions than many other areas. Twenty-eight of the nation's five hundred largest corporations are headquartered in Chicago and its suburbs, including the giant Boeing Company, which arrived in 2001. However, since the late 1990s, it has lost the corporate headquarters of Ameritech, Amoco, Illinois Central, Inland Steel, Marshall Field, Morton International, Montgomery Ward, Fannie May, Bank One, and Leo Burnett. Many of the losses were due to mergers or buyouts. But many large corporations remain headquartered in the Chicago area, including Sears, McDonald's, United Airlines, Motorola, Kraft Foods,

TABLE 6.1.

Employment in Chicago Metropolitan Area by Occupation, 2002

Occupation	No. of Workers
Service	1,762,000
Wholesale and Retail Trade	1,028,000
Manufacturing	638,000
Government	540,000
Finance, Insurance, and Real Estate	526,000
Transportation, Communications, and Public Utilities	300,000
Construction	252,000
Total*	5,046,000

Source: From the files of *Crain's Chicago Business*, 2003, Mark Mandle, staff librarian
*Not including miscellaneous occupations

FIG. 6.10. Corporate headquarters of the Boeing Company along the Chicago River in downtown Chicago, 2005. The company is a leading manufacturer of commercial aircraft and defense products. In 2001, after considering bids from a number of other cities, Boeing selected Chicago for its headquarters. Photograph by Daniel Cutler.

Allstate, Walgreens, Abbott Laboratories, Baxter International, Sara Lee, and Wrigley.

Suburban manufacturing employment has been growing more rapidly than that of Chicago. Table 6.2 shows Chicago's manufacturing employment in 2002 by product category.

The Chicago area is usually the nation's leading producer in many of these fields, including metal wares, confectionery products, surgical appliances, railroad engines and equipment, soap, paint, cosmetics, cans, industrial machinery, steel, commercial printing, and sporting goods. To supply these industries, millions of tons of iron ore, coal, chemicals, petroleum, lumber, paper, and farm products are brought into the area

FIG. 6.11. Corporate headquarters of Motorola, Inc., in Schaumburg, Illinois, 2005. The company is a leading manufacturer of cell phones, broadband equipment, and wireless networks and employs eighty-eight thousand people worldwide. Photograph by Daniel Cutler.

TABLE 6.2.

Manufacturing Employment in Chicago, 2002

Product	Workers
Food and kindred products	30,548
Printing and publishing	26,609
Fabricated metal products	20,967
Electronics	10,268
Industrial machinery and equipment	9,441
Chemicals and allied products	8,988
Paper and allied products	8,280
Apparel and other textiles	6,544
Transportation equipment	6,421
Miscellaneous manufacturing industries	6,165
Furniture and fixtures	5,605
Primary metals	5,489
Rubber and miscellaneous plastics	4,866
Other nondurable goods	3,977
Instruments and related products	3,355
Stone, clay, and glass	2,859
Lumber and wood products	2,423
Petroleum and coal products	1,069
Total	163,885

Source: Adapted from Chicago Department of Planning and Development, *Chicago Fact Book 2002,* "Manufacturing"

annually. To meet the increasing energy needs of the area, Exelon (Commonwealth Edison Company) has greatly expanded its generating capacity, adding a number of nuclear power plants that produce more nuclear power than any other utility in the nation. Over half of the company's energy generation now originates from nuclear power.

Table 6.3 shows the one hundred largest public companies in the Chicago area in 2002, ranked by revenue. The list reveals the diversity of Chicago's enterprise, for only about half of the largest employers are manufacturers. The list includes numerous financial and insurance companies, retailers, transportation companies, and public utilities. Unlike some cities, Chicago's employment is not dominated by a single corporation or just a few giant companies.

Table 6.4 shows the city's employment by industry, and Table 6.5 lists Chicago's top employers.

TABLE 6.3.

Largest Public Companies in Chicago Area, Ranked by 2002 Revenues

Company	Revenues (millions [$])	Company	Revenues (millions [$])
Boeing Co.	$54,069.0	Packaging Corp of America	1,735.9
Sears Roebuck & Co.	41,366.0	Molex Inc.	1,711.5
Kraft Foods Inc.	29,723.0	Wallace Computer Services Inc.	1,545.6
Allstate Corp.	29,579.0	Peoples Energy Corp.	1,482.5
Walgreen Co.	28,681.1	Comdisco Holding Co.	1,415.0
Motorola Inc.	26,679.0	GATX Corp.	1,340.7
Archer Daniels Midland	23,453.6	Hub Group Inc.	1,335.7
Caterpillar Inc.	20,152.0	Tellabs Inc.	1,317.0
Abbott Laboratories	17,684.7	Dade Behring Holdings Inc.	1,281.5
Sara Lee Corp.	17,628.0	Arthur J. Gallagher & Co.	1,101.2
McDonald's Corp.	15,405.7	General Growth Properties Inc.	1,066.3
Exelon Corp.	14,955.0	Federal Signal Corp.	1,057.2
Household Intl. Inc.	14,671.6	Bally Total Fitness Holding Corp.	1,035.9
UAL Corp.	14,286.0	Hollinger Intl. Inc.	1,006.2
Deere & Co.	13,780.0	Aptargroup Inc.	927.0
CNA Financial Corp.	12,286.0	Salton Inc.	922.5
Illinois Tool Works Inc.	9,467.7	Andrew Corp.	864.8
Aon Corp.	8,822.0	Jones Lang LaSalle Inc.	837.8
Baxter Intl. Inc.	8,110.0	First Health Group Corp.	763.6
Smurfit-Stone Container	7,483.0	Career Education Corp.	751.0
Newell Rubbermaid Inc.	7,453.9	Stepan Co.	748.5
Navistar Intl. Corp.	6,764.0	Idex Corp.	742.0
Fortune Brands Inc.	5,677.7	General Binding Corp.	701.7
Tribune Co.	5,384.4	DeVry Inc.	647.6
R. R. Donnelley & Sons Co.	4,754.9	AAR Corp.	638.7
W. W. Grainger Inc.	4,643.9	Metal Management Inc.	631.1
Cow Computer Centers Inc.	4,264.6	Hartmarx Corp.	570.3
Brunswick Corp.	3,711.9	Information Resources Inc.	554.8
United Stationers Inc.	3,701.6	A. M. Castle & Co.	538.1
Equity Office Property Trust	3,612.9	Zebra Technologies Corp.	475.6
Servicemaster Co.	3,589.1	Chicago Mercantile Exchange	453.2
USG Corp.	3,468.0	Central Steel & Wire Co.	450.1
Tenneco Automotive Inc.	3,459.0	Richardson Electronics Ltd.	443.5
Telephone & Data Systems	2,985.4	Aftermarket Technology Corp.	415.9
Pactiv Corp.	2,880.0	Stericycle Inc.	401.5
Old Republic Intl. Corp.	2,756.4	Nuveen Investments Inc.	396.4
Wm. Wrigley Jr. Co.	2,746.3	Tootsie Roll Industries Inc.	393.2
Borgwarner Inc.	2,731.1	Lawson Products Inc.	387.5
Alberto-Culver Co.	2,651.0	APAC Customer Service Inc.	371.2
Anixter Intl. Inc.	2,520.1	Heidrick & Struggles Intl. Inc.	350.7
Unitrin Inc.	2,298.2	First Industrial Realty Trust Inc.	347.0
U.S. Freightways Corp.	2,250.5	John B. Sanfilippo & Son Inc.	343.2
U.S. Cellular Corp.	2,184.5	Whitehead Jewelers	341.0
Ryerson Tull Inc.	2,096.5	Midas Inc.	333.0
FMC Technologies Inc.	2,071.5	FTD Inc.	325.3
IMC Global Inc.	2,057.4	Option Care Inc.	320.5
Equity Residential	1,994.1	Methode Electronics Inc.	319.7
Nicor Inc.	1,897.4	CNA Surety Corp.	316.3
Corn Products Intl. Inc.	1,870.9	Grubb & Ellis Co.	313.5
Hewitt Associates Inc.	1,750.1	AMCOL Intl. Corp.	298.9

Source: Adapted from *Crain's Chicago Business*, May 5, 2003, p. 15

TABLE 6.4.

Ten Largest Industries in Chicago, by
Employment, 2004

Industry	No. of Employees
Health care	132,746
Professional services	124,213
Finance, insurance	123,171
Manufacturing	100,062
Accommodation/food services	88,260
Retail trade	87,754
Administration	83,658
Transportation/warehousing	67,283
Other services	52,393
Educational services	41,029
All industries	1,076,483

Source: Illinois Department of Employment Security,
2004.

TABLE 6.5.

Top Employers in the Chicago Area, 2004

Rank	Employer	No. of Employees
1	U.S. government	88,000
2	Chicago Public Schools	39,402
3	Jewel-Osco	36,749
4	City of Chicago	35,978
5	Cook County	26,505
6	Advocate Health Care	25,293
7	United Parcel Service	19,563
8	State of Illinois	17,222
9	SBC Communications Inc.	17,000
10	United Airlines	15,830
11	Archdiocese of Chicago	15,484
12	Abbott Laboratories	15,300
12	J. P. Morgan Chase Co.	15,300
14	Motorola Inc.	15,000
15	Wal-Mart Stores	14,320

Source: Adapted from Crain's Chicago Business,
October 4, 2004.

Traditionally, industry in the Chicago area was concentrated along the rivers and railroads, with more situated on the South and West sides than on the more residential North Side. In recent years, industrial development has been increasing near expressways, near O'Hare International Airport, and in organized industrial districts. A growing proportion of the area's industrial, commercial, and office establishments, including numerous concerns once situated in the inner city, can now be found outside the city proper. In recent years, the area between downtown and the suburbs suffered heavy losses in factories and jobs—mainly those of blue-collar workers, particularly on the West and South sides of the city. Declining population and jobs led to the loss of thousands of Chicago's shops and stores in the last half of the twentieth century. In the city, manufacturing is now largely in twenty-four industrial corridors and in five planned manufacturing districts. Some of these areas are enterprise zones that allow industry to obtain certain tax advantages.

More than half of the approximately 15,800 manufacturers and more than half of the industrial jobs in the metropolitan area are now outside the city limits of Chicago. Although some suburban industries were established well before the beginning of the last century, most are of recent origin, many having originated after World War II. The shift of industry to the suburbs is attributable to such factors as limited acreage and high land costs in Chicago, as well as to the general problems that currently plague most large cities—congestion, plant obsolescence, high tax and insurance rates, political uncertainties, insensitive government, crime, poor schools, racial conflict, labor problems, and pollution. Although the suburbs are not

FIG. 6.12. Land use in Chicago, 2003. The industrial areas (in black) are aligned mainly along waterways and railroad routes. With the growth of trucking in recent decades, industry has more flexibility in its location. Map courtesy of Chicago Metropolis 2020.

immune to some of these difficulties, the problems are usually less severe. Furthermore, many suburban areas still offer large tracts of vacant land at a relatively reasonable cost—land that meets modern industry's desire for expansive one-story plants and acres of parking and landscaping. Railroad and water sites, which are plentiful in Chicago, are not as essential to our nation's increasingly truck-oriented industries.

Chicago has also lost jobs to small towns, as well as to the Sun Belt—places that often have the advantage of certain living amenities, as well as lower expenses in regard to land, taxes, and wages. Increased foreign competition has likewise cost Chicago jobs, as has the

lack of a proportionate share of U.S. defense contracts.

Chicago-area communities that employ large numbers of industrial workers include Cicero, Bedford Park, Waukegan, North Chicago, Aurora, Melrose Park, Joliet, Skokie, Elk Grove Village, Naperville, Elgin, Chicago Heights, and Schaumburg in Illinois; and Gary, Hammond, East Chicago, and Whiting in adjacent northwestern Indiana. After World War II, much industry moved to the north, northwest, and west suburban areas, generally because of good transportation, desirable environmental factors, and minimal racial problems. More recently, lower-priced and sizable tracts of land, plus improved transportation in the south and southwest suburbs, have made those areas more attractive for industrial plants. Increasingly, suburbanites have been able to earn their livelihood in the suburbs, with only about one-third now commuting to Chicago for their work.

The industrial migration from the city not only has hurt Chicago's economic base but also has increased unemployment among the city's poorly educated and unskilled workers, especially African Americans and Hispanics. These groups find it difficult to accept jobs in suburban areas because they must travel far from their residences in the inner city, although reverse commuting from the city to the suburbs is on the rise. More jobs are now available in the surrounding metropolitan area than in the city itself. In fact, metropolitan Chicago has more jobs than ever; however, their location has changed significantly. Some of the suburban industry is new, but much has relocated from Chicago, causing a net loss of jobs there. The number of manufacturing jobs in the city has been declining at an average rate of about twenty thousand per year. One result of declining manufacturing jobs is that about 20 percent of Chicago's population, mainly members of minority groups, receive some kind of public aid. By contrast, in 1960, only 7 percent of the city's residents were on welfare.

Wholesale and Retail Trade

The dollar volume of Chicagoland's wholesale trade equals that of its manufacturing industries. Chicago is a principal market for grain, machine tools, produce, fish, and flowers. Its giant Merchandise Mart showcases the displays—mainly furniture and home furnishings—of five thousand manufacturers and designers. Across the street from the Merchandise Mart looms the Apparel Center, which opened in 1977. There, several hundred lines of men's, women's, and children's apparel are shown. For the convenience of buyers, the upper floors of the building contain a Holiday Inn.

The Chicago Board of Trade and the Chicago Mercantile Exchange are among the world's largest commodity markets. They have pioneered many new market concepts.

Because of its huge wholesale trade, its accessibility, and its numerous facilities, Chicago has usually ranked as the nation's convention capital. About eighty large conventions and trade shows are held throughout the year; together with tourism, they bring into the city more than $9 billion annually and provide jobs for 150,000 workers. To accommodate the annual influx of approximately 7 million conventioneers and buyers and a total of more than 30 million visitors, Chicago offers 250 hotels and motels, with about thirty thousand rooms; seven thousand restaurants; and numerous exhibition facilities, including the giant McCormick Place—the nation's largest convention center, with 2.2 million square feet (currently in the process of expanding yet again). In recent years many hotels and motels with convention and business meeting facilities have opened in the O'Hare Airport area, along some of the city's expressways, and in the area just north of the Loop. The Chicago area now has eight hotels with more than eight hundred rooms apiece.

Chicago's facilities and location have helped attract the national headquarters of 731 associations, with paid staffs totaling twelve thousand and an annual budget of about $200 million. Among the larger associations headquartered in the

FIG. 6.13. Busy Randolph Street Market in the 1890s in the Haymarket Square area, near the site of the Haymarket Riot of 1886. Chicago Historical Society.

FIG. 6.14. South Water Street, 1905. Between Lake Street and the main stem of the Chicago River, this was the wholesale produce market of Chicago until 1925, when it was closed to make way for the construction of Wacker Drive. The market was moved about three miles to the southwest, around Fourteenth Street and Blue Island Avenue, thereby eliminating some downtown traffic. This newer facility also became obsolete and hopelessly congested. It closed in 2003, and most merchants moved to a new, city-sponsored facility at Twenty-fourth and Wolcott (1900 W.). Photograph by Barnes-Crosby; Chicago Historical Society, ICHi-19201.

FIG. 6.15. South Water Market looking east on Fifteenth Street from Aberdeen Avenue (1100 W.), 1941. It was the major wholesale fruit and vegetable market in the city, with annual sales of about $1 billion. Opened in 1925 to replace the South Water Street Market in downtown Chicago, the market consisted essentially of six long buildings containing 166 virtually identical units. The advent of the long trailer truck severely congested the market streets and prompted periodic proposals for the construction of a new market, which finally opened in 2003. Both the South Water Street Market and the Randolph Street Market declined in importance, partly because of obsolete facilities and the advent of chain supermarkets, which are usually their own wholesalers. The South Water Street Market mainly served restaurants, hotels, hospitals, small retail chains, independent stores, and smaller wholesale markets of the region. Chicago Historical Society, ICHi-04727.

FIG. 6.16. Chicago International Produce Market, which opened in 2003, replacing the South Water Street Market. It is more than four times the size of the old market, less congested, and much more efficient. Photograph by Irving Cutler.

FIG. 6.17. Trading floor of the Chicago Board of Trade, founded in 1848. In this major futures exchange, world prices for a number of commodities are set. Photograph courtesy of the Chicago Board of Trade.

city are the American Medical Association, American Dental Association, American Bar Association, American Library Association, American Marketing Association, International Housewares Association, and the Radiological Society of North America. In addition, the headquarters of three large service organizations—YMCA of the USA, the Lions, and the Rotary—and two of the largest fraternal organizations—the Elks and the Polish National Alliance—are in the area.

Another important aspect of Chicago's economy is its retail trade, $123 billion in 2004, which generally is about half of the dollar volume of the wholesale trade. A hierarchy of retail areas has developed in the city, headed by both downtown and nearby upscale Michigan Avenue. The downtown area is followed by major transit intersections, such as Ninety-fifth and Western, and Irving Park, Milwaukee, and Cicero. The shopping areas scale down in size to the strip developments along some streets and, finally, to the little corner grocery stores. Many of these shopping facilities have had relative declines as the automobile, changing populations, suburban competition, and modern shopping centers—along with the coming of large discounters such as Wal-Mart, Target, and Kmart—have modified old shopping patterns in many of the neighborhoods.

Organized Industrial Districts and Parks

Chicago has been a leader in a modern industrial trend: the development of the organized industrial district and its more modern version, the *industrial park*. These are planned developments designed to physically accommodate industries in a wholesome and functional relationship to each other and to the community, and to provide industries

with such services as transportation, security, utilities, dining facilities, maintenance, financing, and architectural engineering. Industry is provided with a complete location package and can usually either rent or purchase the facility. The accelerating growth of such developments has countered the previous tendency of often locating industry indiscriminately throughout residential areas, a tendency that often resulted in blight.

Chicago's Union Stock Yards and Pullman were pioneering forerunners of organized industrial districts. One of the largest, the Central Manufacturing District, was begun in 1902 to develop a tract of land immediately north of the Union Stock Yards. This industrial development proved so successful that ten others, containing a total of over three hundred industrial plants, were established by the same company in the Chicago metropolitan area, mostly outside the big city.

The Clearing Industrial District was established by the railroads in 1909 in Bedford Park, which is just south of today's Midway Airport. The company operated ten separate industrial tracts that contained more than 275 plants in the southern and western fringes of the city and in some suburbs, before becoming fragmented by the sale of those industrial parks. There are now several hundred industrial parks in the Chicago metropolitan area.

In recent years, the greatest proliferation of industrial parks has been in northern Cook County, especially in the vicinity of O'Hare Airport and Schaumburg, but also in the Oak Brook–Lisle–Naperville–Woodridge area in Du Page County. These areas contain prestigious industrial and office complexes and are near prime residential areas. Unlike the older railway-oriented organized industrial districts, these parks are mainly expressway-oriented. North of Chicago, the communities of Lincolnwood, Skokie, Morton Grove, and Niles also contain numerous high-status industrial parks. One of the parks, Tam-O-Shanter Industrial Fairways in Niles, is built on nine holes of a former championship golf course. Lake and Kane counties in Illinois have also experienced a rapid increase in industrial parks, as have parts of southern Cook County and of Will County in the Joliet-Romeoville-Bolingbrook area, due to low land costs and an expanded expressway network.

By far the largest industrial park in the Chicago area is Elk Grove Business Park, begun as Centex Industrial Park in 1956, northwest of O'Hare International Airport. Unlike earlier industrial districts, it is part of a larger complex—Elk Grove Village—that includes planned residential and commercial areas, as well as industrial sections. Elk Grove Business Park covers 3,584 acres, has about thirty-six hundred plants and offices, employed about one hundred thousand people in 2003, and conforms to the modern trend of well-landscaped one-story buildings with adequate parking facilities for the automobile-oriented workers. As in other developments, the industries are mainly engaged in light manufacturing or service enterprises. The community is directly in the path of possible future airport expansion.

In the city of Chicago, industrial parks have been developed in such areas as the former Stock Yards, Goose Island, the Lake Calumet area, and sites on the West and Southwest sides.

The Calumet Industrial Complex

The heavy industry of the Chicago area is confined largely to the extreme southeastern part of the city and to its east, around the southern end of Lake Michigan beyond Gary

to the Burns Harbor development in Indiana. In Chicago, the six miles along the Calumet River from its mouth to Lake Calumet once contained one of the great industrial complexes of the world. The river was lined with a maze of steel plants, grain elevators, shipping facilities, chemical plants, and other enterprises. This area has undergone major decline in recent years.

Industry began its development on a large scale in the Calumet area over a century ago. Available at low cost were large tracts of vacant, swampy, and sandy land near plenty of fresh water. The tracts were strategically located near a great and growing market but remained outside the built-up urban area. The lake, rivers, and railroads offered virtually unexcelled transportation.

A variety of heavy industries developed. Oil refineries were concentrated around Whiting, Indiana, making it one of the largest inland refinery areas in the world—it includes a huge British Petroleum refinery (formerly Amoco and, even earlier, Standard Oil of Indiana). Major producers of railway equipment were scattered throughout the area, including the plants of Pullman, Union Tank Car, and General American Transportation. Huge soap, paint, chemical, and cement plants were also constructed. Some of these plants were related to the Calumet area's main industry, steel. The Calumet Industrial Complex is the nation's leading steel-producing area and one of the greatest steel centers in the world. Its production is greater than that of Britain, France, or the Ruhr district of Germany, but virtually all of the steel production now takes place in northwestern Indiana rather than in Chicago.

Chicago's steel industry was originally north of downtown on Goose Island, in

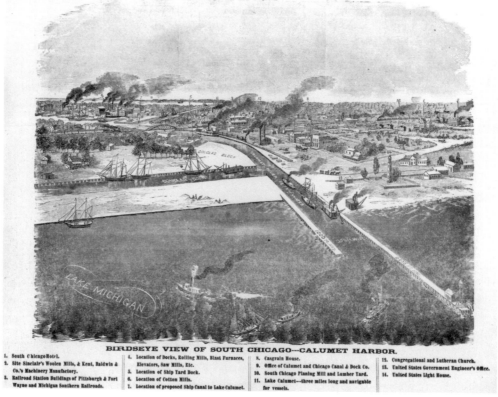

BIRDSEYE VIEW OF SOUTH CHICAGO---CALUMET HARBOR.

1. South Chicago Hotel.	4. Location of Docks, Rolling Mills, Blast Furnaces,	8. Casgrain House.	12. Congregational and Lutheran Church.
2. Site Sinclair's Woolen Mills, & Kent, Baldwin &	Elevators, Saw Mills, Etc.	9. Office of Calumet and Chicago Canal & Dock Co.	13. United States Government Engineer's Office.
Co.'s Machinery Manufactory.	5. Location of Ship Yard Dock.	10. South Chicago Planing Mill and Lumber Yard.	14. United States Light House.
3. Railroad Station Buildings of Pittsburgh & Fort	6. Location of Cotton Mills.	11. Lake Calumet---three miles long and navigable	
Wayne and Michigan Southern Railroads.	7. Location of proposed Ship Canal to Lake Calumet.	for vessels.	

FIG. 6.18. Calumet River and Harbor, from an engraving originally published in 1874. Chicago Historical Society.

the Chicago River. Later it moved to South Chicago, where it spread out along both the Lake Michigan shore and the Calumet River. It also expanded into the sand dune and swamp areas of adjacent Lake County, Indiana, and in the 1960s, farther eastward along the lake into Porter County, Indiana. The area's accessibility to the Lake Superior iron ore ranges by means of low-cost water transportation has been a major advantage.

Today five steel plants operate in the area, although three of them are currently in bankruptcy. Two of these plants rank among the largest in the nation: the Inland Steel plant

(now Inland-Ispat), located next to the smaller LTV plant, established in 1901 on the east side of the Indiana Harbor Canal in East Chicago, jutting a mile and a half out into the lake on artificial land fill; and the Gary Works of U.S. Steel, situated on miles of former sand dunes on the southern shore of Lake Michigan. The establishment of the Gary Works led to the founding of the city of Gary, Indiana, in 1906, and the city's subsequent rapid growth. Today it is Indiana's fifth-largest city. In the 1960s Midwest Steel and Bethlehem Steel were established in the dunes east of Gary in the Burns Harbor area. The Bethlehem Steel plant might have become the largest integrated steel

FIG. 6.19. Looking north from about Ninety-second Street and the Calumet River, 1936. The area shown is mainly the community of South Chicago. Along the lake from the Calumet River to Seventy-ninth Street was the South Works of the U.S. Steel Corporation. The plant was torn down in the 1990s. Northwest of the plant *(upper left)* is the neighboring community of South Shore. Photograph by The Landowner Press and Engraving; Chicago Historical Society, ICHi-03138.

FIG. 6.20. Goose Island, about 1925. This 160-acre island was created in the 1850s, when the North Branch Canal *(right)* was dug from Chicago Avenue to North Avenue through low-lying clay pits, thus creating more waterway frontage and short-circuiting the bend in the North Branch. Before being taken over almost completely by railroads and factories, including a number of tanneries that followed some early meatpacking plants, the island in the 1800s contained the cottages and cabbage patches of more than five hundred immigrant families, mainly Irish. Many of the men of the island served as police officers, firefighters, and ward bosses. One, William E. Dever, became a mayor of Chicago. Halsted Street crosses the southeastern tip of the island and Division Street bisects it in an east-west direction. Chicago Historical Society.

plant in the nation, if earlier plans for its expansion had been implemented. However, in 2003, due to a variety of factors, the company was temporarily placed in bankruptcy and was purchased by International Steel Group, which in 2005 was purchased by Mittal Steel. As a result of the weak steel market and the industry's many problems, Midwest Steel was similarly purchased by U.S. Steel. Further

consolidation and change in ownership are expected. The northwestern Indiana steel plants produce about one-fourth of the nation's steel.

From 1880 until just a few years ago, the South Works of U.S. Steel occupied the Chicago lakefront, from Seventy-ninth Street southward for more than a mile to the mouth of the Calumet River at about Ninety-second Street. At its peak the plant employed almost

FIG. 6.21. Part of the Calumet industrial area of northwestern Indiana, looking north, 1936. In the upper right is the Indiana Harbor area of East Chicago, with its Y-shaped Indiana Harbor Canal *(lower right)*. To the west of the mouth of the canal is the Youngstown Sheet and Tube Company plant (now Mittal Steel), and on the eastern bank is the western tip of the giant Inland-Ispat Steel Company plant, which extends about one and a half miles into the lake on an artificial peninsula. In the center are the oil refineries and storage tanks of East Chicago and Whiting. Whiting is to the north, near the lake, and now contains the huge facilities of the British Petroleum Company. On the extreme left is the city of Hammond. Photograph by Chicago Aerial Survey; Chicago Historical Society.

FIG. 6.22. Interlake Steel's Riverdale, Illinois, steel-making facility in the bend of the Little Calumet River, 1980. The river separated Riverdale from Chicago. Hot metal was shipped to the Riverdale plant in torpedo cars from another company plant about five miles away in Chicago. After Interlake Steel closed the plant for financial reasons, it was purchased by Mittal Steel. Photograph courtesy of Interlake, Inc.

twenty thousand people, but it has recently been torn down due to obsolescence and the depressed steel industry. Its closure had a ripple effect on the adjacent communities, affecting area retail stores, banks, taverns, and other establishments.

The plant had also been an important part of the social life of the workers, with its baseball and bowling leagues, choirs, bands, and more. Although wages and hours in later years were reasonable, work was often dangerous. It is estimated that in the century of the plant's existence, about five hundred men were killed in accidents there. Once the pollution created by the plant is cleaned up, the city plans to develop the large lakefront site into a public park, a residential complex, and an industrial park.

Despite the construction of new steel plants, the expansion of most of the older steel mills, and the installation of the newest technology (including continuous casting and the basic oxygen process), the Chicago area in the past often required more steel than it produced. Its steel plants were sometimes unable to meet the varied demands of the fifteen thousand manufacturing plants in the Chicago area and the thousands more in Chicago's hinterland, including numerous automobile plants. However, in recent years, for a variety of economic and technological reasons and as a result of fierce foreign and domestic competition (including that from other metals), the steel industry has not been operating near its capacity, and there have been layoffs of employees and closings of some marginal facilities. Although the industry now employs far fewer than half the number of steel workers it employed twenty years ago, due to major technological improvements, it can produce more steel than ever before.

The steel industry had been a major employer in the Chicago area, and its presence has undoubtedly aided the establishment of many other industries. But the older steel mills brought appalling air and water pollution; dirt and grime and congestion blighted the surrounding areas. Only in recent years, under public pressure, have strenuous efforts been made to successfully overcome some of the conditions that had led to numerous air pollution alerts. The noxious air conditions were aggravated not only by the emissions of industrial plants and power-generating stations but also by space heating and especially the millions of motor vehicles in the area.

The Chicago area suffered as much of the steel complex became the rust belt and other manufacturers left for other states or foreign lands where costs were lower. But some of this loss was replaced by a growing service economy, which encompasses everything from finance to retail and wholesale trade, and an advantageous housing market, which compares favorably to the higher-cost East and West Coast markets. Yet despite the lower cost of housing, the city still lacks enough affordable housing in the right places

FIG. 6.23. Memorial service in 1939 for ten strikers and sympathizers killed by Chicago police during a May 30, 1937, altercation outside the Republic Steel plant on Chicago's Far South Side. The strike by steelworkers who hoped to unionize the plant is known in labor history as the "Memorial Day Massacre." Chicago Historical Society.

and still lags behind in school performance, which is important in the sale of homes and in performance in industry.

The Changing Role of the Central Business District

Downtown Chicago, where the city first began, is now the heart of a great metropolitan area, but its structure and functions are changing rapidly. Elevated trains still encircle the Loop on their raised tracks as they have since 1897, but missing are the bustle of hundreds of boats on the river, the clanging of the old red streetcars, much of the manufacturing activity, the South Water Street produce

market, and the stately residences flanking Michigan and Wabash avenues. In their place are the ubiquitous motor vehicle, the roaring subway, and the array of numerous new office, hotel, and residential high-rises, occasionally relieved by small plazas.

Chicago's downtown, until recent years, was relatively compact, circumscribed by physical barriers: to the east the lake, to the north and west the river, and to the south a maze of railroad facilities. Enhancing the area's importance was its position as the hub of one of the nation's greatest concentrations of rail, waterway, and road transportation. It was also the focal point of the highly developed internal transit system of the city. For about half a century, the downtown area

FIG. 6.24. Part of the sixty-three-mile network of the Chicago Tunnel Company's narrow-gauge underground freight railroad tunnels, some forty feet below downtown streets. Railroad cars carried coal, ashes, garbage, mail, and a variety of packages between freight terminals and downtown buildings. The tunnels, which underlie the Chicago River in eleven places, were accidentally flooded in 1992, an event that caused major damage to the downtown area. Photograph courtesy of Harold Mayer.

FIG. 6.25. State Street—"that great street"—looking north from Washington Street, with Marshall Field's to the right and Marina City in the background, circa 1970. About ten blocks of the street, from Congress Parkway to Wacker Drive, were later temporarily transformed into the State Street Mall. For many years, the street was one of the world's most highly concentrated shopping areas. Photograph courtesy of Chicago Convention and Tourism Bureau.

even had a network of sixty-three miles of narrow-gauge freight railroad tracks some forty feet below the downtown streets. Over these tracks were carried coal, garbage, and mail, as well as a variety of freight between freight terminals and Loop buildings. These are the underground railroad tunnels, by then essentially abandoned, that were flooded on April 13, 1992.

Lake Street, just south of the river and its wholesale activity, was the main commercial artery of early Chicago. Its major commercial intersection was at Lake and Clark streets. State Street—later to become "that great street"—was a narrow, muddy, shoddy street until Potter Palmer, one of Chicago's most successful retail, wholesale, and real estate entrepreneurs, purchased three-quarters of a mile of land along it. He quickly and dramatically used his influence to have the street widened, drainage improved, public transportation instituted, and commercial structures erected, including a hotel bearing

his name. He persuaded Field, Leiter and Company (the forerunner of Marshall Field's, now Macy's) to move from Lake Street to a new, luxurious store on State Street. By the time of the Chicago Fire of 1871, State Street was already Chicago's "main street."

Although State Street was completely gutted by the fire, it was quickly rebuilt on an even grander scale. The post-Fire building boom helped to develop the modern skyscraper and the world-famous, innovative Chicago school of architecture, which featured many well-known architects. Among the monumental buildings erected in downtown Chicago in the late 1880s were the Auditorium, the Old Chicago Stock Exchange, the Rookery building, and the Monadnock building. In 1891 Maitland's *Dictionary of American Slang* defined the new term *skyscraper* as "a very tall building such as are now being built in Chicago." These were the forerunners of today's high-rise buildings.

FIG. 6.26. Auditorium Building at Michigan Avenue and Congress Parkway (500 S.) in about 1950. Designed by Adler and Sullivan and completed in 1889, the building is one of Chicago's most famous cultural and architectural landmarks—one that has been preserved. The building united a hotel, offices, and an acoustically superb theater in one structure. After about a half century of full and profitable use, the owners declared bankruptcy in 1941. During World War II, the building was used by the United Service Organization and in 1946 became the home of Roosevelt University. With the aid of a public fund-raising drive, the university restored the theater to operation in 1967. Photograph by Ralph Line; courtesy of Municipal Reference Collection, Chicago Public Library.

FIG. 6.27. State Street in the south Loop of the 1960s. A few south Loop streets, including State and Clark, were once the sites of cheap hotels, pawnshops, burlesque and peep shows, betting parlors, and numerous taverns. These streets have since been redeveloped. Photograph by Herb Gaede.

The fire also helped indirectly in the development of Chicago's impressive lakefront Grant Park (originally called Lake Park). Some of the debris from the fire was dumped into the lake, along the original shoreline east of Michigan Avenue. This debris eventually formed the base of much of the park, which today forms the attractive front yard of Chicago's downtown area.

For a while, retail stores were being built in the park. But one of the residents who had an office on Michigan Avenue, Montgomery Ward, recalled that a state law required all of this landfill, from Randolph on the north to Roosevelt on the south, to be open for public use only. He therefore went to the courts and eventually won his case. As a result, all of the commercial structures that had been built in Grant Park had to be torn down. Today the park contains only public facilities, such as the Art Institute, the new Millennium Park,

ball fields, flower gardens, statues, and more. One of the statues is of Montgomery Ward, honoring him for his work in saving the park from commercialization.

The commercial and manufacturing activities of downtown grew with the expansion of the city's population from a half million people in 1880 to well over 3 million a half century later. The growth of downtown was accompanied by the specialization of functions. What was probably the world's most concentrated shopping district stretched for almost a mile along State Street. The wholesale produce area was situated along the main stem of the river; La Salle Street became a major financial center; Market Street was the heart of the garment district; and entertainment facilities were spread along Randolph Street. Smaller enclaves contained concentrations of millinery, florist, furniture,

FIG. 6.28. Michigan Avenue looking north from the new Wrigley Building, 1921. The "Magnificent Mile" had a long way to go when this photograph was taken, but the opening of the Michigan Avenue Bridge the previous year helped initiate rapid development of the street as the site of luxury retail stores, hotels, and office buildings. The Water Tower and the Drake Hotel *(top, left of center)* are the only structures of prominence that still stand. Chicago Historical Society.

music, and other specialty establishments, as well as pawnshops, gambling parlors, and burlesque theaters. Multistory buildings used for light manufacturing were to the west and, to a lesser extent, to the north of the downtown area.

Historically, retail expansion had been slow to develop north of the river, partly because the merchants south of the river feared new competition—at one time they had even burned a bridge that led to North Side establishments. A major breakout of the concentrated downtown commercial area occurred with the opening of the double-deck Michigan Avenue Bridge in 1920. Thus started the development of the "Magnificent Mile," consisting of luxury shops, hotels, and office buildings north of the Loop, a development that coincided with a major downtown building boom in the 1920s. However, with the coming of the Depression and then World War II, virtually all major construction was brought to a standstill.

After almost a quarter century of construction stagnation, the completion in 1957 of the forty-one-story Prudential Building on the air rights over the Illinois Central tracks launched the greatest era of construction that downtown Chicago had yet experienced. The John Hancock Center soars one hundred stories tall. The Sears Tower rose to 110 stories and became the nation's tallest building. It dwarfs other such Chicago giants as the Bank One Building (sixty stories), Marina City (sixty-two stories), Lake Point Tower (seventy stories), Water Tower Place (seventy-four stories), the Aon Building (eighty stories), AT&T Corporate Center (sixty stories), Two Prudential Plaza (sixty-four stories), and 311 South Wacker Drive (sixty-five stories). Measured in feet, three of the four tallest

buildings—and five of the ten tallest—in the United States are in Chicago.

Chicago's downtown business district evidences a viability and growth in employment that few other large city downtowns can match. Downtown employment boasts over one-half million workers, or about 30 percent of the total number of jobs in the city. However, the functions of the downtown area have changed significantly.

Once-critical manufacturing and wholesale activities have declined dramatically in the city, due to economic and technological changes. The structures—often obsolete—in which these activities were conducted are being replaced by office buildings and, increasingly, on the fringe of the Loop, by tall residential buildings. Some buildings, such as the John Hancock Center and Water Tower Place, combine residential, retail, and office functions. The entertainment function of the downtown area (largely a nighttime activity) had also been declining, spreading into the Old Town and New Town areas to the north, and into the suburbs. However, in recent years a new theatrical district is being developed along the Randolph Street corridor in the Loop. There some of the old movie palaces such as the Chicago, Oriental, and Palace have been converted into live theaters, and the Goodman Theater has been added.

Banking remains strong in the downtown area. In recent years, a number of banks have expanded their facilities. Over fifty banks have established branches or representative offices in downtown Chicago, and an increasing number of savings and loan associations have opened downtown branches. Chicago's largest bank, Bank One, has assets of over $256 billion, followed by La Salle Bank with assets of about $65 billion. Bank One, however, is being merged into J. P. Morgan

FIG. 6.29. Double-deck Michigan Avenue Bridge over the Chicago River, which, at its debut in 1920, helped spark the development of the fashionable Magnificent Mile along North Michigan Avenue. Towering above the bridge in this 1972 view are *(left to right)* the Wrigley Building (1921, 1924), the Tribune Tower (1925), and the Equitable Building (1965). Fort Dearborn once stood on a site just west of the bridge, along the south bank of the river. Photograph courtesy of the Chicago Convention and Tourism Bureau.

FIG. 6.30. Examples of Chicago skyscraper architecture, including three of the four tallest buildings in the nation *(left to right):* Sears Tower, the nation's tallest building at 1,454 feet (110 stories), its design consisting of nine modular tubes of varying heights; the twin towers of the sixty-two story (588 feet) Marina City, a concentrated complex of apartments, commercial and recreational facilities, and eighteen-story parking garage; the one-hundred-story (1,127 feet) John Hancock Center, a commercial and residential facility and the city's third-tallest building; the gleaming, white-terra-cotta Wrigley Building (thirty-two stories, 398 feet), built about eighty years ago, a link to an earlier age of Chicago office building architecture; and the eighty-story (1,136 feet) Aon Building, formerly the Amoco Building and the second-tallest building in the city. Photograph courtesy of Chicago Convention and Tourism Bureau.

Chase (as Chase) and will curtail some of its Chicago-based functions.

Banks are the third-largest user of downtown office space, trailing insurance companies, which rank first, and attorneys, who rank second. Other large office-space users in downtown Chicago are accountants and engineers, retailing companies, printing and publishing companies, oil and gas companies, machinery companies, nonprofit groups, communications companies, and stockbrokers. The downtown pays an estimated 40 percent of the entire city's property tax.

Retail growth in the downtown area has been handicapped by the dispersal of many of the higher-income families to the suburbs and the proliferation, toward the perimeter of the

FIG. 6.31. Decades of city grime being removed from the 222 North La Salle building in downtown Chicago. Photograph by Irving Cutler.

city and in the suburbs, of 150 small and large shopping centers geared to the automobile age. Downtown retail business has also been hurt by the concentration of low-income minority groups around the downtown area and by problems of safety, congestion, and parking. In recent years, the numbers of stores and retail workers in the downtown area have declined. The city's proportion of total retail sales in the entire metropolitan area has declined significantly since before World War II. Before the war, State Street had seven large department stores aligned from Randolph to Congress streets, while today there are only three.

An increasing percentage of downtown workers and customers are African American, Hispanic, and Asian, reflecting their greater numbers and affluence, the elimination of racial barriers, good public transportation to the Loop, and the lack of adequate facilities in their own neighborhoods.

Shopping in the old downtown area has been affected by the "new downtown," which has expanded rapidly north of the river in the area of the Magnificent Mile along North Michigan Avenue. Here, high-quality stores, elegant restaurants, and luxury hotels cater to higher-income clientele. Climaxing the opening of numerous new, fashionable facilities along Michigan Avenue was the opening in 1975 of Water Tower Place, a seventy-four-story, $150 million, multiuse building, which contains Marshall Field's (now Macy's) and Lord and Taylor stores, nearly one hundred specialty shops, the 450-room Ritz-Carlton Hotel, and 260 luxury condominiums. The Magnificent Mile now is one of the world's great fashion meccas, with Water Tower Place accounting for almost 40 percent of its retail sales. Since World War II, billions of dollars have been invested in the Magnificent Mile,

its Gold Coast neighborhood to the north and northeast, and in Streeterville to the east.

Streeterville is named after one of Chicago's more colorful squatters, Captain George Wellington Streeter. In 1886 his steamboat ran aground on a sandbar about 400 yards east of the beach at approximately Chicago Avenue (800 N.). As sand drifted about the boat, Captain Streeter invited building contractors to dump their debris on his newly formed land to expand it. Eventually, Captain Streeter claimed about 186 acres of filled-in lakefront as his domain. Despite government opposition, he sold lots and built a small shantytown around his tavern. After years of legal wrangling with the city and nearby residents and in the wake of a number of bloody altercations (one of which resulted in the killing of a policeman in 1918), Captain Streeter was finally evicted from his "District of Lake Michigan" and the shanties were burned. Today Streeterville is a prime residential and office building area and the location of a sizable segment of Chicago's communication media industry.

In sharp contrast to North Michigan Avenue is the relatively recent development, just to the northwest, of shopping and entertainment of a more unusual, arts-and-crafts, faddish, small-shop type. It developed first in Old Town, centered along Wells Street (200 W.), Division Street (1200 N.), and North Avenue (1600 N.), and later, slightly farther north in New Town. The New Town entertainment and shopping facilities extend along Lincoln Avenue, Clark Street, Halsted Street, Broadway, Armitage Avenue, and Clybourn Avenue. Until the turbulent, riotous late 1960s, these establishments catered to many tourists, but now both New

FIG. 6.32. Chicago skyline, Grant Park, and Chicago Harbor, looking northwest from Northerly Island, 2002. Visible at the extreme left is Sears Tower, and at the extreme right, the Aon Center. Photograph courtesy of the City of Chicago/Peter J. Schulz.

and Old Town cater more to the lifestyle of the increasing number of young adults who live in these areas.

As the core of an ever-expanding metropolitan area, the downtown area is by far the front runner in many important categories. It still has the highest concentration of daytime population within the metropolitan area, the highest land values, the greatest building density, and the largest array of services. Downtown has the best accessibility for shoppers and employees, with commuter railroads and the CTA having been augmented by a series of expressways that focus on this important district from most parts of the city and suburbs. The downtown-area residential population has grown very rapidly and is now close to ninety thousand people, with about 40 percent owing their homes.

The importance of downtown is increasing as its outskirts continue to see a tremendous and continuing boom in new office, hotel, and residential buildings and in the conversion of underused facilities into viable residential or commercial facilities. The development and redevelopment boom took place first to the north and then also to the south and west of downtown. Some of the major developments are in the River North and Streeterville areas to the north and in Dearborn Park I and II and Central Station to the south. A smaller but growing number of developments are to the west of downtown.

Within the downtown area itself, the Illinois Center—bounded by the Chicago River on the north, Randolph Street on the south, Michigan Avenue on the west, and the lake on the east—is a major eighty-three-acre multistructure office, residential, and hotel high-rise complex built over the Illinois Central Gulf railroad. It contains three large hotels, including the city's largest, the Hyatt Regency, which has more than two thousand rooms. The complex is said to include about seventy places to eat.

FIG. 7.1. Chicago's lakefront and Michigan Avenue looking northward from Balbo Drive. Visible at the left, in Grant Park, is the Art Institute. In the background, the three tallest buildings are *(left to right)* the John Hancock Center, Two Prudential Plaza (sixty-four stories), and the Aon Center. The buildings to the right in the background are mainly residential facilities. Image by Wernher Krutein; by permission of Photovault.

7

Culture, Education, and Recreation

Recreation Facilities

Chicago's numerous cultural, educational, and recreational facilities are an important facet of the city's economy. Besides being used and enjoyed by local residents, they are a major attraction for nearly nineteen million tourists, almost a million of them from overseas, who come to Chicago each year. These visitors, along with the more than thirteen million business travelers who attend conventions, group meetings, and trade shows and engage in commercial transactions, support numerous jobs in the area.[1]

Chicago has an extensive system of parks, beaches, zoos, forest preserves, sports arenas, and museums. The northern twenty-five of Chicago's thirty miles of lakefront are dedicated to public use only. This lakefront strip contains three major parks, Lincoln Park, Grant Park, and Jackson Park; thirty-three beaches; the nation's largest number of harbor slips, 7,147; one of the oldest and most visited free zoos in the nation, Lincoln Park Zoo; a number of major museums; many lagoons and fishing piers; golf courses, extensive hiking and bicycle trails, and numerous other recreational facilities, including the very popular Navy Pier and Millennium Park. It is

estimated that on a pleasant summer Sunday about a million people use Chicago's lakefront facilities. Annual major lakefront summer events such as the Taste of Chicago, Venetian Night, and the Air and Water Show attract additional millions of people.

The city also contains five large inland parks, Washington, Douglas, Garfield, Columbus, and Humboldt, all connected by a boulevard system. They all have lagoons, field houses, ball fields, picnic facilities, flower gardens, and other features. Chicago has a total of 551 public parks of varying sizes on 6,697 acres. A number of the larger parks were designed by the great landscape architects Frederick Law Olmstead, Jens Jensen, or William Le Baron Jenney.

The Cook County Forest Preserve covers 67,152 acres, of which 3,683 acres are in Chicago. Included in the preserves are horseback riding and bicycle trails, nature centers, toboggan slides, and the well-known Chicago Botanic Garden and Brookfield Zoo.

Chicago is home to a number of professional sports teams, including the Cubs, Sox, Bears, Bulls, Blackhawks, Wolves, and Fire. While the teams through the years have had

FIG. 7.2. Polar bear exhibit at Lincoln Park Zoo. Founded in 1868, the zoo is now one of the most-visited free zoological parks in the country. For two decades during the first half of the twentieth century, the zoo's most famous resident was the gorilla Bushman. Image by Wernher Krutein; by permission of Photovault.

FIG. 7.3. Oak Street Beach at Oak Street and Lake Shore Drive, 1929. On Chicago's fashionable Gold Coast, this most popular beach attracted people from the entire Chicago area. Photograph courtesy of the Chicago Park District Special Collections.

FIG. 7.4. Lakefront, looking south at Northerly Island, the Shedd Aquarium, the Field Museum, Soldier Field, the Burnham Park Yacht Harbor, and McCormick Place, a convention center. Image by Wernher Krutein; by permission of Photovault.

many star players, the one who gained a wide national and international reputation because of his brilliant basketball skills was Michael Jordan of the Chicago Bulls.

Chicago has forty-nine museums, including several of national renown. The latter include the Museum of Science and Industry, the Peggy Notebaert Nature Museum, the Field Museum of Natural History, the Museum of Broadcast Communications, the Shedd Aquarium, the Adler Planetarium, the Chicago Historical Society, and the Oriental Institute. In the fields of art and music, the Art Institute of Chicago, the Museum of Contemporary Art, the Lyric Opera, the Ravinia Music Festival, and the Chicago

Symphony Orchestra rank among the nation's finest. The major museums attract about eight million visitors annually.

The city's and state's top tourist attraction, however, is the new, redeveloped Navy Pier, opened in 1995 at a cost of $187 million. Navy Pier is now a huge entertainment center, complete with fifty shops, many restaurants, a children's museum, three theaters, a ballroom, a huge Ferris wheel, carousel, three exhibition halls, an ice skating rink, and the home port of a number of tour and cruise boats. Its success in attracting a varied clientele of visitors and residents has exceeded expectations, surpassing in a few years of existence the former

FIG. 7.5. Museum of Science and Industry in Jackson Park, one of the nation's most visited museums. Housed in the restored Fine Arts Building of the World's Columbian Exposition of 1893, it contains some seventy-five major exhibit areas, with two thousand displays that explain the principles of science and how they are applied in industry and everyday life. Photograph courtesy of Chicago Convention and Tourism Bureau.

FIG. 7.6. Adler Planetarium and Astronomy Museum, the first modern planetarium in the western hemisphere. Opened in 1930 and funded by Max Adler, a retired executive with Sears, Roebuck and Company, it includes planetarium theaters and one of the world's finest collections of historical astronomy scientific instruments. To the right is a statue of the astronomer Copernicus. Photograph courtesy of the Chicago Convention and Tourism Bureau.

FIG. 7.7. Popular exhibit at the Field Museum of Natural History. Photograph courtesy of Chicago Convention and Tourism Bureau.

tourist attendance leader, the Museum of Science and Industry. Navy Pier is now visited by nearly nine million people annually.

The five-block-long Navy Pier that juts out into Lake Michigan was originally completed in 1916, primarily to handle a portion of the large number of ships that navigated the Great Lakes during that time. Through the years, as shipping declined, the pier served as a place of exhibits, festivals, entertainment, and social events; as the original home of the University of Illinois at Chicago after World War II; and as a training facility for the U.S. Navy during the two world wars. During World War II the pier was the base of operations for two ships converted into small aircraft carriers used to train Navy pilots. One of those who won his Navy pilot wings by successfully completing numerous takeoffs and landings on the carriers would later become President George H. W. Bush.

Beginning to challenge Navy Pier as a tourist draw is the new 24.5-acre Millennium Park, opened in 2004 at a cost of $475 million. Among its facilities are an indoor theater

FIG. 7.8. Navy Pier, 2003. Opened in 1916 to serve Great Lakes shipping, the pier has had a variety of uses through the years and now is a top tourist attraction. Photograph by Irving Cutler.

FIG. 7.9. Riverview Park, the city's major amusement park, about 1960. It opened in 1904 with three rides on the seventy-four-acre site, which had been the home of the German Sharpshooters Club at Western (2400 W.) and Belmont (3200 N.) avenues. The park served a number of generations of thrill seekers with what amounted, in time, to 120 rides, including the popular Bobs, Pair-O-Chutes, Tunnel of Love, and Flying Turns. In 1967 it was sold to commercial interests and is now the site of a strip mall. Photograph courtesy of Harold M. Mayer.

FIG. 7.10. Twenty-four-acre, $475 million Millennium Park in Chicago on July 8, 2004. Between Columbus Drive and Michigan Avenue, the site used to be a rail yard and a parking lot that marred the northwest corner of the otherwise elegant Grant Park. Four years behind schedule, the park officially opened July 16, 2004. Its outdoor Frank Gehry–designed Pritzker Pavilion, with large curving stainless steel panels and trellis, seats eleven thousand people. The subterranean Harris Theater seats fifteen hundred. Other features include the large bean-shaped, reflecting *Cloud Gate*, the two tall Crown Fountains, beautiful landscaping and artwork, and a huge underground parking garage. AP/Wide World Photos.

FIG. 7.11. *Cloud Gate* sculpture *(left)* and the Pritzker Pavilion *(right)* in Millennium Park. Photograph by Daniel Cutler.

and underground parking, galleries, gardens, two large human-faced fountains that spout water, Frank Gehry's huge outdoor Pritzker Pavilion theater, as well as his long, curving BP Bridge, and Anish Kapoor's huge reflecting polished stainless-steel sculpture, "Cloud Gate."

Education

The Chicago metropolitan area, with its thirty-seven colleges and universities, is a major center of higher education. More than seventy Nobel Prize winners have been associated with the University of Chicago alone, and the university was the site where, on December 2, 1942, Enrico Fermi and his colleagues achieved the world's first controlled nuclear chain reaction. DePaul and Loyola universities are among the largest Catholic schools in the country, and the University of Illinois at Chicago, established after World War II, now has twenty-five thousand students. Other state schools are Chicago State University and Northeastern Illinois University. Northwestern University has campuses in Evanston and Chicago. In downtown, Roosevelt University occupies the landmark Auditorium Building in an area that also includes Columbia College, Robert Morris College, Spertus Institute of Jewish Studies, and the downtown campus of DePaul University. A few miles to the south is the Illinois Institute of Technology.

Chicago is also noted for its medical facilities, many of which are operated by the universities. It has six medical schools and three major medical centers. One of every five physicians in the United States has received all or part of his or her training in Chicago.

The city has a number of important specialized libraries that attract scholars in many fields of interest. These include the John Crerar Library in science, the Newberry Library in the humanities, and the Library of International Relations.

Through the years, distinguished educators, artists, and writers have been associated with the city and felt its influence—some for short periods, others for many years. William Rainey Harper, John Dewey, Ella Flagg Young, and Robert Maynard Hutchins were all influential in education. The Chicago "school" of economics included such scholars as Thorstein Veblen, Friedrich von Hayek, Frank H. Knight, and Milton Friedman. The Chicago school of urban sociology, which included William F. Ogburn, Robert E. Park, Ernest W. Burgess, and Louis Wirth, produced a series of classical monographs on cities, with special emphasis on Chicago. Other Chicago schools are less well known but are also influential in their fields.

Chicago is viewed in a myriad of ways by its millions of inhabitants and visitors. As an astute observer wrote in 1974,

> To many people Chicago has been more than a hustling Midwestern city. To some it has meant the world's largest commercial building (the Merchandise Mart), the world's largest grain market (the Board of Trade) and the world's largest farmers' market (the Chicago Mercantile Exchange). To others it has meant the center of the American transportation system, for during the years of extensive train travel no passenger train went through Chicago. A traveler had to change from one train to another or from one station to another. To these travelers Chicago represented an

FIG. 7.12. University of Chicago, looking northeast from Sixtieth Street and Ingleside Avenue. Photograph courtesy of the University of Chicago.

inconvenience to be borne nobly. But they kept coming, for passenger trains arrived and departed almost every minute. To others, it still represents a city of wickedness where vice is rampant, where gangsters rule the municipal government and terrorize the citizens. For some it is the center of the only truly American music, and they come searching for the small bistros which had given rise to jazz in the twenties. For some it is the center of American architecture with the emphasis upon the "Chicago construc-

tion," and they come hoping to find the old buildings of Adler and Sullivan, forgetting that Chicago tears down in order to rebuild. For some few it represents a cultural center, and they come to tramp through some of the world's greatest museums and most beautiful parks. Whatever else it might appear to be, it is a city to be seen, and millions of people pour into the city each year with cameras swinging on their shoulders and wonder in their eyes. It makes no difference

FIG. 7.13. Old Criminal Court building at Dearborn (36 W.) and Hubbard (440 N.), where many important cases were tried, including the famous Leopold and Loeb murder trial in 1924. Carl Sandburg, as a young newspaper reporter, covered cases at the courthouse, and in 1928, Ben Hecht and Charles MacArthur wrote a witty play, *The Front Page,* about their newspaper experiences mainly in this courthouse. The play later was adapted into movies. The building now houses private law firms. Photograph by Irving Cutler.

that many of the old buildings are gone, that many of the gangsters have died, that jazz has since moved to New York, or that the Chicago for which many search is so elusive. Yet visitors and residents alike pursue the legend that is CHICAGO.[2]

The Literary Field

H. L. Mencken, one of the foremost literary critics of the last century, called the city of Chicago "the most civilized in America" and stated that it was culturally "alive from snout to tail."[3] He was referring essentially to Chicago's prominence in many aspects of the literary world. More than a century ago, a Humboldt Park resident, journalist L. Frank Baum (1856–1919), wrote the children's classic *The Wizard of Oz*. Another journalist, Eugene Field (1850–95), produced numerous children's poems, such as "Wynken, Blynken and Nod" and "Little Boy Blue." Ben Hecht (1894–1964), a journalist, novelist, and later a very successful Hollywood screenwriter, wrote *A Thousand and One Afternoons in Chicago*. He later coauthored, with Charles MacArthur, *The Front Page*, a play about their experiences covering cases in Chicago's Criminal Court building. That play has been made into movies three times. Sherwood Anderson (1876–1941) wrote a number of novels, his greatest work being *Winesburg, Ohio*, which explores the frustration and loneliness of small-town life. Edgar Lee Masters (1869–1950), a successful Chicago lawyer, also wrote about small-town life in his sensitive and engaging *Spoon River Anthology*. One of Chicago's most popular poets and authors was Carl Sandburg (1878–1967), whose works include *Chicago Poems, American Songbag*, and his six-volume biography of Abraham Lincoln. He

FIG. 7.14. Carl Sandburg (1878–1967) in 1920, a popular poet, an author, and a two-time recipient of the Pulitzer Prize. Photograph courtesy of Harold M. Mayer.

won the Pulitzer Prize twice and was often considered a poet of the workingman.

A number of prominent Chicago authors wrote extensively on a variety of subjects but focused, in some of their best novels, on such Chicago subjects as communities and ethnic groups. In the 1930s James T. Farrell (1904–79) wrote the *Studs Lonigan* trilogy about growing up as an Irish Catholic "southsider" in the working-class Washington Park neighborhood. Meyer Levin (1905–81) wrote *The Old Bunch*, the definitive book on growing up in the Jewish Lawndale area. Harry Mark Petrakis (1923–) wrote about the Greeks in his *A Dream of*

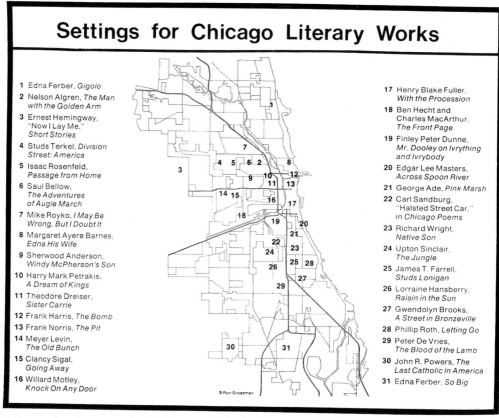

Settings for Chicago Literary Works

1 Edna Ferber, *Gigolo*
2 Nelson Algren, *The Man with the Golden Arm*
3 Ernest Hemingway, "Now I Lay Me," *Short Stories*
4 Studs Terkel, *Division Street: America*
5 Isaac Rosenfeld, *Passage from Home*
6 Saul Bellow, *The Adventures of Augie March*
7 Mike Royko, *I May Be Wrong, But I Doubt It*
8 Margaret Ayere Barnes, *Edna His Wife*
9 Sherwood Anderson, *Windy McPherson's Son*
10 Harry Mark Petrakis, *A Dream of Kings*
11 Theodore Dreiser, *Sister Carrie*
12 Frank Harris, *The Bomb*
13 Frank Norris, *The Pit*
14 Meyer Levin, *The Old Bunch*
15 Clancy Sigal, *Going Away*
16 Willard Motley, *Knock On Any Door*

17 Henry Blake Fuller, *With the Procession*
18 Ben Hecht and Charles MacArthur, *The Front Page*
19 Finley Peter Dunne, *Mr. Dooley on Ivrything and Ivrybody*
20 Edgar Lee Masters, *Across Spoon River*
21 George Ade, *Pink Marsh*
22 Carl Sandburg, "Halsted Street Car," in *Chicago Poems*
23 Richard Wright, *Native Son*
24 Upton Sinclair, *The Jungle*
25 James T. Farrell, *Studs Lonigan*
26 Lorraine Hansberry, *Raisin in the Sun*
27 Gwendolyn Brooks, *A Street in Bronzeville*
28 Phillip Roth, *Letting Go*
29 Peter De Vries, *The Blood of the Lamb*
30 John R. Powers, *The Last Catholic in America*
31 Edna Ferber, *So Big*

© Ron Grossman

FIG. 7.15. Literary geography of Chicago: neighborhood settings of some of Chicago's major literary works. From *Chicago Magazine*, March 1980; map copyrighted by Ron Grossman.

Kings and *Pericles on 31st Street.* Arthur Meeker (1902–70), in *Prairie Avenue,* wrote about the very wealthy on that street. African American life in Chicago is similarly well depicted in some powerful and highly successful writings: Richard Wright (1908–60) wrote the provocative but highly successful novel *Native Son;* Lorraine Hansberry (1930–65) wrote the well-received play *A Raisin in the Sun;* and Gwendolyn Brooks (1917–2000) wrote poetry that depicted the struggles and hopes of African Americans. She won the Pulitzer Prize for poetry in 1950—the first African American to do so. Edna Ferber (1887–1968) won a Pulitzer Prize in 1925 for her novel *So Big,* which portrayed the Dutch immigrants in South Holland, a suburb just south of Chicago.

Novelist Saul Bellow (1915–2005) is the winner of three National Book Awards, a Pulitzer Prize, and the Nobel Prize for Literature in 1976. His novels include *The Adventures of Augie March, Herzog,* and *Humboldt's Gift.* An undergraduate student of the University of Chicago, he later taught there for many years.

One of the most controversial but admired of the Chicago novelists was Nelson Algren (1909–81). He was considered controversial because he wrote about the seamy side of Chicago, including its drunks, prostitutes, and drug addicts in the mainly Polish neighborhoods on the Northwest Side. He won the National Book Award for his novel *A Walk on the Wild Side*. He also wrote *Never Come Morning; Chicago: City on the Make;* and the *Man With the Golden Arm,* which was made into a movie with Frank Sinatra. For many years Algren carried on a romance, sometimes long-distance, with Simone de Beauvoir, the famous French novelist and feminist.

Louis "Studs" Terkel (1912–), an award-winning author, is one of the most popular and best-known literary figures in Chicago, having had for many years his own radio and television shows. His books, many based on interviews, include *Division Street, Hard Times, Working, Race,* and *The Good War,* for which he won the Pulitzer Prize in 1984. *Working* has also been the basis for a play.

Ernest Hemingway (1899–1961) is perhaps the author best known internationally. A native of Oak Park, he spent much of his life overseas. He wrote numerous novels and short stories, many about people living dangerous but courageous lives. He was awarded the Pulitzer Prize in 1952 and the Nobel Prize for Literature in 1954. He became known as the spokesperson of the "lost generation." He participated in World Wars I and II and in the Spanish Civil War. His books include *The Sun Also Rises, For Whom the Bell Tolls, Farewell to Arms,* and *The Old Man and the Sea.* Plagued by ill health, he took his own life in 1961. Also from Oak Park was Edgar Rice Burroughs (1875–1954), who wrote the *Tarzan* series of novels.

FIG. 7.16. Saul Bellow (1915–2005), raised in Chicago's Northwest Side. A leading figure in American literature, he received three National Book Awards, the Pulitzer Prize, and the Nobel Prize for Literature in 1976. Photograph courtesy of the Chicago Jewish Archives.

FIG. 7.17. Nelson Algren (1909–81), an admired but controversial novelist who grew up on Chicago's Northwest Side and wrote about the underside of the city. His novels include *The Man with the Golden Arm* and *A Walk on the Wild Side,* for which he won the National Book Award. Photograph courtesy of Harold M. Mayer.

FIG. 7.18. Studs Terkel, a well-known radio and television personality and the author of a number of books based largely on taped interviews. In 1984 he was awarded the Pulitzer Prize for general nonfiction for his book *The Good War*. Photograph © Nina Subin.

FIG. 7.19. Mike Royko (1932–97), who wrote a nationally syndicated column that appeared in some two hundred newspapers. Known for his biting humor and satire, he was the champion of the little guy and worked to expose corruption, phoniness, and injustice in the power structure. His column appeared in major Chicago newspapers for about thirty-five years. Photograph courtesy of Harold M. Mayer.

Writers whose works were influenced by sojourns in Chicago include George Ade, Willa Cather, Upton Sinclair, Theodore Dreiser, Philip Roth, Willard Motley, and Frank Norris. While many of the writers were also journalists and columnists, a few acclaimed ones became syndicated nationally, including "Ring" Lardner, who specialized in sports; Sydney J. Harris, a thought-provoking columnist; and Mike Royko, sometimes acerbic, with a biting humor that exposed phoniness, fraud, and injustice, and who won the Pulitzer Prize for commentary in 1972. The more prominent of the current writers include playwright, screen writer, and Pulitzer Prize winner David Mamet and crime writers Sara Paretsky and Scott Turow. Other important contemporary writers include Philip Caputo, Leonard Dubkin, Sandra Cisneros, Stewart Dybek, James McManus, Norbert Blei, William Brashler, Larry Heinemann, Andrew Greeley, Eugene Kennedy, and Richard Stern.

Through the years, Chicago has given rise to a variety of periodicals ranging from Harriet Monroe's *Poetry* to Hugh Hefner's *Playboy*. The Chicago school of writers, whose works were strongly influenced by their association with Chicago, has indeed had a strong impact on twentieth- and twenty-first-century American literature.

The Chicago area also has about two hundred live-theater companies scattered throughout the city and suburbs. Many are small, enterprising off-Loop theaters that offer adventurous experimental theater but often struggle financially. Among the theaters that have gained national recognition are the Goodman, Steppenwolf, and Second City. Other viable and successful theaters include Victory Gardens, Northlight, and Chicago Shakespeare Theater. The once flourishing

FIG. 7.20. Looking east on Randolph Street from Clark Street toward the new live-theater district, 2005. A number of the theaters were formerly large movie palaces. Photograph by Irving Cutler.

ethnic theaters have virtually disappeared. In the 1890s there were eleven such German theaters in the city. Of the many noted actors and actresses who performed in these various theaters, the Steppenwolf Theater is especially well known for developing television and movie stars Laurie Metcalf, John Malkovich, John Mahoney, Rondi Reed, Joan Allen, and Gary Sinese.

Chicago was a pioneer in the movie industry and was known as the first "Hollywood." As early as 1896, a narrative film, *The Tramp and the Dog*, was produced in Chicago by the company of "Colonel" William Selig. A movie studio was opened in 1908 by the Essanay Film Manufacturing Company at 1345 West Argyle Street (5000 N.). Its actors included

FIG. 7.21. New home of the Goodman Theater, on Dearborn and Randolph streets in the theater district, 2005. The company had been housed in the Art Institute until 2000. As part of an agreement for the construction of its new home, the Goodman preserved the façades of the Harris and the Selwyn theaters, which occupied a portion of the site and now form the north front of the new theater. Photograph by Daniel Cutler.

Gloria Swanson, Tom Mix, Charlie Chaplin, Wallace Beery, Ben Turpin, and Francis X. Bushman. After enjoying some success in Chicago, the movie industry moved westward after World War I to Hollywood, California, which had climatic and diverse scenery advantages. Nevertheless, through the years, Chicago has been an important locale for the shooting of numerous films and continues to be a major film distribution center. Among those connected with the movie industry who at one time considered Chicago "home" are Ann-Margret, Ed Asner, Barney Balaban, John Belushi, Shelley Berman, Joan Cusack, John Cusack, Severn Darden, Walt Disney,

Roger Ebert, Barbara Harris, Charlton Heston, Amy Madigan, David Mamet, Joe Mantegna, Marlee Matlin, Elaine May, Paul Muni, Bill Murray, Mike Nichols, Kim Novak, Mandy Patinkin, Harold Ramis, Gene Siskel, David Steinberg, Gloria Swanson, Sam Wanamaker, and Johnny Weismuller.

Art

Despite its early reputation as the "hog butcher of the world," the home of shady politics and gangsters, and the "brawling City of the Big Shoulders," Chicago is home to a huge array of art facilities, ranging from world-renowned art museums to hundreds of art galleries, as well as public sculptures by some of the world's most famous artists. Behind the rough surface appearance of Chicago, there were those who strove to bring culture to the city in the form of art. Among those well-known artists who worked in Chicago for varying time lengths are Ivan Albright, Lorado Taft, Augustus Saint-Gaudens, Archibald John Motley Jr., Leonard W. Volk, Richard Hunt, Claes Oldenburg, and Milton Horn.

One of the world's preeminent art museums is the Art Institute of Chicago, which has collections that span five thousand years, encompassing virtually all art media and works from all parts of the world. Its collection of Impressionist and Postimpressionist paintings is among the largest and finest in the world. The museum was founded in 1879 and moved into its present home on Michigan Avenue in 1893. Through the years, it has collected more than three hundred thousand works of art and has developed both a highly rated art school with residential facilities and an extensive library. Its students have included Walt Disney, Grant Wood, Thomas Hart Benton, Ivan Albright, Claes Oldenburg, Georgia O'Keefe, Herblock, and Lorado Taft. The Art Institute of Chicago has a membership of about 120,000, one of the largest memberships of any art museum. In addition to the thousands who attend its numerous art and architecture classes, it attracts about 2 million visitors a year—more when there is a major art exhibit. Many wealthy Chicago art collectors have contributed important art works to the museum.

The Museum of Contemporary Art, founded in 1967, moved to its present home on Chicago Avenue in 1996. It is the only museum in Chicago dedicated almost solely

FIG. 7.22. Art Institute of Chicago on Michigan Avenue, 2003. Founded in 1879, it now has more than three hundred thousand works of art and is one of Chicago's major cultural attractions. It also has a highly rated art school. Photograph by Irving Cutler.

to contemporary art. The museum contains art of all mediums and has a permanent collection of over fifty-six hundred important contemporary art works, including those from internationally famous artists but with an emphasis on Chicago artists.

Among the several other fine art museums in Chicago are the Museum of Contemporary Photography at Columbia College, the David and Alfred Smart Museum of Art, which displays art from the Greeks to the present, and the Museum of the Oriental Institute on the campus of the University of Chicago. The Terra Museum of American Art, which concentrated on the heritage of American artists, has, unfortunately, recently closed. Evanston, in conjunction with Northwestern University, is the site of the Mary and Leigh Block Museum, containing over seven thousand works of art on paper and a sculpture garden that features some significant modern sculptures.

The city also has numerous ethnic museums that exhibit their people's art and culture. Among these museums are the Balzekas Museum of Lithuanian Culture, the Du Sable Museum of African History, the Latvian Folk Art Museum, the Hellenic Museum and Cultural Center, the Mexican Fine Arts Center Museum, the Polish Museum of America, the Spertus Museum of Judaica, the Swedish American Museum of Art, the Ukrainian Institute of Modern Art, and the Ukrainian National Museum. The Mitchell Indian Museum is in Evanston. The essential purpose of these museums is to teach the young about their heritage; to reinforce, nostalgically, the remembrances of the immigrants of their homeland; to preserve the culture of the ethnic group; and to teach outsiders about the group.

The Chicago area has about two hundred fine art, craft, and photography galleries. Although they may be found in virtually all parts of the city and suburbs, the largest concentrations are in River North (just north of the Loop) and, increasingly, in Wicker Park and Bucktown on the Northwest Side. Many of these galleries and local artists are struggling to continue their work, which often depends on the economy, support budgets, and the public's varying support of art.

Chicago is home to many great sculptures, some of which have been produced by the world's best artists. They are typically in parks, plazas, squares, and buildings. Many sculptures honor individuals who have contributed to Chicago or American history, culture, and folklore. They include such varied subjects as Abraham Lincoln, Ulysses Grant, Theodore Thomas, Alexander Hamilton, John Peter Altgeld, General Philip Henry Sheridan, Eugene Field, Mayor Carter Harrison, Mayor John Wentworth, Stephen Douglas, Michael Jordan, Harry Carey, Jack Brickhouse, Marshall Field, Father Marquette, George Pullman, Jane Addams, and Montgomery Ward. Strangely, the Grant statue is standing in Lincoln Park and one Lincoln statue stands in Grant Park. In Oz Park are whimsical statues of the Tin Man and the Cowardly Lion.

Chicago's numerous ethnic and racial groups have statues that honor their heroes. The Germans have Goethe and Schiller; the Danes, Hans Christian Andersen; the Italians, Columbus and Garibaldi; the English, Shakespeare; the Swedes, Linne; the Norwegians, Leif Eriksson; the Poles, Kosciuszko and Copernicus; the Bohemians, Thomas Masaryk; the Mexicans, Juarez; the Scots, Robert Burns; the Jews, Haym Solomon and Henry Horner; and the Puerto Ricans,

Pedro Albizu-Campus. There are also memorials to tragedies such as the Fort Dearborn Massacre, the Haymarket Riot, the Eastland Disaster, the Chicago Fire, the Iroquois Theatre Fire, and the nation's various wars.

A number of the downtown buildings have plazas, a few of which display interesting and unique works of art. In the warmer months, some of the plazas become alive with people and varied activities.

One of the foremost collections of sculptures by world-famous artists is downtown, within a radius of just a few blocks. These include Pablo Picasso's sculpture commonly known as the *Chicago Picasso*, Joan Miro's *Chicago*, Chagall's *Four Seasons*, Alexander Calder's *Flamingo*, Claes Oldenberg's *Batcolumn*, the Buckingham Fountain by Bennett, Parsons, and Frost, Jean Dubuffet's *Monument with Standing Beast*, Milton Horn's *The Spirit of Jewish Philanthropy*, Ivan Mestsovic's *The Bowman and the Spearman*, Edward Kemy's Art Institute lions, and Augustus Saint-Gauden's statue of Abraham Lincoln.

FIG. 7.23. Art in the Loop by distinguished artists. *Top, left to right:* a Picasso sculpture in Daley Plaza; *Flamingo*, a stabile by Alexander Calder in the Federal Center Plaza; and *Universe*, a moving mural by Calder in the lobby of the Sears Tower. The lower photo is *The Four Seasons*, a mosaic by Marc Chagall at the Bank One Plaza (now Chase Plaza). Photograph courtesy of Chicago Convention and Tourism Bureau.

FIG. 7.24. Buckingham Fountain in Grant Park. Donated to the city in 1927 by Kate Sturges Buckingham in memory of her brother Clarence, the fountain is patterned after one at the palace of Versailles and was constructed of Georgia pink marble. It can shoot water to a height of 140 feet and at night is lit in a variety of colors. Irving Cutler collection.

FIG. 7.25. *Batcolumn*, a
108-foot-high sculpture
by Claes Oldenberg.
The sculptor was com-
missioned by the Social
Security Administration
to produce a work
that depicted a facet
of America. The result
stands in the plaza of
the ten-story Chicago
regional headquarters at
600 West Madison Street.
Photograph by Irving
Cutler.

There are also numerous well-known sculptures outside the downtown area. On the South Side are Leonard Volk's tall *Stephen A. Douglas* and probably the most famous and the largest, Lorado Taft's *Fountain of Time,* which stands in Washington Park. The latter depicts more than a hundred people in different walks of life, passing in review before Father Time with a caption that quotes a poem by Austin Dobson: "Time goes, you say. Ah, no. Alas, time stays. We go." Taft also created a grim-looking monument in Graceland Cemetery titled *Eternal Silence.* Also in that cemetery is Louis Sullivan's award-winning Getty Tomb. On the South Side, the Oakwood Cemetery has a tall *Confederate Mound* monument, by an unknown artist, under which an estimated six thousand Confederate soldiers are buried.

Chicago is also noted for its murals. A number of buildings have large lifelike murals that appear to be actual parts of the buildings. Also, many indoor murals depict historic and other interesting subjects, as well as religious themes in churches. The Chicago Board of Trade has an immense five-story mural of Ceres, the Roman goddess of agriculture,

FIG. 7.26. Lorado Taft's huge *Fountain of Time* sculpture in Washington Park, completed in 1923, some fourteen years after it was started. Photograph by Daniel Cutler.

gracing its atrium. At the top of the forty-five-story Board of Trade building is a thirty-foot-high faceless statue, also of Ceres. It is faceless because the prevailing view at the time it was created was that nobody would ever see the details at that height.

In many neighborhoods, but especially in Hispanic areas, are colorful murals, often with political, religious, or nostalgic themes. A recent movement in the school system has been to restore the hundreds of murals that once decorated public schools, some of which are impressive. They were produced in the Depression years of the 1930s by artists who worked for the Works Progress Administration. Many of the murals were marred, painted on, or cemented over. Now that they have been rediscovered, the schools and foundations are holding bake sales and bazaars for money to restore them.

Many groups, individuals, and governmental units have helped to finance, erect, and promote Chicago's monuments, memorials, and murals. Benjamin F. Ferguson, a wealthy lumberman, left an endowment for a sculpture fund that has resulted in the building of seventeen sculptures in Chicago.

Music

Chicago ranks high as a prominent music center—especially in the classical, blues, and jazz fields. The Chicago Symphony Orchestra is rated one of the finest in the world, propelled to the forefront by its earlier directors, Theodore Thomas, Frederick Stock, and Fritz Reiner. George Solti, an acclaimed musical director from 1969 to 1992, and Daniel Barenboim, the current director and a prominent pianist, have in recent decades raised the orchestra to top world status. Since 1904 the orchestra has been housed in Orchestra Hall, which was remodeled, expanded, and renamed *Symphony Center* in 1997. In the summer the orchestra often performs in major American, European, and Asian cities. It also has a summer residency at the Ravinia Music Festival in Highland Park, Illinois. Many suburbs sponsor their own symphony orchestras. In addition, there is a great variety of other musical groups throughout the Chicago area, ranging from the Chicago Sinfonietta to the Music of the Baroque.

FIG. 7.27. Symphony Center, formerly Orchestra Hall, on Michigan Avenue, 2005. It is the long-time home of the renowned Chicago Symphony Orchestra. Photograph by Irving Cutler.

FIG. 7.28. Entrance to the thirty-six-acre Ravinia Park in Highland Park, 2003. Started in 1904 as an amusement park by the adjacent railroad, in 1936 it became the summer home of the Chicago Symphony Orchestra. Each summer, Ravinia presents outdoor programs—symphony, folk, singing, jazz, and ballet—by performers of international repute. It is one of the area's major cultural assets. Photograph by Daniel Cutler.

FIG. 7.29. Civic Opera House on Wacker Drive, 2003. Built by the speculative financier Samuel Insull in 1929, it has housed the highly successful Lyric Opera of Chicago since the 1950s. Photograph by Daniel Cutler.

The Lyric Opera of Chicago is considered one of the best in the country. It is housed in the grand old Civic Opera House on Wacker Drive, along the South Branch of the Chicago River. For years it boasted record subscription numbers and box office receipts. It deftly combines old classical operas with more modern, often venturesome programs. Many other opera and choral groups operate throughout the Chicago metropolitan area.

Chicago is also famous for its blues music. Blues came to Chicago from the Mississippi delta area, transported by thousands of African American migrants from the rural South who arrived during the 1930s and around World War II. In Chicago, urban blues were added to rural blues and, later, were amplified electrically by Willie Dixon, the foremost bluesman. Other popular bluesmen included Muddy Waters, Howlin' Wolf, Little Walter, "Big" Bill Broonzy, and Buddy Guy. Blues music was advanced by Chess Records, a recording company run by Phil and Leonard Chess, a pair of Polish immigrant Jews. The

FIG. 7.30. House of Blues, 2003. At 329 North Dearborn Street, the popular nightspot is part of the Marina City complex. Photograph by Irving Cutler.

FIG. 7.31. Chicago Jazz Festival, held in Grant Park near the city's lakefront, 2005. It is one of many festivals and other events held in the park annually. Photograph by Irving Cutler.

FIG. 7.32. Benny Goodman (1909–86), born in the Maxwell Street area of Chicago. The "King of Swing" performed at Carnegie Hall with his band, one of the first to be racially integrated. Irving Cutler collection.

of the Grant Park Symphony Orchestra and Chorus. Gospel is believed to have been born in Chicago in the 1930s, with such renowned artists as composer-pianist Thomas Dorsey and gospel singer Mahalia Jackson.

The city is also an important jazz center. Like the blues, jazz first arrived in the North from the South, especially from New Orleans around World War I. Among the early African American jazz musicians who came to Chicago were Joe King Oliver, Louis Armstrong, and Jelly Roll Morton. Other prominent African American jazz musicians who lived and performed in Chicago were Earl Hines and Ramsey Lewis. Jazz was soon picked up by such white Chicago-born musicians as Gene Krupa, a pioneering jazz drummer, and Benny Goodman, the "King of Swing." Goodman was born in the Maxwell Street area and helped make jazz danceable and respectable for white audiences with his 1938 performance in Carnegie Hall. The jazz clubs, like the blues clubs, were first most prevalent on the South Side but now are found mainly around downtown and on the North Side, along with smaller numbers of folk, rock, and country music clubs. Some of the important people connected with the folk scene in Chicago include Steve Goodman, Bonnie Koloc, John Prine, Bob Gibson, and "Win" Stracke. Through the years, the various ethnic groups have had their own favorite music, ranging from the Polish polka to the Jewish klezmer music.

Popular vocalists native to Chicago include Mel Torme and Mandy Patinkin. In dance, Ruth Page and Katherine Dunham were, for many decades, the essence of Chicago dance. The city is now also home to the famous Joffrey Ballet.

company was at Michigan Avenue near Cermak Road, and the building is now a Blues museum. Although blues clubs once were concentrated in the African American neighborhoods of the South Side, they now number more than a hundred in the Chicago area and are most prevalent in white North Side trendy neighborhoods. The three-day blues festival held annually in Grant Park draws a crowd of almost half a million. Other large, popular outdoor summer music festivals held annually in the same park are the Gospel Festival, the Jazz Festival, and many ethnic music festivals, as well as the ongoing programs

FIG. 7.33. Aragon Ballroom, at Lawrence and Broadway in Uptown, 2003. For many years it featured big-name bands. A sister ballroom, the Trianon, at Sixty-third Street and Cottage Grove Avenue, was razed years ago. Photograph by Irving Cutler.

Architecture

Chicago is noted for its innovative, distinguished, and diverse architecture. Its buildings range from the balloon-frame houses of its earliest days to the bungalow belts of the early 1900s, to the first skyscrapers. The city is home to some of the tallest buildings in the country—including its tallest—but it owes its stellar reputation to quality and innovation rather than to building size.

Before Chicago's incorporation in 1833, its buildings consisted essentially of a small number of log cabins, often mired in mud. The city's incorporation and the construction of the Illinois-Michigan Canal a few years later spurred land speculation and a building boom. The principal structure became the balloon-frame building, essentially developed in Chicago. Rather than using heavy wooden logs, the balloon cagelike framework used two-by-fours fastened with machine-made nails. The frame was then covered with clapboard siding. This construction was relatively easy, fast, and low cost, and the building, though lightweight, was strong and readily movable, if necessary. The balloon-frame building, in a variety of evolving forms, including the numerous one-story or one-and-a-half-story cottages, became the basic mainstay of Chicago building for many decades. Because of its simplified construction, some of the houses were built by the owners.

Subsequent buildings in Chicago incorporated numerous popular architectural styles, including the large and ornate Queen Anne

FIG. 7.34. Henry B. Clarke House, now at 1855 South Indiana Avenue, is Chicago's oldest dwelling. Built in 1836 by a hardware merchant, it was moved from its original location at Eighteenth Street and Wabash Avenue to 4526 South Wabash Avenue, where it served as a church office. In 1977 it was purchased by the city and moved to its present site in the historic Prairie Avenue district. Photograph by Irving Cutler.

and Victorian styles (generally reserved for wealthier residents); substantial graystones, built of gray limestone, found often near parks and boulevards; ubiquitous two-flats and three-flats; stone or brick row houses; and large apartment buildings, sometimes with courtyards or storefronts on ground level. Buildings also ranged from stately residential hotels for the wealthy to crowded boarding-houses for the masses of arriving immigrants. Some of the houses were overcrowded, leading to inner-city decay. Battles between landlords and tenants were frequent, and much mobility existed, often culminating on May 1 — moving day — when leases commonly

expired. In 1923 citywide zoning laws were enacted to regulate some features of the housing market.

The popular bungalow was built in the early decades of the twentieth century. The eighty thousand such homes that remain in Chicago recently received landmark status on the National Register of Historic Places. The solidly built bungalow largely utilized the basic linear floor plan of the cottage, which was limited by Chicago's narrow lots. All had modern plumbing, electricity, and central heating. The bungalow had two or three bedrooms on one side of the house and a parlor, dining room, and kitchen on the other. Unlike cottages, bungalows were built mainly of brick and had a lower-pitched, overhanging roof. They were primarily one- or one-and-a-half-story single-family rectangular homes with a small front porch, a basement, and a front and back yard. Some of the more expensive and generally more attractive bungalows contained fine woodwork, built-in bookcases, artistic windows, and decorative brickwork. The most famous bungalow is the one at 3536 South Lowe (632 W.), which was the home of the two Mayor Daleys. For many laborers, the bungalow was a step upward residentially and was generally small enough to be affordable, averaging then about eight thousand dollars. Such houses were often found in neighborhoods of particular ethnic traditions. The period that witnessed the bungalow boom also spawned the construction of many courtyard apartment buildings and factory buildings that are now rapidly being converted into condominiums and lofts, mainly in the inner city. After World War II the bungalow lost in popularity to ranches and split-level homes.

The rapid urbanization and outward expansion of the city were aided by the steam engine, the omnibus, the horsecar and, later,

the cable car, the electric trolley, the elevated, and the motor vehicle. Broad rings of parks, connected mainly by residential boulevards, were established near the perimeter of the city. Real estate developers and a few railroads built sizable subdivisions, some mass produced. These tracts of land with new homes were heavily marketed, and their amenities were extolled. They required low down payments, and loans were available from the growing number of savings and loan associations, which were often started by and for different ethnic groups. Although many of these new subdivisions were initially outside the city, many of those were annexed in 1889 when Chicago quadrupled in size.

Despite the craze for single-family homes in the 1920s, about two-thirds of Chicagoans were living in apartments, often in the newly popular U-shaped three-story apartment building that wrapped around a central courtyard, allowing for more windows and thus more light.

The construction of the tall steel-skeleton buildings for which Chicago is noted did not commence until after the Great Fire of

FIG. 7.35. Row of brick bungalows in suburban Cicero, 2003. Thousands of bungalows were built in the early decades of the 1900s, especially on Chicago's Southwest and Northwest sides and in some of the city's closer suburbs. Photograph by Irving Cutler.

FIG. 7.36. Weeghman Park at Clark and Addison (3600 N.) streets, home of the Chicago Federals, 1915. Later the stadium became Wrigley Field, the "friendly confines" of the Chicago Cubs and, until 1970, the Chicago Bears. Photograph by *Chicago Daily News;* Chicago Historical Society, ICHi-24343.

1871. Until the Fire, two-thirds of Chicago's buildings were constructed of wood, and the downtown buildings reached no more than three or four stories high, with the exception of the newly built eight-story Palmer House.

The post-Fire building boom attracted many architects who helped Chicago develop the world's first skyscrapers by using the innovative steel skeleton, elevators, and somewhat later, the floating foundation. The precursor of the true skyscraper was probably

William Le Baron Jenney's twelve-story Home Insurance building, built in 1885, which was soon followed by other monumental high-rise buildings in the 1880s and 1890s.

The post-Fire building era in the late 1880s and early 1900s led to the world-famous, innovative First Chicago School of architecture, which included among its members Louis Sullivan, Dankmar Adler, William Le Baron Jenney, Frank Lloyd Wright, Daniel Burnham, John Wellborn Root, Solon S. Beman, and Henry Hobson Richardson. The Chicago

School not only solved technical problems but also allowed valuable land to be used more intensively by building upward.

Buildings kept getting taller. The tallest building in 1921 was the white terra-cotta Wrigley Building at 398 feet, followed by the Gothic Revival Tribune Tower, at 462 feet, that was built across the street in 1925. The first skyscraper built after World War II was the forty-one-story Prudential Building, erected in 1955 and towering 601 feet. Today the tallest building in the city (and the nation) is Sears Tower. It stands an impressive 1,454 feet tall at 110 stories.

Among the more distinguished of the later-twentieth-century architects in the Second Chicago School are Ludwig Mies van der Rohe, Harry Weese, Stanley Tigerman, Bruce Graham, Bertrand Goldberg, Helmut Jahn, Walter Netsch, Ralph Johnson, and Walter Burley Griffin.

The world-famous architect Frank Lloyd Wright (1867–1959) worked for a while for the firm of Adler and Sullivan before starting his own firm in Chicago in 1893. Flamboyant and romantic in his personal life, he was also the chief exponent of the Prairie School of architecture. He designed many landmark

FIG. 7.37. New Soldier Field. Opened in 1924 as a war memorial, it was built in the style of ancient Greek and Roman stadiums. Through the years, it has hosted the "long count" Dempsey-Tunney fight, the International Eucharist Congress of 1926, the Marian Year Tribute of 1954 attended by 260,000, World Cup soccer games, All-Star football games, and the games of the Chicago Bears. After much controversy, the greatly remodeled Soldier Field opened in 2003. What is essentially a bowl-shaped football field has been placed over the old stadium, and the Grecian Doric colonnades have been preserved. Image by Wernher Krutein; by permission of Photovault.

FIG. 7.38. Wrigley Building, on the river in downtown Chicago, 2005. The terra-cotta-sheathed office building, completed in 1924, houses the headquarters of the William Wrigley Jr. Company. Photograph by Daniel Cutler.

buildings.[4] Among those structures in the Chicago area are the Robie House (1909) in Hyde Park and the Unity Temple (1906) in Oak Park.

Ludwig Mies van der Rohe (1886–1969) left Germany during the Nazi era and became head of the department of architecture at the Illinois Institute of Technology. There he helped design the school's campus, including the innovative Crown Hall. He also designed numerous office buildings in Chicago, as well as the two pioneering "glass house" apartments on Lake Shore Drive (1949–51) that were constructed of glass and steel and became imitated worldwide, exemplifying his dictum that "less is more."

FIG. 7.39. Tribune Tower at 435 S. Michigan Avenue, 2005. Completed in 1925, it houses the offices of the *Chicago Tribune*. The architects, Hood and Howells, submitted the winning design in an international competition held by the newspaper in 1922. The cabin of Chicago's first non–Native American settler, du Sable, was built near the site in 1779. Photograph by Daniel Cutler.

Among Helmut Jahn's (1940–) buildings in Chicago is the daring, innovative cylindrical steel-and-glass James Thompson State of Illinois Center. Jahn also helped design the United Airlines terminal at O'Hare International Airport and the colorful, curvy Northwestern Atrium (now Citicorp Center), which houses a major Metra commuter station.

Walter Burley Griffin (1876–1937) studied under Wright and often followed the latter's Prairie School ideas in the numerous homes he built, especially in the Beverly neighborhood on the Southwest Side. A major accomplishment was his designing of Canberra, Australia, that country's capital.

Walter Netsch (1920–) designed the campus of the University of Illinois at Chicago, as well as the Joseph Regenstein Library at the University of Chicago. In conjunction with Bruce Graham, he also helped design the Inland Steel Building, which was the prototype of innovative structural features.

Bruce Graham (1925–) and the innovative structural engineer Fazlur Kahn (1929–82), both of Skidmore, Owings and Merrill, helped design the nation's tallest building, Sears Tower, as well as the One Magnificent Mile building.

Harry Weese (1925–) and Associates designed numerous buildings, including the Swissôtel (1988), the Seventh Church of Christ Scientist (1968), the four River Cottages along the North Branch of the Chicago River (1990), and the triangular Metropolitan Correctional Center (1973–75).

Bertrand Goldberg (1913–97), who studied under Mies van der Rohe in Germany, is known especially for his distinctive, tall cylindrical buildings along the Chicago River: the twin-tower Marina City (1964–67) and

FIG. 7.40. Frank Lloyd Wright (1867–1959), an internationally famous architect and the chief exponent of the Prairie School of architecture. Among the best known of the 380 buildings that he designed are Taliesin (Spring Green, Wisconsin), Unity Temple (Oak Park), Robie House (Chicago), the Johnson Wax Building (Racine, Wisconsin), the Imperial Hotel (Tokyo), and the Guggenheim Museum (New York). Courtesy The Frank Lloyd Wright Foundation, Taliesin West, Scottsdale, AZ.

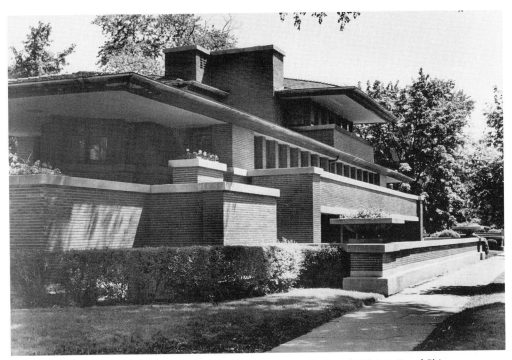

FIG. 7.41. Robie House, at 5757 South Woodlawn Avenue (1200 E.) on the University of Chicago campus, is probably the most famous expression of Frank Lloyd Wright's Prairie School style. The house was built in 1909 for a family in the bicycle business. In 1963 it was designated a National Historic Landmark and recently underwent a major restoration. Tours of the building are given daily. On visiting the home in 1959, Wright said it was his best residential design. Photograph by Daniel Cutler.

the shorter River City (1984–86). Marina City was one of the first "city within a city" structures, with self-contained shopping, entertainment, and parking designed to keep people in the city. He also designed the Raymond Hilliard public housing development.

Stanley Tigerman (1930–) has designed a variety of buildings, including some that are colorful and whimsical, such as the Anti-Cruelty Society Building (1982) and the Illinois Regional Library for the Blind and Physically Handicapped (1975–78). He was also a most active participant in quality low-cost housing and urban renewal developments.

Building on the works of these famed architects, Chicago in the 1990s and early years of the twenty-first century experienced one of the greatest building booms in its history. Mainly residential, the boom surrounded the Loop with largely high-rise residential units. It also moved farther outward, usually with smaller buildings, into adjacent stagnant neighborhoods that were showing signs of decay. The result has been an ever-expanding revitalization and gentrification of the area that surrounds downtown Chicago.

FIG. 8.1. Chicago River from the Rush Street bridge, looking east toward Lake Michigan, about 1869. In the background to the right are the Sturges and Buckingham grain elevators in the Illinois Central terminal complex. Chicago Historical Society.

8 Transportation: External and Internal

From Portage to World Port

In *Planning the Region of Chicago*, Daniel H. Burnham Jr. and Robert Kingery summed up the growth of the city's transportation systems: "At first by water and wagon route, then by railway and finally by motor highway and through the air, the transportation systems of metropolitan Chicago branched out like the arteries of a growing organism, knitting the agricultural settlements and trade centers into an economic unit and joining the Chicago Region with the outside world."[1]

Chicago contains one of the greatest multi-layered transportation networks in the world. Its passenger facilities are among the busiest in the nation, and its freight facilities are geared to handle millions of tons of raw materials annually. It is a major focal point, both for national freight movement and for local traffic interchange. An estimated eighty-six tons of goods per capita are handled annually by the area's transportation network, compared with fifty-four tons per capita nationally.

Chicago's role as a regional, national, and even international center for the various forms of transportation has been one of its greatest assets. However, the relative importance of the various modes of transportation to Chicago has changed through the years.

Water transportation dominated the early era of Chicago; it has been said that Chicago was a port before it was a city. Chicago was blessed with natural waterways, which were used by Native Americans, early explorers, and settlers. But the eventual development of Chicago as an important port depended on a series of manmade improvements, both local and distant. These enhancements included the opening of the Erie Canal in 1825; numerous improvements of the Chicago harbors, starting with the first federal funds in 1833; the completion of the Illinois and Michigan Canal in 1848, the Chicago Sanitary and Ship Canal in 1900, and the Calumet Sag Channel in 1922 (its original sixty-foot width later being widened to 225 feet); and finally, the opening of the modern St. Lawrence Seaway in 1959. These improvements allowed Chicago to take advantage of its location at the junction of major water routes by connecting the city with the Atlantic Ocean and the Gulf of Mexico and, thereby, with the entire world.

Canal and port traffic reached a peak in the 1880s, when the arrivals and clearances of more than twenty-six thousand vessels were

FIG. 8.2. Goodrich Line wharf on the south bank of the Chicago River, east of the Rush Street bridge in 1871, after the Fire. The landing was used by the steamboat company's vessels, from Civil War times until the 1930s, to connect Chicago with ports on both the east and west shores of Lake Michigan. Chicago Historical Society, ICHi-32133.

FIG. 8.3. Construction of the Chicago Sanitary and Ship Canal, 1895, making visible the limestone bedrock that underlies the area. The canal, the "eighth wonder of the world," was opened in 1900 after a decade of construction, which required more earth excavation than the building of the Panama Canal. Chicago Historical Society.

recorded annually for a number of seasons. The banks of the Chicago River in the downtown area were almost continuously lined with wharves during that era. For the next half century, however, water traffic decreased, chiefly because of competition from the railroads. The once flourishing canal barges and the package freight disappeared, although on the whole, the bulk industrial water traffic in iron ore, coal, and limestone for the steel mills continued to increase until the recent closings of the mills.

Water traffic was revived with the completion of the Illinois Waterway in 1933. This waterway made possible barge traffic of a nine-foot draft all the way from Chicago to the Gulf via the Illinois and Mississippi rivers, as well as into a number of the latter's tributaries. In 1959 Queen Elizabeth II and Prince Philip, aboard the royal yacht *Britannia*, led a procession of fifty vessels from Montreal to Chicago to inaugurate the long-awaited opening of the modern version of the St. Lawrence Seaway—an event that was to make Chicago a major world port. Smaller ships had been operating through the old seaway for many years: as early as 1856, the schooner *Dean Richmond* carried a cargo of grain from Chicago to Liverpool.

Water transportation is generally the cheapest form of conveyance, especially for bulk commodities. It also provides substantial savings on manufactured goods, especially if transshipments are eliminated. For example, there is usually an estimated savings of between fifty and sixty dollars in shipping costs on the importation of a foreign automobile via the St. Lawrence Seaway, compared with shipment by water to New York and then by rail to Chicago. An additional benefit for the area is that for every ton of cargo handled by

FIG. 8.4. Straightening of the South Branch of the Chicago River, as seen looking northward from about Eighteenth Street, 1929. The river's wide arc to the east from approximately Congress Street to Eighteenth Street resulted in tight reverse curves in the river, the blockage of through streets that connected the area with the Loop, and awkward track layout for the railroad yards. Straightening the river, accomplished in 1928–30, alleviated some of these problems. Some of the adjacent land was underutilized, and the decline of railroad passenger and freight volume in the area has made much of the land available for redevelopment. Chicago Historical Society.

city dockworkers, an estimated fifty dollars is pumped into the local economy through the generating of jobs and businesses.

The Modern Port of Chicago

Early in Chicago's history, much of the water shipping in the city was handled in the downtown area; today, however, most water freight is handled on the Far South Side, along the six-mile Calumet River and into Lake Calumet. Most of the tonnage is bulk cargo: coal, building materials, chemicals, petroleum, and grain. Such transport, however, has drastically declined due to the depressed industries in this so-called rust belt.

There is some barge shipping along the Chicago River, consisting of the transport of coal for a number of utilities, building materials, petroleum, salt, and a few other products. Several thousand barges enter Chicago waterways annually. Both the South Branch of the Chicago River and its adjoining Chicago Sanitary and Ship Canal are navigable by barge their entire lengths. The North Branch is navigable with at least a nine-foot draft as far as Addison Street (3600 N.) but has relatively little traffic because it dead-ends to the north.

For almost two decades after the opening of the St. Lawrence Seaway in 1959, Chicago normally received between five hundred and eight hundred ships annually, mainly into Lake Calumet (the Illinois International Port District). This traffic consisted of vessels engaged in overseas trade that discharged autos, steel, fish, whiskey, beer, wine, olives, and furniture. The ships carried back scrap metal, machinery, farm equipment, animal and vegetable oils, hides, lumber, and a variety of food products, especially grain, to complete the "topping off" of an overseas vessel. The Calumet area has a number of grain elevators, including two huge ones at Lake Calumet that together can handle some 13 million bushels

of grain brought to them by truck, rail, and barge.

For several reasons, however, the number of foreign ships that reach Chicago annually has dwindled to about 150, with no regularly scheduled overseas service. These factors include the increasing size of ocean freighters (such as container ships), which makes it impossible for them to pass through the St. Lawrence Seaway locks; the tolls charged for transiting the seaway; and the nine-month shipping season through the locks. In addition, the growing use of the low-cost unit train to carry huge quantities of coal, grain, and other bulk commodities has decreased business at the port. The newer, more modern port at Burns Harbor in Indiana, east of Gary, with its excellent lakefront location and varied facilities, has also taken business away from the Port of Chicago.

Lake Calumet Harbor, with its array of transit sheds, scrap facilities, warehouses, tank farms, and grain elevators, was built to handle seventeen freighters at one time.

FIG. 8.5. Indian freighter on the Calumet River, 1969. Photograph by Irving Cutler.

It is now also a free trade zone, which under certain circumstances provides tax advantages. Thus it continues to be the main port of Chicago, especially for international trade. However, shipping at the port has declined drastically in recent years. Much of its income now comes from a variety of industrial plants on its property that are, for the most part, non–water oriented.

Illinois is usually the nation's second-largest exporting state; however, only about 3 percent of this export business moves through the Port of Chicago. The opening in 1980 of the 194-acre Iroquois Landing modern-container facility at the mouth of the Calumet River did little to increase foreign trade to Chicago.

Although inland bulk traffic, conducted mainly by barge, continues to be substantial and makes Chicago a great inland port, the city's hope of becoming a great international port has not been realized. Combined foreign, Great Lakes, and inland waterway annual freight tonnage for the Port of Chicago averages about 25 million tons, with inland waterway barge traffic accounting for almost 90 percent of the total.

Bulk traffic is aided by two canals—the sixteen-mile Calumet Sag Channel and the twenty-eight-mile Chicago Sanitary and Ship

FIG. 8.6. Chicago Harbor, 1968. In the foreground is the Lake Shore Drive bridge over the Chicago River. In the background and to the right is the lock of the Chicago River Controlling Works; to the left is Navy Pier, before overseas shipping to Chicago Harbor was phased out. *Chicago Tribune* file photo. All rights reserved. Used with permission.

FIG. 8.7. Terminal of the Chicago Regional Port District (now the Illinois International Port District) at the south end of Lake Calumet, looking northwest, 1970. At the upper left are two 6.5-million-bushel grain elevators. Just beyond the lower right part of the photo, Lake Calumet joins the Calumet River. Photograph courtesy of the Chicago Regional Port District.

FIG. 8.8. Coal barges on the Chicago Sanitary and Ship Canal. Almost all of the freight on the waterway is of bulk commodities. Photograph by Irving Cutler.

FIG. 8.9. Looking east from the junction of the North Branch and the South Branch of the Chicago River, about 1920. The river was then lined mainly with commercial, industrial, and transportation facilities. Visible in the foreground at the junction are clean water from Lake Michigan and polluted water from the North Branch *(lower left)* flowing into the South Branch. Photograph courtesy of Harold M. Mayer.

FIG. 8.10. Main stem of the Chicago River, looking west through downtown, 1992. The industrial facilities have been replaced by six new hotels and numerous high-rise office and residential buildings. Instead of freighters, numerous recreational and sightseeing boats ply the river. The white building in the center is the 1,250-room Sheraton Chicago Hotel. Photograph by Irving Cutler.

Canal—both vital links in the Lakes-to-Gulf Waterway. The Calumet Sag Channel links the Calumet area waterways with the Chicago Sanitary and Ship Canal, which links the South Branch of the Chicago River with the Illinois and Mississippi rivers. The canals handle bulk barge cargoes and provide scattered facilities with oil, building materials, and other products. Both were originally designed primarily to provide sewage diversion facilities and to reverse the flow of polluted water away from Lake Michigan—Chicago's source of plentiful, low-cost fresh water. The canals and other facilities of the Metropolitan Water Reclamation District of Greater Chicago have helped to protect both Chicago's water supply and its lakefront beaches from the type of pollution that has plagued other Great Lakes cities.

To the east of Chicago, in Indiana, are the ports of Indiana Harbor, Gary, and Burns Harbor (in the Indiana Dunes). The tonnage of these ports consists almost entirely of bulk cargo destined mainly for the steel industry, although the ports also serve grain shipping facilities, oil refineries, and other plants.

The Railroads Spin a Web

The coming of the railroads helped stimulate the rapid growth of Chicago. The first railroad to Chicago was built in 1848—the same year the Illinois and Michigan Canal was completed. At first the railroads were regarded as supplemental to the waterways, and many of Chicago's railroads terminated at or near the waterways of the downtown area. However, they soon surpassed and even supplanted waterway traffic.

In 1848 Chicago's first railroad brought a load of wheat into downtown Chicago from its western terminal at the Des Plaines River, only about ten miles away. By 1852 Chicago was already connected by rail with the East Coast; in 1869 service was inaugurated to the West Coast. Soon railroads came into Chicago by twenty-seven converging routes. As all the railroads terminated in Chicago, the city became the center for the interchange

FIG. 8.11. Park Ridge train station, 1874. The line is now part of the busy Metra–Union Pacific–Northwest commuter line, which runs from downtown Chicago to Harvard and McHenry, Illinois. Photograph courtesy of Harold M. Mayer.

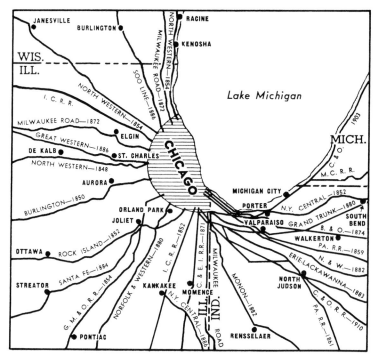

of freight and passengers between different lines. The railroads initially developed a drayage system to haul freight from one line to another. Passengers going beyond Chicago in any direction usually had to take a taxicab to another of Chicago's six downtown passenger stations. The railroads even had their own taxi company, Parmalee, whose sole purpose was to move passengers and their luggage between railroad stations. The terminals were a frenzy of activity most of the day. For publicity purposes, the railroads often had photographers take pictures of celebrities as they alighted from trains. The celebrities included Charlie Chaplin, Elizabeth Taylor, Bob Hope, the Duke and Duchess of Windsor, and hundreds of others.

In time Chicago readily earned the title of "Player with Railroads and the Nation's Freight Handler." While early rail freight consisted mainly of grain, meat, lumber, and animals, today's freight mixture also includes autos, chemicals, coal, machinery, and a great variety of manufactured products. Currently Chicago, served by railroad companies that represent most of the total railroad mileage in the country, is still the world's greatest railroad center.

To facilitate distribution and interchange among the numerous industries and radiating railroads, Chicago developed a web of twelve intersecting belt, switching, and industrial railroads within the 1,754-square-mile Chicago Terminal District. Within this area lie 7,708 miles of track, 131 freight terminal and industrial yards with a capacity of 179,000 cars, thirty-two freight houses, numerous auxiliary facilities, and until the 1970s, six major downtown passenger terminals. On an average day, about every third railroad carload in the country, or 37,500 daily, originates, moves through, or terminates in the Chicago area. The carloads are brought daily by about five hundred freight trains, more than the combined total of New York and St. Louis.

Chicago is the only U.S. city served by all six of the largest railroads—Union Pacific, Burlington Northern Santa Fe, Norfolk Southern, CSX, Canadian National, and Canadian Pacific. The Chicago region is also the largest intermodal (truck-to-rail) hub in the country. It provides about 6 million annual intermodal lifts of trailers or containers onto or off trains, through twenty-one intermodal freight hubs, most of which are on the city's South Side or in the southern suburbs. The rail industry in the area employs about 115,000 people and has an annual payroll of more than $3 billion.

The railroads strongly affected Chicago's growth, its national role, its local land use,

FIG. 8.13. Chicago and Northwestern Railway Depot at Kinzie and Wells streets, about 1885, at the site occupied today by the Merchandise Mart. The station served rail passengers from 1881 to 1911, when it was replaced by the terminal at Madison and Canal streets. Photograph from Union Pacific Historical Collection.

and its settlement patterns. First the railroads brought great numbers of laborers to build the roads; then they brought the permanent settlers who opened up the land. The railroads employed thousands directly, while many more worked in the manufacturing of railroad equipment. By making transportation cheaper, more reliable, and more accessible and by offering service to virtually all parts of the country, the railroads stimulated the growth of agriculture, manufacturing, and commerce in the Chicago area. Many railroads directly fostered industrial development, including the Union Stock Yards in 1865. The railroads also made possible the dispersal of various populations along the commuter routes, into the outlying parts of the city, and into the suburbs. They continue to aid the viability of Chicago's downtown by making it readily accessible to commuters from most parts of the growing metropolitan area.

Although benefiting the city in many ways, the railroads ultimately cut it up into wedges like those of a pie. This division created neighborhood and traffic barriers, as well as noise and pollution problems. In addition, the facilities of the railroads have until recently blocked the expansion of the downtown area to the south and have preempted long stretches of choice lakefront land.

In recent years, rail employment has declined sharply, and the once bustling intercity passenger service has virtually disappeared, except for the Amtrak service. Chicago still leads the nation in the number of long-distance scheduled intercity passenger trains—twenty-five departures daily (carrying more than 2 million passengers annually)—but this is drastically fewer than the many hundreds of such trains that operated daily from the city just a half century ago. Even more passenger-train cuts seem likely. After decades

of debate, the coming of Amtrak has finally led to the consolidation of almost all intercity passenger trains into one terminal, Union Station. This unification eliminated unused terminals and trackage south of the Loop that once served central area passenger stations, manufacturers, and waterway connections and has opened sizable and valuable acreage for development, including the Dearborn Park and Central Station residential complexes. The Grand Central, Central (Twelfth Street), and La Salle Street stations have been demolished. The old Dearborn Street Station is now a shopping mall.

Despite increased competition from other modes of transportation, railway freight volume in the Chicago area continues to hold up well, buoyed by efficient technological changes, labor efficiency, and the introduction of new methods such as the unit train and intermodal shipping.

Unit trains carry one bulk commodity and operate intact from origin to destination, without stopping at intermediate classification yards to break up and make up in the manner of ordinary trains. Intermodal shipping consists of hauling truck trailers on flatcars (TOFCs) or other containers on flatcars (COFCs). The double- and triple-deck auto-rack cars that carry new cars and trucks are an adaptation of the piggyback principle. The railroads are carrying an increasing number of truck trailers, containers, and new autos.

One consequence of changing technology and industrial location, along with the merger of railroads, has been the underutilization of portions of the maze of railroad facilities that occupy thousands of acres of rail rights-of-way and yards in the Chicago area. Some of these yard facilities are outmoded or have

FIG. 8.14. Union Station, on Adams and Canal streets, 2005. Opened in 1924, it was the last major railroad terminal to be built in Chicago. It now handles all Amtrak trains and more than two hundred Metra commuter trains daily. Photograph by Daniel Cutler.

FIG. 8.15. Amtrak Hiawatha Service train leaving for Milwaukee at the Glenview, Illinois, train station, 2005. Amtrak runs seven round trips daily between Chicago and Milwaukee. Photograph by Daniel Cutler.

FIG. 8.16. Milwaukee Road (now Canadian Pacific) freight yards in Bensenville looking southeastward. This area, just south of O'Hare International Airport and near the Tri-State Tollway, has undergone substantial industrial growth in recent decades. Chicago's downtown skyscrapers are visible on the horizon. Photograph by Kee T. Chang; courtesy of the Chicago Association of Commerce and Industry.

been replaced with modern, usually more spacious, less congested facilities farther out, such as those at Markham, Joliet, Proviso, Willow Springs, Bensenville, Rochelle, and Burns Harbor, Indiana. The trend is for the development of huge classification yards even farther beyond the urbanized perimeter. These outlying facilities help alleviate freight car delays that are often associated with the more complex rail network within the Chicago gateway.

Some facilities have been consolidated as a result of mergers. Some of the older, underused, inner-area railyards have been converted into intermodal yards, into new auto-rack yards, or into trucking terminals and other facilities.

In 2003 Chicago and the six major freight-hauling railroads that travel through the midwestern region agreed on an ambitious billion-dollar-plus plan to overhaul the essentially century-old, antiquated railroad infrastructure and inefficient maze of tracks that has resulted in delays and congestion. The aim of the plan is to improve the speed and flow of rail traffic while alleviating auto traffic problems for the city. The plan calls for the elimination of a number of rail spur lines, modernization of track connections and signal equipment, creation of "flyovers" that separate freight from Amtrak and the numerous Metra commuter passenger trains, upgrade of deteriorating rail viaducts, and separation of road and rail traffic via overpasses and underpasses in the city and suburbs. With these improvements, the city plans to continue its century-and-a-half dominance as the railroad hub of the nation.

Road Transportation

Nearly a century ago, the automobile and motor truck began to challenge the dominance of the railroad. The streets, however, proved inadequate for the rapidly increasing number of automobiles. For example, in 1925, with half a million automobile owners in the Chicago region, only thirteen paved gateways led out of the city and only two miles of paved roads could adequately carry four lanes of traffic. Chicago's boulevard system, begun in 1869 to connect the city's parks, was one of the few adequate, though limited, road networks.

The next few decades witnessed a massive road-building program designed to provide for a fivefold increase in the number of

motor vehicles in the next half century. The program called for the widening of many of the major streets, including most of the old diagonal Native American trails, such as Blue Island, Milwaukee, Vincennes, and Archer avenues. The program climaxed in the 1950s and 1960s with the superimposition on the Chicago area's basic street pattern of a coordinated expressway and tollway system of well over five hundred miles. Expressways now radiate from the center of the city in most directions. A proposed, very controversial, and costly Crosstown Expressway project was eventually eliminated from the contemplated road program. It would have provided a circumferential route connecting the major expressways in the city. The expressway would have helped alleviate some of the congestion in the downtown area but would have added greatly to the estimated fifty thousand Chicagoans already displaced from their homes and businesses by the expressway system.

Of the area's three tollway systems, the Indiana and Illinois tollways have exceeded local expectations and have been generally successful financially. In contrast, the 7.8-mile Chicago Skyway, which was hurriedly completed in 1958 to handle the expected dumping of Indiana Toll Road traffic into the already congested southeastern corner of Chicago, was initially a financial disaster. The Chicago Skyway was hurt not only by grossly overestimated traffic projections but also by the subsequent construction of alternate freeway routes. Substantial toll fee increases also hampered traffic growth. However, with the growing congestion on the nearby Dan Ryan Expressway, the opening of five

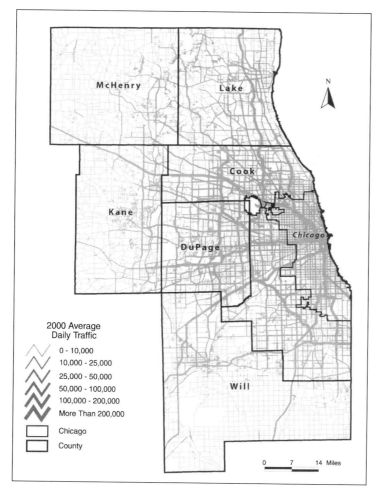

FIG. 8.17. Average daily motor traffic, 2000, as shown by the width of the lines, which represent highways and major streets. The widest lines indicate expressways and tollways. Map courtesy of Chicago Metropolis 2020; data from the Illinois Department of Transportation.

gambling casinos in northwest Indiana, and the residential growth in that area, the Skyway in recent years has become profitable.

It now handles fifty-seven thousand vehicles daily and has undergone major repairs. In 2004 the city granted a ninety-nine-year lease on the Skyway to a private highway company for $1.8 billion. Tolls are now expected to increase through the years.

As in the case of railroading, Chicago has become the nation's largest trucking center, with daily scheduled service to more than fifty-four thousand communities. Trucks now handle over one-fourth of the intercity freight tonnage—about 2 million tons daily. Truck freight has grown steadily, and trucking has exhibited a greater locational flexibility than have the other modes of transportation. Truck terminals have been moving generally outward—away from their former close ties with rail and water facilities and away from congested inner-city areas with their small, poorly located facilities. The movement has

FIG. 8.18. Lake Shore Drive, one of the earliest prototypes of the expressway, looking south toward downtown from Lincoln Park, 1974. In the foreground is Belmont Harbor. Some of Chicago's numerous beaches are visible along the lakeshore. Photograph by Kee T. Chang; courtesy of the Chicago Association of Commerce and Industry.

FIG. 8.19. Chicago-area expressways in 2003, with years of opening listed. The region's first expressway links were easy-to-build segments through open areas that served heavy traffic to the east and to Milwaukee. A toll road network to bypass the city was built in three years, whereas construction of the city's first superhighway through the dense West Side took nearly a decade. Construction was accelerated after the interstate highway program made federal funding available. Radial expressways, intended to make Chicago more accessible from the suburbs, proved "two-way streets" by also drawing businesses and residents outward. Extension of the metropolitan expressway network virtually stalled in the 1990s, and a combination of indecision and relentless urban development has precluded additional links along several logical corridors, such as the Fox Valley in Kane County. © 2004 The Newberry Library; author, Dennis McClendon; from James R. Grossman, Ann Durkin Keating, and Janice L. Reiff, eds., *The Encyclopedia of Chicago* (Chicago: University of Chicago Press, 2004).

FIG. 8.20. Cloverleaf that connects Chicago's major expressways: the Kennedy *(right)*, the Dan Ryan *(left)*, and the Eisenhower *(top and bottom,* where it becomes Congress Parkway). Image by Wernher Krutein; by permission of Photovault.

been particularly noticeable in the southwestern part of the city and in the southwestern suburbs. Large, new terminals have been built, usually in areas that have ready access to expressways and tollways and that lie in proximity to other carriers so as to facilitate the interline exchange of goods. To serve some localized traffic, a number of major companies have established satellite terminals in such cities as Waukegan, Elgin, Aurora, Joliet, and Chicago Heights, where building and operating costs are generally lower and where congestion is less than in Chicago.

There are indications that Chicago has lost some interchange business because of high costs, the emergence of bypass routes, and the rash of recent trucking company mergers that created more "through" routes. Despite the trend toward consolidation of trucking companies, the Chicago area is still served by twelve hundred local trucking firms and almost four hundred intercity carriers. However, the greater flexibility of the trucking industry does not allow Chicago to attain the degree of dominance it enjoys in railroad transportation.

The automobile and an improved road pattern are playing a major role in the location and dispersal of population and economic activities, especially in suburban areas. Settlement no longer has to be aligned along railroad routes. The automobile has made vast new areas accessible for residential, commercial, and industrial uses. The expressway system, in particular, has altered area traffic patterns and has lessened the use of other modes of transportation, notably mass transit. However, the recent rapid escalation of fuel and automobile costs, coupled with the high costs of new homes, has slightly slowed the rapid outward movement of population and renewed some interest in the use of mass transit.

Road congestion is a major problem in the city and suburbs, owing mainly to the tremendous increase in the number of vehicles in the last half century and the comparatively minimal increase in road expansion during that period. Registered vehicles in the six counties in northeastern Illinois surged from fewer than 1.5 million in 1950 to well over 6 million in 2003, a more than fourfold

FIG. 8.21. Kennedy Expressway during the afternoon rush hour, 1977. In the median strip is the CTA rapid transit, and on the overpass is a Chicago and Northwestern Railway (now Metra) double-deck commuter train. Photograph from Union Pacific Historical Collection.

FIG. 8.22. Dan Ryan Expressway looking north toward downtown, with the Sears Tower in the background. Image by Wernher Krutein; by permission of Photovault.

increase. The latter figure includes about 250,000 trucks.

Pipelines

Although pipelines have limited visibility that often masks their crucial importance, they are one of the area's fastest-growing freight transport modes, handling an estimated one-eighth of the freight tonnage of the area. The subterranean network of pipelines into the Chicago area has helped make it a major inland hub for the petroleum and natural gas industry.

The Chicago area has a network of twenty-four pipelines that carry petroleum, natural gas, and refined products; seven underground gas storage facilities; and six active oil refineries. Two of the latter, including the nation's third-largest (owned by British Petroleum), are in the Whiting–East Chicago, Indiana, area. The other four are along the inland waterway network south and southwest of the city. The area's facilities were substantially increased by the opening of the Citgo refinery near Lemont in 1971 and the Mobil Oil refinery near Joliet in 1973. The Chicago area is the nation's largest inland oil refinery center. Most of the area's oil and natural gas are supplied via pipelines from Texas, Oklahoma, Louisiana, Wyoming, Kansas, and Canada. The pipelines range in size from eight inches in diameter to twenty-six-inch Chicap pipelines, which carry oil from Louisiana, and thirty-four-inch Lakehead oil pipelines, which import oil from Canada.

Air Transportation

Transportation did not undergo major changes for thousands of years. Then, introduced in relatively quick succession, were the steamboat, the railroad, the motor vehicle, and, most recently and dramatically, the airplane. As it had with other modes of transportation, Chicago soon became a leading air center.

The first city-owned airport, Ashburn Field, opened in 1916 at Crawford Avenue (4000 W.) and Eighty-third Street. A decade later, in 1926, Chicago Municipal Airport (now Midway) was established at Sixty-third Street and Cicero Avenue (4800 W.) on Chicago's Southwest Side. That year it served more than forty thousand passengers, and Charles Lindbergh was flying mail in and out of the airport a year before his famous solo trans-Atlantic flight.

Midway featured cinder runways, boundary lights, and a revolving beacon for night landings. With many improvements and enlargements over the previous municipal airfield, Midway served as Chicago's main airport for over three decades. For a time it was the busiest airport in the world, handling nearly 10 million passengers a year at its mid-continent location.

Most private planes were handled by nearly three dozen small, scattered airfields that sprang up in the early days of aviation, when airfields were primitive and costs low. Many of these small fields disappeared as they became exceedingly valuable sites for real estate development. For example, Sky Harbor Airport, on the North Shore, is now an industrial park; York Township Airport is a shopping center; and Hinsdale, Elgin, and Chicagoland airports were all sold for commercial development. Many owners of the approximately four thousand small, privately owned planes based in the area are finding it increasingly difficult to secure adequate and convenient airport facilities.

FIG. 8.23. Disabled Meigs Field. Construction crews descended on the lakefront airport in downtown Chicago, and overnight, without warning or explanation, large chunks of the runway were dug up, as shown in this photograph taken Monday, March 31, 2003. Mayor Richard M. Daley, who has favored turning the airport into another lakefront park, had previously agreed to keep the airport open. AP/Wide World Photos.

Many private and commuter planes used Meigs Field, which was opened in 1948 on Northerly Island in Burnham Park. Its convenient location on the lakefront—just a few minutes from the Loop—helped make it one of the busiest single-runway commercial airports in the world. However, due not only to its location on prime recreational land but also to ecological and weather problems and to the technical dangers associated with a lakefront location in an area of increasingly taller buildings, some groups suggested that the facility be phased out. On March 29, 2003, in a highly controversial move, Mayor Richard M. Daley had the runway bulldozed in the dead of night, thus officially closing Meigs Field forever.

The rapid growth of commercial jet aviation generated air traffic in Chicago that soon exceeded Midway Airport's ability to handle it. The largest jets required longer runways than Midway's one square mile of area could provide, and substantial expansion of the field was not feasible because of the built-up area around the airport. Fortunately, the city was able to acquire a huge airfield some eighteen miles northwest of the Loop, which had been developed around the time of World War II as a test field in conjunction with the Douglas Aircraft Company plant on the site. Chicago annexed the territory and developed it as O'Hare Field, spending hundreds of millions of dollars on airport terminals (including a new international terminal), runways, parking facilities, and access roads. More major improvements are contemplated. The field is more than twelve times the size of Midway Airport.

Today, O'Hare International Airport is usually the world's busiest airport, although it is receiving competition for that title from Atlanta's Hartsfield Airport. Over thirty thousand workers are employed at O'Hare. It averages around twenty-five hundred arrivals and departures daily, or about two planes a minute on a twenty-four-hour basis, transporting about two hundred thousand passengers daily. It is served by thirty-eight scheduled carriers, including twenty-five with direct international services. In 2004 those

carriers provided a record 992,471 flights annually. The airport now handles about 75 million passengers in four terminal buildings and over 1.6 million tons of freight annually. It is already overcrowded, despite the periodic expansion of parking, passenger, and cargo facilities. Approximately 50 percent of the passengers are travelers who land at O'Hare to take a connecting flight.

Increased air traffic at O'Hare has brought problems of increased noise and congestion in the air and on the roads that lead to the airport. To help alleviate the parking problem, in 1973 the city opened one of the world's largest

FIG. 8.24. O'Hare International Airport looking southeast toward downtown, 2001. Usually the world's busiest airport, O'Hare handles about 75 million passengers on some 930,000 flights annually. Plans call for the addition of two new runways and the reconfiguration of existing runways. Photograph courtesy of the City of Chicago Department of Aviation.

parking structures, with room for 9,250 vehicles. Additionally, access to the airport was improved with a 7.6-mile extension of the Chicago Transit Authority's Blue Line rapid transit to O'Hare, which runs mainly in the median strip of the Kennedy Expressway.

O'Hare has spawned rapid commercial and industrial development in surrounding areas, as well as substantial suburban residential growth. Numerous hotels and motels have been built to accommodate both air travelers and the growing number of meetings and conventions held in the vicinity of the airport. The economic base of the entire metropolitan area has benefited from the presence of O'Hare International Airport. The aviation industry generates an estimated 340,000 jobs in the Chicago metropolitan area.

A major plan has been proposed by the city of Chicago to expand and improve service at O'Hare. The plan generally provides for the addition of two new runways and the reconfiguration of existing runways. It also provides for direct road access to the airport from the western suburbs. Despite some continuing modifications, the plan is strongly opposed by residents of some of the nearby suburbs, who fear losing their land and homes or who dread the accompanying increase of noise, air pollution, and congestion. The city, however, believes that the expansion of O'Hare is vital because it will bring major economic benefits to the region, allowing O'Hare to retain its status as the world's busiest airport.

Midway Airport started reviving as a major airport in the 1980s, despite the lack of a large number of connecting flights and the reluctance of the major airlines to duplicate facilities at two airports. In 1980 the annual passenger volume was just 1,265,208; by 2002 it had reached 15,681,966, with more than eight hundred flights daily. The tremendous increase in passenger volume is due to a number of factors, including increased congestion at O'Hare, the ten-mile distance of Midway from the Loop (compared with O'Hare's eighteen miles), and much-improved accessibility via the Stevenson Expressway and the new Orange Line Rapid Transit (which runs from the Loop to Midway in about thirty minutes). Probably of greater importance were the coming of a number of low-cost, point-to-point airlines, such as Southwest Airlines and AirTran Airways, and an increase in the range of most planes. Midway Airport is now served by eleven airlines.

The increased traffic has brought major improvements at Midway Airport, including a new terminal, a new parking garage, road improvements, and spacious new airline gates, as well as new restaurants and shops. The airport now offers direct international service, which had ceased more than forty years ago. The once bustling ancillary commercial area of hotels, motels, and restaurants is being rejuvenated as a result of the increased activity at the airport.

Debate has raged for many years regarding the need for a third airport to handle the area's future air transportation growth. The late Mayor Richard J. Daley proposed a third airport in the lake, connected by a causeway to Hyde Park. His son, Mayor Richard M. Daley, proposed an airport in the Southeast Side Calumet district, which would have virtually wiped out the Chicago community of Hegewisch and some industrial plants and which included rechannelization of part of the Calumet River. Both proposals were eventually eliminated as unsound, impracticable, too costly, and too disruptive.

A commission, appointed to find a site for a new airport, recommended five possible locations—four in Illinois and one in Gary, Indiana. The Gary site was the only one with an existing airport and a number of amenities, but it was immediately eliminated, mainly for political reasons—it being in the wrong state. The site finally selected was in Peotone, Illinois, despite being some forty miles south of the Loop but in an area that was still largely rural. The proponents of the plan, who argued that an airport in Peotone would improve the economy of the depressed area to the south of Chicago, were joined by those opposed to the expansion of O'Hare. Some preliminary steps have been taken for the establishment of an airport in Peotone, but it remains a topic of debate. The city of Chicago continues to push for the major expansion of O'Hare International Airport.

The CTA and Its Predecessors

During the years that Chicago remained small in area, people lived close to their places of employment and could usually walk to work or travel by horse and buggy. In 1850, for example, Chicago was less than ten square miles in area, and most of its industry and population were in and around what is now the downtown area. As the city rapidly expanded to its present size of 228 square miles and people and industry spread throughout the city and into the suburbs, internal trans-

FIG. 8.25. Cable cars on Cottage Grove Avenue, 1903. Such cars operated on Chicago streets from 1882 to 1906, when they were replaced by electric trolleys. The Cottage Grove operation was part of what became the world's largest cable car system. Cable cars were pulled on tracks by gripping a moving cable under the roadway. Chicago Historical Society.

FIG. 8.26. Cable cars in the 3800 block of Cottage Grove Avenue en route to "Chicago Day" (free admission) at the World's Columbian Exposition, October 8, 1893. Chicago Historical Society.

FIG. 8.27. Electric trolley cars on Madison Street, looking west from Clinton Street, 1906. These streetcars ran on tracks and were powered electrically by current drawn through a trolley pole from a suspended overhead wire. Chicago Historical Society.

portation for the metropolitan area became a major problem. Through the years, various modes of transportation have been developed to cope with the problem.

Chicago's first mass transportation line was established in 1859, when the city's population passed one hundred thousand. This line consisted of horse-drawn street railway cars on State Street, from Randolph (150 N.) south to Twelfth Street. Aided by numerous extensions that helped spread urbanization, the horsecars dominated the city's public transportation until 1882, when cable cars first rattled and groaned at a speed of up to fourteen miles per hour. Cable cars had a brief life, for in 1892 the electric streetcar was introduced to Chicago. Electric streetcars soon operated throughout the city, along nearly all section-line streets, diagonal streets, and even some half-section streets. A streetcar line was within easy walking distance of nearly everyone in the city. In 1913 the entire fragmented streetcar system was unified under the management of the Chicago Surface Lines, with a resulting track network of about a thousand miles and a passenger count that reached nearly 900 million by 1929.

Also in 1892 the elevated railroad was introduced to Chicago. Originally it ran from downtown south to Thirty-ninth Street, but by 1893 it had been extended to Jackson Park in time for the World's Columbian Exposition. This "El" line was rapidly followed by lines to various parts of the city, with some eventually reaching the northern and western suburbs. Until 1897 the El trains were powered by small steam engines.

El lines converged on the downtown area and swung around the "Loop," a configuration that connected the various independent lines and provided a steel girdle of raised tracks and screeching cars that traversed much of the downtown area. In 1913 the various elevated companies were unified into the Rapid Transit Lines, which created, for the first time, a through route that connected the North and South sides.

The streetcars and, particularly, the fast elevated trains helped populate the far corners of the city and even beyond. High-density apartment buildings were built, especially in the vicinity of the elevated lines. The Loop was particularly accessible, and by 1910 about 750,000 people poured into the downtown area every day by elevated or by streetcar.

While the electric streetcar and the elevated lines were carrying most of Chicago's passengers, a new form of transportation appeared that was to have far-reaching effects—the motor vehicle. The use of the automobile and the bus grew rapidly. In 1917 the Chicago Motor Bus Company began motor bus services, using mainly boulevard routes. Soon its route network encompassed about 170 miles. Equipment included breezy, open-top, double-deck buses that were often also used for pleasure riding, sightseeing, or enjoying a romantic interlude under the stars. By the end of the 1920s, buses were also being used on some routes of the Chicago Surface Lines. A few years later, the electric trolley bus was introduced. By 1958 these two forms of transportation had completely replaced the familiar electric streetcar. However, by the early 1970s the electric trolley bus was phased out, leaving only motor buses as the mode of public mass transportation on Chicago's streets.

Chicago's mass transit system long was hampered by the absence of subway lines. Chicago lagged decades behind some of the large eastern cities in subway construction.

FIG. 8.28. Elevated railroad, which first started operating in Chicago in 1892 with a line that ran from downtown Chicago to the South Side. Thereafter, the El lines expanded rapidly into various parts of the city and eventually into the northern and western suburbs, with all major lines focusing on downtown. Until 1897 El trains were powered by small steam engines. Photograph courtesy of Harold M. Mayer.

FIG. 8.29. Double-deck bus of the Chicago Motor Bus Company, on Michigan Avenue in 1922. The company operated mainly on boulevard routes. The open-top bus was used not only by workers traveling to and from their jobs but also by pleasure seekers and sightseers. Photograph by *Chicago Daily News*; Chicago Historical Society, DN-0074012.

FIG. 8.30. Looking northeast toward the major intersection of State and Madison streets, about 1905, and the different modes of transportation: the horsedrawn carriage, the early automobile, cable cars, and the electric trolley. On the right is the Louis Sullivan–designed Carson Pirie Scott store, and on the left is the store of Mandel Brothers. Chicago Historical Society.

A large part of the problem was physical. In New York the subway was constructed, for the most part, through solid rock that supported the tubes, but in Chicago the subsoil was soft, watery clay, which required thick, steel-reinforced concrete to support the subway tubes.

In 1943 Chicago's first subway, less than five miles in length, was finally opened beneath State Street, and in 1951 the 3.85-mile Milwaukee Avenue–Dearborn Street subway also assumed operation. But while Chicago lagged in subway construction, it was a pioneer in the construction of rapid transit facilities in the median strip of expressways—first, the Eisenhower Expressway in 1958 and, later, the Dan Ryan and Kennedy expressways. The successful five-mile, high-speed, nonstop Skokie Swift service along an abandoned interurban rail line was successfully established in 1964, between the Howard Street rapid transit station (7600 N.) and Dempster Street in Skokie (the Yellow Line). A rapid transit extension to O'Hare International Airport was later constructed (the Blue Line), followed by a line to Midway Airport (the Orange Line).

Meanwhile, the lack of unification of the transit facilities was overcome with the creation in 1947 of the Chicago Transit Authority (CTA). This publicly owned but privately financed agency took over the operations of the Chicago Surface Lines, the Rapid Transit Lines, and the Chicago Motor Coach Company. It now provides transit service throughout Chicago and to thirty-eight nearby suburbs and is the second-largest transit system in the country.

The creation of the CTA brought about improvements in transfer privileges, efficiency of maintenance, and coordination of schedules. But some of the basic problems that had plagued its predecessors also contributed to the CTA's financial troubles, despite repeated increases in fares, which in turn led to a decrease by more than two-thirds of its riders since 1947.

One such problem is that the expensive CTA equipment and facilities are used mainly during the two rush-hour periods and therefore remain idle or underused the remainder of the day and on weekends. Another major challenge to the CTA's economic viability is the increasing competition it faces from private automobiles in the metropolitan area. People insist on the convenience of driving their own automobiles to work, even though public transportation is usually less expensive. The cost discrepancy is especially true if one pays for parking downtown, which many thousands do. As a result of the increase in automobile commuting, about one-sixth of the downtown land area is now devoted to parking. Furthermore, the automobile, for the number of people it carries, is a wasteful fuel

consumer. It is also the major source of the city's air pollution—a problem of growing concern in an area of substantial industry, which at times obscures natural sunlight. Traffic congestion caused by the increasing number of automobiles also slows down public bus transportation, resulting in reduced bus patronage.

Despite the advantages of public transportation, Table 8.1 shows that ridership has continued to decline. Although the major falloff has been in CTA bus ridership, CTA buses still make about a million passenger trips a day over 134 routes, covering 1,937 route miles in Chicago and surrounding suburbs. Ridership on the routes of the elevated-subway rapid transit system, totaling about one-half million passengers daily, has declined only slightly owing to its having its own right-of-way—leading to faster, more reliable service—and to the opening, a few years ago, of the Orange Line to Midway Airport, which brought its total rail trackage to 222 miles.

The CTA operates approximately nineteen hundred buses and eleven hundred rapid transit cars. Despite the conversion of its trains to one-person operation and its implementation of other money-saving measures, the CTA has not been able to operate on the proceeds

TABLE 8.1.

Users of Mass Transportation in Metropolitan Chicago, 1980 and 2000

	1980*	2000
CTA	692,430,041	450,500,000
Pace	38,235,000	38,600,000
Metra	81,395,361	78,700,000
Total	812,060,402	567,800,000

*Numbers include some predecessor lines. The number of riders declined about 30 percent between 1980 and 2000.

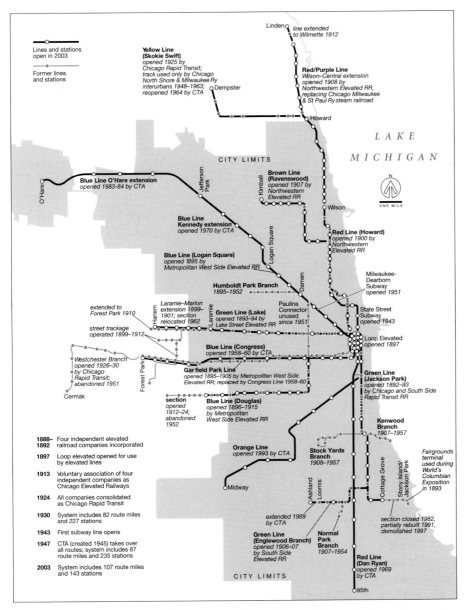

Lines and stations
open in 2003

Former lines
and stations

**Yellow Line
(Skokie Swift)**
opened 1925 by
Chicago Rapid Transit;
track used only by Chicago
North Shore & Milwaukee Ry
interurbans 1948–1963;
reopened 1964 by CTA

Linden ◦ line extended
to Wilmette 1912

Dempster

Red/Purple Line
Wilson–Central extension
opened 1908 by
Northwestern Elevated RR,
replacing Chicago Milwaukee
& St Paul Ry steam railroad

Howard

CITY LIMITS

LAKE

MICHIGAN

N
ONE MILE

Blue Line O'Hare extension
opened 1983–84 by CTA

O'Hare

Jefferson
Park

Kimball

**Brown Line
(Ravenswood)**
opened 1907 by
Northwestern
Elevated RR

Wilson

**Blue Line
Kennedy extension**
opened 1970 by CTA

Logan Square

Red Line (Howard)
opened 1900 by
Northwestern
Elevated RR

Blue Line (Logan Square)
opened 1895 by
Metropolitan West Side Elevated RR

Damen

Humboldt Park Branch
1895–1952

Milwaukee-
Dearborn
Subway
opened 1951

extended to
Forest Park 1910

Harlem

Laramie–Marion
extension 1899–
1901; section
relocated 1962

Laramie

Green Line (Lake)
opened 1893–94 by
Lake Street Elevated RR

Paulina
Connector
unused
since 1951

State Street
Subway
opened 1943

street trackage
operated 1899–1912

Blue Line (Congress)
opened 1958–60 by CTA

Loop Elevated
opened 1897

Westchester Branch
opened 1926–30
by Chicago
Rapid Transit;
abandoned 1951

Forest Park

Garfield Park Line
opened 1895–1905 by Metropolitan West Side
Elevated RR; replaced by Congress Line 1958–60

**Green Line
(Jackson Park)**
opened 1892–93
by Chicago and South Side
Rapid Transit RR

Cermak

section
opened
1912–24;
abandoned
1952

Blue Line (Douglas)
opened 1896–1915
by Metropolitan
West Side Elevated RR

**Kenwood
Branch**
1907–1957

**1888–
1892** Four independent elevated
railroad companies incorporated

1897 Loop elevated opened for use
by elevated lines

1913 Voluntary association of four
independent companies as
Chicago Elevated Railways

1924 All companies consolidated
as Chicago Rapid Transit

1930 System includes 82 route miles
and 227 stations

1943 First subway line opens

1947 CTA (created 1945) takes over
all routes; system includes 87
route miles and 235 stations

2003 System includes 107 route miles
and 143 stations

Orange Line
opened 1993 by CTA

**Stock Yards
Branch**
1908–1957

Midway

Cottage Grove

Stony Island/
Jackson Park

*Fairgrounds
terminal
used during
World's
Columbian
Exposition
in 1893*

section closed 1982,
partially rebuilt 1991,
demolished 1997

extended 1969
by CTA

Ashland

Loomis

**Green Line
(Englewood Branch)**
opened 1906–07
by South Side
Elevated RR

**Normal
Park
Branch**
1907–1954

**Red Line
(Dan Ryan)**
opened 1969
by CTA

CITY LIMITS

95th

FIG. 8.31. Chicago's rapid transit lines, operated by the Chicago Transit Authority, in 2003. Four individual companies built elevated railroads to link outlying city and near-suburban neighborhoods with downtown between 1892 and 1930. Similar construction and equipment standards simplified the unified operation of the lines beginning in 1913, as did public ownership after World War II. The new Chicago Transit Authority closed several lightly patronized branches, reducing a 1947 system of eighty-seven miles to sixty-eight miles by 1958. Four significant expansions since 1969 brought the system to approximately 107 miles by 2003, with several placed innovatively along the median strips of expressways. The most recent, the Orange Line, was built in 1993 to link the neglected Southwest Side and a revived Midway Airport to the Loop. © 2004 The Newberry Library; author, Dennis McClendon; from James R. Grossman, Ann Durkin Keating, and Janice L. Reiff, eds., *The Encyclopedia of Chicago* (Chicago: University of Chicago Press, 2004).

of its fare-box revenues, even with periodic fare increases. The commercial viability of the CTA has been damaged through the years by spiraling labor, fuel, and insurance costs and, especially, increased competition from the automobile. To cover the deficits, the CTA is partially funded by the Regional Transportation Authority, which collects taxes from the metropolitan area to aid mass transit. The CTA also receives federal grants for capital improvements, such as the purchase of new equipment.

Pace, the Suburban Bus System

The smallest of the mass transit systems that serve the Chicago metropolitan area is Pace, the suburban bus system. Its 38-million annual passenger count has held fairly steady through the years. Pace operates 248 fixed routes, with 664 buses in 210 suburbs. It also provides Dial-a-Ride service, "vanpools," and special-event buses throughout Chicago's six-county suburban region, with a small number of routes to Chicago.

FIG. 8.32. Early-twentieth-century traffic jam. Chicago's traffic problems are not new, as this view south on Dearborn Street from Randolph Street, about 1910, shows. Chicago Historical Society, ICHi-04191.

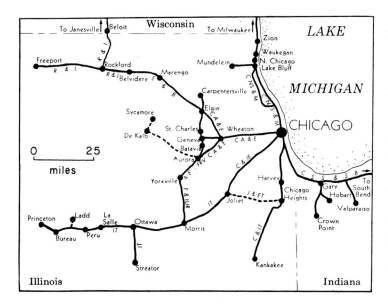

FIG. 8.33. Interurban Electric Railway Network of the Chicago area, 1925, just before the start of its rapid decline. Dashed lines indicate routes abandoned in the early 1920s. The only interurban still operating is the Chicago South Shore and South Bend Railroad. Reproduced, with permission, from Harold M. Mayer and Richard C. Wade, *Chicago: Growth of a Metropolis*, © 1969 by the University of Chicago.

Through the years, Pace has acquired virtually all of the municipal and private passenger bus lines that operate in the suburban area. Although it operates almost twice as many bus routes as the CTA, its routes cover a much larger area (about thirty-five hundred square miles) of low-density population, it has no right-of-way, and it operates where most people drive automobiles. As a result, only about 40 percent of its operating budget is covered by fare-box revenue. The remainder is funded by public subsidies, consisting mostly of local sales tax revenues. In July 2006, Pace is slated to take over the public paratransit operations (service for the handicapped) in Chicago in addition to its current similar service in the suburbs.

Metra, the Commuter Rail System

Table 8.1 shows that the commuter railroads' ridership has changed little in the last two decades. Unlike the commuter rail systems of other cities, Chicago's Metra commuter rail system, whose extensive network converges in the downtown area, has managed to remain in operation and even, on some lines, to grow in ridership. Furthermore, the commuter railroads have improved service by introducing double-deck, air-conditioned cars; by opening a new line; and by extending some lines. They now carry about 150,000 passengers daily. But, as with the CTA, the basic challenges to Metra's economic viability are automobile competition and its limited use in carrying people mainly to and from work. Its commuter function is largely confined to about three rush hours in the morning and about the same number of hours in the late afternoon, five days a week. During the rest of the time, the costly equipment remains largely idle. As a result of this pattern, not enough equipment can be economically justified to always provide every rush-hour rider with a seat.

FIG. 8.34. High-speed Electroliner of the Chicago, North Shore and Milwaukee Railroad in downtown Chicago, about 1950. The company's routes between Chicago and Milwaukee reached their most prosperous period in the 1920s. Thereafter, competition from the automobile brought difficult times, and the railroad ceased operations in 1963. Photograph courtesy of Harold M. Mayer.

Unlike that of the CTA, the total ridership on Metra has held up relatively well in recent years, although results vary among the individual Metra lines, depending on the quality of their service, the population growth of their service areas, the travel-to-work characteristics of their riders, and competitive expressway patterns. Metra, created in 1983, is now one of the world's largest commuter railroad networks. It operates twelve railroad commuter lines over 546 miles of track and serves 230 stations in the six metropolitan-area counties, northwest Indiana, and southern Wisconsin. Those routes that have gained the most passengers serve the fast-growing suburbs to the north, northwest, and west. Table 8.2 shows the annual ridership for the twelve lines. In 2006 the Union Pacific West Line was extended to Elburn, and the Southwest Service Line was extended to Manhattan.

The Metra commuter railroads have, like the CTA and for many of the same reasons, frequently lost money on their commuter service. To combat their financial difficulties, railroads in the past have curtailed service, raised fares, cut costs whenever possible, and abandoned close-in stations to concentrate on longer hauls. In recent years, Metra has also increasingly depended on government aid to alleviate its financial difficulties. Under the Regional Transportation Authority, which has some taxing power, Metra has improved its

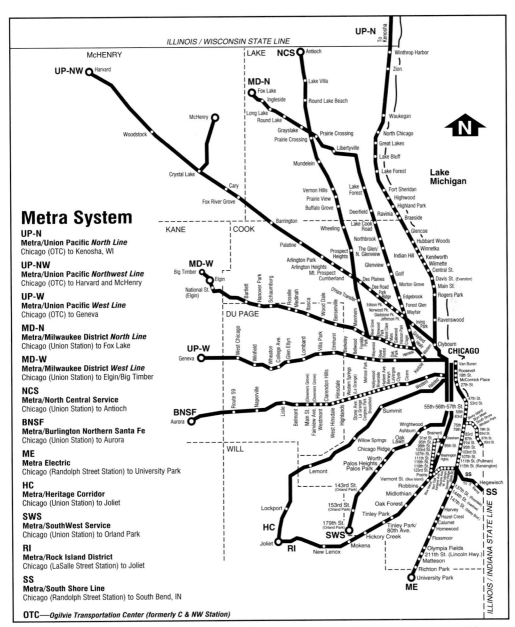

FIG. 8.35. Metra commuter rail system, showing all twelve routes, 2005. The system has averaged about 82 million riders annually. Map courtesy of Metra.

TABLE 8.2.

Users of Metra, 2001

Rail Line	No. of Riders (in millions)
Burlington Northern Santa Fe	14.9
Electric Lines	12.3
Rock Island	9.6
Union Pacific Northwest	9.2
Union Pacific North	8.7
Union Pacific West	7.0
Milwaukee District–North	6.9
Milwaukee District–West	6.4
Chicago South Shore and South Bend	4.0
Southwest Service	1.7
North Central	1.1
Heritage	0.6
Total	82.3

service and financial conditions and has taken over many of the functions and ownership of previously privately owned and operated commuter railroads.

Transportation Trends

The public transportation system in the Chicago area is especially geared to serve the downtown area. Complicating the city's traffic pattern is the dispersal of industry and population into outlying areas at densities usually too low to support adequate mass transportation. Unlike jobs in the downtown areas, where transportation routes converge, jobs in the suburbs are difficult to reach with mass transportation methods. The result is a further decentralization of population and the growing phenomenon of reverse commuting by auto from Chicago to suburban jobs, which often creates two-way rush hour traffic jams. The poor in the city who do not have automobiles find it difficult to commute to

suburban jobs and even more difficult to move near these jobs because of high housing costs.

A number of major plans for improving the area's transportation network have been proposed. These include the further major renovation of the El system, the introduction of new distributor subways, the creation of a riverbank line in the downtown area, southeast and southwest extensions of the Dan Ryan Red Line rapid transit, and the establishment of a new commuter rail line from the south and southwest suburbs to O'Hare and beyond. All of these projects are currently being held in abeyance mainly because of the lack of adequate funding.

The creation in 1974 of the Regional Transportation Authority (RTA) for the six counties of northeastern Illinois was potentially the most important development in the field of public transportation in recent years. This agency has the mandate, backed by some taxing powers, to preserve, coordinate, and improve the operations of the CTA, Metra, and Pace systems throughout the politically fragmented but economically interwoven metropolitan area and to provide regional transportation planning and oversight.

The RTA has helped maintain, expand, standardize, and coordinate suburban bus and commuter rail service. It has helped provide new equipment and financial aid to these carriers, as well as to the CTA. But, like the CTA, it has been plagued by frequent and severe financial crises due chiefly to escalating costs and inadequate funding sources. The RTA has also been handicapped by political wrangling and persistent opposition from some of the suburban areas, especially those more distant from the city. It has, however, helped improve service and been instrumental in keeping some of the suburban bus routes and commuter railroads from ceasing operations completely. Since the advent of the RTA, suburban bus service has showed its largest percentage increase in ridership, although the passenger load per bus is still small in comparison with that of the CTA. To meet its financial requirements, fares throughout the RTA system have often been increased and attempts have been made to render the entire transit system more efficient and economical. However, much more remains to be done, especially in integrating the three mass transit systems.

The extensive multimodal mass transit system—consisting of commuter railroads, suburban bus lines, and the giant Chicago Transit Authority, with its elevated, subway, and bus lines—has long been instrumental in establishing the layout of the Chicago area and in preserving the viability of the downtown area. In recent decades, the growing use of the automobile, the establishment of an expensive expressway network, the dispersal of population into areas of lower population density, and escalating costs have resulted in declining ridership and financial difficulties for the mass transit system. However, the energy and pollution crisis, renewed government interest in mass transportation due to its relative cheapness and efficiency, and the establishment of the Regional Transportation Authority to aid mass transit are all examples of trends that hold some promise of reversing, or at least stabilizing, the steady decline of mass transportation in the Chicago area.

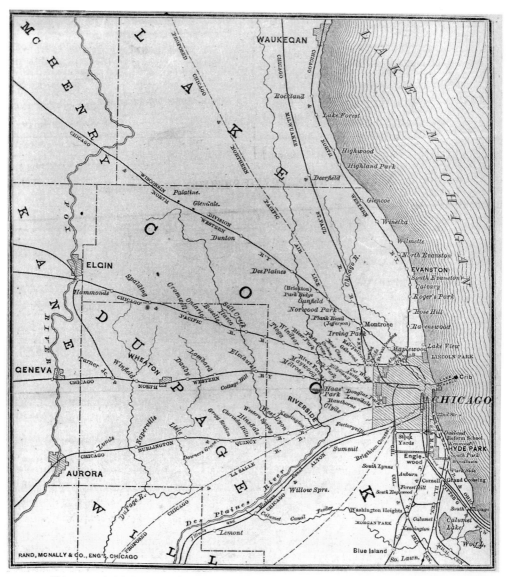

FIG. 9.1. Chicago and vicinity on a suburban real estate promotion map, 1873. Chicago Historical Society.

9 Expansion of the Chicago Metropolitan Area

Suburban Growth

The Chicago metropolitan area is a mosaic of six counties and hundreds of variegated, competitive, and fiercely independent communities that stretch approximately from the Wisconsin state line to northwestern Indiana. The area has a total population of over 8 million, with about 36 percent of the people living in the city of Chicago—down from 80 percent residing there in 1900. While Chicago did lose population for the first time in the 1960–1990 period, the sprawling suburban "outer city" now has more people, more jobs, a faster rise in political power, and an immensely greater growth potential than the slower growing but still powerful city of Chicago. The city gained 4 percent in population in the 1990–2000 decade, whereas the outer city gained about 8 percent.

This result is much improved from the census of 1980, which showed that Chicago had lost 11 percent of its population in the previous decade, while the remainder of the metropolitan area gained about 12 percent. The 1970 census showed a loss of 5 percent for Chicago and a huge 31-percent increase for the remainder of the metropolitan area.

The huge movement to the suburbs consisted largely of white families with school-age children leaving their homes in the city, although about half of the new immigrants to the Chicago area now settle directly in the suburbs. The movement from the suburbs to the city, on the other hand, was comparatively small and involved young adults without families and older adults with grown children. The movement of these groups back to the city has, however, accelerated in recent years.

Although a few suburbs are almost as old as Chicago, rapid suburban growth around the city of Chicago is largely a phenomenon of the post–World War I period. Chicago itself is, in fact, largely an amalgamation of suburbs that, in years past, found it advantageous to be annexed to the city to acquire needed services. Suburbs annexed by Chicago make up many of its communities—Lake View, Hyde Park, Jefferson Park, Washington Heights, Roseland, Rogers Park, West Ridge, Norwood Park, Austin, Edison Park, Morgan Park, Clearing, Mt. Greenwood, and a number of others. In the last three-quarters of a century, however, annexation of suburban areas by Chicago has been minimal because the remaining suburbs have preferred not to

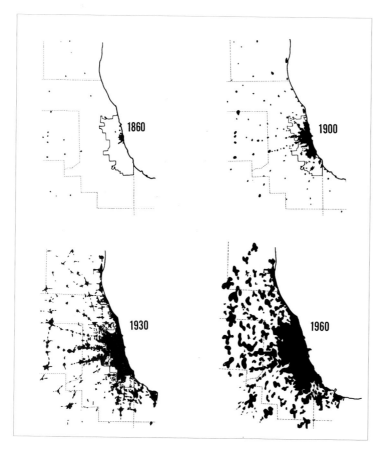

FIG. 9.2. Metropolitan growth moving outward from Chicago, 1860–1960. From Pierre De Vise, *Chicago's People, Jobs, and Homes,* vol. 1 (Chicago: Department of Geography, De Paul University, 1964).

become politically attached to the big city, with its multiplicity of problems.

The growth of Chicago's suburbs has been closely related to development of transportation facilities. Some early communities were established along the waterways; later, ribbons of suburbs developed along the railroads. A few of the early settlements were recreation-resort communities, and a very few were all-temperance communities. More recently, with the advent of the motor vehicle and expressways, suburban settlement has become extremely diffuse.

Before the coming of the railroads there were a few water-oriented communities and a

number of small farm-service villages outside Chicago. With the relatively fast transportation provided by extended streetcar lines and railroads, however, people could, for the first time, live some distance from downtown Chicago and still commute there to work. The railroads radiated out from downtown, and stops were located every few miles. Around these stops, homes and often a few shops were built and the nucleus of a suburb developed. More than a century ago, settlements that resembled widely spaced beads on a string had grown up along the main commuter railroads. Along the Northwest Line of the Chicago and North Western Railway (now Metra Northwest Lines), the communities of Des Plaines, Palatine, and Barrington were already incorporated; and along the North Line of the Chicago and North Western Railway (now Metra North Line), the communities of Evanston, Wilmette, Winnetka, Glencoe, Highland Park, and Lake Forest were established. The villages were small, usually numbering only a few hundred people, since the inhabitants had to live close to the local railroad station.

The increasing use of the automobile, especially after World War I, resulted in a rapid increase in suburban growth. The growth was substantially slowed during the Great Depression of the 1930s and around World War II, but thereafter it increased at an unprecedented rate. At first the automobile chiefly allowed people to reside farther from the commuter railroad stations; later, after improvements in roads, it allowed them to commute to work independently of the railroads. The result was a surge of population outward from the city into the interstitial areas between the railroad radials.

Examples of rapid suburban growth are numerous. To the north of Chicago, Skokie was a small village with a population of 783 in 1920. Its truck-farming economy served the Chicago market. The general exodus to the suburbs and improved transportation, especially the opening of the Edens Expressway in 1951, resulted in an increase in Skokie's population to sixty-three thousand by 2000. To the south of Chicago, the planned community of Park Forest, which was farmland until the late 1940s, now has a population of twenty-four thousand. Similarly, Oak Lawn to the southwest increased from 3,483 in 1940 to more than fifty-five thousand today,

and Addison to the west increased from 819 in 1940 to more than thirty-six thousand today.

In recent years, one of the largest developments of new housing construction has been recorded in the southwest suburb of Naperville. The population of Naperville increased from 12,933 in 1960 to 128,358 in 2000, making it the fourth-largest city in Illinois. Other communities that have led in housing construction and population growth in recent decades include Hoffman Estates, Wheeling, Elk Grove Village, Vernon Hills, Palatine, Buffalo Grove, Schaumburg, Crystal Lake, Grayslake, Gurnee, and Hanover Park to the north and northwest; Bloomingdale, West Chicago, Carol Stream, and Glendale Heights to the west; and to the south and southwest, Bolingbrook, Woodridge, Romeoville, Orland Park, and Tinley Park. The large industrial satellite cities of Joliet, Aurora, Elgin, and Waukegan have also had substantial population growth in the last decade. (See Appendix F for population data.)

There are many reasons for the slow growth of the population of Chicago and, conversely, for the rapid growth in the suburban population (a pattern occurring across the nation). The central city itself is nearly fully occupied and has limited space for further growth; indeed, expressway construction and slum clearance have decreased the population density of Chicago. In addition, many inhabitants of the central city moved to the suburbs to escape its real or sometimes perceived negative aspects—racial conflict, slums, crime, high taxes, congestion, poor schools, and other problems.

The last half century was, on the whole, a period of prosperity. Automobiles, highways, and homes were built at an unprecedented rate. The "open space, good life" attractions of the suburbs, some real and some imaginary,

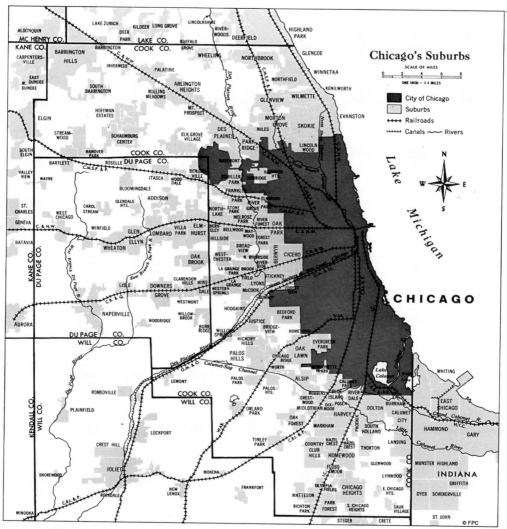

FIG. 9.3. Chicago's suburbs, 1958. Until recent decades, Chicago's suburban growth was largely aligned along the railroad routes that radiated from the city. With the advent of the motor vehicle, the land between the railroad routes began to be urbanized also. Reproduced, with permission, from Margaret S. Rátz and Charles H. Wilson, *Exploring Chicago* (Chicago: Follett Publishing, 1958).

held strong appeal for young and growing families. Improved transportation, higher standards of living, increased leisure, industrial decentralization, government financial aid, and mass construction of homes all helped accelerate the movement to the suburbs.

In some instances, migration to the suburbs is undoubtedly a response by whites to the approach of African Americans and Hispanics; in other cases, it is a flight of either the wealthier classes from the poorer classes or of the more "Americanized" from ethnic groups. The small sizes of most suburbs make possible a more homogeneous group of people with their own "kind" than is possible in the big city. Even housing may take the form of look-alike structures put up by a single developer in a single effort.

The amount of urbanized land continues to grow. It increased from 1,270 square miles in 1980 to 1,717 square miles in 2000. Largely urbanized stretches now radiate outward from the Loop, especially along the commuter rail lines. In some directions, the built-up areas extend about fifty miles from Chicago's Loop—beyond Waukegan, the Fox River valley cities, Joliet, University Park, and Gary, Indiana. Between the railroad radials, urbanization has been filling in rapidly; the movement outward is often discontinuous. Patches of open space occur because of "leap-frogging"—the skipping over of some land by developers who decide to target more distant land because it is more readily available or has certain amenity and cost advantages.

Suburban Characteristics

The suburbs of Chicago are far from uniform. They may differ from each other as much as the individual communities within the city of Chicago differ. In fact, parts of Chicago are more suburban in character than some suburbs, and some suburbs are more densely populated than the average Chicago community. Chicago's suburbs are rich and poor, new and old, planned and unplanned, white-collar and blue-collar, industrial and dormitory, black and white, close in and far out, populated by young and by old, successful and unsuccessful, observant of or lacking community tradition, homogeneous and heterogeneous in population—and everything in between. Their residents often differ markedly in race, religion, and ethnic background, as well as in educational and vocational levels. In economic level, they range from Kenilworth, which had a median family income in 1999 of well over two hundred thousand dollars, to Ford Heights, whose median family income was $17,500. Yet despite their differences, the suburbs exhibit certain general patterns and trends:

1. Their population density is lower than that of Chicago, as the homes generally occupy larger acreage. Chicago's average population density per square mile is about 12,700 persons, but the city's residential density profile resembles a volcano with a crater of very low density in the heart of the central business district, followed by a sharp rise around downtown, and a gradual decline toward the periphery. In the suburbs the density per square mile averages slightly less than five thousand, although it varies substantially owing to differences in zoning laws and their enforcement. A community's zoning laws control residential density and reflect the attitudes and socioeconomic status of its inhabitants, the transportation facilities, and—an increasingly important consideration—the availability and cost of land.

2. The population density of suburbs generally decreases as their distance from

Chicago increases. Some of the older, larger, closer suburbs, such as Evanston, Oak Park, and Cicero, built largely in an earlier period and having good rapid transit connections to Chicago, have relatively high population densities between nine thousand and twelve thousand per square mile. In a way, such suburbs are simply extensions of the city, with population density decreasing somewhat outward from the city. Like Chicago, their deteriorated commercial cores are being rejuvenated, particularly in Evanston.

3. There is an accelerating trend toward building multiple-dwelling units in some suburban areas. In the 1960s alone, some 150,000 multiple-dwelling units in the form of apartments, cooperatives, and condominiums were constructed. Such units help circumvent high land costs, add to local tax revenue, and often better meet the needs of certain groups, such as singles, young couples, and older people. The rapidly rising cost of single-family homes has priced them out of the range of many families.

4. Another trend has been the development of planned, highly self-sufficient communities that embody separate compatible locations for residential, commercial, industrial, and recreational functions. Prime examples are Elk Grove Village (near O'Hare Airport) and University Park (thirty-two miles south of the Loop). Other suburbs are reserving areas for industrial and commercial use with the aim of broadening their tax base. Some smaller planned developments are being built around recreational facilities, including artificial lakes and golf courses. A growing trend is the development of senior residential complexes, such as the sizable Sun City in Huntley, McHenry County.

5. A crescent of relatively economically self-sufficient, large, industrial satellite cities grew up in an arc lying about thirty-five miles from the Loop, which generally follows the route of the Elgin, Joliet, and Eastern Railway (Chicago Outer Belt Line). These cities, at or near the intersection of the belt line and railroads that radiate from Chicago, include Waukegan–North Chicago, Elgin, Aurora, Joliet, Chicago Heights, and Gary. Each of these industrial communities was heavily populated first by immigrants primarily from eastern and southern Europe and later by growing numbers of African Americans and Hispanics.

6. Industry and commerce, as well as population, are decentralizing. During recent decades, Chicago has lost thousands of manufacturing establishments, while the suburbs have gained thousands. Consequently, increasing numbers of suburbanites are working in the suburbs. At one time the majority of suburbanites worked in Chicago. But by 1980 nearly two-thirds of the suburban workforce no longer commuted to Chicago; instead, they remained in their home suburb or, increasingly, traveled to other suburbs for employment. That trend is continuing.

The percentages of suburban commuters vary somewhat by income and occupation. The suburbs with the highest proportion of rail commuters to Chicago are high-income, white-collar bedroom communities, such as Winnetka, Glencoe, Western Springs, Hinsdale, and Flossmoor. Conversely, industrial communities, which are large consumers of labor, such as Whiting, Melrose Park, Northlake, Bedford Park, and the more distant communities of Aurora, Elgin, Joliet, North Chicago, and Waukegan, supply few commuters. In addition, in 2000 more than 20 percent of Chicago's workforce was employed in the suburbs, compared with 7 percent in 1960—the big gain being in blue-collar jobs that the suburbs otherwise might have difficulty filling. But the major increase in suburban workers has been in the white-collar category. Suburban commercial office jobs have shown a steady increase through the years, as have research, technology, and service jobs. Table 9.1 shows the projected change in employment by county from 2000 to 2030, based on a preliminary report of the Northeastern Illinois Planning Commission, the official planning body for the six counties of northeastern Illinois. By percentage, it is projected that the outlying counties will have grown much more rapidly in employment than will Cook County.

7. To a much greater degree than Chicago, the suburban area is strongly oriented toward the automobile. The expressway network, in particular, has extended and opened areas for residential, commercial, and industrial development, while occasionally even reducing commuting time. Residential expansion has been stimulated in the vicinity of almost all of the expressways. Commercial developments, especially in the form of office buildings, have risen near sections of the Ronald Reagan Tollway and, to the north and northwest, along the corridors of the Tri-State Tollway,

the Northwest Tollway, and the Kennedy and Edens expressways.

There is little effective public transportation for the newer commuting patterns of inter-suburban movement and reverse commuting from Chicago to the suburbs—as compared with the old, traditional journey from the suburbs to Chicago's center. The Regional Transportation Authority for the six counties of northeastern Illinois has provided some of the public transportation needed to cope with the new patterns, mainly by establishing numerous new suburban Pace bus routes. In a period of higher fuel and automobile costs, commuters with access to good public transportation are in an advantageous position. Workers from the inner city often find it difficult and costly to commute to jobs in the suburbs and too expensive to live in the suburbs.

8. In general, the suburbs have a substantially higher median income and higher educational and professional job level than the city of Chicago. The suburbs have a much smaller foreign-born and African American population. Chicago's African American population has increased rapidly in recent decades, until it now comprises about 36 percent of the population. During the same period, the number of

TABLE 9.1.
Preliminary 2030 Forecasts of Population and Employment, by County and Region

	Cook	Du Page	Kane	Lake	McHenry	Will	Region
Population							
2000 Base	5,376,743	904,169	404,119	644,357	260,076	502,266	8,091,730
2030	5,989,296	972,847	676,077	860,896	437,903	1,085,079	10,022,098
Employment							
2000 Base	2,856,895	651,378	206,376	354,729	105,147	164,859	4,339,384
2030	3,354,892	826,071	331,352	459,333	162,705	420,636	5,554,989

Source: Northeastern Illinois Planning Commission

FIG. 9.4. Corporate offices of Peapod Inc., a food distribution company, along the Edens Expressway in Skokie, 2005. Since World War II many companies have located their offices and research facilities in well-landscaped suburban sites, often along expressways, which allow for both exposure and accessibility. Photograph by Irving Cutler.

African Americans in the suburban area has increased slowly to around 9.3 percent of the total suburban population, up from 5 percent in 1980. African Americans now live in over half of the nearly three hundred municipalities in the Chicago metropolitan area. However, the majority of African Americans are concentrated in fewer than twenty suburbs. In Du Page, McHenry, and Porter counties, African Americans still number only about 3 percent or less of the total population. Another developing socioeconomic characteristic is that the newer, more distant suburbs have a younger population than the older, closer suburbs, partially due to lower home costs.

In the past decade, however, the number of people who live in poverty in the inner-ring suburbs has increased noticeably. This change is attributable mainly to immigration from Mexico, to gentrification that displaces the poor from city neighborhoods, and to the dispersal of former residents of demolished Chicago public housing.

9. The past growth trends of the suburban areas have varied widely, as is shown in Table 9.2. The Northeastern Illinois Planning Commission made long-range preliminary projections of population growth for the area for the period from 2000 to 2030, which shows an increase of about 24 percent. The projections were based on such factors as current housing prices, highway corridors, employment location, and local and county government plans. As shown in Table 9.1, all of the six metropolitan counties are projected

to grow by 2030. The slowest growth is projected in the two most populous counties, Cook and Du Page, while the other counties, lying partially on the rural fringe, are expected to grow by anywhere from 34 percent to more than 100 percent for Will County (south of Cook County). In 2005 the commission projected that by 2030 the six-county population will exceed 10 million and that there will be 5.5 million jobs. The 2000 U.S. census recorded somewhat more than 8 million residents with about 4.3 million jobs in the region.

10. Although the rapid suburban growth immediately after World War II has slowed, the suburban area is still growing at an average of about twenty-five square miles per year, expanding into farmland and vacant areas. In recent decades, many inner-ring suburbs have demonstrated a small gain or even losses in population; middle-ring suburbs have tended to show modest gains; and outer suburbs are generally growing very rapidly. Little land remains for new development in suburban Cook County.

11. While suburban living offers many advantages, it also has certain drawbacks. These disadvantages may include poor public transportation, long commuting distances, and inadequate facilities for sewage and water, especially if the suburb is new or has grown rapidly. Initially, there may be a shortage of schools, churches, and shopping facilities. School taxes may be high, since the suburbs, particularly the newer ones, usually contain a high proportion of young couples with growing families. In time the children grow up and leave home, marry, and often settle in Chicago or in newer communities farther out from Chicago, where the school-building cycle is repeated. The older suburb may then decline in population and find itself saddled with an overabundance of deteriorating schools and other facilities. At the same time, the older suburb may lack facilities for the elderly, such as low-cost housing.

12. The suburban areas of Chicago can be divided broadly into north, west, and south sectors. These sectors generally differ in rate of growth, economic and social status, and industrial development. Within each sector, too, there are noticeable, though usually less pronounced, differences.

North Suburban Growth Patterns

The north suburban area includes those suburbs in north Cook County, Lake County, and adjacent sections of McHenry County.

TABLE 9.2.
Metropolitan Population by County, 1950–2000

County	1950	1960	1970	1980	1990	2000
Cook	4,508,792	5,129,725	5,493,766	5,253,190	5,141,375	5,376,743
Du Page	154,599	313,459	490,882	658,177	843,067	904,169
Kane	150,388	208,246	251,005	278,405	348,590	404,119
Lake	179,097	293,656	382,638	440,372	559,392	644,357
McHenry	50,656	84,210	111,555	147,724	215,945	260,076
Will	134,336	191,617	247,825	324,460	398,706	502,266
Lake (Indiana)	368,152	513,269	546,253	522,965	481,635	484,584
Porter (Indiana)	40,076	60,279	87,114	119,816	138,243	146,798

Source: Adapted from U.S. Census data

This area ranks higher economically, socially, and educationally than either the western or southern suburbs. Although the northern suburban area contains numerous communities over a century old, it is also the area that has grown the most since World War II.

Population has long been aligned along the three major commuter railroads in the area, but buildup in the sectors between the railroad lines has been rapid in recent years. In addition to well-established transportation facilities, the northern suburbs have certain aesthetic attractions. They include the inland lake area, with its numerous small lakes and ponds that were developed first as a recreational area and later as sites for permanent homes; rolling topography, particularly in the areas to the northwest, around Barrington; and most important, the Lake Michigan shoreline, which is further enhanced by the picturesque North Shore ravines that stretch from Winnetka to Waukegan. Just south of the Lake County line are the Chicago Horticultural Society's beautiful botanic gardens and the rejuvenated Skokie Lagoons. This long-settled lakeshore area, with its attractive physical features, good rail transportation, and freedom from obnoxious industry, contains the greatest number of high-income suburbs in the Chicago area.

Of the forty-three Chicago-area communities with median family incomes of more than a hundred thousand dollars in 1999, thirty are in the north and northwest suburbs, including the top three: Kenilworth, Winnetka, and Glencoe, all of which are aligned along the lake. Also having a median family income of well above a hundred thousand dollars annually are the lakeshore suburbs of Lake Bluff, Lake Forest, Highland Park, and Wilmette. Unlike communities farther inland, the lakeshore suburbs have now largely achieved maturity; coupled with a relatively low birth rate, their prospects for population growth are very limited. But the suburbs just to the west of the long-established lakeshore suburbs, such as Skokie, Glenview, Northfield, Northbrook, and Deerfield, have grown very rapidly in recent decades because of the availability of land, the opening of the Edens Expressway with its profusion of office buildings, and the proximity of these communities to the prestigious shoreline suburbs.

Aligned northwest, in the corridor of the former Chicago and North Western Railway, are another group of long-established suburbs—Park Ridge, Des Plaines, Mt. Prospect, Arlington Heights, Palatine, Barrington, and Crystal Lake. These towns are generally populated by families with more modest income than those of the North Shore. Unlike the North Shore suburbs, these communities have grown rapidly in recent years, especially those near O'Hare International Airport, which include Schaumburg, Elk Grove Village, Hoffman Estates, Streamwood, and Hanover Park. This area contains many newly erected prestigious office and hotel complexes, as well as one of the world's largest enclosed shopping centers under one roof—Woodfield Mall in Schaumburg. The village of Schaumburg increased in population from only 986 in 1960 to 75,386 in 2000. Arlington Heights, the largest community of the area, grew from about nine thousand in 1950 to 76,031 in 2000.

Between 1950 and 1980, the population of this northwest corridor, sometimes referred to as the "golden corridor," more than quadrupled. The growth can be attributed to readily available land and a good transportation system, which includes the old Chicago and North Western railroad (now Metra

FIG. 9.5. Bahá'í House of Worship in Wilmette, started in 1920 and completed in 1953. It annually attracts thousands of visitors from all over the world. Photograph by Irving Cutler.

FIG. 9.6. Architectural award–winning North Shore Congregation Israel, designed by Minoru Yamasaki. The pioneer synagogue in Glencoe, on the North Shore, was started in 1920 as a branch of the Chicago Sinai Congregation. The present temple, along the lakefront, was dedicated in 1964. Photograph by Irving Cutler.

Northwest Line) and the Milwaukee Road railroad (now Metra/Milwaukee District North Line), together with the Kennedy Expressway–Northwest Tollway, the Tri-State Tollway, and the Lake Street extension of the Eisenhower Expressway (U.S. 290). In 1996 the Metra/North Central Service line was added to provide service from Antioch to Union Station in Chicago. In addition, the proximity of O'Hare Airport has attracted a great number of industrial and commercial enterprises.

The areas around O'Hare International Airport and Woodfield Mall are the employment nodes of the corridor. The communities around the airport employ more than two hundred thousand people in over five thousand industries, with Elk Grove Village alone employing about one hundred thousand persons. Employment is provided not only by industrial concerns but also by a growing number of hotels and office buildings. The area around O'Hare International Airport contains over fifty office buildings with more than 6 million square feet of office space.

In the corridor, approximately seven or eight miles northwest of the airport, is the younger, rapidly growing Woodfield area of Schaumburg, Hoffman Estates, and Rolling Meadows—where new office buildings dot the landscape and where room for growth is still substantial. In 1980 the Woodfield area contained sixty-three office buildings with a combined 6.5 million square feet of space. With one exception, all the office buildings have been built since 1965.

The northwest corridor contains the offices and other facilities of about three hundred of *Fortune*'s five hundred largest corporations, including corporate headquarters of United Airlines, Sears Holdings, Allstate,

Kraft, Illinois Tool Works, Walgreens, Motorola, USG, Fortune Brands, and Baxter International. These buildings are usually in well-landscaped industrial parks or office complexes. The spectacular growth of the area has created such problems as increased traffic congestion, greater noise and air pollution from airplanes, and water shortages (alleviated somewhat by new water allocation and distribution systems from Lake Michigan). A major problem is a shortage of workers, especially blue-collar workers. The extension of the CTA rapid transit line to O'Hare International Airport helped alleviate some of this problem. The extension has also given impetus to the construction of residential, commercial, and industrial facilities along its route.

There are few lower-income suburbs north of Chicago. Among them are North Chicago, Park City, Highwood, Round Lake Park, and Waukegan. These communities help supply some of the blue-collar workers urgently needed by industry. The African American population is small and is concentrated in Evanston, Waukegan–North Chicago, and Zion, with other communities having very few, if any, African Americans.

Light industry has expanded rapidly in the northern suburban areas of Chicago, often having relocated from the city. There is virtually no heavy industry in the northern sector. Much of the light industry falls within the growing fields of electronics, chemicals, and pharmaceuticals. Research and office facilities also are increasing rapidly.

Major centers of employment are in Evanston, North Chicago–Waukegan, Skokie, Deerfield, Palatine, Niles, Hoffman Estates, Elk Grove Village, Schaumburg, Arlington Heights, Wheeling, Des Plaines, and Northbrook. One of the largest cities in the northern suburbs is Evanston, which had a population of 74,239 in 2000. It is an attractive, tree-lined community of homes, apartments, and condominiums, with some industrial areas and a distinguished educational facility, Northwestern University. It is a transitional city between Chicago to the south and the wealthier lakeshore suburbs to the north.

The frontier of urbanization to the north has now pushed deeply, but by no means solidly, into Lake County. Much of the northern third of the county running to the Wisconsin state line is still partially rural in character, but new developments have been appearing with increasing frequency. The amount of farmland in Lake County dwindled from 173,000 acres

in 1950 to a mere thirty-nine thousand acres in 2002.

Lake County is one of the most heterogeneous of counties, both physically and in population diversity. It is a blend of a variety of urban communities and some sizable rural areas. The county is divided by the Des Plaines River as it flows south from Wisconsin into Cook County. West of the river, the landscape is characterized by rolling topography, declining areas of farmland, and numerous small lakes whose shores harbor small, moderate-income communities and resort areas. In the northwest corner of the county are the Chain

FIG. 9.7. Fountain Square in downtown Evanston, about 1930. City Hall is the towered building on the left, and the Marshall Field store, one of the first suburban branches of a downtown Chicago department store, is in the center background. Extensive recent construction has revitalized downtown Evanston, making it a busy and vibrant area once again. Photograph by Childs; Chicago Historical Society.

FIG. 9.8. Looking north at the Northwestern University campus in Evanston, 1988. The university was founded in 1851 and has an enrollment of about twelve thousand, including those students in its Chicago facilities. It is highly rated in numerous fields, among them journalism, business, law, medicine, and music. The right side of the photo includes a large addition to the Evanston campus, created in the 1960s through the filling in of seventy acres of Lake Michigan. Photograph courtesy of Northwestern University.

of Lakes State Park, the winding Fox River, and Fox Lake. In the center of the county are the neighboring cities of Mundelein and Libertyville, which have grown rapidly in recent decades. To their south is the small community of Long Grove, with its many antique and specialty shops. Just to the south of Long Grove, straddling the Cook County line, is Buffalo Grove, the home of many young families. Its population has exploded from 1,492 in 1960 to 42,909 in 2000.

To the east of the Des Plaines River, especially along Lake County's twenty-four

miles of Lake Michigan shoreline, are some of the wealthiest commuter suburbs in the metropolitan area, including Highland Park, Lake Forest, and Lake Bluff. Also fronting the lake is the Great Lakes Naval Training Center, founded in 1917 in North Chicago. It is now the only naval boot camp in the country, graduating more than fifty thousand recruits a year, plus thousands of naval specialists. The first African American naval officers were commissioned there during World War II. More than a million sailors were trained there during World War II. In recent years the huge seventeen-hundred-acre base has been headed by female commanders.

Also situated along the lake, between Highland Park, Highwood, and Lake Forest, a few miles south of the Great Lakes Naval Training Center, was the seven-hundred-acre Ft. Sheridan. It was in operation from 1887 to 1994 and was built on land donated to the army by the Commercial Club of Chicago, which wanted the army nearby during the period of violent labor strife that occurred toward the end of the nineteenth century. Originally a cavalry base, it later trained hundreds of thousands of soldiers in various skills and shipped them off to fight in all the wars from the Spanish American War to the Viet Nam conflict. In later years it was mainly an administrative base and housed a number of army schools. Soldiers and their families lived in what resembled a small residential community. After its closing in 1994, the land was divided among the neighboring communities and converted into a very expensive residential community of new and old homes near the lake, with some homes selling for over $1 million.

North Chicago and Waukegan are heavily industrialized satellite cities along the lake. To their north, near the Wisconsin border, are the Illinois Beach State Park and the city of Zion. From its start in 1901 until 1935, Zion was a religious community with a communal society and theocratic government. Today it has a population of about twenty-three thousand and is basically residential but was once the site of a large nuclear power plant, now closed.

The dense population in the eastern part of Lake County distinguishes it as the third-most populous county in Illinois. Minorities

FIG. 9.9. Entrance to the seventeen-hundred-acre Great Lakes Naval Training Station in North Chicago, 2004. The base was established in 1911 and now is the only Navy boot camp in the country. During World War I it turned out about one hundred thousand sailors, and during World War II, more than a million. Photograph by Irving Cutler.

FIG. 9.10. Zion Hotel in Zion, Illinois. From its founding in 1900 until 1935, Zion was a strict religious community founded and run by the Christian Catholic Apostolic Church, which prohibited its residents from smoking, drinking, and card playing and trains from stopping there on Sunday. The church built a large lace factory, a brick plant, and a cookie-baking facility, all of which went into receivership in 1933. Later, the church's three-story, 350-room hotel was given to the Village of Zion, which ran it unsuccessfully for a time before demolishing it. Photograph by Herb Gaede.

constitute about 21 percent of the county's population, with about twice as many Hispanics as African Americans. A large blue-collar workforce is available in the county for industrial development.

New population growth in the county has been stimulated by a number of factors: the growth of industry, including huge developments by two medical supply–pharmaceutical companies, Baxter International and Abbott Laboratories; the opening of two regional shopping centers, Lakehurst in Waukegan (now demolished) and Hawthorne Center (including the adjacent New Century Town community in Vernon Hills); the building of

the Great America theme recreational park; and the establishment of the huge Gurnee Mills shopping outlet in Gurnee. The county also contains Ravinia Park, one of the nation's foremost summer music centers.

The Waukegan–North Chicago–Gurnee complex, aided especially by rapid industrial growth, has led to a population increase from 48,671 in 1950 to 152,653 in 2000. By far the largest industrial employer in this area is Abbott Laboratories. Other large employers include Medline Industries, WMS Gaming, and Federal Chicago. Growth in the county had been limited somewhat by the lack of adequate water and sewage facilities and by the presence of large estates. Growth has been rapid in the county, partly because land is still available in large sections, often from the estates of wealthy Chicagoans who purchased farms years ago and are now willing to sell them.

McHenry County to the northwest has the smallest population of any of the metropolitan-area counties in Illinois, or 260,076 in 2000. Its largest city, Crystal Lake, had only thirty-eight thousand people in 2000. Agriculture is a significant industry there, as is milk production. The economic base, however, has gradually shifted to manufacturing, and today the majority of its workers are employed in blue-collar occupations. Because of its geographic remoteness, its immediate growth prospects are somewhat limited, despite recent residential developments and the establishment of the large Sun City retirement village in Huntley.

West Suburban Growth Patterns

The suburbs west of Chicago are more mixed in their characteristics than the suburbs to the north and northwest. Because of Chicago's narrow east-west width, this area includes those suburbs that are closest to the Loop, in some places only about six to eight miles away, such as Cicero, Berwyn, and Oak Park. These old, sizable, mature suburbs have had very little room for growth in recent decades. While Berwyn and Oak Park are mainly residential, Cicero is a large industrial employer. Oak Park, somewhat similar in makeup to the community of Evanston to the north, is a transitional community that shares characteristics of both the big city and suburbia. It is noted for its beautifully shaded streets and its many homes designed by Frank Lloyd Wright, a one-time Oak Park resident. Former residents also include Ernest Hemingway

and Edgar Rice Burroughs, the author of the *Tarzan* books. Like Evanston, Oak Park has a large number of apartment buildings, some condominium buildings, excellent transportation to Chicago, and an increasing African American population.

At the far west, almost forty miles from the Loop, are a string of satellite communities that are aligned along the Fox River in extreme eastern Kane County. The largest of these communities (from north to south) include Carpentersville, Elgin, St. Charles, Geneva, Batavia, and Aurora.

All of these communities had a substantial population increase in recent decades. These residential-industrial communities originated largely because of their location along the river. The river was also the locale of many summer homes and hotels frequented by Chicagoans. A sizable industrial base, especially in larger cities like Elgin (94,487) and Aurora (142,150), combined with the greater distance of these communities from Chicago, contributed to their self-sufficiency in employment and thus relatively little need for commuting to Chicago. The Elgin area hosts the facilities of such companies as Simpson Electric, U.S. Can, Amtec Precision Products, Elgin Sweeper, Chicago Rawhide, and Illinois Tool Works. Nearby, the Aurora area includes the facilities of such companies as Caterpillar, Westell, National Metalwares, and Emerson Power Transmission.

In recent years, the frontier of urban expansion from Chicago has reached well beyond the Fox Valley area to Elburn and Sugar Grove, leaping over some rural farmland and second-growth prairies. Fox Valley Center, a major regional shopping center, opened in Aurora in 1975. It is part of the Fox Valley Villages, a planned residential, commercial,

FIG. 9.11. Lake Street at Harlem Avenue, part of the central business district of Oak Park in the late 1920s. A Marshall Field store is on the left. Chicago Historical Society.

and industrial community on the western edge of Du Page County.

Downtown Aurora is also undergoing improvement, evidenced by the construction of the Water Street Mall, the restoration of the Paramount Theater, and the construction of a new civic center. To the north in Elgin, downtown rehabilitation also is taking place, with a new city hall having been built as part of a civic center complex. Elgin also has the Grand Victoria Casino, whose taxes have helped finance some infrastructure projects, as has the Hollywood Casino in Aurora. A few miles to the north of Elgin, in West Dundee, is the huge Spring Hill Mall Shopping Center, which was opened in 1980.

Between the suburbs on the periphery of Chicago and the Fox valley suburbs is an area that has grown rapidly since World War II—western Cook County and all of Du Page County. Western Cook County is now almost entirely urbanized. It contains a number of industrial-residential communities, such as Melrose Park, Franklin Park, and Maywood. Riverside is an especially attractive western suburb; it was one of the nation's first planned communities, having been laid out in 1868 by the noted landscape architect Frederick Law Olmsted. Riverside was constructed in a park-like fashion, with generous lots and winding roads that conform to the meandering Des Plaines River, which it straddles. In western Cook County, over 75 percent of the residents of Maywood, Bellwood, and Broadview are African American. Fifty-four percent of the population of Melrose Park is Hispanic. In 2000 there were 46,557 Hispanics living in

Aurora, about a third of its population. That group constitutes the third-largest Hispanic population in the metropolitan area. Cicero, with its 66,299 Hispanics, representing 77 percent of its population, has the second-largest Hispanic population.

Du Page County, lying due west of Chicago, has urbanized very rapidly. In 1950 far more than half the land there was still devoted to agriculture and its entire county population numbered only 154,599. Since then, the amount of its agricultural land has declined steeply and its population has climbed to over nine hundred thousand. Between 1970 and 1980, the population rose 34.9 percent, the largest percentage of any Illinois county in the Chicago metropolitan area. Today it is the second most populous county in Illinois.

Du Page County has the highest median family income in the state. In 2000 a number of its cities had annual median family incomes of over one hundred thousand dollars, including Oak Brook, Hinsdale, and Burr Ridge. Also, the value of homes and the median school years completed were higher in Du Page County than in any other county in the Chicago metropolitan area.

Employment is growing in Du Page County. Communities with fairly sizable employment figures include Addison—thirty-five thousand; Hinsdale—eighteen thousand; Lisle—twenty-four thousand; Wheaton—twenty-five thousand; Naperville—sixty-five thousand; and Oak Brook—sixty-one thousand. Some jobs are in commerce and manufacturing; however, a growing number of nationally known laboratories, research centers, and corporate offices have settled in the county. These facilities are aligned mainly along the Ronald Reagan Tollway (formerly the East-West Tollway) corridor, with major foci in Oak Brook to the east and in the Naperville area to the west.

Oak Brook, incorporated as a small village in 1958, has about nine thousand residents living in large homes that commanded a median price of about $620,000 in 2003. Although it is noted for its polo fields and golf courses, Oak Brook is also a major office building and shopping center complex. Many thousands of workers and shoppers flood the village daily, and about seventy of *Fortune Magazine*'s five hundred largest companies are headquartered or have office representation in Oak Brook. Companies who have headquarters there include Ace Hardware, Federal Signal, and McDonald's. Numerous hotels dot the area, and Oak Brook Shopping Center, the second-largest regional shopping center in the metropolitan area, is there. The mall's sales are usually exceeded only by those of the Woodfield Mall in Schaumburg. A short distance to the north lies the Yorktown Shopping Center in Lombard, and farther north is the Stratford Square shopping center in Bloomingdale. The latter's developers also built substantial nearby residences.

Farther west, along some five miles of the Ronald Reagan Tollway corridor in the vicinity of Naperville, is an even more recent, rapidly growing cluster of research centers and office parks. It includes the Fermi National Accelerator Laboratory, with the world's largest high-energy particle accelerator. This research and office corridor, like Oak Brook, has grown rapidly because of available open land and stable residential communities with such growing amenities as hotels, shopping centers, and excellent transportation that provides easy access to O'Hare International Airport or downtown Chicago by automobile.

Less than ten miles to the south, in the southern tip of Du Page County, is the thirty-seven-hundred-acre Argonne National Laboratory. It is one of the world's leading atomic energy research and development centers.

Residents, although beginning to settle throughout Du Page County, are still predominantly aligned along the two major commuter railroads that serve the county. Along the route of the Chicago and North Western Railway (now the Metra West Line)—also previously served by the now-defunct Chicago, Aurora, and Elgin Railroad—are the sizable communities of Elmhurst, Villa Park, Lombard, Glen Ellyn, and Wheaton. Wheaton is especially noted for its religious institutions, while Lombard is known for its annual lilac festival. Larger cities farther south, along the Metra/Burlington Northern Santa Fe Railroad (which generally parallels the Ronald Reagan Tollway), include Hinsdale, Downers Grove, and the rapidly growing, more distant communities of Lisle and Naperville. Naperville, incorporated in 1857, is the oldest community in Du Page County. It is noted for its interesting memorial Riverwalk along the Du Page River. The Lisle area is the site of the Morton Arboretum, a privately endowed, beautiful outdoor nature preserve, consisting of thousands of trees and smaller plants. A number of communities that are not along the main commuter railroads have also grown rapidly and become sizable in the last decade or two. These include, in particular, Addison, Carol Stream, Bloomingdale, Hanover Park, Glendale Heights, and Woodridge.

The high-rises that have been recently built in Wheaton, Hinsdale, Oak Brook, and other communities exemplify the increasingly urbanized nature of the area. The growing population has encountered increased traffic congestion and problems associated with garbage and sewage disposal. In recent years, the water supply of the county has been improved and the forest preserve area has been greatly expanded.

Minorities have a small but growing presence in Du Page County. African Americans comprise a mere 3 percent of the population, and Hispanics, only 9 percent. The low numbers may be traceable to early restrictive practices, high home values, and the scarcity of blue-collar industrial employment opportunities.

Du Page County remains a mosaic of the old and new. Old towns with quiet streets shaded by majestic trees are experiencing renewed growth that sometimes matches that of the new residential municipalities. And scattered around the rapidly disappearing cornfields are sleek new office buildings, busy shopping centers, and vital new industrial concerns. In 1950, when Du Page County employed only about fifteen thousand persons, it was clearly a "bedroom" of Chicago. In 2000, with employment of more than 650,000 persons, a majority of its residents now work within their own county. In recent decades, Du Page County had the greatest percentage increase in jobs of any of the counties of the Chicago metropolitan area.

South Suburban Growth Patterns

The southern sector of suburbs forms a large arc that stretches from Will County in the southwest through southern Cook County in the south, and into Indiana's Lake and Porter counties in the southeast. Although the very size of this sector allows for great diversity, in general, this area contains the suburbs with the lowest median income, the lowest home value, the lowest levels of schooling, the highest proportion of minorities, and the greatest amount of heavy industry. It also probably has greater growth potential than that of the other sectors, although thus far no major new employment complex, like those in Oak Brook, O'Hare, or Woodfield, has been developed.

The area southwest of Chicago that borders the city of Joliet in Will County was at one time one of the slowest-growing suburban segments of the metropolitan area. Will County, for example, was still more than two-thirds farmland in 1970. It was handicapped both by its distance from the Loop and by one of the poorest transportation systems to downtown Chicago of any sector. The later opening of several expressways in that area, plus its

position as one of the few remaining suburban areas with plentiful, relatively cheap land, has contributed to its rise as one of the fastest-growing areas around Chicago. Because homes are comparatively moderate in price, many blue-collar workers have relocated there from the South Side of Chicago after African Americans moved into their neighborhoods. As yet, few African Americans live in the distant southwest suburbs, with the exception of Joliet, where in the year 2000 African Americans comprised about 18 percent of the population.

Some of this southwest area is aesthetically attractive, featuring rolling topography and morainic features, especially the Mount

FIG. 9.12. Metropolitan area expanding into the cornfields southwest of Chicago. The development is along the Stevenson Expressway, the opening of which in 1964 helped stimulate a building boom in the area. From Rutherford H. Platt, *Open Land in Urban Illinois*, 1971. Used with permission of Northern Illinois University Press.

Forest–Palos area. The proximity of modern expressways, such as the Stevenson and interstates 57, 355, and 80, has allowed residents now to enjoy a greater range of employment opportunities. In addition, there are multiple industrial centers, such as those at Bedford Park, Alsip, and Joliet. The Joliet region has benefited from the development of the Jefferson Square Mall, the Louis Joliet Mall, two casinos, and a growing petrochemical complex along the Illinois Waterway. Joliet, with a population of about 106,000, has a fairly strong industrial base, with a number of large manufacturers, such as Caterpillar, Ecolab, B.P. Amoco Chemical, and Kemlite. Its location along the Chicago Sanitary and Ship Canal also benefits the area. However, Joliet, once known as the city of "Steel and Stone," has lost those two major industries.

Among the faster growing communities to the southwest are Frankfort, Justice, Tinley Park, Lockport, Orland Park, Lemont, Oak Forest, New Lenox, Plainfield, Romeoville, Bolingbrook, and Oak Lawn. For example, the population of Orland Park increased from 2,592 in 1960 to 51,077 in 2000. During the same period, Tinley Park increased from 6,392 to 48,401.

Due south of Chicago in southern Cook County, spilling over into Will County in an area served by the Illinois Central Gulf and Rock Island railroads (now Metra), exist a large number of small and medium-sized communities. Most are older, mature suburbs, but a number were developed after World War II. A few older communities, such as Blue Island, Harvey, and Chicago Heights, have been highly industrialized for about a century.

Among the larger industrial employers in Harvey are Allied Tube and Conduit, and Fuchs Lubricant. In Chicago Heights, the larger employers include Ford, Thrall Car Manufacturing, UGN, CFC International, and Calumet Heights Steel. Many communities are a combination of industrial and residential development, containing a population with a low-to-moderate income range and educational level. The suburbs of Ford Heights, Robbins, Phoenix, and Dixmoor, for example, rank among the poorest in the Chicago area. However, there are a few notable exceptions, especially the residential suburbs of Flossmoor and Olympia Fields. In income, these two commuter communities lying along the Illinois Central Gulf Railroad (Metra Electric) rank among the top twenty suburbs in the Chicago area.

An interesting moderate-income suburb is Park Forest, established in 1947 as one of the first large carefully planned communities in the country. It was developed essentially by a single corporation. It consists of a series of neighborhood units united by common community and service facilities, including a shopping center that recently has been undergoing redevelopment. Park Forest offers abundant open spaces, curved streets, and a mixture of townhouse apartments, cooperatives, and single-family homes. Its 2000 population was 23,462. Adjoining it in Will County is an even newer planned community, University Park (formerly Park Forest South).

After a long period of slow growth, the area due south of Chicago is now developing more rapidly. This increase is due in part to the construction of modern expressways in the area, the availability of cheap land, and the mitigation of some drainage problems in the eastern section. In recent years, many of the long-established Dutch and German farmers of the area have sold their land. Today virtually none of the onion set farmers of Dutch ancestry remain in that area.

FIG. 9.13. Curvilinear streets of the post–World War II planned community of Park Forest, 1952. The community is about thirty miles south of the Loop. Photograph by Owen Kent; Chicago Historical Society, ICHi-07481.

Some of the growth has been due to an influx of African Americans into the area, continuing the southward movement of African Americans from the heart of Chicago. Many were attracted to the area by jobs in industry. Despite the south suburban area having the largest percentage of African Americans of any suburban sector around Chicago, some communities there have few, if any, African Americans. The few communities that do contain large percentages of African American residents include Dixmoor, Harvey, University Park, Markham, Dolton, Chicago Heights, Ford Heights, Riverdale, Phoenix,

and Robbins. The population of the latter four communities is almost entirely composed of African Americans.

Across the state line, in adjacent Lake County, Indiana, is an area quite different from other sectors around Chicago. This is a region of heavy industry: steel, in particular, and oil refining and chemical manufacturing to a lesser extent. This narrow industrial corridor fronts Lake Michigan and encompasses part of the Indiana Dunes. Surface drainage is poor, and pollution problems have been precipitated by heavy industry in the area.

Northern Lake County contains the industrial cities of Hammond, Whiting, East Chicago, and Gary. Gary, with a 2000 population of 102,798, and Hammond, with 83,048 people, are among the largest cities in the eight-county metropolitan area. Unlike the more rural southern portion of Lake County, Indiana, this is an area of stagnant residential growth and, in some instances, of declining population brought on at least partially by declining industry. All four of the cities have lost population since 1960: all but Whiting have suffered substantial population declines. Gary's population, for example, has declined 42 percent since 1960.

As a whole, the area ranks low in median income, home values, and educational levels. Sizable African American communities live in Gary and East Chicago: in Gary, African Americans comprise 84 percent of the population, and in East Chicago they comprise 36 percent of the population. A substantial Hispanic population also lives in northern Lake County, especially in East Chicago, where, in the year 2000, 51 percent of the population was Hispanic. East Chicago, with a population of 32,414 in 2000, is divided into two parts by railroads and the Indiana Harbor Ship Canal. The "twin cities" comprise an eastern part, Indiana Harbor, where African Americans and Hispanics, for the

FIG. 9.14. Broadway, the main north-south artery of Gary, 1908. The tracks are those of an electric trolley line. The community had been incorporated in 1906 on U.S. Steel land in conjunction with the building of the company's huge, new steel plant in the dunes area, along the Lake Michigan shoreline. The community was named for the chairman of the board of the corporation, Elbert H. Gary. The corporation usually contributes half of the tax revenues of the city. Chicago Historical Society.

most part, live and have their own business area, and a western part, usually identified as East Chicago, which is largely white and possesses its own business district.

Less than ten miles south of Gary, along Interstate 65, lies the community of Merrillville, Indiana. Established in the 1960s, by 2000 it had grown in population to 30,560. Many of the residents are white steel workers who moved out of Gary and were followed by many of their doctors, lawyers, churches, clubs, stores, and restaurants. Merrillville is also the site of a large shopping and entertainment center.

Lying farther east, Porter County, Indiana, remains the least populated of the eight metropolitan counties. It had 146,798 persons in 2000, compared with adjacent Lake County's 484,564. Its population increased about 10 percent in the 1990s. All of the cities of Porter County are small. Its growth, however, has been accelerating, largely as a result of the construction, within recent decades, of two huge steel mills. They flank the new deep-water Port of Indiana, at Burns Harbor on the lakeshore, east of Gary. One of the largest cities, Valparaiso, numbering 27,428 people in 2000, is perched on the Valparaiso Moraine and is a manufacturing and university center, as well as the county seat. Somewhat larger, with a population of 33,496, is the relatively new community of Portage, incorporated in 1959. It spans three miles of Lake Michigan shoreline and includes much of the two steel mills. The importance of the steel industry to both Lake and Porter counties is evidenced by almost half of all the employed residents of each county having occupations associated with the primary metals industry. In recent years, however, employment in that depressed industry has declined sharply.

Indiana Dunes National Lakeshore

Porter County contains the Indiana Dunes State Park and most of the Indiana Dunes National Lakeshore. The latter has been described as "America's first urban national park." Years of bitter conflict raged before federal legislation finally authorized it in 1966, thanks to the dedicated efforts of Senator Paul Douglas of Illinois and others. Conservationists, who wished to preserve more of the scenic dunes for the benefit of the burgeoning population of the metropolitan area, were opposed by commercial and industrial leaders, who argued that development of industry in this strategic location would stimulate economic growth. After recent land acquisitions, the Indiana Dunes National Lakeshore occupied about thirteen thousand acres, including ten miles of Lake Michigan shoreline—about one fourth of Indiana's entire lakefront. In addition to long beaches, the park includes high dunes, wooded ravines, tree graveyards, interdunal lagoons and swamps, arctic bogs, tropical orchids, desert cactus, and interesting wildlife, as well as historic and cultural features.

About ninety years ago, Professor Eliot R. Downing described the wildlife of the dunes in its natural setting.

It is an extensive stretch of wild country with plenty of cover in which small animals find shelter; it is consequently also the haunt of some of the larger predaceous animals now near extinct elsewhere hereabouts. In the last five years I have found the gray timber wolf there once, foxes several times, raccoons, porcupines, rattlesnakes, and nearly every year the bald eagle has been nesting somewhere in the region .... Just as the flora of the dunes is a curious mixture of southern and northern species,

FIG. 9.15. Sand dune and varied vegetation in the West Beach section of the Indiana Dunes National Lakeshore, 2003. Photograph by and used with permission of Henning H. Sorensen.

FIG. 9.16. First large gathering of citizens to preserve the Indiana dunes. The meeting was held in 1917 on the site of the present Indiana Dunes State Park and was sponsored by the Prairie Club of Chicago. Chicago Historical Society.

FIG. 9.17. Tour group learning about the formation, flora, and fauna of the Indiana dunes, 2001. Irving Cutler collection.

like the cactus and arbutus, that grow side by side, so there are found animals there as neighbors that represent the desert conditions of the Southwest and the pine barrens of the North. Such representatives of usually widely separate faunas are the six lined lizard that runs to cover with such celerity and the ruffed grouse that as a rule only nests in the pine forest several hundred miles farther north. Yet both these animals are quite common in "the dunes." . . . Because of the congenial cover afforded by the evergreen thickets and the abundant food, many birds are found during the spring and fall migrations, staying days and weeks in the dunes, that would not loiter at all in the Chicago region were it not for the attractions of this particular section.[1]

Some of the wildlife of the dunes area has vanished owing to encroachment by man, but still left are an estimated forty different mammals, including the raccoon, opossum, weasel, muskrat, skunk, and white-tail deer, as well as between 250 and 300 species of birds.

The National Lakeshore park in the Chicago urban complex is also unique in a number of other respects.

The Indiana Dunes National Lakeshore is America's first urban park. It is within easy driving distance of millions of Americans . . . . [It] is a mosaic park where great industrial complexes, residential communities and a web of railroad tracks and highways are interspersed with areas of great physical beauty which remain substantially untouched by man. Though the Lakeshore's land holdings are not contiguous, they include the recreational, aesthetic, and historical elements which typify all of our country's great parks.[2]

Regional Shopping Centers

In addition to the ubiquitous supermarket, the retail heart of many Chicago suburban areas is the automobile-oriented regional

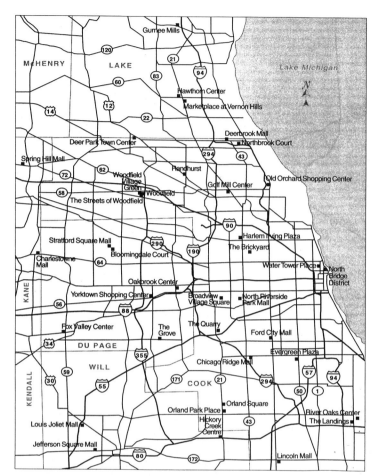

FIG. 9.18. Major Chicago area shopping malls, 2002. Map courtesy of the National Research Bureau.

shopping center. These huge, modern shopping complexes usually contain from two to six major department stores and from fifty to two hundred specialty stores (the majority of which are stores of regional or national chains). Chicago's department store giants have well over fifty stores in these suburban centers. The centers are surrounded by acres of parking space, with some being able to accommodate as many as ten thousand cars. Few have adequate public transportation.

These shopping centers constitute, in some instances, the new downtowns of suburbia. The retail industry has, accordingly, accommodated itself to these new retail complexes. In addition to retail activities, there are usually numerous professional services, recreational facilities, and often, cultural events. The centers are also often the gathering places for various age groups. Design and landscaping are usually attractive, with many centers having enclosed malls for more convenient and pleasurable shopping.

The Chicago area now contains twenty-seven regional shopping centers and more than one hundred smaller plaza-type centers. The first regional shopping centers in the area were opened about a half century ago, but until 1960, there were only four in the area. These were well spaced, at least fifteen miles apart, and were more than a dozen miles from the Loop. However, between 1960 and 1980, twenty-three additional major regional shopping centers were opened.

Many of the centers are now near each other, with overlapping remote boundaries. In the western suburbs, Hillside (opened in 1956), Oak Brook (1962), Yorktown (1968), and North Riverside (1976) malls are just a few minutes' drive from one another. To the north of Chicago, in the vicinity of Golf Road along a stretch of only about seventeen miles, four major regional shopping centers coexist: Old Orchard (1956), Golf Mill (1960), Randhurst (1962), and Woodfield (1971). The pattern of the opening of the new centers, as illustrated by these cases, has generally been an ever-outward movement toward the periphery of the metropolitan area. Some of the newer centers, in areas where large tracts of land are available, are the hubs of a complementary residential development, such as the New Century Town adjacent to Hawthorn Center, or the Fox Valley Villages development that includes Fox Valley Center. The shopping center often is a catalyst for important residential and commercial growth, like that which has occurred around the Woodfield and Oak Brook shopping centers. Some centers have been established prematurely, in sparsely populated areas, and are counting on rapid population growth to increase their market potential.

FIG. 9.19. Westfield Old Orchard Shopping Center in Skokie, 2005. The mall was opened in 1956 on ninety-eight acres of what were formerly picnic grounds. The center contains five major department stores and about seven thousand parking spaces. Photograph by Daniel Cutler.

The community that contains the regional shopping center usually finds that its roads have become more congested and that it has to provide additional police and fire protection; however, this challenge is usually more than compensated for by greatly increased real estate and sales tax revenue, as well as improved shopping and employment opportunities for its residents. Adjacent communities often feel the adverse effect of the shopping center, for not only do their streets usually bear some of the increased traffic, but their shopping facilities suffer from the competition of the new, modern center. As a consequence, many neighboring communities have strongly opposed the development of large shopping centers. In a few rare cases, adjoining suburbs have agreed to share, in some fashion, the revenue generated by a new shopping center.

A new major shopping center can also adversely affect an old, established suburban downtown. This has been the case in such communities as Chicago Heights, Aurora, Oak Park, Waukegan, and Evanston. Evanston, for example, although larger in population than adjacent Skokie, has only about half the retail sales of Skokie, which contains the busy Westfield Old Orchard Shopping Center. Similarly, Park Ridge has only about half the retail sales of the adjacent, smaller community of Niles, which contains the Golf Mill Shopping Center. Likewise, Oak Brook, with only one-sixth the population of Oak Park, has substantially greater retail sales due to the presence in Oak Brook of the huge Oak Brook Shopping Center. Some major suburban shopping centers not only compete with long-established suburban downtown stores but also attract customers from the city of Chicago.

The Rural-Urban Fringe

The number of acres used for farming around Chicago continues to decline as urbanization expands outward from the central city. The once-productive truck and dairy farms of Cook County have largely disappeared. The other counties of the metropolitan Chicago area still have varying, but rapidly declining, farmland, as urban sprawl continues to move ever-outward, taking over productive farmland.

The change of an area from rural to urban generally follows a pattern, with accompanying problems. First, there is an influx of nonfarm, rural residents.

They come to the countryside for cheaper land and lower taxes, sunshine and open spaces, room to relax and enjoy outdoor living, a safe and healthy environment in which to raise their children, a place to grow a garden and perhaps a few chickens, refuge during misfortune, and a home in their declining years.

The change in the rural scene often begins when a farmer sells off a front lot or two or perhaps a front tract or an acre or so. The price the farmer received was high compared with the value per acre of his farm as a whole. Because of this, other farmers are induced to sell off their frontages. More houses follow. Later, entire farms are broken up into tracts and subdivided. The change continues and as the years go by, country roads begin to look like residential streets. As the nonfarm population grows land is bought for gas stations and roadside stores and shops, then for other business and industrial uses.[3]

If the area is unincorporated and without adequate government regulations, new

FIG. 9.20. Twenty-eight acres of farmland for sale in Lake County, Illinois, 1969. The land, with its broken silo and grazing horses, had been neglected for farming because the land was worth much more as a future housing development, which it ultimately became. Photograph by Irving Cutler.

construction may be substandard, creating a honky-tonk atmosphere, and the natural environment may be defaced. This intrusion of nonfarm rural residents often creates problems that virtually force farmers out. Whereas an eighty-acre farm may contain one family, an eighty-acre subdivision may hold 120 families. Without adequate advance planning and zoning, the farmers may find their schools suddenly overcrowded; new problems of water, sewage disposal, and drainage arise; increased traffic results; and higher taxes are levied. Often there is a time lag before the subdivision assumes its full tax load, and the farmer may be assessed at land values similar to those of subdivisions. Highway relocations may divide farms. There may also be zoning disputes. Also, the lack of large, undivided, or expandable farms makes it difficult for farmers to take full advantage of large cost-reducing farm machinery or other improvements. Thus some of the urban-area farmers produce vegetables because such crops typically are more profitable on small parcels of land than is the production of grain. However, much of the farmland left in the area is still devoted to growing corn, soybeans, oats, winter wheat, hay, and alfalfa and to dairy farming.

The aggressive farmer may feel himself hemmed in as far as expansion is concerned. He may even have to put up fencing against trespassers. He may have to use his land more intensively in order to pay the

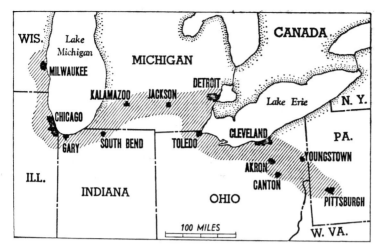

FIG. 9.21. Twenty-first-century "megalopolis" *(shaded area)*, predicted by some planners. The "Midwest megalopolis" forms the western part. *Chicago Tribune* graphic. All rights reserved. Used with permission.

higher taxes. Necessary farm services are often curtailed as an area becomes more urbanized, and a farmer so isolated may encounter difficulty, for example, in arranging for a truck to collect his milk. The result of these problems, plus the attraction of high land prices, is that the farmer sells his land.[4]

However, as Jean Gottman points out in *Megalopolis,*

Actually very few farmers are deeply disappointed when urban interests buy them out for thousands of dollars per acre. For agricultural purposes the soil itself is generally worth no more than a fraction of the selling price. The sale of the land may mean giving up a favorite spot, but even the old homestead loses its appeal when all the farms around it go into industry, residential developments, and shopping centers. The capital gain that comes when a farmer surrenders to the city is a handsome reward. He naturally feels much better about the deal than the suburbanite who

follows him with a split-level on an 80 foot lot and a thirty-year mortgage. The "poor farmer" can grieve at his leisure on Miami Beach while the "rich city slicker" works the rest of his able lifetime to pay for taking the land.[5]

In time, this distant "exurbia" becomes suburbia, and another tier of suburbs develops around Chicago. Since 1960 the average annual loss of farmland in the Chicago metropolitan area has been about seventeen thousand acres. At first only the small farms around Chicago were adversely affected; now urbanization is expanding into areas of larger farms, some fifty or more miles from the city.

Midwest Megalopolis

By early in the twenty-first century, it is likely that the suburbs of Chicago will have virtually merged with the suburbs of Milwaukee and other large communities to form a giant, mainly urbanized area whose basic framework is clearly evident. Chicago is now the nucleus of this large developing urbanized sprawl—a Midwest megalopolis—that stretches almost three hundred miles from approximately Elkhart, Indiana, to Green Bay, Wisconsin. This urbanizing area, encompassing about six thousand square miles, is roughly L-shaped. It extends around the southern and western shores of Lake Michigan, through such cities as South Bend, Gary, East Chicago, Hammond, Chicago, and its suburbs, and then farther northward through Waukegan, Kenosha, and Racine to Milwaukee and beyond. This area of developing urban coalescence already contains a population of over 10 million people. The dominance of the Chicago area is evident in that the city now contains almost one-third of this population and its surrounding metropolitan area contains more than another third of the total population of the megalopolis.

The orderly, harmonious, and efficient development of the emerging megalopolis, with its changing scope and nature of urban settlement, is a major task confronting the Chicago area.

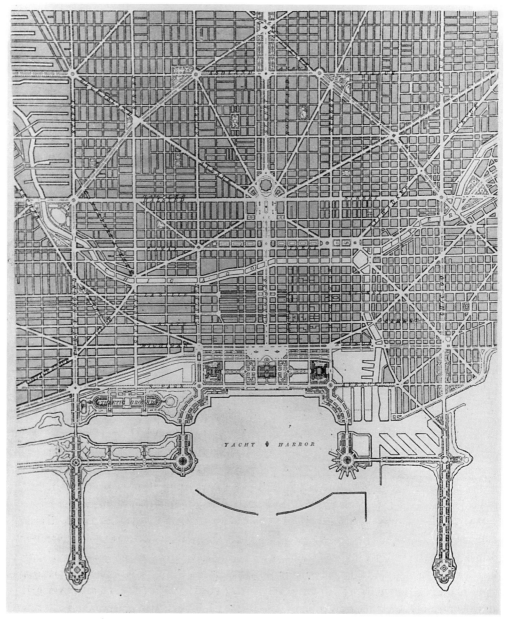

FIG. 10.1. Portion of Burnham's Plan of Chicago, 1909. Some of the important proposals shown on the map have been implemented, generally in accordance with the plan; they include Northerly Island, Grant Park, and Navy Pier *(from left to right at the bottom of the map)*, the straightening of the South Branch of the Chicago River, the widening of major streets, and the construction of the Eisenhower Expressway. The campus of the University of Illinois at Chicago is now in the area of Burnham's proposed monumental civic center plaza, around Halsted and Congress streets. From *Plan of Chicago, 1909*; Chicago Historical Society.

10 Planning for the Future

Problems and Principles

Chicago is plagued by the problems that confront most large cities today: inadequate housing, pollution, traffic, racial discord, unemployment, high welfare numbers, crime, substandard schools, conflicts over land use, and limited recreation facilities. The city has made extensive efforts and has achieved good progress in some of these fields, but problems remain. For example, billions of dollars have been spent on new expressways and rapid transit service, yet acute traffic problems remain and may even be getting worse. Public and private slum clearance projects have been extensive, yet slums and limited affordable housing persist. Chicago has developed a fine recreational system of parks, beaches, and some of the best museums in the country, yet sufficient readily accessible recreational facilities are not available in many areas. Because of high costs and uncertain tax sources, the financing of improvements is becoming increasingly difficult. The same problems, on a smaller scale, now also affect many other parts of the metropolitan area whose destinies are inextricably interwoven with that of the city proper.

Some of the factors influencing Chicago's long-standing problems include the rapid growth of the metropolitan area, changing lifestyles and technology, governmental shortcomings, an inadequate tax base, and a lack of adequate foresight. All have resulted in Chicago's haphazard growth. In the beginning there was no plan for Chicago, yet once a city is developed and populated, it is most difficult to change. Unraveling the chaos to improve an area's livability requires substantial planning, dedication, and financial contribution.

A plan to support the optimal development of the area should be based on certain principles and objectives: (1) the community should decide "where it wants to go," that is, prepare goals based on the citizens' ideals for a better community and better living; (2) the plan should be a blueprint to guide future development, as well as to correct the mistakes of the past; (3) it must try to anticipate future population trends and technological innovations; (4) it should be flexible, comprehensive, and practical regarding financing and implementation; and (5) the plan should encompass human aspects, as well as physical conditions—for a city is really the sum of its people.

The Burnham Plan

Fortunately, Chicago has been a pioneer in city planning, and some of its finest features are the result of such foresight. In 1869 Frederick Law Olmsted laid out the basic park and connecting boulevard system that has served Chicago so well for more than a century. A semicircular basic park pattern was developed in which Jackson and Washington parks on the South Side and Lincoln Park on the North Side were linked by a belt of boulevards that also connected Humboldt, Garfield, and Douglas parks on the West Side.

In 1893 the World's Columbian Exposition gave Chicago a glimpse of the advantages of urban design that incorporated an orderly arrangement of structure and space. Sixteen years later, in 1909, the renowned architect Daniel H. Burnham (who presided over the construction of the World's Columbian Exposition) and Edward H. Bennett proposed a monumental long-range *Plan of Chicago* that introduced comprehensive city planning to Chicago and the nation.

The Burnham Plan was primarily encouraged and financed by the Commercial Club, the members of which included many of Chicago's foremost business and civic leaders, whose interests converged. Although Burnham did not adequately foresee such problems as housing, neighborhood redevelopment, and the enormous effects of the automobile, his plan was boldly imaginative, metropolitan in scope, and comprehensive in its incorporation of the advanced concepts of the time. It viewed Chicago, primarily, as a dynamic industrial and commercial city. It was designed to free industry and commerce from congestion and to transform the city into an agreeable place in which to work

and live—a city that would be aesthetically pleasing as well as convenient and practical. It stressed the "city beautiful" trend toward wide, tree-lined boulevards, parks, vistas, and civic centers. It became the official plan of Chicago and guided public improvements for many years. Although not all of Burnham's specific suggestions were implemented, some outstanding features of present-day Chicago were either proposed or advanced by the plan and almost a billion dollars has been expended in its implementation. Much of its success can be credited to such men as Charles H. Wacker and Walter D. Moody whose promotional and education efforts helped to gain public support for the plan and to carry necessary bond issues. *The Wacker Manual*, a noteworthy civics textbook, explained the plan to two generations of local schoolchildren, as follows:

Major recommendations and achievements of the Burnham Plan include:

1. The creation of a regional highway system extending up to sixty miles outside the city—a metropolitan approach which has been at least partially implemented by the expressway system. The highways were to be spatially unifying, bringing together the city center, the neighborhoods, and the suburban areas.

2. The widening of major thoroughfares, including the section-line streets. Michigan Avenue was bridged and partially double-decked, Canal Street was widened, Ogden Avenue was extended, and the mile-long Roosevelt Road viaduct and the double-deck Wacker Drive were built.

3. The consolidation of major railway terminals, now almost fully achieved and much improved from the past. The Union Station was built as the plan suggested.

4. The construction of new docks and navigation facilities. Navy Pier was built, Lake Calumet developed, the South Branch of the Chicago River straightened, and a number of new bridges constructed.

5. The development of a continuous lakefront park has been largely achieved, with twenty-five miles of the city's twenty-nine miles of lakeshore devoted to recreational and cultural facilities, including numerous parks, beaches, yacht basins, and museums. Only one (Northerly Island) of the string of contemplated offshore islands has been completed.

6. The substantial extension of the outlying forest preserves, especially along the river floodplains, as a permanent greenbelt around the metropolitan area. The plan helped in the creation of the Cook County Forest Preserve system.

An incidental but far-reaching result of the Burnham Plan was the organization of planning on a permanent basis. The plan stimulated the development of two groups: one devoted to the city's planning, the other committed to planning on a more regional basis. From these earlier agencies evolved the city's present policy-making Chicago Plan Commission and its administrative arm, the Department of Planning and Development. Six counties of the northeastern part of the state are served by a similar agency, the Northeastern Illinois Planning Commission.

Later Chicago Planning

Through the years, other measures were taken to ensure the orderly development of Chicago, but none of them has, as yet, matched the overall impact of the Burnham Plan. Since the 1920s the Plan's high civic goals have been hampered by racial and, occasionally, class conflict, by the increasing self-sufficiency of the suburban areas, and by shifting population and industry.

In 1923 Chicago's first zoning ordinance was passed. Two decades later, a complete land use survey of Chicago was finished. The documents based on this survey provided planners with significant factual information, which has been updated periodically. Special agencies were created to deal with specific problems. These groups included the Medical Center Commission, aimed at redeveloping the area that surrounds Cook County Hospital; the Urban Renewal Agency, formed to undertake slum clearance and redevelopment and to aid in the conservation and rehabilitation of rundown areas; the Chicago Area Transportation Study, created to develop a comprehensive transportation plan (and which now acts in conjunction with the Northeastern Illinois Planning Commission); and the city's Department of Environment.

In 1946 the Chicago Plan Commission published a map of the Preliminary Comprehensive City Plan of Chicago. The plan recommended patterns of residential, commercial, industrial, recreational, and transportation development. Included were designated boundaries for 514 self-contained neighborhoods, each centered around an elementary school, and fifty-nine larger community units, each centered around a high school. The document has served as a general guide for subsequent activities in urban renewal, zoning, and public works.

In 1956 Daniel Burnham Jr. and Robert Kingery coauthored *Planning the Region of Chicago*, which took into account the rapid growth of the suburbs. In 1966, after prolonged study and discussion, the city proposed

FIG. 10.2. Downtown Chicago and adjacent areas looking northeast from approximately Taylor Street (1000 S.), 2002. To the far right are Grant Park and Monroe Harbor, and to the left are the new and old post office buildings and the 110-story Sears Tower, the nation's tallest building. Photograph by Aerial Images Photography.

the Comprehensive Plan of Chicago, designed to guide Chicago's growth into the 1980s and to alleviate some of the city's most pressing problems. This plan, more than any of the previous efforts, concentrated on human and economic elements. It stated some rather obvious basic aims, such as improving the quality of family life and the environment, expanding opportunities through economic develop-

ment, providing for efficient movement of people and goods, and planning for proper land use. The plan did not, however, deal with the serious problem of racial segregation or the continued movement of whites to the suburbs.

To supplement the basic plan, the Department of Planning and Development published a lavishly illustrated, detailed program for each of sixteen geographic areas of Chicago. Each community plan (complete with colorful, detailed maps) recommended specific improvements in the various facets of the area, such as housing, shopping, schools, recreation, transportation, industry, public safety, and health. Once the plans had been discussed by members of each community and had been officially approved by the city, appropriate improvements were to be adopted as part of the capital improvements program of Chicago.

The proposed Comprehensive Plan did not receive official city approval, largely because of political, community, and racial bickering. As a consequence, only small parts of the plan were implemented. The laissez-faire approach to planning in Chicago led one critic to observe, "Bend the zoning a little. Give the big money boys a tax break. Bring on the skyscrapers. Build more expressways. Let the cement mixers roll." Conflicts between public and private interests were frequent. Engineering solutions were often much easier to surmount than social problems.

Nevertheless, this plan, later city plans, and the Chicago 21 Plan of 1973 (proposed by a nonprofit organization composed mainly of business and real estate people) have helped bring about and guide many major changes and improvements to the city. They include the stabilization and growth of the city's central area through the construction of thousands of new residential units and numerous new office and hotel buildings; the building of the huge Illinois Center development, which employs thousands; and the opening of the South Loop, which now contains such developments as Printers Row, Dearborn Park I and II, and Central Station. State Street has also been rejuvenated, and the Magnificent Mile of Michigan Avenue has grown in commercial importance.

The planning generally recommended high-density communities along the lakefront, in the downtown area, and along mass transportation routes; low-density housing in the outlying parts of the city; and medium-density development in between. In some areas there would be a mix of housing.

A major aim was to have more people — including many members of nonminority groups — live, shop, work, and seek entertainment in the central area. In addition to substantial housing and commercial development in or near the Loop, the plan proposed a variety of public transportation improvements; more open space, especially along the lakefront; and the preservation of certain landmarks.

Two elaborate waterfront development plans have been proposed by the city itself. In 1973 the city published the Lakefront Plan of Chicago, which was designed to improve the ecological aspects of the lake and lakeshore. The following year, the Riveredge Plan of Chicago proposed the improvement of the one-and-a-half-mile trunk of the Chicago River that runs from Lake Michigan to Wolf Point at the junction of the North and South branches of the river. In 1990 the city published two other planning documents, the Downtown Corridor and the North Branch Riverwalk.

The Riveredge Plan proposed the development of recreational and open spaces along both sides of the river. It included a type of grand pedestrian promenade along part of its north bank, a new landfill park near the river mouth, and significant artwork, as well as other cultural and historical attractions. Appropriate public and private Riveredge developments, including residential buildings,

FIG. 10.3. Richard M. Daley (1942–), the current mayor of Chicago. The son of the late mayor Richard J. Daley and a graduate of the De Paul University law school in 1968, the younger Daley has served in the Illinois senate and as the Cook County state's attorney. He was elected Democratic mayor of Chicago in 1989 and is now serving his fifth term in that office. He is known to pay a visit to his father's grave in Holy Sepulchre Cemetery every election morning. Photograph courtesy of the Office of the Mayor.

were encouraged by the plan. Efforts were to be made to improve the water quality of the river and its use for recreational as well as commercial purposes. No significant financial arrangements were made to carry out either of these elaborate plans for the waterfront, but many of the improvements have been at least partially completed. For example, the recent rebuilding of Wacker Drive incorporated aspects of the plan.

Chicago's planning, development, and investments in recent decades have concentrated on the central area of the city, often neglecting many poorer parts. The city has been renewing itself from its core outward. The vitality of the downtown area, however, has helped in the renovation of some of the choice nearby areas, such as the Near North Side, Lincoln Park, West Town, Logan Square, Near West Side, Lower West Side, and Near South Side. These areas are increasingly inhabited by essentially white middle- and upper-income persons, mainly professionals—young couples, singles, and empty nesters (some returning from the suburbs). Often poor minority groups are replaced in the process, and they crowd into poorer neglected areas, aggravating already crowded conditions.

Away from the city center is a huge crescent of mainly African American and Hispanic residents, many having arrived in the city at the time manufacturing jobs were moving away. This largely economically depressed section, between the central area and the remaining old ethnic communities to the southwest and northwest, especially needed sound planning to improve its residential, educational, and shopping facilities, as well as employment opportunities. Some improvements have occurred in this area, and some of it is being gentrified.

Improvements to the city's central area are substantial. In addition to the housing, commercial, river, and lakefront improvements, a number of other developments contribute to the area's growing vibrancy. Navy Pier, with its variety of activities, has been converted into Chicago's most popular entertainment attraction. A new live theater row has been created along Randolph Street, between State and Wells streets, often through the conversion of old movie palaces. Toward the southern end of the Loop are the large Harold Washington Library Center and new developments sponsored by a number of educational institutions. In the northwest corner of Grant Park is the new Millennium Park, with its large outdoor and indoor theaters and a substantial underground parking garage, all in a beautifully landscaped setting. Farther south is the new museum campus, with the renovated Soldier Field nearby. And in the last fifteen years, under Mayor Richard M. Daley's program, some three hundred thousand new trees and countless flowers have been planted throughout the city, especially in major arterial median strips, and thousands of acres of new park land have been established.

Planning for the Metropolitan Area

The metropolitan area has both localized and widespread planning problems. Often the two are interwoven. A planner of a new suburban development would have to seriously consider a number of important questions.

As the planner gazes out over the rural-urban fringe he must face such questions as: Where should schools be located? How much land should be set aside for each school? Where should major thoroughfares be located? How should interstitial areas between thoroughfares be laid out—with winding street patterns, or grids, or some other design? What areas should be zoned for apartments, for large-lot single-family dwellings, for small-lot single-

FIG. 10.4. Harold Washington Library Center, which opened in 1991 at 400 South State Street in downtown Chicago. It replaced the main Chicago Public Library at 78 E. Washington, which dates to 1897 and is now the Cultural Center. Photograph by Irving Cutler.

family structures? Should land be set aside for shopping centers? If so, how much and where should it be located? Will there be a need for land for industrial uses? (If so, it should be demarcated in large parcels—at least a few hundred acres—zoned to keep other users out and situated near railways, main highways, and on land which is not too valuable.) The general thinking by planners now is that at least five percent of a city's land should be set aside for recreational purposes. Hence, the need for deciding what parts of the farmland to be annexed should be devoted to parks, golf courses, wildlife refuges, or other types of recreational uses. Additional questions deal with matters like positioning of storm sewers in such a manner that heavy rains and melting snow can run off with no flooding. Rural land adjoining a city usually is not faced with a serious problem at this point (unless it is in a valley bottom) since most of the earth's surface is covered with soil into which much of the water seeps. Water which isn't absorbed by the soil often is retarded in its run off by pasture grasses or other ground cover. But when such land is transformed into city, it is almost entirely resurfaced—and water proofed. Roofs, streets, driveways, and sidewalks absorb no water—neither do they impede its run off. Heavy rains and melting snow produce volumes of water that must be quickly conducted away to prevent flooding.[1]

Many of the problems of the Chicago metropolitan area defy purely local solutions. Rainwater falling in one community may create flood problems for other communities; traffic problems in the heart of the central city may cause expressway backups all the way

into the suburbs; and disease, pollution, and crime do not stop at political boundaries. The major obstacle to solving these problems is that although the area has a certain socioeconomic unity, it is a fragmented, overlapping, disorganized, political checkerboard—often offering inadequate, conflicting, and uncoordinated solutions at the local level. The "real Chicago" encompasses more than twelve hundred governmental units, ranging from counties to mosquito abatement districts, and even crosses state lines. This multiplicity of government has led to an absence of coordination and efficiency in road construction, the use of open space, water control, mass transit development, air pollution control, and refuse disposal. It has also resulted in increased costs because each community, regardless of its size, must usually provide for its own police and fire protection, garbage disposal, schools, and other services. Attempts to consolidate some local governmental units and to eliminate duplicate layers of government in order to provide a more efficient structure are usually met with strong opposition. This opposition is based on several things, including fierce local independence; distrust of larger governmental units; apprehension about Chicago's dominance; racial antipathy; and fear of the loss of jobs, patronage, and political power.

Probably the most disruptive political boundary is that between Chicago and its suburbs, despite both having problems that neither can solve alone. Chicago provides employment and a variety of cultural and recreational services for suburban commuters who do not share proportionately in the cost. The suburbs, for their part, generally refuse to become enmeshed in the many problems and burdens of the central city. Political party rivalry has often widened the gap between Chicago and the surrounding areas—in recent decades Chicago has consistently voted Democratic, while the suburbs generally have tended to vote Republican. Racial, religious, and economic differences between Chicago and the suburbs have also been divisive.

Fortunately, the trend toward cooperation among the numerous governmental units is growing. Chicago supplies water to about 115 other communities, and the Metropolitan Water Reclamation District of Greater Chicago—a pioneer in certain aspects of regional planning for the area—handles the sewage of 125 cities and villages. Groups of suburbs have formed cooperative pacts to provide such services as police, fire, and health protection; library cooperation; joint purchasing; transit improvement; refuse disposal; water supply; and street construction and maintenance. Some suburbs on occasion have even considered the possibility of merging so as to pool tax dollars, provide better services, and exercise uniform control over development. The Comprehensive Plan of Chicago has been developed in a metropolitan context and recommends principles of development for the metropolitan area.

The agency officially designated by the state of Illinois to guide the development of the six Illinois counties in the Chicago area is the Northeastern Illinois Planning Commission (NIPC), created in 1957. Shortly thereafter, the private nonprofit Chicago Regional Planning Association, which had been established in 1925 to plan for the greater Chicago area, was merged into the new commission. The commission is becoming increasingly important in general planning for the six counties in the area. Although it is largely an advisory agency funded by voluntary contributions from state, county, municipal, and private sources, it also receives occasional federal grants for specific projects. However, the agency's lack

of financial independence and its dependence on uncertain sources for funding have handicapped it since its inception.

The commission has thirty-four members. Five are appointed by the governor, five by the mayor of Chicago, three by the president of the Cook County Board, and one by each of the other five counties. In addition, the RTA, Metra, Pace, the CTA, and the Metropolitan Water Reclamation District of Greater Chicago each appoints a member, and the mayors and village presidents of all municipalities outside Chicago elect eight members to represent the suburbs. In addition, there are two park district and one wastewater representative. The NIPC conducts research into such problems as flooding, water supply, recreation, open space, industrial development, housing, land use, population growth, and refuse disposal and then makes reports and recommendations. It also assists local governments with their problems and planning and tries to coordinate efforts. Finally, it reviews and makes recommendations on requests for federal funds, which, in many years, exceed billions of dollars. It has further prepared a comprehensive regional plan for the area.

To guide future development of the suburban area, the commission drafted the so-called finger plan. This Comprehensive General Plan, adopted in 1968, was selected from eleven alternative plans that were considered after extensive study and consultation with community groups.

The finger plan called for the orderly development of the suburban area along the major transportation routes, or "fingers," radiating out of Chicago. Communities were to concentrate most of their industrial, commercial,

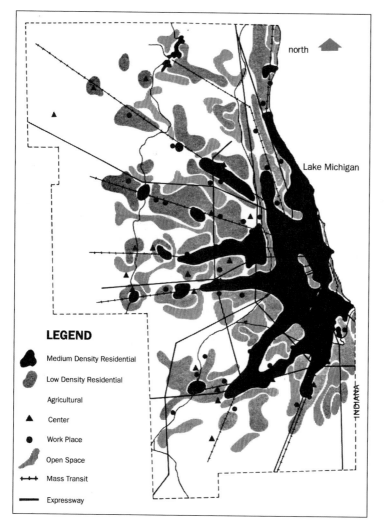

FIG. 10.5. "Finger plan" for the future development of the Chicago area, as proposed by the Northeastern Illinois Planning Commission in the late 1960s. Map courtesy of the Northeastern Illinois Planning Commission.

educational, medical, and other service facilities, as well as high-density residential areas (including skyscraper complexes), along the corridors of the main transportation routes. Residential areas of decreasing density would be placed farther out, although close enough to transportation facilities. In the wedges between the corridors, open space and recreational facilities would absorb pollution.

The plan was designed as a framework to maximize the use of land and transportation facilities and to prevent the entire area from being covered by unplanned, congested, and polluted urbanization. It was formulated to enhance accessibility by centralizing transportation facilities in each corridor. Owing, however, to various conflicting economic and political pressures and to the lack of adequate enforcement powers, the plan was not implemented and encroachment on the open-space areas has continued.

In 1976 the NIPC updated its Comprehensive General Plan of 1968 to reflect the important and rapid changes that had taken place in the intervening years. These changes included chronic high inflation, energy shortages, tight government budgets, escalating suburban land costs, widespread environmental concerns, and housing abandonment in older neighborhoods. The updated plan envisioned better synchronization of land use, transportation, and utility services to minimize further environmental incursions and larger capital expenditures.

In lieu of further urban encroachment into even more distant farm areas, accompanied by heavy expenditures for new roads, utilities, and schools, the 1976 updated plan recommended improvements, redevelopment, and maintenance of or increases in population in existing cities. These communities included satellite cities and suburbs, as well as Chicago, where established public facilities and services are underutilized and population had declined. Urban investments were to be concentrated in municipal areas, not in unincorporated areas, and the trend toward lack of investment in built-up municipalities was to be discouraged and reversed. This policy, if implemented, would help conserve open space, revitalize existing urban areas, and guide new growth into compact, economical forms, while countering some of the problems of high energy and building costs.

Thus, in recent years, Chicago has had many elaborate official plans—the Comprehensive Plan of 1966; the "finger plan" and its later update, the Lakefront Plan; the Riveredge Plan; and others—all presented with much fanfare and colorful illustrative material. While some of these plans have produced certain results, most in recent years have become bogged down and stymied by the realities of political maneuvering and expediency, racial conflict, self-interest, and financial difficulties.

There have been three more recent plans. In 1992 the NIPC adopted the "Strategic Plan for Land Resource Management." It contained seventy-two recommendations for improving life in the six counties of northeastern Illinois. The plan addresses, in some detail, the environment, transportation, land use, wastewater facilities, the greenway network, and agricultural areas. The recommendations also include suggestions for future capital programs, the balancing of jobs and housing, and definition of the role government is to play in implementing these recommendations. A 2005 NIPC comprehensive plan reemphasizes its previous planning principles and urges communities to consider "compact growth," such as mixed-use development that would allow residents to live nearer the places where they work.

The most recent plan to deal with the region in detail is *The Metropolis Plan: Choices for the Chicago Region*. It was published in 2002 by the Commercial Club, the same organization that created Daniel Burnham's highly successful 1909 Plan of Chicago. The Metropolis Plan aims to provide for the orderly development of the Chicago region to the year 2030.[2]

The plan predicts that by the year 2030, the Chicago region will grow by 1.6 million people and will add about eight hundred thousand new jobs and a million additional automobiles. This change is forecast to take place in a region that has more than twelve hundred units of local government, including six counties, 293 municipalities, 113 townships, 306 school districts, and hundreds of other special units that range from forest preserve districts to water reclamation districts. There is one governmental unit for every six thousand people—at least five times the per capita number of governmental units of other large cities, such as New York and Los Angeles.

The provisions of the Metropolis Plan include investment in regional cities that have faced difficult conditions, such as Joliet, Aurora, and Waukegan; creation of a broader range of housing options, partially through adjustment of restrictive zoning ordinances; improvements in transportation across the board, with emphasis on public transit (especially), freight handling, and the provision of areas for walking and biking; and better coordination of land use and transportation. The plan also calls for the restoration and protection of open space, including prairie resources, wetlands, woodlands, and farmland. It would use economic incentives in ways that encourage local governments, businesses, and individuals to make decisions that benefit the region.

Some of the more important detailed recommendations of the plan include the expansion of O'Hare International Airport and improvements in its western access; the continuation of plans for an airport in south suburban Peotone; expansion of Metra commuter rail lines; placement of new residential developments, including affordable housing, near job centers; reformation of the tax structure; and creation of a Regional Growth and Transportation Commission to fund, plan, and coordinate physical, economic, and transportation growth in all of northeastern

Illinois through the merger of a multiplicity of agencies into a single agency responsible for regional planning and development.

Legislation approved in 2005, and to be implemented within three years, creates a new Regional Planning Board, its fifteen members to be appointed by mayors and county officials, with a third representing Chicago, a third suburban Cook County, and a third the collar counties (fast-growing Kendall County being represented for the first time as the seventh metropolitan-area county). The plan also calls for the eventual merger of the staffs of the two regionwide planning agencies—the Chicago Area Transportation Study and the Northeastern Illinois Planning Commission. Consolidation will allow the region to speak with one voice on such vital matters as transportation and land use.

The changes should better match road and transit projects with land use decisions and provide the region with a stronger voice in applying for federal funds. However, the new board will have no authority over local annexation and zoning decisions.

The Challenge

In less than two centuries, the Chicago area has been transformed from a virtual wilderness into the nucleus of a burgeoning megalopolis. Crude cabins have been replaced by soaring skyscrapers, muddy trails by multilane expressways, canoes by the ocean freighters of the world, and a handful of settlers by over eight million people of every race, religion, and nationality.

Step by step, millions of people fired by ideals, ambitions, and an indomitable "I Will" spirit built the city. They utilized its important locational assets and overcame its natural deficiencies. They drained its marshes, built

FIG. 10.6. Beginning of construction of the slated ninety-two-story Trump Tower along the Chicago River in downtown Chicago, September 2005. The *Chicago Sun-Times* building was formerly at the site. Photograph by Daniel Cutler.

canals, and reversed its rivers. Despite the devastation of a catastrophic fire, periods of crime and corruption, and economic downturns, they developed major industrial, commercial, and transportation facilities and created outstanding universities, medical centers, and cultural institutions. Internationally known leaders in the scientific, literary, educational, and social fields flourished in the Chicago area.

Though the area's accomplishments have been great, significant challenges remain. Unfortunately, "bigger" did not always lead to "better." Rapid, largely uncontrolled urban sprawl, coupled with changing socioeconomic conditions, often exacerbated old problems

and created new ones, such as Chicago's loss of people and jobs that resulted in an inadequate tax base. Although some of Chicago's problems are indigenous, many are common to most metropolises and, on the whole, Chicago's progress compares favorably with that of most other large American cities.

In the future, the dynamism and innovation that have characterized Chicago in the past will be increasingly vital in order for it to flourish. As the metropolitan area and its problems grow, bold, imaginative, large-scale plans are essential, along with the commitment and ability to carry them out. In an age of technological advancement characterized

FIG. 10.7. Chicago River, where the city started less than two centuries ago. Photograph courtesy of the City of Chicago/Peter J. Schulz.

by splitting the atom, digital communications, and landing on the moon, the resolution of major urban problems certainly appears attainable. In such areas as housing, transportation, ecology, education, government, public safety, and racial relations, the technology and concepts necessary to provide for wholesome growth and development in a pleasant environment already exist or can be created. As Daniel H. Burnham, one of Chicago's greatest dreamers and planners, counseled almost a century ago, "Make no little plans; they have no magic to stir men's blood and probably will not be realized. Make big plans, aim high in hope and worth, remembering that a noble, logical diagram once recorded will never die, but long after we are gone will be a living thing, asserting itself with ever-growing insistency. Remember that our sons and grandsons are going to do things that would stagger us."

Appendixes
Notes
Selected Bibliography
Index

Appendix A: Chicago Population

Area and Population of Chicago, by Decade

Year	Area of Chicago (square miles)	Population Chicago	Metropolitan Area*
1830	0.4	est. 50	—
1840	10.2	4,470	35,616
1850	9.3	29,963	115,285
1860	17.5	112,172	259,384
1870	35.2	298,977	493,531
1880	35.2	503,185	771,250
1890	178.1	1,099,850	1,391,890
1900	189.6	1,698,575	2,084,750
1910	190.2	2,185,283	2,702,465
1920	198.2	2,701,705	3,394,996
1930	207.2	3,376,438	4,449,646
1940	212.9	3,396,808	4,569,643
1950	212.9	3,620,962	5,177,868
1960	212.9	3,550,404	6,220,913
1970	227.3	3,369,357	6,981,347
1980	228.1	3,005,072	7,102,328
1990	228.1	2,783,726	7,261,176
2000	228.4	2,896,016	8,091,719

*The numbers in this column refer to the Chicago Standard Metropolitan Statistical Area, which consists of McHenry, Lake, Cook, Du Page, Kane, and Will counties in Illinois. Its area is 4,653 square miles.

TABLE A.2.

People per Square Mile

	1980	2000
Chicago	13,173	12,680
Metropolitan Chicago	1,526	1,739
United States	64	80

TABLE A.3.

Population and Incomes of Some Racial and Ethnic Groups in Chicago

	Population (%) 1980	2000	Median Household Income, 1999 ($)
Caucasian	44	31	49,276
African American	39	36	29,103
Hispanic	14	26	36,661
Asian American	2	2	40,503
Overall	—	—	38,625

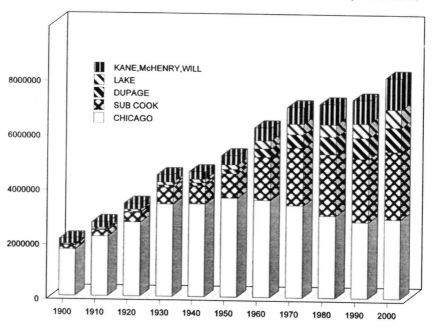

Population Growth in Northeastern Illinois, 1900-2000

Appendix B: Chicago Weather and Climate

TABLE B.I.

Average Temperature and Precipitation in Chicago, by Month

	Average Temperature (°F)	Average Precipitation (inches)	
		Rainfall	Snowfall
January	24.3	1.85	9.7
February	27.4	1.59	8.1
March	36.8	2.73	8.0
April	49.9	3.75	1.2
May	60.0	3.41	Trace
June	70.5	3.95	0.0
July	74.7	4.09	0.0
August	73.7	3.14	0.0
September	65.9	3.00	0.0
October	55.4	2.62	0.4
November	40.4	2.20	2.6
December	28.5	2.11	9.7

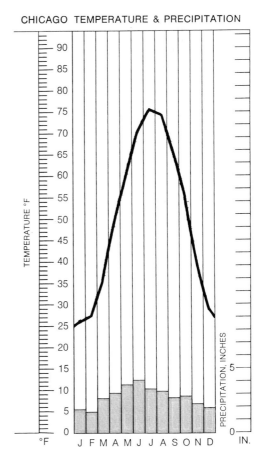

CHICAGO TEMPERATURE & PRECIPITATION

Average annual temperature, 49.2°F (about 6 percent colder than the world mean)

Highest recorded temperature, 105°F. July 24, 1934

Lowest recorded temperature, -27°F. January 20, 1985

Average annual precipitation, 34.44 inches (about six inches less than the world mean)

Days per year with precipitation of 0.01 inch or more, 122

Average annual snowfall, 39.7 inches. Greatest seasonal snowfall, 89.7 inches, 1978–79. Greatest single snowfall, 23 inches, January 26–27, 1967.

Average annual relative humidity: 7 AM, 75 percent; 1 PM, 58 percent

Average annual percentage of possible sunshine, 57 percent; summer, 68 percent; winter, 44 percent

Average annual wind speed, 10.4 miles per hour. The wind blows from the southwest more than from any other direction.

Appendix C: General Facts about Chicago

The name *Chicago* is seemingly derived from *Che-ca-gou*, the name applied by local Native Americans to the strong-smelling wild onions of the mud flats where Chicago began.

The latitude of the city is 41°50' N., and the longitude, 87°37' W.

Chicago is on the waterway that connects the Great Lakes–St. Lawrence Seaway with the Mississippi Waterway.

The airline distance from Chicago to New York City is 714 miles; to Washington, DC, 596 miles; and to San Francisco, 1,859 miles.

The metropolitan area is about 285 miles northeast of the center of population of the United States and about 150 miles north of the center of the greatest industrial region on earth.

It is also near the heart of the largest food-producing region on earth.

Chicago's altitude is 578.5 feet above sea level. The highest point is at Ninety-second Street and Western Avenue — 672.4 feet.

The geographic center of the city is at approximately 3700 South Honore Street (1832 W.).

Chicago has 3,775 miles of streets and 63.7 miles of expressways.

The city's lake shoreline extends for twenty-nine miles.

More than half the nations of the world have fewer people than metropolitan Chicago.

Metropolitan Chicago has 3 percent of the U.S. population but accounts for about 4 percent of the nation's gross national product.

More than 70 million people live within a five-hundred-mile radius of Chicago. Within this area about 40 percent of the nation's manufacturing and one-third of its wholesale and retail sales are found.

In 2002 metropolitan Chicago had retail sales of $106 billion.

The median family income in Chicago in 1978 was $19,468; in 2000 it was $38,625.

Chicago has 1,061,928 housing units of all kinds, with more than a third of them owner-occupied and almost three-quarters more than forty years old. About 24 percent of all Chicago families live in single-family houses; 35 percent live in buildings with two, three, or four apartments; and the remainder live in larger apartment or condominium buildings.

The daily per-capita consumption of water is 335 gallons, and the average daily pumpage is 977 million gallons. Sixty-five miles of tunnels under the lake and the land supply not only the 4,232 miles of water mains in Chicago but also those in about 125 suburbs.

Sewer facilities extend forty-three hundred miles in the city.

Park land covers 7,143 acres of the city. There are 551 parks, thirty-one beaches, and nine yacht harbors with 7,147 slips.

Passenger motor vehicles number 1,202,460, with 80,657 trucks.

Forty-six movable and thirty-nine fixed bridges span waterways in Chicago.

Places of worship in Chicago number more than two thousand, with the most numerous being Protestant churches, followed by Roman Catholic churches.

Chicago has 493 public elementary schools and 95 public high schools; 267 parochial elementary schools and 45 parochial high schools; 11 public colleges, of which 7 are city community colleges; and 20 major private colleges.

The Chicago area is home to the American Medical Association, American Hospital Association, Radiological Society of North America, American College of Surgeons, American Dental Association, and six area medical schools. One of every five doctors in the United States has received all or part of their training in Chicago.

About 30 percent of adults over twenty-five years of age have a bachelor's degree, compared with 24 percent in the United States as a whole.

The lowest median age by region in the metropolitan area is 31.5 years in Chicago; the highest is 35.2 years in Du Page County.

The average life expectancy in Chicago is 70.4 years. For the United States as a whole, it is 77 years of age.

Chicago has eighty-nine hospitals of all types, with the largest as of 2003 being Rush Medical Center (723 beds), Advocate Christ (662 beds), Northwestern Memorial (661 beds), University of Chicago (523 beds), and Stroger Cook County (525 beds).

There are 233 physicians per 100,000 people in metropolitan Chicago. The figure for the United States is 155.

Metropolitan Chicago has 475 cemeteries, with almost half in Cook County. Oakwood Cemetery, on the South Side, is the oldest, and Rosehill Cemetery, on the North Side, is the largest.

Although crime has declined steadily overall in recent years, the number of homicides still remains high—449 in 2004, down from 593 in 2003—most being associated with gangs and drugs.

Chicago has a mayor-council form of government, with fifty aldermen in the city council.

Cook County, in which Chicago is located, has 592 political administrative units, more than any other county in the United States.

In 2004 Chicago had 12,643 policemen and 4,802 firefighters.

The Chicago flag is white, with two blue stripes and four red stars. The white, a composite of all colors, represents the composite of nationalities living in peace. The top white represents the North Side; the middle white, the West Side; and the bottom white, the South Side. The blue strips represent the magnificent waterways—Lake Michigan, the Chicago River, and the great canal. The stars represent Fort Dearborn (1803), the Chicago Fire (1871), the World's Columbian Exposition (1893), and A Century of Progress (1933).

Appendix D:
Significant Dates in Chicago History

ca. 11,500 BC	Last glacier receded from the area.
ca. 10,000 BC	Glacial Lake Chicago broke through its confining moraines to drain southwest into the Illinois and Mississippi rivers.
1673	Marquette and Jolliet explored the region, claiming the land for New France.
1696	Father Pierre Pinet established the short-lived Mission of the Guardian Angels.
1779	First home and fur-trading station were built by Jean Baptiste Point du Sable.
1803	Fort Dearborn was erected.
1812	Fort Dearborn Massacre. Fifty-three settlers were killed by Native Americans.
1816	Fort Dearborn was rebuilt.
1830	Surveyor James Johnson plotted out the town of Chicago.
1831	Cook County was organized with Chicago as the county seat. Allied Native American tribes ceded Illinois land.
1833	Chicago, with 350 inhabitants, was incorporated as a town.
1837	Chicago, with a population of about four thousand, was incorporated as a city; William B. Ogden served as its first mayor.
1845	First permanent school building was erected near Madison and State streets.
1847	McCormick, inventor of the reaper, started making farm implements in Chicago.
1848	Chicago Board of Trade was founded.
	Illinois-Michigan Canal was opened.
	Chicago and Galena Union Railroad was built.
1851	The Chicago area's first university, Northwestern, was founded.
1854	Cholera claimed 1,424 victims.
1855	The city began raising the level of streets up to twelve feet.
	"Beer riots" occurred after enforced closing of saloons on Sunday.
1856	Chicago Historical Society was founded.
	Fort Dearborn was demolished.

1859	First horse-drawn railway line went into operation.
1860	Abraham Lincoln was made a presidential candidate in the Wigwam.
1865	Union Stock Yards were established south of the city's boundary.
1866	Cook County Hospital was founded.
1867	A sanitary water system was installed.
1868	Lincoln Park Zoo opened.
1870	Loyola University opened.
	Predecessor of Chicago Cubs baseball team was founded.
1871	Great Chicago Fire of October 8–10.
1872	An ordinance outlawed wooden buildings in the downtown area.
1873	Chicago Public Library was formed.
1877	Railroad strike resulted in violence.
1879	Art Institute of Chicago was incorporated.
1880	George Pullman built his car shop and the town of Pullman.
	U.S. Steel South Works opened.
1881	Marshall Field and Company was founded.
1882	Cable car system began operation.
1885	The nine-story Home Insurance Building, major progenitor of the true skyscraper, was erected.
1886	Violence during Haymarket Riot killed seven policemen.
	Adler and Sullivan's Auditorium building opened.
1889	Hull House was founded by Jane Addams.
	Annexations increased the area of the city from 36 to 168 square miles.
	Chicago Sanitary District was established.
1891	Chicago Symphony Orchestra was formed.
	Typhoid fever epidemic killed about two thousand.
1892	University of Chicago opened.
	The first elevated trains began operation.
1893	Carter H. Harrison was elected mayor for a fifth term. He was assassinated by a disgruntled office seeker.
	World's Columbian Exposition opened.
1894	Field Museum of Natural History was founded.
	Pullman car plant strike led to a railroad strike.
1897	Chicago Loop was encircled by new El lines.
1898	St. Vincent's College was founded. It was renamed DePaul University in 1907.
1900	Chicago Sanitary and Ship Canal opened; the flow of the Chicago River was reversed.
1903	White Sox baseball team was founded.
	Iroquois Theater fire killed 602 people.
1904	Riverview amusement park opened.
1906	Freight tunnels began service.
	Cable car system ended service.

1909	The Chicago Plan was originated by Daniel Burnham and Edward Bennett.
1910	Comiskey Park opened.
	Garment workers went on strike.
1911	Present-day City Hall and County Building were completed.
	Carter H. Harrison Jr. was elected mayor for a fifth term.
1912	Police raids shut down the South Side Levee vice district.
	An ordinance officially approved Maxwell Street Market.
1914	Weeghman (later Wrigley) Field opened.
1915	Excursion steamer *Eastland* was overturned in the Chicago River, killing 812 people.
1916	Municipal Pier (later called Navy Pier) was completed.
1918	Influenza epidemic killed thousands.
1919	A bloody race riot left fifteen Caucasians and twenty-three African Americans dead.
	Chicago Mercantile Exchange was founded.
1920	New Michigan Avenue Bridge was completed.
	Blackhawks hockey team was founded.
	Bears football team was founded as Decatur Staleys.
1921	Chicago's first radio station, KYW, started broadcasting.
1922	Calumet-Sag Channel was completed.
1923	Indiana Dunes State Park opened.
1924	Despite Prohibition, fifteen breweries and twenty thousand retail alcoholic beverage outlets were operating illegally in Chicago.
	Soldier Field opened.
1925	Relocated South Water Street produce market opened.
1927	Chicago's first municipal airport (later called Midway Airport) opened.
	Buckingham Fountain was dedicated.
1929	Seven gangsters were killed in the St. Valentine's Day Massacre.
	Chicago Stadium opened.
1930	Adler Planetarium and Shedd Aquarium were dedicated.
	Merchandise Mart was built.
1931	Al Capone was sentenced to eleven years in prison for income tax evasion.
1933	Museum of Science and Industry officially opened in the former Fine Arts Building of the World's Columbian Exposition of 1893.
	Mayor Anton Cermak was fatally shot.
1933–34	Century of Progress Exposition ran successfully for two years.
1934	Gulf to Lakes Inland Waterway opened with Chicago as the northern terminus.
	John Dillinger was killed by the FBI next to the Biograph Theater.
	International Amphitheater opened in Union Stock Yards.
	Brookfield Zoo was founded.

1937   Eleven were killed in a labor dispute at Republic Steel.

Chicago Housing Authority (CHA) was founded.

1940   Illinois Institute of Technology was formed through the merger of Armour Institute of Technology and Lewis Institute.

1941   West Side Medical Center district was established.

1942   World's first atomic reaction was achieved at the University of Chicago.

1943   Chicago's first passenger subway opened beneath State Street.

1945   Roosevelt University was established. It opened in 1946 in the historic Auditorium Building.

1947   Chicago Transit Authority started operating.

1948   Meigs Field opened on landfill built for the Century of Progress Exposition.

1950   Chicago's population peaked at 3,620,962.

1953   Chicago became the world's steel capital.

1954   Lyric Opera of Chicago started.

1955   O'Hare Airport opened.

1957   Northeastern Illinois Planning Commission was founded.

1958   Fire at Our Lady of Angels School killed ninety students and three nuns.

1959   St. Lawrence Seaway opened.

1960   McCormick Place opened.

1962   Robert Taylor public housing high-rise buildings opened on the South Side with forty-four hundred units.

1965   University of Illinois at Chicago Circle opened.

1966   Indiana Dunes National Lakeshore was established.

1967   Record twenty-three-inch snowfall of January 26–27 paralyzed the city.

1968   Riots and fires occurred in parts of Chicago's West Side following assassination of Dr. Martin Luther King Jr.

Disorders erupted during the Democratic National Convention.

1971   Stockyards closed.

McCormick Place reopened after the original building was damaged by fire in 1967.

1972   Chicago Botanic Gardens opened.

1974   U.S. tallest building, Sears Tower, opened.

Regional Transportation Authority (RTA) was established.

1975   Mayor Richard J. Daley died while serving a record sixth term.

Tunnel and Reservoir (Deep Tunnel) project began.

1979   Record total winter snowfall of 89.7 inches crippled the city.

Jane M. Byrne was elected Chicago's first female mayor.

1983   Harold Washington was elected Chicago's first African American mayor.

Metra rail and Pace suburban bus systems were established.

1987   Mexican Fine Arts Center Museum opened.

1989   Navy Pier was renovated.

1991	New Comiskey Park opened. It was renamed U.S. Cellular Field in 2003.
1992	The "Great Chicago Flood" poured 124 million gallons of water into downtown Chicago.
1994	United Center opened.
1995	An extended heat wave contributed to the death of more than seven hundred city residents.
1996	Demolition of CHA high-rises began.
1998	Chicago Bulls won their sixth NBA championship in eight years.
1999	Peggy Notebaert museum opened.
2003	Mayor Richard M. Daley was elected to a fifth term.
	Fire in an office building owned by Cook County killed six.
	Meigs Field was closed, and the remodeled Soldier Field opened.
	Twenty-one people were killed in the E2 nightclub stampede after pepper spray was used during an altercation.
2004	The twenty-four-acre Millennium Park opened in the northwest corner of Grant Park.

Appendix E: Chicago Historic Sites

This list of the more important historic sites in Chicago is slightly modified and enlarged from one prepared by the Municipal Reference Library of the City of Chicago. Wherever it is known that suitable memorial plaques and historical markers have been erected, that fact is shown. The list is in approximate chronological order.

Chicago Portage (Harlem Avenue and Forty-ninth Street). Near this site began the portage used by Marquette and Jolliet in 1673 between the Des Plaines River and the South Branch of the Chicago River, about six miles to the northeast.

Marquette Cabin (north end of the Damen Avenue bridge at Twenty-sixth Street; wooden cross marker). Near this spot stood a cabin at which Jacques Marquette, a priest of the Society of Jesus, arrived on December 14, 1674. He spent the ensuing winter there. In September 1673, Louis Jolliet and Father Marquette had first passed this spot.

Guardian Angel Mission (North Branch of the Chicago River, at Foster Avenue). Near this site, from 1696 to 1699, stood Father Pinet's Mission of the Guardian Angel.

There he conducted his evangelical labors among the Miami Indians.

Fort Dearborn (southwest corner of Michigan Avenue and Wacker Drive; landmark plaque). One of the military posts established by Thomas Jefferson to protect the new frontier, Fort Dearborn was constructed under the supervision of Captain John Whistler in 1803 near the mouth of the Chicago River. The fort was destroyed by Native Americans on August 16, 1812, the day after the Fort Dearborn Massacre. A second Fort Dearborn was built in 1816 and stood until 1856.

Du Sable Cabin (northeast corner of Michigan Avenue and the Chicago River). Near this site stood the du Sable cabin, later remodeled into the Kinzie mansion, 1789–1832, successively the home of Jean Baptiste Point du Sable, the French trader Le Mai, and John Kinzie. There the city's first white child, Ellen Marion Kinzie, was born in 1805.

Old Vincennes Road. This historic trail into Chicago from the south, now Vincennes Avenue, was originally used by Native Americans to unite all villages of the

Potawatomi nation. It later became the thoroughfare from the Ohio and Wabash river settlements.

Little Fort Road (head of Wells Street and Lincoln Avenue). Here began the Little Fort Road, now Lincoln Avenue, a Native American trail that became the main road to Little Fort, or Waukegan, the first important settlement north of Chicago.

Fort Dearborn Massacre. In 1812 the garrison at Fort Dearborn, under the command of Captain Nathan Heald, evacuated the fort and marched southward along the lake to a point now marked by a tablet at Eighteenth Street and Prairie Avenue, where it was attacked by Native Americans. Fifty-three were killed, including several women and children, on August 15.

Antoine Ouilmette Home (west of Michigan Avenue on the north bank of the Chicago River.) Near this site stood the home of the French interpreter Antoine Ouilmette, after whom the suburb Wilmette was named. Following the Fort Dearborn Massacre (1812), Ouilmette was one of Chicago's few white inhabitants.

Indian Boundary Line. In 1816 Native Americans ceded land from Lake Calumet on the south to Rogers Avenue on the north. Rogers Avenue from Sheridan Road to Ridge Avenue was part of the Indian Boundary Road.

Jean Baptiste Beaubien Home (southwest corner of Randolph Street and Michigan Avenue). On this site, then the lakeshore, Beaubien, an early settler, built in 1817 a "mansion" to which he brought his bride, Josette La Framboise. It remained their home until 1845.

Sauganash Hotel (southeast corner of Lake Street and Wacker Drive). The popular hotel, built in 1827 by Mark Beaubien, was the site of an 1833 meeting to incorporate Chicago. The building was destroyed by fire in 1851.

Wolf Point. This elbow of land, formed by the junction of the North Branch of the Chicago River with the main river, was the site of Chicago's first tavern, Wolf Tavern, built in 1828 by James Kinzie.

Billy Caldwell's House (State Street and Chicago Avenue). Here stood the home of Billy Caldwell, a half-breed Potawatomi known as "Sauganash" (The Englishman). The house was built in 1828 by the U.S. Department of Indian Affairs in recognition of Caldwell's friendly efforts to preserve peace.

"Cobweb Castle" (north side of Chicago River near the foot of State Street). Near this site of Wolcott (now State) Street stood Agency House, known as "Cobweb Castle." It was the home of Dr. Alexander Wolcott, a government Indian agent at Chicago (1819–30).

City's First Church and First Methodist Church. On June 14, 1831, the Rev. Jesse Walker and ten members founded a church and held their first services in a log cabin at Wolf Point on the North Branch of the Chicago River. Today the congregation is the Chicago Temple–First United Methodist Church at Washington and Clark streets.)

Green Bay Road (north end of Michigan Avenue Bridge). From this point, Green Bay Road ran northwesterly to Clark Street and North Avenue and followed Clark Street's present route to the vicinity of Peterson Avenue. This road connected Fort Dearborn with Fort Howard at Green Bay, Wisconsin.

City's First Baptist Church (southwest corner of South Water and Franklin streets). Near this site Chicago's first Baptist church held services in the Temple Building. The congregation was organized on October 19, 1833, by Rev. Allen B. Freeman.

City's First Catholic Church (southwest corner of State and Lake streets). On this site, old St. Mary's, Chicago's first Catholic church, was erected in 1833 and was dedicated in October of that year. Father John Mary Iranaeus St. Cyr was the first pastor.

City's First Presbyterian Church (near southwest corner of Lake and Clark streets). Near this spot in 1833 was erected Chicago's first Presbyterian church, organized June 26, 1833, by Rev. Jeremiah Porter. The building was dedicated January 4, 1834.

First Post Office (near the corner of Lake Street and Wacker Drive; memorial plaque). Near this site in 1833, the log store of John S. C. Hogan was this section's only post office, serving settlers from miles around. Eastern mail was delivered once a week from Niles, Michigan.

Green Tree Tavern (northeast corner of Milwaukee Avenue and Lake and Canal streets). Built near this site in 1833 and opened by David Clock, the tavern was renamed Stage House in 1835, Chicago Hotel a few years later, and afterward Lake Street House.

Old Treaty Elm (intersection of Rogers, Kilbourn, and Caldwell avenues). The tree that stood here until 1933 marked the northern boundary of the Fort Dearborn Reservation, the trail to Lake Geneva, the center of Billy Caldwell's (Chief Sauganash) reservation, and the site of the Indian Treaty of 1833.

South Water Street (now Wacker Drive between State and Clark streets). This was Chicago's main business street in 1834, connecting the village with Fort Dearborn. It also was the site, years before, of a trading post with the local Native Americans.

Dearborn Street Drawbridge (Dearborn Street at the Chicago River). This first drawbridge over the Chicago River was constructed in 1834 by Nelson R. Norton. A primitive wooden affair, three hundred feet long with a sixty-foot opening, it was removed after a vote by the Common Council in 1839.

"Hubbard's Folly" (corner of La Salle Street and South Water Street, now Wacker Drive; memorial plaque.) On this site about 1834, Gurdon S. Hubbard built Chicago's first warehouse for storing pork and other pioneer produce. Because of the size and substantial construction of the building, early skeptics called it "Hubbard's Folly."

First U.S. Land Office (south side of Lake Street between Clark and Dearborn streets). Near this site the first U.S. Land Office was erected in 1835.

First City Cemeteries (near the lake and Twenty-third Street). This was the site of one of Chicago's first two cemeteries and comprised sixteen acres. It was laid out in August 1835 and enclosed in September, after which burials elsewhere on the South Side were forbidden.

Chicago's Oldest House (landmark plaque). This home, said to be the oldest house in Chicago, was built by Henry B. Clarke in 1836 at Michigan Avenue and Sixteenth Street. John Chrimes bought it in 1871 and moved it to 4526 Wabash Avenue. In 1977 it was moved again to 1855 S. Indiana

Avenue in the vicinity of its original site. It is now in the Prairie Avenue Historic District.

Saloon Building (southeast corner of Lake and Clark streets). The Saloon Building was so called because of the upper-floor salon, where entertainment took place. The Common Council leased one of the rooms, and the building functioned as the city hall from 1837 to 1842.

First Mayor's House (block bounded by Erie, Rush, Ontario, and Cass [now Wabash Avenue]). In the center of this block, Chicago's first mayor, William B. Ogden, built a home in 1837. It was the city's first house designed by an architect.

Toll Bridge (Ninety-second Street and Calumet River). This bridge, in use from 1839 to 1843, was built of planking and timbers by means of the barge principle of construction. Gideon M. Jackson was the first toll man.

First Wheat Cargo (north bank of river near Rush Street). Near this site stood Newberry and Dole's warehouse. In 1839 on the brig *Osceola,* the first cargo of wheat was shipped from the port of Chicago.

Stagecoach Office (southwest corner of Dearborn and Lake streets). On this site Frink and Walker, successors to Dr. John Temple, a pioneer stagecoach operator, built their terminal and office about 1840. Temple had begun his line in 1834.

Washington Square (Dearborn Street, Delaware Place, Clark Street, and Walton Place). This area was deeded to Chicago in 1842 on the condition that it be enclosed with "a handsome post, board, or picket fence within five years and kept enclosed forever as a public square." Later it became known as "Bughouse Square."

First City Hospital (just north of North Avenue on Clark Street). Near this site stood Chicago's first city hospital, built in 1843 and originally used as a rest house for smallpox patients, on ground purchased for a cemetery. Burned in 1845, it was rebuilt the same year.

First City-Owned School (southeast corner of Madison and Dearborn streets; memorial plaque). On this site was erected in 1844 a two-story frame building, Chicago's first city-owned school. It was known as "Old District School" and sometimes called the "Rumsey School."

Historic Cow Path (under 100 West Monroe Street). This areaway, measuring 10 by 117 by 18 feet, is reserved forever as a cow path by the terms of the deed of Willard Jones in 1844, when he sold portions of the surrounding property.

St. Paul's Church (southwest corner of Ohio and La Salle streets). On this site in 1846–48 stood the first St. Paul's Evangelical Lutheran Church and Chicago's first Lutheran parochial school. Pastor Selle preached the first Lutheran sermon here on Easter Sunday, April 12, 1846.

McCormick Reaper Works (north bank of the Chicago River just east of Michigan Avenue). On this site in 1847 Cyrus Hall McCormick began his reaper factory. International Harvester (now Navistar International Corporation) is the industrial giant that grew from this first factory, and its home office was, for many years, in the Equitable Building, now on the site of the original factory.

First Permanent Theater (south side of Randolph Street, a little east of Dearborn Street). John B. Rice built Chicago's first permanent theater in 1847, a forty-by-eighty-foot frame building modeled after an old coliseum. He paid twenty-five dollars as a monthly license for operating it.

First Board of Trade (Clark and Wacker; memorial plaque). Near this spot in 1848 was held the first session of the Board of Trade of the City of Chicago, now the world's largest grain exchange.

First Cattle Market (Madison Street and Ogden Avenue). From Bull's Head Stockyards, established here in 1848, began Chicago's journey to become the world's greatest livestock and packing center.

First Railway Depot (southwest corner of Canal and Kinzie streets; memorial plaque). Here stood Chicago's first railway depot, a wooden structure built in 1848 by the Galena and Chicago Union Railroad. From its cupola, the president and dispatchers watched trains advance across the prairie.

First Plank Road. This southwestern road was constructed in 1848 from Chicago to Doty's Tavern in Riverside, a distance of ten miles. It generally parallels what is now Ogden Avenue. By 1852 it extended to Naperville, connecting with a network of southwestern improved roads.

Chicago's First Synagogue (Clark Street between Quincy and Adams streets; plaque on Kluczynski Federal Building). On this site stood Chicago's first synagogue. It was dedicated in 1851, with Rabbi Ignatz Kunreuther in charge of the congregation.

Grave of David Kennison (Lincoln Park near Wisconsin and Clark streets). A granite boulder marks the grave of David Kennison, the last survivor of the Boston Tea Party. He died in 1852 at the age of 115.

Junction Grove (Sixty-third and La Salle streets). In 1852, around this intersection of the Michigan Southern Railroad with the Rock Island Railroad, started the settlement called Junction Grove, later named Chicago Junction, and finally, Englewood.

St. Patrick's Church (northwest corner of Adams and Des Plaines; landmark plaque). Constructed during 1852–56, it is the oldest church building in Chicago and one of the few buildings to escape the Great Fire of 1871.

First Black Church (Jackson Boulevard and Federal Street). Here stood Quinn Chapel, an African Methodist Episcopal Church, named in honor of Bishop William P. Quinn. The building, dedicated on November 20, 1853, was Chicago's first black house of worship and a civic and social center.

Blue Island Plank Road. Built in 1854, the road ran north on the line of Western Avenue to Blue Island Avenue, thence into the heart of the city. Thirteen miles long, it was a direct route for heavy southern transportation.

Lakeview House (northwest corner of Grace Street and Sheridan Road). On this site stood the first lakeside hotel. Built by James H. Reese and Elisha E. Hundley and opened July 4, 1854, it became the center of a fine residential section.

Grand Crossing (Seventy-fifth Street and Woodlawn Avenue). A collision here of two trains in 1854 prompted a legal requirement that all trains stop at this intersection. It also resulted in the development of a village nearby.

Chicago's First High School (748 W. Monroe Street). Chicago's first high school was completed in 1856 in accordance with a Common Council ordinance of 1855.

Andersonville School (southwest corner of Foster Avenue and Clark Street). In the northeastern corner of the subdivision called Andersonville stood the Andersonville School. There, in 1857, arrangements were made for Lake View Township's first election.

The Wigwam (southeast corner of Lake Street and Wacker Drive; plaque on building). A temporary wooden building erected in 1860 for the Republican National Convention, the Wigwam was where Abraham Lincoln was first nominated for the presidency.

Camp Douglas. Camp Douglas, built in 1861 during the Civil War, was a training ground for Union soldiers and later a Confederate prison. It covered sixty acres along Cottage Grove Avenue, Thirty-first and Thirty-third streets, and Giles Avenue.

Grave of Stephen A. Douglas (east end of Thirty-fifth Street). A Democratic leader and U.S. senator, Douglas died June 3, 1861. In 1868 a monument was erected to his memory, and his body was placed in the crypt at its base. The tomb is in Illinois' smallest state park, on land once part of Douglas's fifty-three-acre estate.

Refuge for Slaves (9955 Beverly Avenue). South of what was then Chicago, in the midst of the prairie, stood the Gardner Home and Tavern. Built in 1836, it was bought by William Wilcox in 1844 and became a refuge for slaves during the Civil War.

Lind Block (northwest corner of Randolph Street and Wacker Drive). This building, one of Chicago's first "skyscrapers," was built in the 1860s, ninety feet high with seven stories. It is celebrated for its escape from the Chicago Fire.

Camp Fry (Clark Street and Diversey Parkway). On a site once known as Wright's Grove, Camp Fry was an assembly and mustering point for Civil War troops.

The 132nd and 134th Illinois Infantry Regiments were organized there in 1864.

Mrs. Lincoln's Home (1238 West Washington Street). On this site stood the home Abraham Lincoln's widow bought in 1866 and occupied for about a year with her son Tad.

Old Water Tower (Chicago and Michigan avenues; landmark plaque). This gothic-style standpipe housing, completed in 1869, marks the establishment of Chicago's second water works and stands as a memorial to the Chicago Fire of 1871.

Mrs. O'Leary's Home (558 De Koven Street; landmark plaque). On this site stood the home and barn of Mrs. O'Leary, where the Chicago Fire of 1871 is said to have started. Although there are many versions of the origin of the fire, the real cause has never been determined. The Chicago Fire Academy now occupies this site, which also includes a sculpture, *Pillars of Fire,* by Egon Weiner.

Limits of the Chicago Fire. The northern limits of the Fire of 1871 extended along the line of Fullerton Avenue, from Lincoln Park on the east to the Chicago River on the west. The last building burned was the frame house of Dr. John Foster, near the northeast corner of Belden Avenue, Sedgwick, and Clark streets.

Ogden Home (60 West Walton Place; plaque in building). The home of Mahlon D. Ogden was the only house in the path of the Chicago Fire that was not burned. It is now the site of the Newberry Library.

Lake View Town Hall (northwest corner of Halsted and Addison streets). On this site stood the town hall of the Township of Lake View, a two-story building erected in 1872. When the area was a separate municipality, the building was its "City Hall."

Calaboose (approximately Byron and Clark streets). On this site stood the calaboose, or jail, of the original town of Lake View. It was a predecessor of the Little Jail at the old Town Hall.

Union Stock Yards Gate (Exchange Avenue at Peoria Street; landmark plaque). The gate, erected in 1875, is one of the few visual reminders of Chicago's past supremacy in the livestock and meatpacking industries.

Pullman (approximately 103rd Street to 115th Street and Cottage Grove Avenue eastward to the Lake Calumet area; landmark plaque). The first completely planned company town in the United States, erected by George M. Pullman in the early 1880s.

Prairie Avenue. This street, from about Eighteenth Street south for a few blocks, around the end of the nineteenth century contained the mansions of many of Chicago's elite, including Marshall Field, George Pullman, Philip Armour, William Kimball, and John Glessner. The Glessner House, 1800 S. Prairie Avenue, designed by H. H. Richardson in 1886, has a landmark plaque. The main street of the Prairie Avenue Historic District now is lined with newly constructed, expensive houses and condominiums.

Haymarket Square (Randolph Street between Halsted and Des Plaines streets). Here, on May 4, 1886, a bomb was thrown into a group of policemen who had come to disperse a labor protest meeting. Many people died, including seven policemen. The bomb thrower was never positively identified, but eight anarchist leaders were convicted and four were later hanged. Of a nearby historic landmark monument that once included a memorial statue of a policeman, only the pedestal still stands. In 2005 a memorial sculpture depicting the event was dedicated on the exact spot of the incident.

Hull House (800 S. Halsted Street, now part of the University of Illinois at Chicago campus; landmark plaque). One of the most important and influential social settlement complexes in America was established here by Jane Addams in 1889.

Eugene Field Home (4242 Clarendon Avenue). In 1895 Eugene Field bought a home on this site in Buena Park. After enlarging and remodeling the building, Field called his place "The Sabine Farm."

Iroquois Theater Fire. On December 30, 1903, 602 people died when fire started on the stage of the theater on Randolph Street near State Street. Many audience members, crowded around the exits, could not escape because the doors opened inward.

Steamer Eastland *Disaster* (plaque at La Salle Street and Wacker Drive). The worst disaster in Chicago history occurred on July 24, 1915. Loaded with Western Electric employees and their families, who were bound for an outing at Michigan City, Indiana, the ship *Eastland* capsized in the Chicago River near La Salle Street, killing a reported 844 people.

Michigan Avenue Bridge (Michigan Avenue and Wacker Drive; numerous memorial plaques and stoneworks). The bridge opened in 1920, near the sites of Fort Dearborn, the du Sable cabin, the start of the Green Bay Trail, and the McCormick Reaper Works.

First Nuclear Reaction (South Ellis Avenue between Fifty-sixth and Fifty-seventh streets; landmark plaque). On this site on December 2, 1942, the first self-sustaining controlled nuclear reaction was conducted under the grandstands of Stagg

Field Stadium. The site contains a twelve-foot-high bronze sculpture by Henry Moore titled *Nuclear Energy*.

Democratic National Convention Violence (across the street from the Chicago Hilton and Towers Hotel in the 700 block of south Michigan Avenue). A bloody tear-gas altercation in Grant Park in 1968 took place between thousands of demonstrators and police. Many police officers and demonstrators were hurt as the police shoved hundreds of protesters into paddy wagons.

The "Great Chicago Flood" (Kinzie Avenue bridge and the North Branch of the Chicago River). In 1992 a river bridge protection piling was pounded into part of a sixty-two-mile-long system of freight tunnels, thereby unleashing 124 million gallons of water. The water deluged much of the Loop, including City Hall and the Marshall Field store on State Street, resulting in damage and business losses of about a billion dollars.

E2 Nightclub Disaster. On February 17, 2003, at 2347 S. Michigan Avenue, twenty-one patrons died during a stampede for the doors after pepper spray was used during an altercation.

Appendix F: Statistical Data for Incorporated Communities of the Chicago Area

Place	Population			Median Household Income ($), 1999	Distance from Loop (miles)
	2000	1980	1960		
Cook County					
Alsip	19,725	17,134	3,770	47,963	19
Arlington Heights	76,031	66,116	27,878	67,807	27
Barrington	10,168	9,029	5,434	83,085	37
Barrington Hills	3,915	3,631	1,726	145,330	38
Bedford Park	574	988	737	49,722	15
Bellwood	20,535	19,811	20,729	52,856	13
Berkeley	5,245	5,467	5,792	58,984	15
Berwyn	54,016	46,849	54,224	43,833	10
Blue Island	23,463	21,855	19,618	36,520	18
Bridgeview	15,335	14,155	7,334	42,037	15
Broadview	8,264	8,618	8,588	47,651	13
Brookfield	19,085	19,395	20,429	52,636	13
Buffalo Grove	42,909	22,230	1,492	80,525	29
Burbank	27,902	28,461	—	49,388	13
Burnham	4,170	4,030	2,478	39,053	21
Calumet City	39,071	39,673	25,000	38,902	23
Calumet Park	8,516	8,788	8,448	45,357	16
Chicago	2,896,016	3,005,072	3,550,440	38,625	—
Chicago Heights	32,776	37,026	34,331	36,958	28
Chicago Ridge	14,127	13,473	5,748	44,101	17
Cicero	85,616	61,232	69,130	38,044	8
Country Club Hills	16,169	14,676	3,421	57,701	29
Countryside	5,991	6,538	—	45,469	15

Statistical Data for Incorporated Communities of the Chicago Area *(continued)*

Place	Population 2000	Population 1980	Population 1960	Median Household Income ($), 1999	Distance from Loop (miles)
Cook County (continued)					
Crestwood	11,251	10,712	1,213	45,813	19
Des Plaines	58,720	53,568	34,886	53,638	21
Dixmoor	3,934	4,175	3,076	26,677	20
Dolton	25,614	24,766	18,746	48,020	20
East Hazel Crest	1,607	1,362	1,457	43,000	22
Elk Grove Village	34,727	28,907	6,608	62,132	22
Elmwood Park	25,405	24,016	23,866	43,315	11
Evanston	74,239	73,706	79,283	56,335	12
Evergreen Park	20,821	22,260	24,178	53,514	14
Flossmoor	9,301	8,423	4,624	94,222	26
Ford Heights	3,456	5,347	3,270	17,500	30
Forest Park	15,688	15,177	14,452	44,103	10
Forest View	778	764	1,042	46,000	11
Franklin Park	19,434	17,507	18,322	46,688	15
Glencoe	8,762	9,200	10,472	164,432	21
Glenview	41,847	30,842	18,132	80,730	20
Glenwood	9,000	10,538	882	53,894	24
Golf	451	482	409	136,742	20
Hanover Park	38,278	28,850	451	61,358	30
Harvey	30,000	35,810	29,071	31,958	20
Harwood Heights	8,297	8,228	5,688	43,288	15
Hazel Crest	14,816	13,973	6,205	50,576	23
Hickory Hills	13,926	13,778	2,707	54,779	19
Hillside	8,155	8,279	7,794	50,774	14
Hodgkins	2,134	2,005	1,126	36,090	18
Hoffman Estates	49,495	38,258	8,296	65,937	29
Hometown	4,467	5,324	7,479	39,512	14
Homewood	19,543	19,724	13,371	57,213	24
Inverness	6,749	4,046	—	141,672	33
Justice	12,193	10,552	2,803	50,254	18
Kenilworth	2,494	2,708	2,959	200,001	16
La Grange	15,608	15,681	15,285	80,342	14
La Grange Park	13,295	13,359	13,793	58,918	15
Lansing	28,332	29,039	18,098	47,554	26
Lemont	13,098	5,640	3,397	70,563	29

Statistical Data for Incorporated Communities of the Chicago Area *(continued)*

Place	Population 2000	Population 1980	Population 1960	Median Household Income ($), 1999	Distance from Loop (miles)
Cook County (continued)					
Lincolnwood	12,359	11,921	11,744	71,234	11
Lynwood	7,377	4,195	255	56,554	29
Lyons	10,255	9,925	9,936	44,306	12
Markham	12,620	15,172	11,704	41,592	24
Matteson	12,928	10,223	3,225	59,583	30
Maywood	26,987	27,998	27,330	41,942	11
Melrose Park	23,171	20,735	22,291	40,689	12
Merrionette Park	1,999	2,054	2,354	36,278	17
Midlothian	14,315	14,274	6,605	50,000	22
Morton Grove	22,451	23,747	20,533	63,511	16
Mount Prospect	56,265	52,634	18,906	57,165	24
Niles	30,068	30,363	20,393	48,627	16
Norridge	14,582	16,483	14,087	47,787	15
Northbrook	33,435	30,735	11,635	95,665	24
Northfield	5,389	5,807	4,005	91,313	19
Northlake	11,878	12,166	12,318	48,406	16
North Riverside	6,688	6,764	7,989	43,856	11
Oak Forest	28,051	26,096	3,724	60,073	25
Oak Lawn	55,245	60,590	27,741	47,585	15
Oak Park	52,524	54,887	61,093	59,183	9
Olympia Fields	4,732	4,146	1,503	94,827	26
Orland Park	51,077	23,045	2,592	67,574	26
Palatine	65,479	32,166	11,504	63,321	31
Palos Heights	11,260	11,096	3,775	69,907	22
Palos Hills	17,665	16,654	3,766	52,329	18
Palos Park	4,689	3,150	2,169	78,450	21
Park Forest	23,462	26,222	29,993	47,579	30
Park Ridge	37,775	38,704	32,659	73,154	18
Phoenix	2,157	2,850	4,203	29,643	20
Posen	4,730	4,642	4,517	49,470	20
Prospect Heights	17,081	11,808	—	55,641	25
Richton Park	12,533	9,403	933	48,299	30
Riverdale	15,055	13,233	12,008	38,321	19
River Forest	11,635	12,392	12,695	89,284	10
River Grove	10,668	10,368	8,464	40,050	12

Statistical Data for Incorporated Communities of the Chicago Area *(continued)*

Place	Population 2000	Population 1980	Population 1960	Median Household Income ($), 1999	Distance from Loop (miles)
Cook County (continued)					
Riverside	8,895	9,236	9,750	64,931	11
Robbins	6,635	8,119	7,511	24,145	20
Rolling Meadows	24,604	20,167	10,879	59,535	27
Rosemont	4,224	4,137	978	34,663	20
Sauk Village	10,411	10,906	4,687	46,718	31
Schaumburg	75,386	52,319	986	60,941	30
Schiller Park	11,850	11,458	5,687	41,583	15
Skokie	63,348	60,278	59,364	57,375	13
South Chicago Hts.	3,970	3,932	4,043	39,639	29
South Holland	22,147	24,977	10,412	60,246	23
Stickney	6,148	5,893	6,239	42,772	10
Stone Park	5,127	4,273	3,038	39,787	14
Streamwood	36,407	23,456	4,821	65,076	33
Summit	10,637	10,110	10,374	38,132	13
Thornton	2,582	3,022	2,895	46,778	26
Tinley Park	48,401	26,171	6,392	61,648	29
Westchester	16,824	17,730	18,092	58,928	14
Western Springs	12,493	12,876	10,838	98,876	16
Wheeling	34,496	23,266	7,169	55,491	27
Willow Springs	5,027	4,147	2,348	58,322	19
Wilmette	27,651	28,229	28,268	106,773	15
Winnetka	12,419	12,772	13,368	167,458	18
Worth	11,047	11,592	8,196	42,723	19
Du Page County					
Addison	35,914	28,836	6,741	54,090	20
Bartlett	36,706	13,254	1,540	79,718	32
Bensenville	20,703	16,124	9,141	54,662	20
Bloomingdale	21,675	12,659	1,262	67,365	25
Burr Ridge	10,408	3,833	299	129,507	19
Carol Stream	40,438	15,472	836	64,893	27
Clarendon Hills	7,610	6,857	5,885	84,795	20
Darien	22,860	14,968	—	74,836	21
Downers Grove	48,724	39,274	21,154	65,539	22
Elmhurst	42,762	44,251	36,991	69,794	17

Statistical Data for Incorporated Communities of the Chicago Area *(continued)*

Place	Population 2000	Population 1980	Population 1960	Median Household Income ($), 1999	Distance from Loop (miles)
Du Page County (continued)					
Glendale Heights	31,765	23,163	173	56,258	23
Glen Ellyn	26,999	23,649	15,972	80,730	23
Hinsdale	17,349	16,726	12,859	104,551	18
Itasca	8,302	7,948	3,564	69,864	24
Lisle	21,182	13,625	4,219	59,129	26
Lombard	42,322	37,295	22,561	60,015	21
Naperville	128,358	42,330	12,933	88,771	30
Oak Brook	8,702	6,641	324	146,537	19
Oak Brook Terrace	2,300	2,285	1,121	59,148	18
Roselle	23,115	16,948	3,581	65,254	28
Villa Park	22,075	23,185	20,391	55,706	19
Warrenville	13,363	7,519	3,134	62,430	30
West Chicago	23,469	12,550	6,854	63,424	32
Westmont	24,554	16,718	5,997	51,422	21
Wheaton	55,416	43,043	24,312	75,385	26
Willowbrook	8,967	4,953	157	56,725	19
Winfield	8,718	4,422	1,575	89,060	28
Wood Dale	13,535	11,251	3,071	57,509	22
Woodridge	30,934	22,322	542	61,944	25
Kane County					
Aurora	142,990	81,293	63,715	54,861	39
Batavia	23,866	12,574	7,496	68,656	37
Carpentersville	30,586	23,272	17,424	54,526	42
East Dundee	2,955	2,618	2,221	61,219	41
Elburn	2,756	1,224	960	67,788	45
Elgin	94,487	63,798	49,447	52,605	38
Geneva	19,515	9,881	7,646	77,299	37
Hampshire	2,900	1,735	1,309	58,519	53
Montgomery	5,471	3,363	2,122	51,028	41
North Aurora	10,585	5,205	2,088	58,577	39
St. Charles	27,896	17,492	9,269	69,424	37
Sleepy Hollow	3,553	2,000	311	91,279	44
South Elgin	16,100	6,218	2,624	67,323	37
Sugar Grove	3,909	1,366	326	75,856	46
West Dundee	5,428	3,502	2,530	62,540	42

Statistical Data for Incorporated Communities of the Chicago Area *(continued)*

Place	Population 2000	Population 1980	Population 1960	Median Household Income ($), 1999	Distance from Loop (miles)
Lake County					
Antioch	8,788	4,419	2,268	56,481	53
Bannockburn	1,429	1,316	466	150,415	30
Deerfield	18,420	17,430	11,786	107,194	27
Deer Park	3,102	1,368	476	149,233	34
Fox Lake	9,178	6,831	3,700	46,548	53
Grayslake	18,506	5,260	3,762	73,143	44
Gurnee	28,834	7,179	1,831	75,742	39
Hawthorn Woods	6,002	1,658	239	132,720	36
Highland Park	31,365	30,611	25,532	100,967	26
Highwood	4,143	5,452	4,499	42,993	27
Island Lake	8,153	2,293	1,639	63,455	44
Lake Bluff	6,056	4,434	3,494	114,521	33
Lake Forest	20,059	15,245	10,687	136,462	31
Lake Villa	5,864	1,462	903	65,078	49
Lake Zurich	18,104	8,225	3,458	84,125	37
Libertyville	20,742	16,520	8,560	88,826	37
Lincolnshire	6,108	4,151	555	134,259	31
Lindenhurst	12,539	6,220	1,259	74,841	47
Long Grove	6,735	2,013	640	148,150	32
Mundelein	30,935	17,053	10,562	69,651	38
North Barrington	2,918	1,475	282	146,251	39
North Chicago	35,918	38,774	22,938	38,180	38
Park City	6,637	3,673	1,408	36,508	38
Riverwoods	3,843	2,804	96	158,990	29
Round Lake	5,842	2,644	997	58,051	47
Round Lake Beach	25,859	12,921	5,011	59,359	46
Round Lake Heights	1,347	1,192	—	54,706	47
Round Lake Park	6,038	4,032	2,565	44,896	45
Vernon Hills	20,120	9,827	123	71,297	31
Wadsworth	3,083	1,104	—	86,867	44
Wauconda	9,448	5,688	3,227	57,805	42
Waukegan	87,901	67,653	55,719	42,335	39
Winthrop Harbor	6,670	5,438	3,848	62,795	47
Zion	22,866	17,861	11,941	45,723	46

Statistical Data for Incorporated Communities of the Chicago Area *(continued)*

Place	Population 2000	Population 1980	Population 1960	Median Household Income ($), 1999	Distance from Loop (miles)
McHenry County					
Algonquin	23,276	5,834	2,041	79,730	44
Cary	15,531	6,640	2,530	76,801	43
Crystal Lake	38,000	18,590	8,314	66,872	49
Fox River Grove	4,862	2,515	1,866	66,469	41
Harvard	7,996	5,126	4,248	44,363	70
Hebron	1,038	786	701	46,607	66
Huntley	5,730	1,646	1,143	60,456	51
Lake in the Hills	23,152	5,651	2,046	73,312	46
Marengo	6,355	4,361	3,568	50,214	56
McCullom Lake	1,038	947	759	54,693	54
McHenry	21,501	10,908	3,336	55,759	53
Richmond	1,091	1,068	855	48,299	61
Woodstock	20,151	11,725	8,897	47,871	57
Will County					
Beecher	2,033	2,024	1,367	51,250	37
Bolingbrook	56,321	37,261	—	67,852	28
Braidwood	5,203	3,429	1,944	54,375	60
Channahon	7,235	3,734	—	71,991	48
Crest Hill	13,329	9,252	5,887	45,313	37
Crete	7,346	5,417	3,463	67,671	32
Frankfort	10,391	4,357	1,135	83,055	32
Joliet	105,597	77,956	66,780	47,761	39
Lockport	15,191	9,017	7,560	59,179	36
Manhattan	3,330	1,944	1,117	55,559	43
Mokena	14,583	4,578	1,332	74,703	32
Monee	2,924	993	646	58,625	36
New Lenox	17,771	5,792	1,750	67,697	36
Peotone	3,385	2,832	—	56,404	42
Plainfield	13,038	4,485	1,788	80,799	37
Rockdale	1,888	1,913	2,183	39,954	41
Romeoville	21,153	15,519	1,272	60,737	32
Shorewood	7,686	4,714	3,574	76,842	44
Steger	9,682	9,269	499	43,275	30
University Park	5,134	4,424	6,432	45,659	54
Wilmington	6,662	6,245	4,210	50,652	34

Statistical Data for Incorporated Communities of the Chicago Area *(continued)*

Place	Population 2000	Population 1980	Population 1960	Median Household Income ($), 1999	Distance from Loop (miles)
Lake County, Indiana					
Cedar Lake	9,279	8,754	5,766	43,987	43
Crown Point	19,806	16,455	8,443	52,889	44
Dyer	13,895	9,555	3,993	63,045	31
East Chicago	32,414	39,786	57,669	26,538	22
Gary	102,746	151,953	178,320	27,195	30
Griffith	17,334	17,026	9,483	50,030	32
Hammond	83,048	93,714	111,698	35,528	22
Highland	23,546	25,935	16,284	69,975	28
Hobart	25,363	22,987	18,680	47,759	38
Lake Station	13,948	14,294	9,309	36,984	35
Lowell	7,505	5,827	—	49,173	50
Merrillville	30,560	27,677	—	49,545	38
Munster	21,511	20,671	10,313	63,243	26
New Chicago	2,063	3,284	—	32,759	33
St. John	8,362	3,974	—	71,378	35
Schererville	24,851	13,209	2,875	59,243	33
Whiting	5,137	5,630	8,137	34,972	18
Porter County, Indiana					
Burns Harbor	766	920	—	53,929	41
Chesterton	10,488	8,531	4,335	55,530	47
Hebron	3,596	2,696	—	46,103	55
Ogden Dunes	1,313	1,489	—	76,924	39
Portage	33,496	27,409	11,822	47,500	39
Porter	4,972	2,988	—	50,625	45
Valparaiso	27,428	22,247	15,227	45,799	53

Source: U.S. Census data.

Notes

2. The Physical Setting

1. Wallace W. Atwood and James Goldthwait, *Physical Geography of the Evanston-Waukegan Region,* Illinois State Geological Survey Bulletin 7 (Urbana: University of Illinois, 1908), 4.

2. Cowles quoted in S. T. Mather, *Report on the Proposed Sand Dunes National Park, Indiana* (Washington, DC: Department of the Interior, National Park Service, 1917), 44.

3. The Evolution of Chicago

1. Milo M. Quaife, *Checagou: From Indian Wigwam to Modern City, 1673–1835* (Chicago: University of Chicago Press, 1933), 36.

2. Patrick Shirreff, *A Tour Through North America; Together with a Comprehensive View of Canada and the United States* (Edinburgh: Oliver and Boyd, 1835), 226.

3. John Lewis Peyton, *Over the Alleghenies and Across the Prairies. Personal Recollections of the Far West One and Twenty Years Ago (1848)* (London: Simpkin, Marshall, 1869), 325–29.

4. Joseph Kirkland and John Moses, *History of Chicago* (Chicago: Munsell, 1895), 1:119.

5. Herman Kogan and Robert Cromie, *The Great Fire: Chicago 1871* (New York: Putnam, 1971), 9.

6. George W. Steevens, *The Land of the Dollar* (New York: Dodd, Mead, 1897), 144.

4. People and Settlement Patterns: The Europeans

1. Graham Hutton, *Midwest at Noon* (Chicago: University of Chicago Press, 1946), 143–44.

2. Jane Addams, *Twenty Years at Hull House* (New York: Macmillan, 1910), 81–82.

3. Melvin G. Holli and Peter d'A. Jones, *Ethnic Chicago,* 4th ed. (Grand Rapids, MI: Eerdman, 1995), 65.

4. Richard Lindberg, *Passport's Guide to Ethnic Chicago: A Complete Guide to the Many Faces and Cultures of Chicago,* 2nd ed. (Lincolnwood, IL: Passport Books, 1997), 24.

5. Lawrence J. McCaffrey, *The Irish Diaspora in America* (Bloomington: Indiana University Press, 1976), 84.

6. Harvey Warren Zorbaugh, *The Gold Coast and the Slum* (Chicago: University of Chicago Press, 1929), 149–50.

7. Rudolph A. Hofmeister, *The Germans of Chicago* (Champaign, IL: Stipes, 1976), 202.

8. Andrew Jacke Townsend, "The Germans of Chicago," *Deutsch-Amerikanische Geschichtsblatter* 32 (1932): 141. Reprinted from PhD diss., University of Chicago, 1927.

9. Holli and Jones, *Ethnic Chicago,* 98–102.

10. A. E. Strand, *A History of the Norwegians of Illinois* (Chicago: John Anderson, 1905), 180.

11. Ernst W. Olson, ed., *History of the Swedes of Illinois* (Chicago: Engberg-Holmberg, 1908), 1:311.

12. Ulf Beijbom, *Swedes in Chicago: A Demographic and Social Study of the 1846–1880 Immigration* (Stockholm: Historiska Institutionen at University of Uppsala–Chicago Historical Society, 1971), 95.

13. Bessie Louise Pierce, *A History of Chicago* (Chicago: University of Chicago Press, 1957), 3:28.

14. Morris A. Gutstein, *A Priceless Heritage* (New York: Block, 1953), 38–39.

15. Seymour Jacob Pomrenze, "Aspects of Chicago Russian-Jewish Life, 1893–1915," *The Chicago Pinkus*, ed. Simon Rawidowicz (Chicago: College of Jewish Studies, 1952), 130–31.

16. Louis Wirth, *The Ghetto* (Chicago: University of Chicago Press, 1928), 232–33.

17. Hyman L. Meites, ed., *History of the Jews of Chicago* (Chicago: Jewish Historical Society of Illinois, 1924), 150–51.

18. Lindberg, *Passport's Guide*, 90.

19. Ira Berkow, *Maxwell Street* (Garden City, NY: Doubleday, 1977), 10–11.

20. *The Sentinel's History of Chicago Jewry, 1911–1961* (Chicago: Sentinel, 1961), 127.

21. Czechoslovak National Council of America, *Panorama: A Historical Review of Czechs and Slovaks in the United States of America* (Cicero, IL: Czechoslovak National Council of America, 1970), 33.

22. Residents of Hull-House, *Hull-House Maps and Papers* (New York: Crowell, 1895), 117.

23. Edward R. Kantowicz, *Polish-American Politics in Chicago, 1888–1940* (Chicago: University of Chicago Press, 1975), 31–32.

24. Kantowicz, *Polish-American Politics*, 22.

25. City of Chicago, Department of Development and Planning, *Chicago's Polish Population: Selected Statistics* (Chicago, 1976), 1–2.

26. David Fainhauz, *Lithuanians in Multi-Ethnic Chicago until World War II* (Chicago: Lithuanian Library Press and Loyola University Press, 1977), 99.

27. "The Second Generation," *Juanimas* (Chicago), December 1–15, 1940.

28. Rudolph Vecoli, "Chicago's Italians Prior to World War I: A Study of Their Social and Economic Adjustment," (PhD diss., University of Wisconsin, 1962), 16–17.

29. Humbert S. Nelli, *Italians in Chicago, 1880–1930* (New York: Oxford University Press, 1970), 66.

30. Ronald P. Grossman, *The Italians in America* (Minneapolis: Lerner, 1966), 28.

31. Grossman, *Italians in America*, 25.

32. City of Chicago, Department of Development and Planning, *Chicago's Italian Population: Selected Statistics* (Chicago, 1976), 2.

33. Edith Abbott, *The Tenements of Chicago, 1908–1935* (Chicago: University of Chicago Press, 1936), 95–96.

34. Zorbaugh, *The Gold Coast and the Slum*, 159–61, 164–65, 166, 170.

35. Jayne Clark Jones, *The Greeks in America* (Minneapolis: Lerner, 1969), 55.

36. George A. Kourvetaris, *First and Second Generation Greeks in Chicago* (Athens, Greece: National Center of Social Research, 1971), 49.

37. Abbott, *Tenements of Chicago*, 97.

38. Andrew T. Kopan, "Education and Greek Immigrants in Chicago, 1892–1973: A Study in Ethnic Survival" (PhD diss., University of Chicago, 1974), 152.

39. Theodore Saloutos, *The Greeks in the United States* (Cambridge, MA: Harvard University Press, 1964), 267.

40. Lindberg, *Passport's Guide*, 206.

41. Amry Vandenbosch, *The Dutch Communities of Chicago* (Chicago: Knickerbocker Society of Chicago, 1927), 75–76.

42. Cynthia Linton, ed., *The Ethnic Handbook: A Guide to the Cultures and Traditions of Chicago's Diverse Communities* (Chicago: Illinois Ethnic Coalition, 1996), 177.

43. Mike Royko, *Boss: Richard J. Daley of Chicago* (New York: Dutton, 1971), 24–25.

44. Royko, *Boss*, 26.

5. People and Settlement Patterns: Recent Migration and Trends

1. Allen H. Spear, *Black Chicago: The Making of a Negro Ghetto, 1890–1920* (Chicago: University of Chicago Press, 1967), 91.

2. St. Clair Drake and Horace R. Cayton, *Black Metropolis: A Study of Negro Life in a Northern City* (New York: Harcourt, 1945), 1:73.

3. Spear, *Black Chicago*, 174–75.

4. Drake and Cayton, *Black Metropolis*, 1:78–79.

5. Drake and Cayton, *Black Metropolis*, 1:80.

6. Harold M. Mayer and Richard C. Wade, *Chicago: Growth of a Metropolis* (Chicago: University of Chicago Press, 1969), 406–10.

7. Gerald William Ropka, "The Evolving Residential Pattern of the Mexican, Puerto Rican, and Cuban Population in the City of Chicago" (PhD diss., Michigan State University, 1973), 132.

8. Cynthia Linton, ed., *The Ethnic Handbook: A Guide to the Cultures and Traditions of Chicago's Diverse Communities* (Chicago: Illinois Ethnic Coalition, 1996), 57.

9. Linton, *Ethnic Handbook*, 94.

6. The Economy of Chicago

1. James Parton, "Chicago," *Atlantic Monthly* 19 (March 1867): 325–45.

7. Culture, Education, and Recreation

1. Department of Planning and Development, *Chicago Fact Book 2003* (City of Chicago, 2003), 58.

2. Kenny J. Williams, *In the City of Men* (Nashville: Townsend Press, 1974), 5.

3. Mencken quoted in Kenan Heise, *Chicago the Beautiful: A City Reborn* (Chicago: Bonus Books, 2001), 249.

4. F. Richard Ciccone, *Chicago and the American Century: The 100 Most Significant Chicagoans of the Twentieth Century* (Chicago: Contemporary Books, 1999), 369–73.

8. Transportation: External and Internal

1. Daniel H. Burnham Jr. and Robert Kingery, *Planning the Region of Chicago* (Chicago: Chicago Regional Planning Association, 1956), 81.

9. Expansion of the Chicago Metropolitan Area

1. Downing quoted in S. T. Mather, *Report on the Proposed Sand Dunes National Park, Indiana* (Washington, DC: Dept. of the Interior, National Park Service, 1917), 93–94.

2. Jean Komaiko and Norma Schaeffer, *Doing the Dunes* (Beverly Shores, IN: Dunes Enterprises, 1973), 5.

3. U.S. Department of Agriculture, *The Why and How of Rural Zoning*, Agriculture Information Bulletin 196 (Washington: Government Printing Office, 1958), 1.

4. Irving Cutler, *The Chicago-Milwaukee Corridor: A Geographic Study of Intermetropolitan Coalescence*, Studies in Geography 9 (Evanston: Northwestern University, Department of Geography, 1965), 126–27.

5. Jean Gottman, *Megalopolis* (New York: Twentieth Century Fund, 1961), 131, 133.

10. Planning for the Future

1. John W. Alexander, *Economic Geography* (Englewood Cliffs, NJ: Prentice Hall, 1963), 639–40.

2. Chicago Metropolis 2020, *The Metropolis Plan: Choices for the Chicago Region* (Chicago: Commercial Club, 2002), 1–36.

Selected Bibliography

1. Introduction

Alinsky, Saul D. *Reveille for Radicals*. Chicago: University of Chicago Press, 1946.

Andreas, Alfred T. *History of Chicago*. 3 vols. Chicago: A. T. Andreas, 1884–86.

Berry, Brian J. L., et al. *Chicago Transformations of an Urban System*. Cambridge, MA: Ballinger Publishing Co., 1976.

Bishop, Glen A., and Gilbert, Paul T. *Chicago's Accomplishments and Leaders*. Chicago: Bishop Publishing Co., 1932.

Bonner, Thomas N. *Medicine in Chicago, 1850–1950*. New York: American Book–Stratford Press, 1957.

Bross, William. *History of Chicago*. Chicago: Jansen, McClurg & Co., 1876.

Campbell, Edna Fay, Fanny R. Smith, and Clarence F. Jones. *Our City — Chicago*. New York: Charles Scribner's Sons, 1930.

Chicago Department of Development and Planning. *Historic City: The Settlement of Chicago*. Chicago, 1976.

——. *The People of Chicago: Who We Are and Who We Have Been*. Chicago, 1976.

Chicago Department of Planning and Development. *Chicago Fact Book 2003*. Chicago, 2003.

Chicago Department of Public Works, Bureau of Maps and Places. *Atlas of City of Chicago*. Chicago, 1977–78.

Chicago Fact Book Consortium. *Local Community Fact Book: Chicago Metropolitan Area 1990*. Chicago: University of Illinois at Chicago, 1995.

Ciccone, F. Richard. *Chicago and the American Century: The 100 Most Significant Chicagoans of the Twentieth Century*. Chicago: Contemporary Books, 1999.

Commission of Chicago Historical and Architectural Landmarks. *Chicago Landmarks, 1980*. Chicago, 1980.

——. *Landmark Neighborhoods of Chicago, 1981*. Chicago, 1981.

Condit, Carl W. *Chicago 1910–29: Building, Planning, and Urban Technology*. Chicago: University of Chicago Press, 1973.

——. *Chicago 1930–70: Building, Planning, and Urban Technology*. Chicago: University of Chicago Press, 1974.

Cronin, William. *Nature's Metropolis: Chicago and the Great West*. New York: W. W. Norton & Co., 1991.

Currey, Josiah Seymour. *Chicago: Its History and Its Builders: A Century of Marvelous Growth*. 5 vols. Chicago: S. J. Clark Publishing Co., 1912.

Cutler, Irving, ed. *The Chicago Metropolitan Area: Selected Geographic Readings*. New York: Simon & Schuster, 1970.

Dedmon, Emmett. *Fabulous Chicago*. 2nd ed. New York: Atheneum, 1981.

Drell, Adrienne, ed. *20th Century Chicago: 100 Years, 100 Voices*. Chicago: Chicago Sun-Times, 2000.

Duis, Perry R. *Challenging Chicago: Coping with Everyday Life, 1837–1920*. Chicago: University of Illinois Press, 1998.

Farr, Finis. *Chicago: A Personal History of America's Most American City*. New Rochelle, NY: Arlington House, 1973.

Federal Writers Project. *Illinois: A Descriptive and Historical Guide*. 2nd ed. Chicago: A. A. McClurg & Co., 1947.

Fiedler, D. E., ed. *The Chicagoland Atlas*. Arlington Heights, IL: Creative Sales Corp., 1980.

Furer, Howard B. *Chicago: A Chronological and Documentary History, 1784–1970*. Dobbs Ferry, NY: Oceana Publications, 1974.

Gilbert, Paul, and Charles Lee Bryson. *Chicago and Its Makers*. Chicago: Felix Mendelsohn, 1929.

Goode, J. Paul. *The Geographic Background of Chicago*. Chicago: University of Chicago Press, 1926.

Graham, Jory. *Chicago—An Extraordinary Guide*. Chicago: Rand McNally & Co., 1968.

——. *Instant Chicago. How to Cope*. Chicago: Rand McNally & Co., 1973.

Grossman, James R., Ann Durkin Keating, Janice L. Reiff, eds. *The Encyclopedia of Chicago*. Chicago: University of Chicago Press, 2004.

Grossman, Ron. *Guide to Chicago Neighborhoods*. Piscataway, NJ: New Century Publishers, 1981.

Halper, Albert, ed. *The Chicago Crime Book*. Cleveland: World Publishing Co., 1967.

——. *This Is Chicago: An Anthology*. New York: Henry Holt & Co., 1952.

Hansen, Harry, ed. *Illinois: A Descriptive and Historical Guide*. New York: Hastings House, 1974.

Havighurst, Robert J. *The Public Schools of Chicago: A Survey for the Board of Education of the City of Chicago*. Chicago: Chicago Board of Education, 1964.

Hayner, Don, and Tom McNamee. *Streetwise Chicago: A History of Chicago Street Names*. Chicago: Loyola University Press, 1988.

Heise, Kenan. *Chaos, Creativity and Culture*. Salt Lake City: Gibbs Smith Publisher, 1998.

——. *Chicago the Beautiful: A City Reborn*. Chicago: Bonus Books, Inc., 2001.

——. *The Chicagoization of America, 1893–1917*. Evanston: Chicago Historical Bookworks, 1999.

Heise, Kenan, and Mark Frazel. *Hands on Chicago*. Chicago: Bonus Books, Inc., 1987.

Herrick, Mary J. *The Chicago Schools: A Social and Political History*. Beverly Hills, CA: Sage Publications, 1971.

History of Chicago, A: Its Men and Institutions. Chicago: Inter Ocean, 1900.

Horowitz, Helen Lefkowitz. *Culture & the City: Cultural Philanthropy in Chicago from the 1800s to 1917*. Lexington: University Press of Kentucky, 1976.

Jensen, George Peter. *Historic Chicago Sites*. Chicago: Creative Enterprises, 1953.

Johnson, Cut, and R. Craig Sautter. *Wicked City, Chicago: From Kenna to Capone*. Highland Park, IL: December Press, 1994.

Karlen, Harvey. *The Governments of Chicago*. Chicago: Courier Publishing Co., 1958.

Kiang, Ying Cheng. *Chicago*. Chicago: Adams Press, 1968.

Kirkland, Joseph. *The Story of Chicago*. 3 vols. Chicago: Dibble Publishing Co., 1892–94.

Lewis, Lloyd, and Henry Justin Smith. *Chicago, the History of Its Reputation*. New York: Harcourt, Brace & Co., 1929.

Lindberg, Richard. *Return to the Scene of the Crime*. Nashville: Cumberland House Publishing, 1999.

Longstreet, Stephen. *Chicago, 1860–1919*. New York: David McKay Co., 1973.

McManis, John T. *Ella Flagg Young and a Half-Century of the Chicago Public Schools*. Chicago: A. C. McClurg & Co., 1916.

McNamee, Tom, and Don Hayner. *Metro Chicago Almanac*. Chicago: Bonus Books and Chicago Sun-Times, 1991.

McPhaul, John J. *Deadlines and Monkeyshines: The Fabled World of Chicago Journalism*. Englewood Cliffs, NJ: Prentice Hall, 1962.

Mark, Norman. *Chicago: Walking, Bicycling, and Driving Tours of the City.* Chicago: Chicago Review Press, 1977.

Masters, Edgar Lee. *The Tale of Chicago.* New York: G. P. Putnam's Sons, 1933.

Mayer, Harold M. *Chicago: City of Decisions.* Papers on Chicago 1. Chicago: Geographic Society of Chicago, 1955.

Mayer, Harold M., and Richard C. Wade. *Chicago: Growth of a Metropolis.* Chicago: University of Chicago Press, 1969.

Miller, Donald L. *City of the Century: The Epic of Chicago and the Making of America.* New York: Simon & Schuster, 1996.

Nash, Jay Robert. *People to See: An Anecdotal History of Chicago's Makers and Breakers.* Piscataway, NJ: New Century Publishers, 1981.

Northeastern Illinois Planning Commission. *A Social Geography of Metropolitan Chicago.* Chicago, 1960.

Olcott's Land Values Blue Book of Chicago & Suburbs. Chicago: George C. Olcott & Co., 1980.

Pacyga, Dominic A., and Ellen Sherrett. *Chicago: City of Neighborhoods.* Chicago: Loyola University Press, 1986.

Pierce, Bessie Louise, ed. *As Others See Chicago: Impressions of Visitors, 1673–1933.* Chicago: University of Chicago Press, 1933.

———. *A History of Chicago.* 3 vols. New York: Alfred A. Knopf, 1937–57.

Poole, Ernest. *Giants Gone: Men Who Made Chicago.* New York: McGraw Hill Book Co., 1943.

Rex, Frederick. *Mayors of the City of Chicago from March 4, 1837, to April 13, 1933.* Chicago: Municipal Reference Library, 1947.

Schackleton, Robert. *The Book of Chicago.* Philadelphia: Penn Publishing Co., 1920.

Smith, Henry Justin. *Chicago, A Portrait.* New York: D. Appleton–Century Co., 1931.

Swanson, Stevenson, ed., and the staff of the Chicago Tribune. *Chicago Days: 150 Defining Moments in the Life of a Great City.* Chicago: Contemporary Books, 1997.

Wagenknecht, Edward. *Chicago.* Norman: University of Oklahoma Press, 1964.

Winslow, Charles S. *Historical Events of Chicago.* Chicago: Soderlund Printing Service, 1937.

2. The Physical Setting

Atwood, Wallace W., and James Goldthwait. *Physical Geography of the Evanston-Waukegan Region.* Illinois State Geological Survey Bulletin 7. Urbana: University of Illinois, 1908.

Benton, Chris. *Chicagoland Nature Trails.* Chicago: Contemporary Books, 1978.

Bretz, J. Harlan. *Geology of the Chicago Region.* Part 1, *Geology of the Chicago Region*, 1939; Part 2, *The Pleistocene*, 1955. Bulletin no. 65. Urbana: Illinois State Geological Society.

Cain, Louis P. *Sanitation Strategy for a Lakefront Metropolis.* De Kalb: Northern Illinois University Press, 1978.

Cowles, Henry C. *The Plant Societies of Chicago and Vicinity.* Bulletin no. 2. Chicago: Geographic Society of Chicago, 1901.

Cox, Henry J., and John H. Armington. *The Weather and Climate of Chicago.* Bulletin no. 4. Chicago: Geographic Society of Chicago, 1914.

Cressey, George B. *The Indiana Sand Dunes and Shore Lines of the Lake Michigan Basin.* Bulletin no. 8. Chicago: Geographic Society of Chicago, 1928.

Dubkin, Leonard. *My Secret Places: One Man's Love Affair with Nature in the City.* New York: Laird McKay and Co., 1972.

Duddy, Edward A. *Agriculture in the Chicago Region.* Chicago: University of Chicago Press, 1929.

Fryxell, F. M. *The Physiography of the Region of Chicago.* Chicago: University of Chicago Press, 1927.

Greenberg, Joel. *A Natural History of the Chicago Region.* Chicago: University of Chicago Press, 2002.

Knight, Robert, and Lucius H. Zeuch. *The Location of the Chicago Portage of the Seventeenth Century.* Chicago: University of Chicago Press, 1920.

Salisbury, Rollin D., and William C Alden. *The Geography of Chicago and Its Environs.* Bulletin no. 1. Chicago: Geographic Society of Chicago, 1899.

Schmid, James A. *Urban Vegetation.* Research Paper no. 161. Chicago: University of Chicago, Department of Geography, 1975.

Shelford, Victor E. *Animal Communities in Temperate America, As Illustrated in the Chicago Region: A Study in Animal Ecology.* Bulletin no. 5. Chicago: Geographic Society of Chicago, 1913.

Wilman, H. B. *Summary of the Geology of the Chicago Area.* Circular 460. Urbana: Illinois State Geological Survey, 1971.

3. The Evolution of Chicago

Andrews, Wayne. *Battle for Chicago.* New York: Harcourt, Brace & Co., 1946.

Angle, Paul M. *The Great Chicago Fire, October 8–10, 1871, Described by Eight Men and Women Who Experienced Its Horrors and Testified to the Courage of Its Inhabitants.* Chicago: Chicago Historical Society, 1971.

Asbury, Herbert. *Gem of the Prairie: An Informal History of the Chicago Underworld.* Garden City, NY: Garden City Publishing Co., 1942.

Badger, R. Reid. *The Great American Fair: The World's Columbian Exposition and American Culture.* Chicago: Nelson-Hall, 1979.

Bancroft, Hubert Howe. *The Book of the Fair: An Historical and Descriptive Presentation Viewed through the Columbian Exposition at Chicago in 1893.* 2 vols. Chicago: Bancroft Co., 1895.

Burg, David F. *Chicago's White City of 1893.* Lexington: University Press of Kentucky, 1976.

Chicago Department of Public Works. *Chicago Public Works: A History.* Chicago: Rand McNally & Co., 1973.

Chicago Plan Commission. *Housing in Chicago Communities.* 75 vols. Chicago, 1940.

Colbert, Elias, and Everett Chamberlain. *Chicago & the Great Conflagration.* Chicago: J. S. Goodman & Co., 1871.

Cromie, Robert, and Archie Lieberman. *Chicago.* Chicago: Rand McNally & Co., 1980.

David, Henry. *History of the Haymarket Affair.* New York: Farrar & Rinehart, 1936.

Demaris, Ovid. *Captive City.* New York: Lyle Stuart, 1969.

Duis, Perry. *Chicago: Creating New Traditions.* Chicago: Chicago Historical Society, 1976.

Fanning, Charles. *Finley Peter Dunne and Mr. Dooley: The Chicago Years.* Lexington: University Press of Kentucky, 1978.

Fehrenbacher, Don E. *Chicago Giant: A Biography of "Long John" Wentworth.* Madison, WI: American History Research Center, 1957.

Ginger, Ray. *Altgeld's America: The Ideal Versus Changing Realities.* New York: Funk & Wagnall Co., 1958.

Green, Paul H., and Melvin G. Holli, eds. *The Mayors: The Chicago Political Tradition.* Carbondale: Southern Illinois University Press, 1987.

Harrison, Carter H. *Stormy Years.* Indianapolis: Bobbs-Merrill Co., 1935.

Hirsch, Susan E., and Robert I. Goler. *A City Comes of Age: Chicago in the 1890s.* Chicago: Chicago Historical Society, 1990.

Illinois Archaeological Survey. *Chicago Area Archaeology.* Bulletin no. 3. Urbana: University of Illinois, 1961.

Kennedy, Eugene. *Himself! The Life and Times of Mayor Richard J. Daley.* New York: Viking Press, 1978.

Kinzie, Juliette A. *Wau-Bun.* Chicago: Rand McNally & Co., 1901.

Knudtson, Thomas. *Chicago, The Rising City.* Chicago: Chicago Publishing Co., 1975.

Kobler, John. *Capone: The Life and World of Al Capone.* New York: G. P. Putnam's Sons, 1971.

Kogan, Herman, and Robert Cromie. *The Great Fire: Chicago 1871.* New York: G. P. Putnam's Sons, 1971.

Kogan, Herman, and Rick Kogan. *Yesterday's Chicago.* Miami: E. A. Seemann Publishing Co., 1976.

Kogan, Herman, and Lloyd Wendt. *Chicago: A Pictorial History*. New York: Bonanza Books, 1958.

Kreinberg, Lew, and Charles Bowden. *Street Signs Chicago: Neighborhood and Other Illusions of Big-City Life*. Chicago: Chicago Review Press, 1981.

Larson, Erik. *The Devil in the White City*. New York: Crown Publishers, 2003.

Lohr, Lenox Riley. *Fair Management, the Story of A Century of Progress Exposition: A Guide for Future Fairs*. Chicago: Cuneo Press, 1952.

Lowe, David. *Lost Chicago*. Boston: Houghton Mifflin Co., 1975.

———. *The Great Chicago Fire*. New York: Dover Publications, 1979.

Mark, Norman. *Mayors, Madams, & Madmen*. Chicago: Chicago Review Press, 1979.

McIlvaine, Mabel, ed. *Reminiscences of Chicago During the Civil War*. New York: Citadel Press, 1967.

McNulty, Elizabeth. *Chicago—Then and Now*. San Diego: Thunder Bay Press, 2000.

Merriam, Charles Edward. *Chicago: A More Intimate View of Urban Politics*. New York: Macmillan Co., 1929.

O'Connor, Len. *Clout: Mayor Daley and His City*. Chicago: Henry Regnery Co., 1975.

Quaife, Milo M. *Checagou: From Indian Wigwam to Modern City, 1673–1835*. Chicago: University of Chicago Press, 1933.

———. *Chicago and the Old Northwest, 1673–1835*. Chicago: University of Chicago Press, 1913.

Quimby, George Irving. *Indian Life in the Upper Great Lakes, 11,000 BC to AD 1800*. Chicago: University of Chicago Press, 1960.

Rakove, Milton. *Don't Make No Waves—Don't Back No Losers*. Bloomington: Indiana University Press, 1975.

Reckless, Walter C. *Vice in Chicago*. Chicago: University of Chicago Press, 1933.

Royko, Mike. *Boss: Richard J. Daley of Chicago*. New York: E. P. Dutton, 1971.

Sawyers, June Skinner. *Chicago Portraits: Biographies of 250 Famous Chicagoans*. Chicago: Loyola University Press, 1991.

Schaaf, Barbara C. *Mr. Dooley's Chicago*. Garden City, NY: Anchor Press–Doubleday, 1977.

Smith, Henry Justin. *Chicago's Great Century, 1833–1933*. Chicago: Consolidated Publishers, 1933.

Stead, William T. *If Christ Came to Chicago: A Plea for the Union of All Who Love in the Service of All Who Suffer*. Chicago: Laird & Lee Publishers, 1894.

Wendt, Lloyd, and Herman Kogan. *Big Bill of Chicago*. Indianapolis: Bobbs-Merrill Co., 1953.

———. *Lords of the Levee*. Indianapolis: Bobbs-Merrill Co., 1943.

4 and 5. People and Settlement Patterns

Abbott, Edith. *The Tenements of Chicago, 1908–1935*. Chicago: University of Chicago Press, 1936.

Abrahamson, Julia. *A Neighborhood Finds Itself*. New York: Harper & Brothers, 1959.

Addams, Jane. *Twenty Years at Hull House*. New York: Macmillan, 1910.

Adelman, William J. *Pilsen and the West Side*. Chicago: Illinois Labor History Society, 1977.

Allswang, John M. *A House for All Peoples: Ethnic Politics in Chicago, 1890–1936*. Lexington: University Press of Kentucky, 1971.

Beijbom, Ulf. *Swedes in Chicago: A Demographic and Social Study of the 1846–1880 Immigration*. Trans. Donald Brown. Stockholm: Historiska Institutionen at University of Uppsala–Chicago Historical Society, 1971.

Berkow, Ira. *Maxwell Street*. Garden City, NY: Doubleday & Co., 1977.

Blei, Norbert. *Neighborhood*. Peoria: Ellis Press, 1987.

Bowly, Devereux, Jr. *The Poorhouse: Subsidized Housing in Chicago, 1895–1976*. Carbondale: Southern Illinois University Press, 1978.

Chicago Commission on Race Relations. *The Negro in Chicago. A Study of Race Relations and a Race Riot.* Chicago: University of Chicago Press, 1922.

City of Chicago, Department of Development and Planning. *Chicago's Black Population: Selected Statistics.* Chicago, 1975.

———. *Chicago's German Population: Selected Statistics.* Chicago, 1976.

———. *Chicago's Irish Population: Selected Statistics.* Chicago, 1976.

———. *Chicago's Italian Population: Selected Statistics.* Chicago, 1976.

———. *Chicago's Polish Population: Selected Statistics.* Chicago, 1976.

———. *Chicago's Spanish-Speaking Population: Selected Statistics.* Chicago, 1973.

Cutler, Irving. *Jewish Chicago: A Pictorial History.* Chicago: Arcadia Publishing Co., 2000.

———. *The Jews of Chicago: From Shtetl to Suburb.* Urbana: University of Illinois Press, 1996.

Czechoslovak National Council of America. *Panorama: A Historical Review of Czechs and Slovaks in the United States of America.* Cicero, IL, 1970.

De Vise, Pierre. *Chicago's Widening Color Gap.* Chicago: Interuniversity Social Research Committee, 1967.

Drake, St. Clair, and Horace R. Cayton. *Black Metropolis: A Study of Negro Life in a Northern City.* 2 vols. New York: Harcourt, Brace & World, 1970.

Duncan, Otis Dudley, and Beverly Duncan. *The Negro Population of Chicago: A Study of Residential Succession.* Chicago: University of Chicago Press, 1957.

Eastwood, Carolyn. *Near West Side Stories: Struggles for Community in Chicago's Maxwell Street Neighborhood.* Chicago: Lake Claremont Press, 2002.

Eshel, Shili, and Roger Schatz. *Jewish Maxwell Street Stories.* Chicago: Arcadia Publishing Co., 2004.

Fainhauz, David. *Lithuanians in Multi-Ethnic Chicago until World War II.* Chicago: Lithuanian Library Press and Loyola University Press, 1977.

Frazier, Franklin E. *The Negro Family in Chicago.* Chicago: University of Chicago Press, 1932.

Garraghan, Gilbert. *Catholic Church in Chicago, 1673–1871.* Chicago: Loyola University Press, 1921.

Greeley, Andrew M. *Neighborhood.* New York: Seabury Press, 1977.

Grossman, Ronald P. *The Italians in America.* Minneapolis: Lerner Publications Co., 1966.

Grove, Lori, and Laura Kamedulski. *Chicago's Maxwell Street.* Chicago: Arcadia Publishing Co., 2002.

Gutstein, Morris A. *A Priceless Heritage.* New York: Block Publishing Co., 1953.

Heimovics, Rachel Baron. *The Chicago Jewish Source Book.* Piscataway, NJ: New Century Publishers, 1981.

Hofmeister, Rudolph A. *The Germans of Chicago.* Champaign, IL: Stripes Publishing Co., 1976.

Holli, Melvin G., and Peter d'A. Jones, eds. *Ethnic Chicago.* 4th ed. Grand Rapids, MI: Wm. B. Eerdmann Publishing Co., 1995.

Holt, Glen E., and Dominic A. Pacyga. *Chicago: A Historical Guide to the Neighborhoods, the Loop and South Side.* Chicago: Chicago Historical Society, 1979.

Horwich, Bernard, *My First Eighty Years.* Chicago: Argus Books, 1939.

Hucke, Matt, and Ursula Bielski. *Graveyards of Chicago.* Chicago: Lake Claremont Press, 1999.

Jones, Jayne Clark. *The Greeks in America.* Minneapolis: Lerner Publications Co., 1969.

Kantowicz, Edward R. *Polish-American Politics in Chicago, 1888–1940.* Chicago: University of Chicago Press, 1975.

Koenig, Harry C., ed. *A History of the Parishes of the Archdiocese of Chicago.* Vols. 1 and 2. Chicago: Archdiocese of Chicago, 1980.

Kopan, Andrew T. "Education and Greek Immigrants in Chicago, 1892–1973: A Study in Ethnic Survival." PhD diss., University of Chicago, 1974.

Kourvetaris, George A. *First and Second Generation Greeks in Chicago.* Athens, Greece: National Center of Social Research, 1971.

Lane, George A. *Chicago Churches and Synagogues: An Architectural Pilgrimage.* Chicago: Loyola University Press, 1981.

Lindberg, Richard. *Passport's Guide to Ethnic Chicago: A Complete Guide to the Many Faces and Cultures of Chicago.* 2nd ed. Lincolnwood, IL: Passport Books, 1997.

Linn, James Weber. *Jane Addams.* New York: D. Appleton–Century Co., 1935.

Linton, Cynthia, ed. *The Ethnic Handbook: A Guide to the Cultures and Traditions of Chicago's Diverse Communities.* Chicago: Illinois Ethnic Coalition, 1996.

McCaffery, Lawrence J. *The Irish Diaspora in America.* Bloomington: Indiana University Press, 1976.

Meites, Hyman L., ed. *History of the Jews of Chicago.* Chicago: Jewish Historical Society of Illinois, 1924.

Nelli, Humbert S. *Italians in Chicago, 1880–1930: A Study in Ethnic Mobility.* New York: Oxford University Press, 1970.

Olson, Ernst W. *History of the Swedes of Illinois.* 2 vols. Chicago: Engberg-Holmberg Publishing Co., 1908.

Philpott, Thomas Lee. *The Slum and the Ghetto: Neighborhood Deterioration and Middle Class Reform, Chicago 1880–1930.* New York: Oxford University Press, 1978.

Poles of Chicago, 1837–1937. Chicago: Polish Pageant, 1937.

Pomrenze, Seymour Jacob. "Aspects of Chicago Russian-Jewish Life, 1893–1925." In *The Chicago Pinkus*, edited by Simon Rawidowicz. Chicago: College of Jewish Studies, 1952.

Residents of Hull-House. *Hull-House Maps and Papers.* New York: Thomas Y. Crowell & Co., 1895.

Ropka, Gerald William. "The Evolving Residential Pattern of the Mexican, Puerto Rican, and Cuban Population in the City of Chicago." PhD diss., Michigan State University, 1973.

Roth, Walter. *Looking Backward: True Stories from Chicago's Jewish Past.* Chicago: Chicago Jewish Historical Society and Academy Chicago Publishers, 2002.

Saloutos, Theodore. *The Greeks in the United States.* Cambridge, MA: Harvard University Press, 1964.

Samors, Neal, Mary Jo Doyle, Martin Levin, and Michael Williams. *Chicago's Far North Side: An Illustrated History of Rogers Park and West Ridge.* Chicago: Rogers Park–West Ridge Historical Society, 2001.

Shanabruck, Charles. *Chicago's Catholics: The Evolution of an American Identity.* South Bend, IN: University of Notre Dame Press, 1981.

Schiavo, Giovanni. *The Italians in Chicago: A Study in Americanization.* Chicago: Italian American Publishing Co., 1928.

Sentinel's History of Chicago Jewry, 1911–1961, The. Chicago: Sentinel Publishing Co., 1961.

Sentinel's History of Chicago Jewry, 1911–1986, The. Chicago: Sentinel Publishing Co., 1986.

Short, James F., Jr. *The Social Fabric of the Metropolis: Contributions of the "Chicago School of Urban Sociology."* Chicago: University of Chicago Press, 1971.

Suttles, Gerald D. *The Social Order of the Slum. Ethnicity and Territory in the Inner City.* Chicago: University of Chicago Press, 1968.

Spear, Allan H. *Black Chicago: The Making of a Negro Ghetto, 1890–1920.* Chicago: University of Chicago Press, 1967.

Strand, A. E. *A History of the Norwegians of Illinois.* Chicago: John Anderson Publishing Co., 1905.

Thrasher, Frederic M. *The Gang.* Chicago: University of Chicago Press, 1927.

Townsend, Andrew Jacke. "The Germans of Chicago." *Deutsch-Amerikanische Geschichtblatter* 32 (1932). Reprinted from PhD diss., University of Chicago, 1927.

Travis, Dempsey J. *An Autobiography of Black Chicago.* Chicago: Urban Research Institute, 1981.

Tuttle, W. M., Jr. *Race Riot: Chicago in the Red Summer of 1919.* New York: Atheneum, 1970.

Vandenbosch, Amry. *The Dutch Communities of Chicago.* Chicago: Knickerbocker Society of Chicago, 1927.

Vecoli, Rudolph. "Chicago's Italians Prior to World War I: A Study of Their Social and Economic Adjustment." PhD diss., University of Wisconsin, 1962.

Wirth, Louis. *The Ghetto*. Chicago: University of Chicago Press, 1928.

Zorbaugh, Harvey Warren. *The Gold Coast and the Slum*. Chicago: University of Chicago Press, 1929.

6. The Economy of Chicago

Adelman, William J. *Touring Pullman*. Chicago: Illinois Labor History Society, 1972.

Appleton, John B. *The Iron and Steel Industry of the Calumet District*. University of Illinois Studies in the Social Sciences, vol. 13, no. 2. Urbana: University of Illinois, 1925.

Barrett, James R. *Work and Community in the Jungle: Chicago's Packinghouse Workers 1894–1922*. Urbana: University of Illinois Press, 1987.

Berry, Brian J. L. *Commercial Structure and Commercial Blight*. Research Paper no. 85. Chicago: University of Chicago, Department of Geography, 1963.

Bird's-Eye Views and Guide to Chicago. Chicago: Rand McNally & Co., 1898.

Breese, Gerald W. *The Daytime Population of the Central Business District of Chicago*. Chicago: University of Chicago Press, 1949.

Buder, Stanley. *Pullman: An Experiment in Industrial Order and Community Planning 1880–1930*. New York: Oxford University Press, 1967.

Carter, Peter. *Mies van der Rohe at Work*. New York: Praeger Publishers, 1974.

Casson, Herbert N. *Cyrus Hall McCormick*. Chicago: McClurg & Co., 1909.

Cohen, Elizabeth. *Making a New Deal: Industrial Workers in Chicago, 1919–1939*. Cambridge: Cambridge University Press, 1990.

Corplan Associates, IIT Research Institute. *Technological Change: Its Impact on Industry in Metropolitan Chicago*. 8 vols. Chicago: IIT Research Institute, 1964.

Darby, Edwin. *The Fortune Builders*. Garden City, NY: Doubleday & Co., 1986.

De Meirleir, Marcel J. *Manufactural Occupance in the West Central Area of Chicago*. Research Paper no. 11. Chicago: University of Chicago, Department of Geography, 1950.

Hayes, Dorsha B. *Chicago: Crossroads of American Enterprise*. New York: Julian Messner Publishers, 1944.

Heise, Kenan, and Michael Edgerton. *Chicago: Center for Enterprise*. 2 vols. Woodland Hills, CA: Windsor Publications, Inc., 1982.

Hines, Thomas S. *Burnham of Chicago: Architect and Planner*. Chicago: University of Chicago Press, 1974.

Hoyt, Homer. *One Hundred Years of Land Values in Chicago 1830–1933*. Chicago: University of Chicago Press, 1933.

Industrial Chicago. 6 vols. Chicago: Goodspeed Publishing Co., 1891–96.

Kornblum, William. *Blue Collar Community*. Chicago: University of Chicago Press, 1974.

Leech, Harper, and John Carroll. *Armour and His Times*. New York: D. Appleton–Century Co., 1938.

Lindsay, Almont. *The Pullman Strike*. Chicago: University of Chicago Press, 1942.

McDonald, Forrest. *Insull*. Chicago: University of Chicago Press, 1997.

Morrison, Hugh. *Louis Sullivan: Prophet of Modern Architecture*. New York: W. W. Norton & Co., 1935.

Randall, Frank A. *History of the Development of Building Construction in Chicago*. Urbana: University of Illinois Press, 1949.

Solomon, Ezra, and Zarko G. Bilbija. *Metropolitan Chicago: An Economic Analysis*. Glencoe, IL: Free Press, 1959.

Solzman, David M. *Waterway Industrial Sites, A Chicago Case Study*. Research Paper no. 107. Chicago: University of Chicago, Department of Geography, 1966.

Twombly, Robert C. *Frank Lloyd Wright: An Interpretive Biography*. New York: Harper & Row, 1973.

University of Chicago Center for Urban Studies. *Mid-Chicago Economic Development Study*. 3 vols. Chicago: Mayor's Committee for Economic and Cultural Development, 1966.

Wendt, Lloyd. *Chicago Tribune: The Rise of a Great American Newspaper*. Chicago: Rand McNally & Co., 1979.

Wendt, Lloyd, and Herman Kogan. *Give the Lady What She Wants!* Chicago: Rand McNally & Co., 1952.

Werner, Morris R. *Julius Rosenwald*. New York: Harper & Brothers, 1939.

Wille, Lois. *At Home in the Loop: How Clout and Community Built Chicago's Dearborn Park*. Carbondale: Southern Illinois University Press, 1997.

7. Culture, Education, and Recreation

Andrews, Clarence A. *Chicago in Story: A Literary History*. Iowa City: Midwest Heritage Publishing Company, 1982.

Bach, Ira J., ed. *Chicago's Famous Buildings*. 3rd ed. Chicago: University of Chicago Press, 1980.

Bach, Ira J., and Mary Lackritz Gray. *A Guide to Chicago's Public Sculptures*. Chicago: University of Chicago Press, 1983.

Bach, Ira J., and Susan Wolfson. *Walking Tours of Chicago's Architecture*. 5th ed. Chicago: Chicago Review Press, 1994.

Bailey, Janet. *Chicago Houses*. New York: St. Martin's Press, 1981.

Bernstein, Arnie. *Hollywood on Lake Michigan: 100 Years of Chicago and the Movies*. Chicago: Lake Claremont Press, 1998.

Block, Jean F. *Hyde Park Houses: An Informal History, 1856–1910*. Chicago: University of Chicago Press, 1978.

Christiansen, Richard. *A Theater of Our Own: A History and a Memoir of 1001 Nights in Chicago*. Evanston: Northwestern University Press, 2004.

Condit, Carl W. *The Chicago School of Architecture: A History of Commercial and Public Building in the Chicago Area, 1875–1925*. Chicago: University of Chicago Press, 1964.

Dale, Alzina Stone. *Mystery Reader's Walking Guide, Chicago*. Lincolnwood, IL: Passport Books, 1995.

Drury, John. *Old Chicago Houses*. Chicago: University of Chicago Press, 1941.

Fogel, Henry, Konrad Strauss, and Mark Kluge. *Chicago Symphony Orchestra in the Twentieth Century*. Chicago: Chicago Symphony Orchestra, 2000.

Garf, John, and Steve Skorpad. *Chicago's Monuments, Markers and Memorials*. Chicago: Arcadia Publishing Co., 2002.

Holden, Greg. *Literary Chicago: A Book Lover's Tour of the Windy City*. Chicago: Lake Claremont Press, 2001.

Junior League of Evanston. *An Architectural Album: Chicago's North Shore*. Evanston, 1988.

Krantz, Leslie J. *Chicago Art Review*. 2nd ed. Chicago: Chicago Review Press, 1980.

Lowe, David. *Chicago Interiors*. Chicago: Contemporary Books, 1979.

Lyric Opera of Chicago. *Lyric Opera of Chicago, 1954–1963*. Chicago: R. R. Donnelly, 1963.

Museum of Science and Industry. *A Guide to 150 Years of Chicago Architecture*. Chicago: Chicago Review Press, 1985.

Pruter, Robert. *Chicago Soul*. Urbana: University of Illinois Press, 1991.

Riedy, James L. *Chicago Sculpture*. Urbana: University of Illinois Press, 1986.

Sawyers, June Skinner, and Sue Telingator. *The Chicago Arts Guide*. Chicago: Chicago Review Press, 1993.

Swanson, Warren L., and Leonard F. Miska. *Recreation Guide to Chicago and Suburbs*. Chicago: Chicago Review Press, 1981.

Tallmadge, Thomas Eddy. *Architecture in Old Chicago*. Chicago: University of Chicago Press, 1946.

Travis, Dempsey J. *An Autobiography of Black Jazz*. Chicago: Urban Research Institute, 1983.

Williams, Kenny J. *Prairie Voices: A Literary History of Chicago from the Frontier to 1893*. Nashville: Townsend Press, 1980.

Williams, Kenny J., and Bernard Duffey, eds. *Chicago's Public Wits: A Chapter in the American Comic Spirit*. Baton Rouge: Louisiana State University Press, 1983.

8. Transportation: External and Internal

Chicago Area Transportation Study. *Final Report*. 3 vols. Chicago, 1959, 1960, 1962.

Chicago Freight Tunnels, The. Chicago: Chicago Tunnel Terminal Corp., 1928.

Davis, James L. *The Elevated System and the Growth of Northern Chicago*. Studies in Geography 10. Evanston: Northwestern University, Department of Geography, 1965.

Draine, Edwin H. *Import Traffic of Chicago and Its Hinterland*. Research Paper no. 81. Chicago: University of Chicago, Department of Geography, 1963.

Fellman, Jerome D. *Truck Transportation Patterns of Chicago*. Research Paper no. 12. Chicago: University of Chicago, Department of Geography, 1950.

Hansen, Harry. *The Chicago*. Rivers of America Series. New York: Farrar & Rinehart, 1942.

Helvig, Magne. *Chicago's External Truck Movements*. Research Paper no. 90. Chicago: University of Chicago, Department of Geography, 1964.

Hill, Libby. *The Chicago River: A Natural and Unnatural History*. Chicago: Lake Claremont Press, 2000.

Hilton, George W., and John F. Due. *The Electric Interurban Railways in America*. Stanford, CA: Stanford University Press, 1960.

Illinois. Governor's Transportation Task Force. *Public Transportation in Northeastern Illinois*. Chicago, 1973.

Lind, Alan R. *Chicago Surface Lines: An Illustrated History*. Park Forest, IL: Transport History Press, 1974.

Mayer, Harold M. *The Port of Chicago and the St. Lawrence Seaway*. Research Paper no. 49. Chicago: University of Chicago, Department of Geography, 1957.

———. *The Railway Pattern of Metropolitan Chicago*. Chicago: University of Chicago, Department of Geography, 1943.

Middleton, William D. *North Shore: America's Fastest Interurban*. San Marino, CA: Golden West Books, 1968.

———. *South Shore: The Last Interurban*. San Marino, CA: Golden West Books, 1970.

Putnam, James Williams. *The Illinois and Michigan Canal: A Study in Economic History*. Chicago: University of Chicago Press, 1918.

Quaife, Milo M. *Chicago's Highways Old and New: From Indian Trails to Motor Road*. Chicago: D. F. Keller & Co., 1923.

Ranney, Edward. *Prairie Passage: The Illinois and Michigan Canal Corridor*. Urbana: University of Illinois Press, 1998.

Solzman, David M. *The Chicago River. An Illustrated History and Guide to the River and Its Waterways*. Chicago: Wild Onion Books, 1998.

Taaffe, Edward J. *The Air Passenger Hinterland of Chicago*. Research Paper no. 24. Chicago: University of Chicago, Department of Geography, 1952.

Tank, Deane, Sr., and Theodore J. Karamanski. *Maritime Chicago*. Chicago: Arcadia Publishing Co., 2000.

Young, David. *Chicago Aviation: An Illustrated History*. De Kalb: Northern Illinois University Press, 2003.

9. Expansion of the Chicago Metropolitan Area

Ahmed, G. Munir. *Manufacturing Structure and Patterns of Waukegan–North Chicago*. Research Paper no. 46. Chicago: University of Chicago, Department of Geography, 1957.

Andreas, Alfred T. *History of Cook County, Illinois: From the Earliest Period to the Present Time*. Chicago: A. T. Andreas, 1884.

Bach, Ira J. *A Guide to Chicago's Historic Suburbs, on Wheels and on Foot*. Chicago: Swallow Press, 1981.

Canine, Gerald C., ed. *Chicagoland's Community Guide, 17th Annual Edition*. Chicago Law Bulletin Publishing Co., 1981.

Chamberlain, Everett. *Chicago and Its Suburbs.* Chicago: T. A. Hungerford & Co., 1874.

Cramer, Robert E. *Manufacturing Structure of the Cicero District, Metropolitan Chicago.* Research Paper no. 27. Chicago: University of Chicago, Department of Geography, 1952.

Cutler, Irving. *The Chicago-Milwaukee Corridor: A Geographic Study of Intermetropolitan Coalescence.* Studies in Geography 9. Evanston: Northwestern University, Department of Geography, 1965.

Ebner, Michael H. *Creating Chicago's North Shore.* Chicago: University of Chicago Press, 1988.

Federal Writers Project. *The Calumet Region Historical Guide.* Gary, IN: Garman Printing Co., 1939.

Franklin, Kay, and Norma Schaeffer. *Duel for the Dunes: Land Use Conflict on the Shores of Lake Michigan.* Urbana: University of Illinois Press, 1983.

Harper, Robert A. *A Recreational Occupance of the Moraine Lake Region of Northeastern Illinois and Southeastern Wisconsin.* Research Paper no. 14. Chicago: University of Chicago, Department of Geography, 1950.

Johnson, Charles B. *Growth of Cook County: A History of the Large Lake-Shore County That Includes Chicago.* Chicago: Board of Commissioners of Cook County, 1960.

Kenyon, James B. *The Industrialization of the Skokie Area.* Research Paper no. 33. Chicago: University of Chicago, Department of Geography, 1954.

Klove, Robert C. *The Park Ridge–Barrington Area: A Study of Residential Land Patterns and Problems in Suburban Chicago.* Chicago: University of Chicago, Department of Geography, 1942.

Komaiko, Jean, and Norma Schaeffer. *Doing the Dunes.* Beverly Shores, IN: Dunes Enterprises, 1973.

Lane, James B. *"City of the Century": A History of Gary, Indiana.* Bloomington: Indiana University Press, 1978.

League of Women Voters of Chicago. *The Key to Our Local Government: Chicago, Cook County Metropolitan Area.* 4th ed. Chicago: Citizens Information Service of Illinois, 1978.

Miller, John J. *Open Land in Metropolitan Chicago.* Chicago: Midwest Open Land Association, 1962.

Moore, Powell A. *The Calumet Region. Indiana's Last Frontier.* Indianapolis: Indiana Historical Bureau, 1959.

Northeastern Illinois Planning Commission. *Open Space in Northeastern Illinois.* Technical Report no. 2. Chicago, 1962.

——. *Suburban Fact Book.* Chicago, 1973.

Platt, Rutherford H. *Open Land in Urban Illinois.* De Kalb: Northern Illinois University Press, 1971.

Stetzer, Donald Foster. *Special Districts in Cook County: Toward a Geography of Local Government.* Chicago: University of Chicago, Department of Geography, 1975.

10. Planning for the Future

Burnham, Daniel H., and Edward H. Bennett. *Plan of Chicago.* Chicago: Commercial Club, 1909.

Burnham, Daniel H., Jr., and Robert Kingery. *Planning the Region of Chicago.* Chicago: Chicago Regional Planning Association, 1956.

Chicago Department of Development and Planning. *Chicago 21: A Plan for the Central Area Communities.* Chicago, 1973.

——. *The Comprehensive Plan of Chicago.* Chicago, 1966.

——. *The Lakefront Plan of Chicago.* Chicago, 1972.

——. *The Riveredge Plan of Chicago.* Chicago, 1974.

Chicago Land Use Survey. Vol. 1, *Residential Chicago.* Vol. 2, *Land Use in Chicago.* Chicago: Chicago Plan Commission, 1942, 1943.

Chicago Metropolis 2020. *The Metropolis Plan: Choices for the Chicago Region.* Chicago: Commercial Club, 2002.

Chicago Plan Commission. *Forty-four Cities in the City of Chicago.* Chicago, 1942.

———. *Master Plan of Residential Land Use of Chicago*. Chicago, 1943.

Hillman, Arthur, and Robert J Casey. *Tomorrow's Chicago*. Chicago: University of Chicago Press, 1953.

Meyerson, Martin, and Edward C. Banfield. *Politics, Planning, and the Public Interest*. Glencoe, IL: Free Press, 1955.

Midwest Open Land Association. *Preservation of Open Space Areas*. Chicago, 1966.

Moody, Walter D. *Wacker's Manual of the Plan of Chicago*. Chicago: H. C. Sherman & Co., 1911.

Moore, Charles. *Daniel Burnham: Architect, Planner of Cities*. 2 vols. New York: Houghton Mifflin Co., 1921.

Northeastern Illinois Metropolitan Area Local Governmental Services Commission. *Governmental Problems in the Chicago Metropolitan Area*. Edited by Leverett S. Lyon. Chicago: University of Chicago Press, 1957.

Northeastern Illinois Planning Commission. *The Comprehensive Plan for the Development of the Northeastern Illinois Counties Area*. Chicago, 1968.

———. *Summary of Census 2000: Profiles of General Demographic Characteristics for Counties, Townships and Municipalities in Northeastern Illinois*. Chicago, 2001.

Ranney, Victoria Post. *Olmsted in Chicago*. Chicago: Open Land Project, 1972.

Rossi, Peter H., and Robert A. Dentler. *The Politics of Urban Renewal: The Chicago Findings*. New York: Free Press of Glencoe, 1961.

Simpson, Dick, ed. *Chicago's Future: An Agenda for Change*. Champaign, IL: Stipes Publishing Co., 1976.

Wille, Lois. *Forever Open, Clear and Free: The Historic Struggle for Chicago's Lakefront*. Chicago: Henry Regnery Co., 1972.

Fiction, Poetry, Reflections

Ade, George. *Chicago Stories*. Chicago: Henry Regnery Co., 1963.

Algren, Nelson. *Chicago: City on the Make*. Garden City, NY: Doubleday, 1951.

———. *Man with the Golden Arm*. Garden City, NY: Doubleday, 1949.

Anderson, Sherwood. *Windy McPherson's Son*. New York: Cape, 1916.

Bellow, Saul. *Adventures of Augie March*. New York: Viking Press, 1953.

———. *Humboldt's Gift*. New York: Viking Press, 1975.

Brashler, William. *City Dogs*. New York: Harper & Row, 1976.

Brooks, Gwendolyn. *Maud Martha*. New York: AMS Press, 1953.

Brown, Frank London. *Trumbull Park*. Chicago: Henry Regnery Co., 1959.

Casey, Robert J. *Chicago Medium Rare*. Indianapolis: Bobbs-Merrill Co., 1952.

Cather, Willa. *Lucy Gayheart*. New York: Alfred A. Knopf, 1935.

Cleaver, Charles. *Early Chicago Reminiscences*. Fergus Historical Series no. 19. Chicago: Fergus Printing Co., 1882.

Cook, Frederick F. *Bygone Days in Chicago*. Chicago: A. C. McClurg & Co., 1910.

Dreiser, Theodore. *The Financier*. New York: Harper & Brothers, 1912.

———. *Sister Carrie*. New York: Doubleday, Page & Co., 1900.

Dybek, Stuart. *The Coast of Chicago*. New York: Vintage Books, 1991.

Farrell, James T. *Studs Lonigan: A Trilogy*. New York: Vanguard Press, 1935.

Ferber, Edna. *So Big*. Garden City, NY: Doubleday, Page & Co., 1924.

Field, Eugene. *Sharps and Flats*. New York: C. Scribner's Sons, 1900.

Fuller, Helen Blake. *The Cliff Dwellers*. New York: Harper & Brothers, 1893.

Gale, Edwin O. *Reminiscences of Early Chicago*. Chicago: F. H. Revell Co., 1902.

Halper, Albert. *On the Shore: Young Writer Remembering Chicago*. New York: Viking Press, 1934.

Hansberry, Lorraine. *Raisin in the Sun*. New York: Random House, 1959.

Harris, Frank. *Bomb*. Chicago: University of Chicago Press, 1963.

Hecht, Ben. *Gaily, Gaily*. Garden City, NY: Doubleday, 1963.

Hecht, Ben, and Charles MacArthur. *The Front Page*. New York: Covici-Friede, 1928.

Herrick, Robert. *The Web of Life*. New York: Irvington Publishers, 1900.

Howland, Bette. *Blue in Chicago*. New York: Harper & Row, 1978.

Kotlowitz, Alex. *Never a City So Real*. New York: Crown Journeys, 2004.

Kupcinet, Irv. *Kup's Chicago*. Cleveland: World Publishing Co., 1962.

Levin, Meyer. *Compulsion*. New York: Simon & Schuster, 1956.

———. *The Old Bunch*. New York: Viking Press, 1937.

Liebling, Abbott J. *Chicago: The Second City*. New York: Alfred A. Knopf, 1952.

Maday, Tom, and Sam Landers, eds. *Great Chicago Stories*. Chicago: Two Press Publishing Co., 1994.

Masters, Edgar Lee. *The Tale of Chicago*. New York: G. P. Putnam's Sons, 1933.

Meeker, Arthur. *Chicago with Love*. New York: Alfred A. Knopf, 1955.

———. *Prairie Avenue*. New York: Alfred A. Knopf, 1949.

Morley, Christopher D. *Old Loopy: A Love Letter for Chicago*. Chicago: Argus Book Shop, 1937.

Motley, Willard. *Knock on Any Door*. New York: D. Appleton–Century Co., 1947.

Norris, Frank. *The Pit*. New York: Doubleday, Page & Co., 1903.

Paretsky, Sara. *Guardian Angel*. New York: Delacorte Press, 1992.

———. *Windy City Blues*. New York: Delacorte Press, 1995.

Petrakis, Harry Mark. *A Dream of Kings*. New York: D. McKay & Co., 1966.

———. *Pericles on 31st Street*. Chicago: Quadrangle Books, 1965.

Port Chicago Poets. Chicago: Chicago International Manuscripts, 1966.

Powers, John R. *The Last Catholic in America*. New York: Saturday Review Press, 1973.

Roth, Philip. *Letting Go*. New York: Random House, 1962.

Sandburg, Carl. *Chicago Poems*. New York: H. Holt & Co., 1916.

Sinclair, Upton. *The Jungle*. New York: Doubleday, Page & Co., 1906.

Smith, Alston J. *Chicago's Left Bank*. Chicago: Henry Regnery Co., 1953.

Smith, Mark. *The Death of the Detective*. New York: Avon, 1977.

Starkey, David, and Richard Guzman. *Smokestacks and Skyscrapers: An Anthology of Chicago Writing*. Chicago: Wild Onion Books, 1999.

Stern, Richard. *Pacific Tremors*. Evanston, IL: TriQuarterly Books, Northwestern University Press, 2001.

Terkel, Louis (Studs). *Division Street: America*. New York: Pantheon Books, 1967.

———. *Hard Times: An Oral History of the Great Depression*. New York: Pantheon Books, 1970.

Turow, Scott. *Personal Injuries*. New York: Farrar, Straus and Giroux, 1999.

———. *Presumed Innocent*. New York: Farrar, Straus and Giroux, 1987.

Williams, Kenny J. *In the City of Men*. Nashville: Townsend Press, 1974.

Wright, Richard. *Black Boy*. New York: Harper & Brothers, 1937.

———. *Native Son*. New York: Harper & Brothers, 1940.

Index

Irving Cutler, an emeritus professor of geography at Chicago State University, is the author or coauthor of six books, including *Urban Geography* and the award-winning *The Jews of Chicago: From Shtetl to Suburb*. Cutler has served as a consultant to government agencies, written and produced film scripts about urban affairs, participated in radio and television programs, curated museum exhibits about Chicago, and given many tours and talks about various aspects of Chicago. A former president of the Geographic Society of Chicago, he sits on the boards of directors of a number of historical and geographic societies.